THE ART OF READING SCRIPTURE

THE ART OF READING SCRIPTURE

Edited by

Ellen F. Davis and Richard B. Hays

WILLIAM B. EERDMANS PUBLISHING COMPANY
GRAND RAPIDS, MICHIGAN / CAMBRIDGE, U.K.

Wm. B. Eerdmans Publishing Co.
2140 Oak Industrial Drive N.E., Grand Rapids, Michigan 49505 /
P.O. Box 163, Cambridge CB3 9PU U.K.
www.eerdmans.com

Printed in the United States of America

11 10 09 08 07 06   10 9 8 7 6 5 4

Library of Congress Cataloging-in-Publication Data

ISBN-10: 0-8028-1269-4
ISBN-13: 978-0-8028-1269-8

Scripture translations not otherwise identified are the authors' own.

Contents

A Living Tradition

Reading Difficult Texts

Selected Sermons

Acknowledgments

This volume of essays owes its existence to the vision and the generous support of Wallace Alston and Robert Jenson of the Center of Theological Inquiry (Princeton, New Jersey). Over a period of four years, they hosted and participated in a conversation among the authors that generated many of the ideas in this book. We thank them and all the members of the Scripture Project for deep and extended interaction among theological disciplines that is a rare and precious experience.

Our conversation was enriched by the contributions of two participants who are not represented by essays in this volume: Professor Robin Darling Young, of the Catholic University of America, and Professor J. Ross Wagner, of Princeton Theological Seminary. Each played a crucial role in the formation of the group's thinking, and we record our gratitude to them. Professor Young, with her expertise in Eastern patristic sources, played an indispensable part in encouraging us to consider the Christian tradition's understanding of the multiple senses of Scripture and to recognize that the early Christians encountered the Bible as a living word. Professor Wagner, who joined us initially as an observer, soon became an integral part of our dialogue through his gift for summarizing and synthesizing the salient ideas that emerged from our meetings.

At one meeting, Margaret Adams Parker shared her extensive knowledge of visual art as a form of scriptural interpretation, and she has kindly allowed us to reproduce one of her woodcuts in this volume. Many friends and colleagues provided helpful critiques of earlier drafts of the Nine Theses; among these, a special word of thanks goes to Professor A. Katherine Grieb, of Virginia Theological Seminary, and to the Reverend Fleming Rutledge for offering suggestions that materially improved the final version. Brad Trick and David Moffitt, doctoral students at Duke, provided timely help in overseeing the transliteration of Hebrew and Greek phrases in the volume's essays and in preparing the Scripture index.

Beyond his own involvement in the Scripture Project, our Dean, L. Gregory Jones, generously provided the staff assistance that made editing this volume pleasurable work. Our debt to Carol Shoun, editorial assistant to the faculty of Duke Divinity School, is impossible to calculate. Without her careful tending at every stage of production, this book would be published only sometime in the indefinite future, and it would not read nearly so well.

ELLEN DAVIS and RICHARD HAYS
The Divinity School
Duke University
Confession of St. Peter, 2003

Contributors

Gary A. Anderson
Professor of Old Testament
University of Notre Dame

Richard Bauckham
Professor of New Testament Studies and Bishop Wardlaw Professor
University of St. Andrews

Brian E. Daley, SJ
Catherine F. Huisking Professor of Theology
University of Notre Dame

Ellen F. Davis
Associate Professor of Bible and Practical Theology
Duke Divinity School

Richard B. Hays
George Washington Ivey Professor of New Testament
Duke Divinity School

James C. Howell
Senior Minister
Myers Park United Methodist Church, Charlotte, N.C.

Robert W. Jenson
Senior Scholar for Research
Center of Theological Inquiry, Princeton, N.J.

William Stacy Johnson
Arthur M. Adams Associate Professor of Systematic Theology
Princeton Theological Seminary

L. Gregory Jones
Dean and Professor of Theology
Duke Divinity School

Christine McSpadden
Priest
Episcopal Diocese of California

R. W. L. Moberly
Reader in Theology
University of Durham

David C. Steinmetz
Amos Ragan Kearns Professor of the History of Christianity
Duke Divinity School

Marianne Meye Thompson
Professor of New Testament Interpretation
Fuller Theological Seminary

Abbreviations

ANF	*Ante-Nicene Fathers*
BA	Bibliothèque Augustinienne
BCP	*Book of Common Prayer*
CCath	Corpus Catholicorum
CCSG	Corpus Christianorum: Series graeca
CCSL	Corpus Christianorum: Series latina
CF	Cistercian Fathers
CWS	Classics of Western Spirituality
EBS	Encountering Biblical Studies
FC	Fathers of the Church
GTI	Guides to Theological Inquiry
Herm	Hermeneia
JSNTSup	Journal for the Study of the New Testament: Supplement Series
LCC	Library of Christian Classics
LLA	Library of Liberal Arts
LXX	Septuagint
NC	Narrative Commentaries
NIB	*The New Interpreter's Bible*
NJPS	*Tanakh: The Holy Scriptures: The New JPS Translation according to the Traditional Hebrew Text*
NRSV	New Revised Standard Version
OBT	Overtures to Biblical Theology
OTL	Old Testament Library
PG	Patrologia graeca [= Patrologiae cursus completus: Series graeca]
RSV	Revised Standard Version
SBT	Studies in Biblical Theology
SMRT	Studies in Medieval and Reformation Thought
THL	Theory and History of Literature
TPINTC	TPI New Testament Commentaries
WBC	Word Biblical Commentary

Introduction

A cartoon in the *New Yorker* shows a man making inquiry at the information counter of a large bookstore. The clerk, tapping on his keyboard and peering intently into the computer screen, replies, "The Bible? . . . That would be under self-help."[1]

As the cartoon suggests, in postmodern culture the Bible has no definite place, and citizens in a pluralistic, secular culture have trouble knowing what to make of it. If they pay any attention to it at all, they treat it as a consumer product, one more therapeutic option for rootless selves engaged in an endless quest of self-invention and self-improvement. Not surprisingly, this approach does not yield a very satisfactory reading of the Bible, for the Bible is not, in fact, about "self-help"; it is about *God's* action to rescue a lost and broken world.

If we discount the story of God's gracious action, what remains is decidedly *non*therapeutic. We are left with a curious pastiche of ancient cultural constructions that might or might not be edifying for us, in the same way that the religious myths of any other ancient culture might or might not prove interesting or useful. Indeed, some postmodern readers have come to perceive the cultural alienness of the Bible and to find it dangerous and oppressive.

The difficulty of interpreting the Bible is felt not only in secular culture but also in the church at the beginning of the twenty-first century. Is the Bible authoritative for the faith and practice of the church? If so, in what way? What practices of reading offer the most appropriate approach to understanding the Bible? How does historical criticism illumine or obscure Scripture's message? How are traditional readings to be brought into engagement

---

1. Cartoon by Peter Steiner, *New Yorker,* 6 July 1998, p. 33.

with historical methodologies, as well as feminist, liberationist, and post-modernist readings? The church's lack of clarity about these issues has hindered its witness and mission, causing it to speak with an uncertain voice to the challenges of our time. Even where the Bible's authority is acknowledged in principle, many of our churches seem to have lost the art of reading it attentively and imaginatively.

In order to address these problems, the Center of Theological Inquiry (Princeton, New Jersey) convened a group of fifteen scholars and pastors who met periodically over a period of four years (1998-2002) under the collective name "The Scripture Project." The group's individual members contributed expertise in the fields of Old Testament, New Testament, systematic and historical theology, and parish ministry. Our aim was to overcome the fragmentation of our theological disciplines by reading Scripture together. As one member of the group remarked, at one time the church's great interpreters of Scripture (such as Origen, Augustine, Aquinas, Calvin, and Luther) did not think of themselves narrowly as specialists in Old or New Testament or in theology or church history; for them, the interpretation of the Bible was a seamlessly integrated theological activity that spoke directly to the needs of the church. Thus what we were doing, he joked, was assembling a group of fifteen specialists to function corporately as a "Complete Theologian." The joke captured something of the truth, and it became for us a working description of the ideal we were pursuing. In seeking to explore, to exemplify, and to nurture habits of reading Scripture theologically, we hoped to recover the church's rich heritage of biblical interpretation in a dramatically changed cultural environment.

In the course of our consultation, the conviction grew among us that reading Scripture is an *art* — a creative discipline that requires engagement and imagination, in contrast to the Enlightenment's ideal of detached objectivity. In our practices of reading the Bible, we are (or should be) something like artists. This conviction carries two corollaries, the bad news and the good.

The bad news is that, like every other true art form, reading Scripture is a difficult thing to do well. Strangely, we do not often mention this difficulty in church, in sermons or in teaching. Our attitude seems to be that the interpretation of Scripture is a cut-and-dried kind of thing. In most liberal churches, it hardly seems worth discussing. But even in more Bible-oriented churches, there is little acknowledgment of the fact that making good sense of the Bible and applying that sense wisely to our lives is a hard thing to do. The disciplines of attentiveness to the word do not come easily to us, accustomed as we are to user-friendly interfaces and instant gratification. (It is worth noting that recognition of the difficulty of interpretation is one of the huge differences between Christians and Jews; Jews have always revered the reading of Scripture as the greatest and most difficult of all art forms.)

But in recognizing that scriptural interpretation is an art, there lies good news as well. Like every other form of art, reading Scripture has the potential for creating something beautiful. Interpretations of Scripture are not just right and wrong, although at times such categories are useful and necessary. But perhaps ultimately a more adequate way of judging our readings is the way we judge works of art — according to the standards of beauty. To what extent do our readings reveal the intricacy, the wondrous quality of what the biblical writers call *ma'asei Adonai,* "the works of the LORD"? To what extent do they draw us toward something, a way of being that is — to use Paul's language — more "lovely," more "gracious," more "excellent," "noble," "worthy of praise" (Phil 4:8)?

Our readings will produce such beauty precisely to the extent that they respond faithfully to the antecedent imaginative power of God, to which the Bible bears witness. We normally say that God relates to us through God's power for love, for compassion, and so on — and of course that is true. But consider this: imagination is the capacity to envision the existence of something that does not yet exist; we see this in the imagination of the artist. So it makes sense to say that the creation of the world, the covenant between the Creator of heaven and earth and an old man named Abraham, the creation of a nation of priests out of a band of runaway slaves, the incarnation of the Godhead in human flesh, the explosion of death's finality, the inclusion of the Gentiles in God's covenant with Israel — all these and more are remarkably imaginative acts on God's part, acts through which God envisions and effects something totally new, totally unimaginable before it was brought into being. If we are faithful readers of the stories of these imaginative acts, we will find our own imaginations expanded and transformed. Scripture will claim us and make us into new people.

If reading Scripture is an art, there follows one more conclusion: we learn the practice of an art through apprenticeship to those who have become masters. Learning to read Scripture well and imaginatively must be done at the feet of those who have gone before us and performed, in their lives of embodied faithfulness, beautiful interpretations of Scripture. For that reason, we in the Scripture Project immersed ourselves in the history of biblical interpretation, paying special attention to the patterns and practices of reading that have characterized the lives of the saints — those whom the church has recognized as the most astute and faithful exemplars of Scripture's meaning.

As our consultation progressed, the group found growing agreement on a set of core affirmations about the interpretation of Scripture. We now set these affirmations forth at the beginning of this book in the form of "Nine Theses on the Interpretation of Scripture." These theses hardly answer all questions about how to read the Bible, but we believe they do provide substantial guidance for the church. Each thesis is accompanied by questions for ongoing discussion, indicating that even as we find agreement on these fundamental affirmations, we recognize the need for continued debate and reflection within the framework defined by our common convictions. In the spirit of seeking to hear the word of God together, we offer these theses to the wider community of faith as a basis for further conversation about the interpretation of Scripture.

The essays that follow both amplify and model the approach to Scripture recommended in the Nine Theses. They were not written, however, in order to explicate the theses. The project evolved in the other direction: the essays, originally presented as working papers to the group, provoked the discussions from which the Nine Theses were distilled. It is our hope that these essays, revised and refined in light of the Scripture Project's conversations, may now continue to provoke fruitful discussion within church and academy.

The essays in part I, "How Do We Read and Teach the Scriptures?" provide a theoretical framework for our interpretive approach. Ellen Davis, "Teaching the Bible Confessionally in the Church," articulates the need for the church "to learn afresh to acknowledge the Bible as the functional center of its life."[2] Davis's proposal for "confessional" reading reimagines the ways the Bible has characteristically been taught in our seminaries and congregations. Robert Jenson, "Scripture's Authority in the Church," reframes the usual debates about biblical authority by insisting that "our common life is located *inside* the story Scripture tells."[3] But does Scripture really tell a single, overarching story in which we can live? Richard Bauckham, "Reading Scripture as a Coherent Story," discusses the problem of unity and diversity within the Bible and contrasts the grand biblical narrative with the totalizing "metanarratives" characteristic of modernity. Finally, David Steinmetz, "Uncovering a Second Narrative: Detective Fiction and the Construction of Historical Method," develops an engaging analogy that sheds light on the ways in which Christian biblical interpreters have reread Israel's story in light of Scripture's "second narrative" — the compelling disclosure, at the end, of "what the story was about all along."[4]

2. Ellen F. Davis, "Teaching the Bible Confessionally in the Church," p. 9.
3. Robert W. Jenson, "Scripture's Authority in the Church," p. 30.
4. David C. Steinmetz, "Uncovering a Second Narrative," p. 57.

The diverse essays in part II, "A Living Tradition," trace some of the ways the Bible has been interpreted in the Christian tradition and reflect on the fresh possibilities created by the collapse of the conventional interpretive paradigms of modernity and Christendom. Brian Daley poses the question, "Is Patristic Exegesis Still Usable?" and answers it through some observations on early Christian readings of the Psalms. Noting that "modern historical criticism — including the criticism of biblical texts — is *methodologically* atheistic," Daley argues that we have much to learn from the Fathers and their "hermeneutic of piety."[5] James Howell, "Christ Was like St. Francis," examines how particular human lives can embody and illumine the meaning of the biblical text. "The gospel is incarnational, even messy, and we learn as much from the foibles of saints as from their luminous moments of genuine imitation of Christ."[6] The next two essays move from the history of interpretation to the problem of interpretation in our time. Stacy Johnson, "Reading the Scriptures Faithfully in a Postmodern Age," proposes a trinitarian hermeneutical model that offers a movement "beyond foundations, beyond totality, and toward the Other."[7] While Johnson focuses on theology's dialogue with postmodern philosophy, Christine McSpadden, "Preaching Scripture Faithfully in a Post-Christendom Church," contributes a more concrete reflection on the practical task of preaching at a time when the preacher can no longer presume a congregation's familiarity with Scripture and Christian categories. She sees in this challenging situation "the rare historical opportunity to communicate good news that is heard as good and as news once again."[8] Finally, Greg Jones, "Embodying Scripture in the Community of Faith," explores how scriptural interpretation takes shape in community, focusing particularly on St. Augustine and Martin Luther King Jr. as exemplary readers whose interpretations were nurtured by — and in turn gave nurture to — particular communities of faith.

While part I provides theoretical perspectives and part II explores practices of reading in the church, past and present, part III, "Reading Difficult Texts," moves to the actual constructive work of exegesis, giving particular attention to passages that for one reason or another present interpretive difficulties for the church in our time. Ellen Davis, "Critical Traditioning: Seeking an Inner Biblical Hermeneutic," begins by showing that the biblical writers

---

5. Brian E. Daley, SJ, "Is Patristic Exegesis Still Usable?" pp. 72, 79.

6. James C. Howell, "Christ Was like St. Francis," p. 103.

7. William Stacy Johnson, "Reading the Scriptures Faithfully in a Postmodern Age," p. 110.

8. Christine McSpadden, "Preaching Scripture Faithfully in a Post-Christendom Church," p. 142.

themselves faced the problem of interpreting difficult texts; their hermeneutical strategies, then, should offer important clues for our reading of such texts. Critical traditioning, Davis suggests, "denotes the willingness to engage in radical rethinking of a formerly accepted theological position"; in this exercise of "profound, even godly, humility," we may "learn something previously unimaginable about the fundaments of life with God."[9] This proposal is amplified by the other essays in the section. Walter Moberly, "Living Dangerously: Genesis 22 and the Quest for Good Biblical Interpretation," engages what is surely one of the strangest and most daunting texts in the Bible. The terrifying story of Abraham's near sacrifice of his son Isaac reveals, in Moberly's reading, that right worship of God entails "a rigorous, searching, critical, purifying process in which what one holds most dear and God-given may be precisely that which must in some sense be relinquished if faith is to be genuine."[10] Gary Anderson, "Joseph and the Passion of Our Lord," offers a multilayered reading of the Joseph story as a typological prefiguration of the story of Christ; in both narratives, "it is precisely the *culpability* of the brothers or the disciples that allows them to experience and ponder the miracle of their forgiveness."[11] Richard Hays, "Reading Scripture in Light of the Resurrection," takes up the New Testament's resurrection narratives — those stories most notoriously offensive to modernist rationality — and points to three Gospel passages in which the resurrection of Jesus is explicitly linked with unlocking the meaning of Scripture. Walter Moberly, "How Can We Know the Truth?" explores John 7:14-18 as a key to biblical epistemology. If we take the claim of this text seriously, it transposes interpretation "into a different key by envisaging a particular mode of being — faith — as the enabling factor in inquiry."[12] In the concluding exegetical probe, Marianne Meye Thompson, "'His Own Received Him Not,'" undertakes a reading of the footwashing story in John 13, showing that its soteriological and ethical dimensions can be held in unity only if we read its theological message whole. The story, "set in the larger context of Scripture, reveals the tenacity of human resistance to the self-giving love of God."[13] Precisely for that reason, John 13 undercuts all human pretensions to power and domination.

Finally, because the Scripture Project was centrally concerned not just with academic theology but also with the use of Scripture in the life of the church, we the editors include in part IV several examples of our own ser-

---

9. Ellen F. Davis, "Critical Traditioning," pp. 170, 177.

10. R. W. L. Moberly, "Living Dangerously," p. 197.

11. Gary A. Anderson, "Joseph and the Passion of Our Lord," p. 214.

12. R. W. L. Moberly, "How Can We Know the Truth?" pp. 256-57.

13. Marianne Meye Thompson, "'His Own Received Him Not,'" p. 273.

mons. We offer them not as models of rhetorical style or sermon design: while we both preach with some regularity, neither of us is an expert homiletician. Rather, we offer them as illustrations of "practical biblical theology," and we have chosen these particular sermons because in our judgment they exemplify in various ways the kind of interpretive approach that the Nine Theses commend. Our selections encompass biblical texts of different types and genres: Genesis, the Psalms, Daniel, the Gospel of Luke, and Romans. Each sermon is followed by a few remarks from the preacher that point to the interpretive issues we consider most significant.

This volume proposes a quiet revolution in the way the Bible is taught in theological seminaries. At the same time, it also calls pastors and teachers in the churches to rethink their practices of using the Bible. Yet we do not understand the Scripture Project as a solitary voice in the wilderness; in recent years a number of other scholars and theologians have called for a recovery of an unapologetically theological approach to biblical interpretation. An annotated bibliography at the end of this volume provides a few suggestions for further reading along these lines. It is our hope that the Nine Theses, together with the essays in this book, might stimulate and strengthen a gathering new consensus about the need for the church to recover its own heritage of biblical interpretation — and to reclaim its conviction that the Old and New Testaments of the Christian Bible tell the true story of God's gracious action to redeem the world. Most of all, it is our hope that this volume will encourage readers to pursue the demanding but ultimately joyful art of reading Scripture.

Nine Theses on the Interpretation of Scripture
The Scripture Project

1. Scripture truthfully tells the story of God's action of creating, judging, and saving the world.

God is the primary agent revealed in the biblical narrative. The triune God whom Christians worship is the God of Israel who called a people out of bondage, gave them the Torah, and raised Jesus of Nazareth from the dead. This same God is still at work in the world today. God is not a projection or construct of human religious aspiration. Readers who interpret the biblical story reductively as a symbolic figuration of the human psyche, or merely as a vehicle for codifying social and political power, miss its central message. Scripture discloses the word of God, a word that calls into existence things that do not exist, judges our presuppositions and projects, and pours out grace beyond our imagining.

> *For ongoing discussion:* How is the biblical story of God's action related to God's continuing work in the contemporary world? How is the affirmation that God is at work in the world to be related to widespread evil and human suffering?

2. Scripture is rightly understood in light of the church's rule of faith as a coherent dramatic narrative.

Though the Bible contains the voices of many different witnesses, the canon of Scripture finds its unity in the overarching story of the work of the triune God. While the Bible contains many tensions, digressions, and subplots, the biblical texts cohere because the one God acts in them and speaks through them: God is the author of Scripture's unity for the sake of the church's faithful proclamation and action.

1

For ongoing discussion: How are nonnarrative portions of Scripture to be understood in light of the claim that Scripture is a coherent dramatic narrative? How do we understand the character of the Bible's unity in and through its polyphony? the character of God's speech through Scripture? of God's authorship? How do we understand particular texts that seem theologically or morally problematic — does God speak through *all* the texts of Scripture?

3. Faithful interpretation of Scripture requires an engagement with the entire narrative: the New Testament cannot be rightly understood apart from the Old, nor can the Old be rightly understood apart from the New.

The Bible must be read "back to front" — that is, understanding the plot of the whole drama in light of its climax in the death and resurrection of Jesus Christ. This suggests that figural reading is to be preferred over messianic proof-texting as a way of showing how the Old Testament opens toward the New. Yet the Bible must also be read "front to back" — that is, understanding the climax of the drama, God's revelation in Christ, in light of the long history of God's self-revelation to Israel. Against the increasingly common contention that Christians should interpret "the Hebrew Bible" only in categories that were historically available to Israel at the time of the composition of the biblical writings, we affirm that a respectful rereading of the Old Testament in light of the New discloses figurations of the truth about the one God who acts and speaks in both, figurations whose full dimensions can be grasped only in light of the cross and resurrection. At the same time, against the assumption that Jesus can be understood exclusively in light of Christian theology's later confessional traditions, we affirm that our interpretation of Jesus must return repeatedly to the Old Testament to situate him in direct continuity with Israel's hopes and Israel's understanding of God.

For ongoing discussion: How is "figuration" related to traditional understandings of allegory and typology? How do we honor claims about the centrality of Christ while honoring the abiding significance of Israel? How do we deal with New Testament texts that appear to say that Israel has been rejected by God and superseded by the church?

4. Texts of Scripture do not have a single meaning limited to the intent of the original author. In accord with Jewish and Christian traditions, we affirm that Scripture has multiple complex senses given by God, the author of the whole drama.

The authors and editors of the canonical texts repeatedly gave new contexts and senses to earlier traditions, thereby initiating the process of discerning multiple senses within the text. The medieval "fourfold sense" is a helpful reminder of Scripture's multivalence. The church's traditions of biblical interpretation offer models and guidance about how the fuller sense of Scripture should be understood. This does not entail a rejection of historical investigation of biblical texts. Indeed, historical investigations have ongoing importance in helping us to understand Scripture's literal sense and in stimulating the church to undertake new imaginative readings of the texts.

> *For ongoing discussion:* How, then, do we learn from modern historical interpretations of Scripture while also drawing on the church's premodern traditions of biblical interpretation? Should either modern or premodern traditions be privileged in the church's reading of biblical texts? What criteria ought to be employed to provide some determinacy to the interpretation of particular texts?

5. The four canonical Gospels narrate the truth about Jesus.

The Gospels, read within the matrix of Scripture from Genesis to Revelation, convey the truth about the identity of Jesus more faithfully than speculative reconstructions produced by modernist historical methods. The canonical narratives are normative for the church's proclamation and practice.

> *For ongoing discussion:* How are the four portraits of Jesus related to one another? To what extent are historical investigations necessary or helpful in understanding Jesus? How is the entirety of Scripture necessary to an accurate portrayal of Jesus? To what extent is a right understanding of the whole of Scripture necessary to an appropriate understanding of the identity of Jesus?

6. Faithful interpretation of Scripture invites and presupposes participation in the community brought into being by God's redemptive action — the church.

Scriptural interpretation is properly an ecclesial activity whose goal is to participate in the reality of which the text speaks by bending the knee to worship the God revealed in Jesus Christ. Through Scripture the church receives the good news of the inbreaking kingdom of God and, in turn, proclaims the message of reconciliation. Scripture is like a musical score that must be played or sung in order to be understood; therefore, the church interprets Scripture by forming communities of prayer, service, and faithful witness.

The Psalms, for example, are "scores" awaiting performance by the community of faith. They school us in prayer and form in us the capacities for praise, penitence, reflection, patient endurance, and resistance to evil.

> *For ongoing discussion:* What does "participation in the community" entail? Does it require particular creedal or sacramental understanding? At what point does a community lose its status as an identifiably Christian community? How does the disunity of the church affect the interpretation of Scripture?

7. The saints of the church provide guidance in how to interpret and perform Scripture.

From the earliest communities of the church, through whose scriptural interpretation we received the Christian Bible, to the present communities of biblical interpreters, generations of Christians have received this book as a gift from God and sought to order their lives according to the witness of Scripture. This chain of interpreters, the communion of the saints, includes not only those officially designated as saints by the churches but also the great cloud of witnesses acknowledged by believers in diverse times and places, including many of the church's loyal critics. This communion informs our reading of Scripture. We learn from the saints the centrality of interpretive virtues for shaping wise readers. Prominent among these virtues are receptivity, humility, truthfulness, courage, charity, humor, and imagination. Guidance in the interpretation of Scripture may be found not only in the writings of the saints but also in the exemplary patterns of their lives. True authority is grounded in holiness; faithful interpretation of Scripture requires its faithful performance.

> *For ongoing discussion:* How much of a gap can be endured between one's right interpretation of Scripture and one's failure in performance (e.g., churches that practice racial exclusion or unjust divisions between rich and poor)? How do we understand what goes wrong when the Bible is used as an instrument of oppression and division?

8. Christians need to read the Bible in dialogue with diverse others outside the church.

There is a special need for Christians to read Scripture in respectful conversation with Jews, who also serve the one God and read the same texts that we call the Old Testament within a different hermeneutical framework. There are also diverse others to whom we need to listen and from whom we need to learn. This includes critics who charge us with ideological captivity rather than fidelity to God.

> *For ongoing discussion:* How do we pursue the tasks of learning (again) to read Scripture faithfully in the church while also being in dialogue with those outside? How should we understand and engage people who find themselves, in some sense, simultaneously inside and outside a fragmented church?

9. We live in the tension between the "already" and the "not yet" of the kingdom of God; consequently, Scripture calls the church to ongoing discernment, to continually fresh rereadings of the text in light of the Holy Spirit's ongoing work in the world.

Because the narrative of Scripture is open to a future that God will give, and because our vision is limited by creaturely finitude and distorted by sinfulness, we lack the perspective of the finished drama as we seek to live faithfully in the present. Yet we trust that the story is moving to a final consummation in which God will overcome death and wipe away every tear from our eyes. Knowing that we do not see ourselves and our world from God's point of view, we are grateful for the gifts of Scripture and community and for the possibilities of mutual correction in love that they offer. We are also grateful for Scripture's promise that the Spirit of God will lead us into truth, which gives us hope that our speech and practice might yet be a faithful witness to the righteous and merciful God who is made known to us in Jesus Christ.

> *For ongoing discussion:* If the story has not yet reached its conclusion, does this have implications for understanding the relationship between Scripture's identification of God and the claims made by other religious traditions? How are our fresh rereadings to be distinguished from interpretations of Scripture that purport to separate the "kernel" of the gospel from the "husk" of cultural accretions? To what standards of accountability are we called in order to keep our rereadings faithful to the God of Jesus Christ?

HOW DO WE READ AND TEACH THE SCRIPTURES?

Teaching the Bible Confessionally in the Church

Ellen F. Davis

One day about six years ago I sat around a table dreaming with a group of theologians, biblical scholars, and scholars in secular disciplines who regularly enter into dialogue between their own disciplines and theology. We were Catholics and Protestants, the latter representing a broad spectrum of reformed traditions. Our enviable task was to identify the kinds of theological inquiry that should be pursued and funded in order to provide solid intellectual grounding for this stage of the church's life. We did not need to worry about raising funds or administering projects; we were asked only to imagine what would most benefit the church. Somewhat to our surprise, it took no more than an hour — probably an academic record — for us to agree on the most fundamental need, namely, to learn again to read and teach the Bible confessionally within mainstream North American and European Christianity.

By "confessional" reading and teaching, we did not mean interpreting in accordance with a particular doctrinal statement, such as the Westminster Confession. Rather, we identified the need for the church to learn afresh to acknowledge the Bible as the functional center of its life, so that in all our conversations, deliberations, arguments, and programs, we are continually reoriented to the demands and the promises of the Scriptures. Reading the Bible confessionally means recognizing it as a word that is indispensable if we are to view the world realistically and hopefully. We acknowledge it as a divine word that is uniquely powerful to interpret our experience. But more, we

A form of this essay appeared in *Anglican Theological Review* 84 (2002): 25-35. Permission granted.

allow ourselves to be moved by it, trusting that it is the one reliable guide to a life that is not, in the last analysis, desperate. Reading the Bible confessionally means reading it as the church's Scripture, and the meeting I have described was the origin of the Scripture Project.

This essay summarizes my own goals as a teacher of Bible in a seminary context; it is at the same time intended to provide guidelines for the kind of teaching that would in my judgment be most effective in congregational settings. Since most clergy do the bulk of their teaching in the pulpit, it is important to note at the outset that everything of substance here applies equally to preaching and classroom teaching of the Bible.

In brief, teaching Christians to read the Bible confessionally means equipping them to do three things: to read with a primarily theological interest; to read with openness to repentance; and to read with an understanding of the Old Testament witness to Christ.

I. Reading with a Theological Interest

One of the watershed moments in my self-awareness as a teacher of Scripture occurred a few years ago when I moved to a new teaching position. Looking at the long-established catalogue description of the introductory Old Testament course, I realized that it projected a course I did not intend to teach. The description stated that the course would emphasize the historical and religious background of the biblical text, presumably referring both to social-historical studies of ancient Israel and to study of the literary history of the biblical text. I wrote the following as a substitute: "The Old Testament will be examined as a rich and complex witness to Israel's faith." The difference between these catalogue entries undoubtedly reflects a difference in personal background between me and my predecessors, a difference in our particular interests and skills. But even more, it represents a generational difference in our perceptions of where the present struggle is for the church as it attempts to read the Bible as the word of God.

An earlier generation of biblical scholars rightly perceived that people who read the Bible were looking for theological meaning but did not take with sufficient seriousness the historical character of the Bible — or, more likely, knew nothing of it. The challenge facing that generation was to demonstrate convincingly how it is that the "words of Torah [come to us] through human language," as the ancient rabbis said: how deeply the biblical texts are embedded in a particular culture; how they reflect current events; how they are shaped and in some ways limited by the Zeitgeist as well as by the Holy Spirit.

I am myself profoundly indebted to this historical work and draw upon it daily in my teaching. Nonetheless, in the present intellectual climate, I believe the Bible is often read "too historically" — that is, too narrowly so. Many students in mainstream Protestant seminaries study the Bible as if its aim were to give us insight into ancient ideologies and events. Yet a confessional reading sees in the Bible a different aim: first of all, to tell us about the nature and will of God, to instruct us in the manifold and often hidden ways in which God is present and active in our world; and second, to give us a new awareness of our selves and our actions, to show us that in everything, we have to do with God. In a word, the Bible's aim is to do theology.

Since the Bible is about human life in the presence of God, it follows that teaching the Bible confessionally is not primarily a matter of conveying historical information. The teacher's task is to impart the information and the conceptual framework, but even more, the imaginative skills for wondering fruitfully about the ultimate facts of life: love, sin, redemption, forgiveness — facts that can be pondered and confirmed as true, yet never really explained, and certainly not explained away. The Bible confronts us with facts that are peculiar in this way: the better we understand them, the more we wonder about them. So teaching the Bible confessionally means enabling people to wonder wisely and deeply. Wondering is the business of scholars and preachers, just as it is of Sunday school children. My own sermons and lectures are generated by the things I wonder about: Why is this verse phrased the way it is? Can I afford to let my worldview shift or expand in response to this miracle story? Can I afford not to? How can the church responsibly yet profoundly appropriate this apocalyptic vision?

The capacity for fruitful theological wondering resides chiefly in the imagination. Theologian Garrett Green has argued persuasively that in many instances the biblical term "heart" (לֵב, *lev;* καρδία, *kardia*) refers to what we call imagination.[1] This notion wonderfully illuminates the use of that word in the eucharistic liturgy: "Lift up your hearts" — lift up your imaginations, open them toward God. Yet an aroused imagination is not in itself a holy state, for the "heart" can be healthy or perverted. Perhaps it is in tacit recognition of this fact that Anglican eucharistic worship begins with the Collect for Purity:

Almighty God, to you all hearts are open, all desires known, and from you no secrets are hid: Cleanse the thoughts of our hearts by the inspiration

---

1. Garrett Green, *Imagining God: Theology and the Religious Imagination* (San Francisco: Harper & Row, 1989), pp. 109-10.

Amen!!)

of your Holy Spirit, that we may perfectly love you, and worthily magnify your holy Name, through Christ our Lord.[2]

The Collect for Purity introduces the Ministry of the Word. Thus we ask that when the appointed lections are read, we may be changed in order to hear them with healthy "hearts." Yet at the same time, the church understands that through the action of the Holy Spirit, "the word of the Lord" may itself be an agent of cleansing for our imaginations. Therefore, the subsequent reading of Scripture is part of God's gracious answer to the Collect for Purity.

Correct.'y a rule

In addition to imaginations fit for the reading of Scripture, students also need literary skills, and these are often of a different kind than their earlier studies have required of them. Most new seminarians are schooled in textbooks, operators' manuals, and plot-driven novels. They know how to skim for content, yet relatively few of them are experienced with literary complexity. Moreover, the Bible is the last place they expect their reading skills to prove inadequate, since most entering students think they know what is there, even if they have never actually read it. So the first task that confronts them — or should confront them — is to learn to read in a radically different way. One of my students in the introductory Old Testament course put the problem succinctly about eight weeks into the first semester: "When we started, I thought the problem was that I read too slowly. Now I see that the problem is, I read too fast." Making mileage through the text invariably impedes movement into what Barth rightly calls "the strange new world within the Bible." Slowing down, we can begin to see how the (sometimes frustratingly) complex literary artistry of the Bible conveys theological meaning.

The most difficult aspect of the Bible's literary complexity is its use of symbols. The Bible speaks often in symbolic, or imaginative, language for the simple reason that the realities of which it speaks exceed the capacity of ordinary, "commonsense" discourse. Symbols are inherently ambiguous, and necessarily so; their continuing validity depends on their ability to take on new meanings in new situations and in light of new insights and challenges. The nature of biblical language bears on some of the deepest problems with which the church is currently wrestling. For example, as I argue in another essay in this volume,[3] the symbolic representation of holiness as set forth in Leviticus bears on the sexuality debate: in the purity legislation (Lev

---

2. *The Book of Common Prayer* of the Episcopal Church, USA (1979), p. 355.
3. Ellen F. Davis, "Critical Traditioning."

11–19), Israel symbolizes its understanding of the boundaries that God established at creation. The question that troubles the church is whether or not that symbolism is open to radical theological reinterpretation. Interpretation of symbols is the church's most serious and most consequential business. Precisely such a reinterpretation of the purity legislation marked the split between synagogue and church in the first century. Many rightly fear that the community that worships the God of Israel may once more split or fragment over this issue.

"God the Father" is another biblical symbol whose interpretation and continuing validity are much debated. Aware that symbols always originate and function within particular social contexts, feminist theologians rightly raise the question, Do we wish to perpetuate the androcentric bias of ancient social systems? The question is valid, but in this case the canonical context of the symbol also needs to figure in the debate. Here the crucial point is that long before Jesus and the New Testament writers took up the symbol of God the Father, the Hebrew Scriptures had already supplied images of fatherhood that make this a potent symbol of suffering love. Most obvious is Malachi's representation of God, the Father of contemptuous children, crying out: "And if I am a father, then where is my honor?" (Mal 1:6). Since, in the Christian ordering of the Bible, Malachi is the last book of the Old Testament, this pained question receives an immediate answer in the good news of Jesus Christ, the faithful Son.

Several indelible images of human fathers in the Old Testament also inform the gospel's use of the symbol God the Father. First among them is Abraham, a father against all odds, journeying to Moriah to sacrifice his "only son" Isaac. That Abraham is torn between two demanding and irresistible loves is indicated by the narrative in the simplest way. His immediate response when God calls — "Here I am" (Gen 22:1) — is echoed and matched by his exquisite attention to the boy: "Here I am, my son" (Gen 22:7). A second unforgettable image is David, the betrayed father, mourning the son who perished making war against him: "My son Absalom, my son, my son Absalom! If only I had died instead of you! Absalom, my son, my son!" (2 Sam 19:1 Heb). Perhaps the most complex image of a human father's suffering love is that of Job. The overly careful father of the first chapter, anxiously seeking to ward off any harm that might befall his party-loving children (Job 1:5), is transformed through much grief into the carefree father of the final chapter, bestowing on his daughters frivolous names and (contrary to "patriarchal" custom) an inheritance — apparently, just because they are pretty! Thus "father" is already a highly condensed expression of love that suffers unimaginably and yet finds resources to love still more and in unexpected ways — all this before the symbol is taken up and expanded by Jesus and the evangelists![4]

It is largely in response to the literary complexity of the Scriptures that some seminary faculties are placing increasing emphasis on the study of biblical languages. I am one of those who believe that it is best to enter this strange new world within the Bible by becoming radically uncertain about the language spoken there — at first, uncertain of every letter. But as one progresses a few weeks or months into language study, the *theological* fascination becomes obvious. Biblical statements that seemed straightforward now become curious; they become the ground from which new questions spring up. Does divine compassion appear in a new light when one learns that the Greek word implies intestinal activity and the Hebrew word evokes the maternal womb? It is the business of published translations to resolve ambiguities, but those who read in the original language revel in them. Jonah proclaimed: "Another forty days and Nineveh is inverted!" (Jonah 3:4). Was his prophecy of doom subsequently annulled by God's predictable mercy (4:2), or was his prophecy of conversion fulfilled?

The more small uncertainties we are willing — or constrained by "ignorance" — to entertain, the more texture appears in the text. That is why it is instructive for senior-level teachers periodically to teach beginning languages. It was a first-year Hebrew student (a struggling one) who altered my reading of Gen 11:1: "And all the earth was one language and one [set of] words." The standard translation regularizes the phrasing thus: "Now the whole earth *had* one language and the same words" (NRSV). But what my student helped me see — after successfully resisting my effort to "correct" his translation — is that the Hebrew phrasing is a reductio ad absurdum. The world in its bewildering complexity is revealed to be nothing more than talk. And when that talk gets too pretentious — "Come on, let's build us a city and a tower with its head in the heavens" (Gen 11:4) — God undoes the pretension with perfect irony: "Come on, let's go down and there make a mess of their language . . ." (Gen 11:7).

Study of Greek and Hebrew gives us a fruitful unsettledness about the language of the Bible. And as we take that unsettledness to heart, then we may gradually become unsettled in our own language. The church would be hugely blessed if its teachers, preachers, and theologians were to suffer a loss of fluency in speaking about how things stand with us, before God. We live in

---

4. For a good general discussion of Old Testament usage of the metaphor of God the Father, see Marianne Meye Thompson, *The Promise of the Father: Jesus and God in the New Testament* (Louisville: Westminster/John Knox, 2000), pp. 35-55.

an age of glibness. It is hard to imagine that in all human history words have ever been so plentiful, so lightly considered, and so deceptive as they became in the course of the twentieth century. A survivor of Auschwitz says that all words have become for her suspect or ridiculous — not just the calculated rhetoric of political camouflage but ordinary expressions that seem to require no thought: "I'm dying for a cup of tea."

However, that most appalling example may not be the best general proof that "our language is broken," as Barbara Brown Taylor argued in her recent Beecher Lectures.[5] Our language is broken by our denial of its uncertainty. Mass media journalists, politicians, academics all speak and write copiously and, moreover, authoritatively; their jobs depend upon it. Maybe their jobs depend upon their sounding more certain than they are about what is true. At any rate, it is rare to find a piece of journalism, of political rhetoric, or even of academic writing that clearly evidences the struggle to express the truth "about what it is to be human and hungry in a fallen world full of wonders."[6]

Yet theologians and preachers are distinguished from workers in these other categories because we are specifically charged by the community of faith to do that necessarily uncertain work. If we are glib in the face of what is mysterious and never fully known, then the church is misled. But if study of the biblical languages has created a lively awareness of the awkwardness, the inadequacy, the slipperiness — and the potential richness — of words woven together, then the church may be well served by those of us who stammer on her behalf.

Cultivating unsettledness about biblical language and unsettledness about our own — these are good reasons for studying Hebrew and Greek. But perhaps the best reason is the most obvious: reading in the original languages slows us down, and reading the text more slowly is essential for learning to love the Bible. As we know from other areas of experience, giving careful attention is not just an outcome of love; it is part of the process of growing in love. We love best those for whom we are obligated to give regular, often demanding, care: a child, an animal, a sick or elderly person, a plot of land or an old house. Inching patiently through the Greek or Hebrew text is best seen as "an act of charity"[7] — ultimately, charity toward God. Poring over every syllable, frustration notwithstanding, we affirm the ages-old conviction of the

---

5. Barbara Brown Taylor, *When God Is Silent* (Cambridge, Mass.: Cowley, 1998), p. 39.

6. Taylor, *When God Is Silent*, p. 110.

7. For this phrase I am indebted to my teaching colleague and former Hebrew student, Amy Laura Hall.

faithful that these words of Scripture are indeed "some molten words perfected in an oven seven times."[8]

II. Reading with Openness to Repentance

Acquiring literary competency with Scripture should make us suspicious of our interpretations. "The hermeneutics of suspicion" has become a byword in contemporary biblical scholarship, the chief object of suspicion being the text itself, viewed as a social product. But if we are reading from a confessional perspective — that is, as members of a community that regularly confesses its sins as well as its faith — then it is well to begin by suspecting our own interpretations. Most of them have probably not been reconsidered in a long time — years in our own lives, generations in the church. Whenever we pick up the Bible, read it, put it down, and say, "That's just what I thought," we are probably in trouble. The technical term for that kind of reading is "proof-texting." Using the text to confirm our presuppositions is sinful; it is an act of resistance against God's fresh speaking to us, an effective denial that the Bible is the word of the living God. The only alternative to proof-texting is reading with a view to what the New Testament calls *metanoia*, "repentance" — literally, "change of mind."

One of the important literary features of the canon is the way its multivoiced witness exposes the tendency to read the Bible "for ourselves," in Dietrich Bonhoeffer's phrase, that is, in order to maintain our self-interest.[9] The book of Jonah sounds an "anti-prophetic" note in Israel's face: "So you think the oracles against the nations (e.g., Isa 13–23; Jer 46–51; Ezek 25–32) mark the end of God's concern for the Gentiles? Rethink that." The divine speeches in Job counter an anthropocentric reading of Genesis 1: "So you think the P(riestly) creation account means that the whole world was created for human beings and their self-gratification? Wrong again."

Because the Bible speaks with multiple voices, it attests to the perpetual struggle of the faith community to test different perspectives. Some of these voices are complementary, probably reflecting gradual shifts in Israel's religious perception; they allow us as readers gradually to broaden our vision. Other voices stand in sharp disagreement and press us hard to examine en-

---

8. This rendering of Ps 12:7 (Heb) is that of poet Jacqueline Osherow, *Dead Men's Praise* (New York: Grove, 1999), p. 53.

9. Dietrich Bonhoeffer, *No Rusty Swords*, trans. C. H. Robertson et al. (London: Collins, 1970), p. 181, cited in Fowl and Jones, *Reading in Communion: Scripture and Ethics in Christian Life* (Grand Rapids: Eerdmans, 1991), p. 140.

trenched positions.[10] In other words, the canon itself models for us a process of *metanoia* within the community of faith, and this is one of the best reasons to trust its witness.[11]

For Christians, the ultimate goal of *metanoia* is that our minds be conformed to the mind of Christ (1 Cor 2:16; cf. Rom 12:2). Such conformity is an eschatological state that we can now only dimly imagine: "It does not yet appear what we shall be. But we know that when he appears we shall be like him, for we shall see him as he is" (1 John 3:2). And in our present state of sin, seeking immediate identification — "What would Jesus do?" — may be dangerously self-deceptive if it leads us to ignore the incomparability of Jesus' sinless life to our own. The Old Testament is the best hedge against overhasty identification with Jesus. For it offers something the Gospels do not, namely, a wide range of developed human characters whose stories clarify where we now are, both as individuals and as a community. The New Testament writers are of course counting on us to know those stories and to make full use of them in the lifelong work — and suffering — of being conformed to the mind of Christ. When teaching, preaching, and liturgy are designed well, those stories are being brought regularly to mind, so that Christians who are struggling precisely in their lack of "conformity" may find guidance and sympathetic companionship.

I recently preached at the ordination of a deacon. Being a lectionary preacher, I took as my text the Old Testament passage that *The Book of Common Prayer* rubric says is "ordinarily" used on that occasion, the call of Jeremiah (Jer 1:4-9). Immediately after the service, one of the participating priests looked at me with evident disappointment and said, "It's too bad you didn't talk about Jesus." Very likely I had overemphasized the difficulty of ordained ministry, and the sermon did not adequately convey the gospel message, found in both Testaments, that God is "very find-able in troubles" (Ps 46:2 Heb). But if I correctly understood his objection, it was to my choice of Jeremiah rather than Jesus as a model for Christian ministers. If that was indeed the objection, then I stand by my choice. Jeremiah's story is a model of faithful ministry because, like Jesus', it recounts persistence — decades-long in Jeremiah's case — in an "impossible" calling that meets with steady rejection. However, Jeremiah also shows us something about our present situation as ministers of the gospel that Jesus' story cannot, precisely because Jesus did not know sin in the same way that every other human being knows it. The book of Jeremiah has an essential place in the Christian Bible because it

---

10. See my essay "Critical Traditioning."
11. See Thesis 2, "Nine Theses on the Interpretation of Scripture."

shows us at the same time a long history of *resistance* to God, beginning with Jeremiah's first response to God's call: "Ahhh, Lord YHWH . . . look, I don't even know how to speak; I'm just a kid!" In Jeremiah's repeated "complaints," we hear his prolonged accusation against God for depriving him of friends and family and subjecting him to ceaseless pain. The complaints meet with God's sharp rebuke, which is also without analogue in Jesus' story:

> If you race with runners, and they weary you,
>   then how will you compete with horses?
> And if you count on a peaceful land,
>   then how will you do in the (wild) majesty of the Jordan?
>
> (Jer 12:5)

My point is that Jeremiah's ministry is a resource in a different way than is Jesus' own for those who are still struggling with their resistance to God — and that is probably every minister of the gospel. And the same point could be made with respect to every fully developed character in the Old Testament: Abraham, Jacob, Moses, David, Elijah, Job. None of these comes on the scene as a finished character, a completely satisfactory "holy man." As Eric Auerbach[12] and others have enabled us to see, one of the things that distinguishes biblical narrative from classical epic is the fact that biblical characters change. They are often substantially different at the end of the story than at the beginning, whereas "*pius* Aeneas" and "wily Odysseus" are not. As with Jeremiah, so with each of these biblical characters we see a movement away from personal absorption and toward God, a movement that could rightly be termed *metanoia,* or in Hebrew, *teshuvah,* "turning" — that is, repentance.

III. Reading with an Understanding of the Old Testament Witness to Christ

Probably the most far-reaching issue separating traditional and modern (or postmodern) biblical interpretation is whether — and if so, how — to read the Old Testament as a witness to Jesus Christ. The answer to that question is fundamentally theological, yet we must render it in a way that reflects an awareness of the complex historical issues involved. Among the relevant historical factors is, of course, the history of modern biblical scholarship. Historical criticism and studies of the literary and linguistic practices of the biblical

---

12. Eric Auerbach, "Odysseus' Scar," in *Mimesis* (Princeton: Princeton University Press, 1953).

writers have affected the way everyone — conservative, liberal, and postliberal — reads the text. Further (as I shall argue in the final section of this essay), our answer must also reflect an awareness of the long history of Jewish interpretation. As Christian interpreters of Scriptures we share with Jews, we must acknowledge that these shared texts have only rarely served as common ground between church and synagogue — and that only in the last two or three decades, at most. Rather, they have consistently been, as a rabbi with whom I study put it, "the texts that divide us."

My own teaching, almost all of which takes place in explicitly Christian settings, follows from acceptance of the consensus of virtually all premodern interpreters that it is legitimate — indeed, necessary — for Christians to find in the Old Testament a witness to the One who "came to fulfill the Law and the Prophets" (Matt 5:17). However, in discerning this witness, I regularly and instinctively eschew certain options from the Christian past. It never occurs to me to suggest that God's "Come on, let *us* go down there and make a mess of their language . . ." (Gen 11:7) is a reference to the Trinity. My training leads me to see a literary perspective as more helpful than a doctrinal one at this point. The divine resolve mocks the human boast: "Come on, let us build ourselves a city and a tower . . ." (Gen 11:4).

The characteristic of the text that allowed premodern readers to trace the Old Testament witness to Christ is one treated at length above, namely, the prominence of symbolic, or poetic, language. With respect to the Old Testament witness to Christ, what is important about language that engages the imagination is that it has the potential to create over time a vision that is both clear and open. It often takes years — maybe hundreds of them — for the vision to become clear, for fruitful interpretations to be sorted from misleading ones. After a lapse of six centuries, the crucifixion clarified the enigma of exilic Isaiah's fourth Servant Song (Isa 52:13–53:12). The biblical canon itself testifies to the fact that expectations based on historically specific prophetic language were often disappointed, at least in the first instance, and then became subject to reinterpretation (e.g., the eighth-century Isaiah's Immanuel prophecy; Jeremiah's seventy years until deliverance from Babylon, reinterpreted in Daniel and again in Christian tradition as setting the time for the first and second comings of Christ). Moreover, it is important to recognize that it is not only prophetic poetry that bears witness to Christ. The New Testament writers range through the whole canon, drawing especially on the Psalms[13] and the wisdom tradition, to clarify the meaning of the Christ event.

---

13. "David," understood as author of the Psalms, is also viewed as a prophet by the New Testament writers.

Yet, as the Gospels show, the best interpretation retains the poetic openness of the original and thus continues to beget a religious vision that has suppleness as well as clarity.

Until the present generation, Christians have generally believed that reading the Old Testament as a witness to Jesus Christ means that the New Testament illumines the Old. But far less attention has been given, even among biblical scholars, to the necessary converse of that view — namely, that the New Testament itself can be understood only in light of a profound theological reading of the Old Testament. In one of his last writings, Dietrich Bonhoeffer states it sharply: "I still read the New Testament far too little on the basis of the Old," and further: "I don't think it is Christian to want to get to the New Testament too soon and too directly."[14] That lapidary statement points to a tenet of Bonhoeffer's theology that increasingly informed his work in the last years of his life: Study of the Old Testament enables us to hear the demand and the harsh warning that run all through the New Testament. Yet we have been trained not to hear it, by too much soft-pedaling in Sunday school and from the pulpit. In a sermon on a hard saying from the gospel — "It is easier for a camel to go through the eye of a needle than for a rich man to enter the kingdom of God" (Mark 10:25) — I heard a preacher surmise that "Needle's Eye" is the name of a narrow mountain pass in Palestine. So Jesus is saying that the passage takes skill (especially with the rich man's entourage) but can be accomplished. However, a plain-sense reading would set this saying against the background of Amos's threats against the rich "who are at ease in Zion and confident on the hill of Samaria" (Amos 6:1), warning that they will be first to experience God's wrath.

Moreover, finding continuity with the witness of the Old Testament makes it possible to preach parts of the New Testament that would otherwise leave the preacher speechless. The book of Revelation, probably the bloodiest book in the Bible, and the wildest, seems stylistically and temperamentally very far removed from the "home turf" of the narrative of Jesus in Palestine or the pastoral and doctrinal discourse of Paul. In fact, the closest analogues are the apocalyptic visions of Ezekiel, Zechariah, and Daniel. Further, the language of Revelation is thick with allusion: words and phrases from the Hebrew Scriptures echo on every page. It is pertinent also that Revelation is a book that is in toto addressed to the imagination.[15] The training in reading

---

14. Dietrich Bonhoeffer, *Letters and Papers from Prison* (London and Glasgow: SCM, 1953), pp. 93, 50.

15. This insight is the point of departure for Eugene H. Peterson, *Reversed Thunder: The Revelation of John and the Praying Imagination* (San Francisco: Harper & Row, 1988).

symbolic language that the Old Testament affords is mandatory before advancing even one sentence into John's vision, which aims to raise our sights to the ultimate destination of the Christian journey, the heavenly Jerusalem. However, the inference one must draw from John's allusive style is that we cannot conceive of that goal — let alone reach it — without having firmly in mind a picture of where we have been and where we now are, as set forth in the Hebrew Scriptures.

Yet reading the New Testament "on the basis of the Old" is a practice that ramifies beyond our understanding of individual passages or even an entire book. Preaching and teaching more deeply from the Old Testament is instrumental in correcting misapprehension of the gospel message as a whole. Here I highlight one crucial point at which the Old Testament challenges a common misreading of that message, namely, in an exclusive focus on "salvation" as though that were the single theme of the gospel and the Christian life: "Are you saved?"

That question — or its more subtle counterparts found in the Protestant and Catholic "mainstream" — puts me, or what God has done for me, at the center of religious interest. Yet the Old Testament clarifies the fact that the Bible as a whole is relentlessly *theo*centric. Its pervasive focus is not salvation, either personal or corporate, but rather revelation of the nature and will of God. From a biblical perspective, salvation is a subcategory of revelation — or better, salvation is a consequence of revelation fully received. This is a regular pattern in the Bible: when God's Person or Presence is made known to some human agent and God's will is fully accepted and therefore becomes operative in our world, then salvation is what happens for God's people. The culmination of the pattern is Jesus' perfect knowledge of his Father, demonstrated in his obedient life and his death, through which salvation comes to the whole world. But consider also the shape of Torah. Salvation per se is the subject of perhaps 20 chapters (of the 187 chapters of the Pentateuch), the stories of Noah and the exodus being key instances. What dominates this foundational story is the increasingly clear revelation of God's character, demonstrated as covenant faithfulness to "every living being" (Gen 9:10), and to Israel in particular. Further, God's will is revealed, first in creation, then through the covenants with Noah, with Abraham's family, and with all Israel at Sinai. The Sinai teaching — and its lengthy recapitulation in Moab (Deut 1:5) — occupies the remainder of Torah.

So salvation is the keynote of the first 15 chapters of Exodus (although the theme of God's revelation, to Moses and to Pharaoh, is also present here). These chapters contain what is to Christians probably the most familiar story in Torah, and certainly the part that Hollywood has judged to have most cinematic value. (The recent animated blockbuster *The Prince of Egypt* never gets beyond it.) The revelation of God's will and the story of Israel's early responses to it — both obedient and disobedient — occupy about 120 chapters: the rest of Exodus, Leviticus, Numbers, and Deuteronomy. God's revelation to Moses leads to salvation for Israel in Egypt, and that leads to more revelation for Israel at Sinai. Where the center of gravity falls within Torah is clear.

A similar balance is found in the Prophets, arguably where the center of gravity falls in the Christian Old Testament. The theme of salvation is of course frequent in the Prophets, and most notably in Isaiah, whose name itself means "YH[WH] will save." But the whole prophetic corpus is nothing other than a persistent revelation of God's nature and will for Israel in the face of Israel's devastating rejection of God and, eventually, in the face of Israel's own terrible suffering.

What does this focus on revelation within the Old Testament signify for a "good reading" of the New Testament? Here is one possibility: Adequate apprehension of the gospel requires that we amplify our vocabulary for talking about God beyond the firm but (sadly) hackneyed truth that God is Love. The Old Testament establishes with equal firmness, in Leviticus and again in "the evangelical Prophet" Isaiah, that God is holy, an affirmation that underlies the first petition of the prayer our Lord taught the disciples. In both Torah and Prophets, it is clear that the proper response to God's holiness is human obedience. Surely Jesus' own submission to death on a cross is just such an obedient response to God's holiness. We have been saved through grace — this is often the first affirmation we make as Christians awakening to the wonder of the life we share with God. But if the fruits of salvation are to be evidenced in the world, then the affirmation of salvation needs to be followed by the question, What form of obedience does Christian discipleship now require?

Conclusion: Reading in Dialogue with Jews

The danger of Christians reading the Bible confessionally is that we run the risk of reading alone. One of the positive elements to appear within the last generation or two of Christian seminary students is a growing awareness that Christians are not the only ones who read the first three-quarters of the Bible[16]

---

16. I do not include the Apocrypha in this reckoning, as it is not part of the primary canon of either Jews or Protestant Christians.

from a faith perspective. My own students frequently voice their discomfort with an unwarranted "Christianizing" of the Old Testament.[17]

Since in the preceding section of this essay I have argued for reading the Old Testament as a witness to Jesus the Christ, I want here to address what is in my judgment the most troubling objection that could be raised to my argument, namely, that it excludes the possibility of "read[ing] Scripture in respectful conversation with Jews."[18] Failing to address that objection would undercut the first two elements of my argument as well, or at least it would belie my own reasons for mounting the arguments. With respect to the first — reading the Bible with a primarily theological interest — I should note that my initial fascination with the Bible was prompted and encouraged by Jewish teachers whose own interest was theological, and much of my subsequent education has proceeded and continues to proceed in conversation with Jewish colleagues. With respect to the second element of my argument — reading with openness to repentance — I shall suggest here that one of the forms of repentance most necessary for Christian theological interpreters to exercise, not just personally but on behalf of the tradition, is demonstrating theological respect for and, indeed, gratitude toward Jews.

Christian biblical interpretation is dangerous when it is pursued in ignorance or disregard of the long history of Jewish interpretation, and also Jewish martyrdom. (These two must be considered together, because they are inextricably bound in the minds and the lives of many Jews.)[19] The danger is

17. For some, discomfort begins with the term "Old Testament" itself. Yet I still entitle my introductory course for seminarians "Old Testament Interpretation," because that term is more accurate for most Christian interpretation than the recently popularized phrase "Hebrew Scriptures." This is for two reasons. First, while Jewish confessional readings almost invariably take their interpretive cues from the Hebrew text and often involve sophisticated wordplay in that language, this style of reading is largely foreign to Christian interpretation. Second, Christian theological interpreters, especially preachers, do inevitably read the Old Testament directionally, as "open[ing] toward the New" (see Thesis 3). Accordingly, the modifier "Old" does not in this instance mean "outdated." Rather, it affirms a long-established authority that commends respect, like "old money."

18. See Thesis 8.

19. Daniel Boyarin offers a compelling and consequential example in the person of Rabbi Akiva, the greatest Jewish teacher of antiquity. Boyarin argues that Akiva's midrashic teachings and the account of his martyrdom (while being flayed by Roman soldiers, he recited the Shema and interpreted "with all your soul" for his students, who witnessed the execution) both reflect "a way of reading and living in the text of the Bible, which had and has profound implications for the life of the reader. If my reading has any cogency, R. Akiva is represented in the tradition as having died a martyr owing to his way of reading. Moreover, his model had profound implications for the development of martyrology. All through the Middle Ages, Jews went enthusiastically to a martyr's death with R. Akiva's words on their lips." Daniel Boyarin, *Intertextuality and the Reading of Midrash* (Bloomington: Indiana University Press, 1990), p. 128.

real and present, because the long history of traditional (i.e., theological) Jewish interpretation is widely overlooked in Christian theological education.[20] If it is treated at all, it is as a specialized subject for advanced students. But in fact, my experience is that beginning Bible students can be both inspired and instructed by even a slight introduction to Jewish interpretation — for example, a section from *Midrash Rabbah* (the compilation of midrashic teachings on various books of the Bible) or a passage from Rashi's commentary on the Torah. Especially, they respond with interest and sometimes relief to a tradition in which more than one possible meaning is routinely entertained. Such exposure is a welcome counter to the impression that many seminarians seem to take from their introductory Bible course, that a given text is a puzzle with only one solution — an impression that often makes biblical study oppressive rather than exhilarating.[21]

In order for Christian seminarians to see that biblical interpretation can be genuinely dangerous, it is important for them to be exposed also to the "confessional anti-Semitism" that has been, from ancient to modern times, a persistent element of Christian theology and therefore of Jewish history. A vivid example of such interpretation has recently been made available to teachers and scholars through publication of the *Bibles moralisées*, elaborately illustrated volumes produced for wealthy European patrons from the late twelfth century through the fifteenth century. In these volumes, biblical texts are interpreted visually and verbally at both literal and allegorical levels; the detailed illustrations are accompanied by brief commentary based on the Glossa Ordinaria, the standard medieval "one-volume commentary" on the Bible.[22] A steady theme of both illustrations and commentary is the passing of God's favor from *Synagoga*, sometimes depicted as a woman skulking away in shame, to *Ecclesia*, who is crowned as a queen. This work has enabled my students to see (literally) for the first time how the medieval church read the Bible in relation to Jews and to see that biblical interpretation played a role in the often tragic fate of European Jewry in those centuries — indeed, arguably, even up to the twentieth century.

Christian confessional interpretation of the Bible has historically been

20. One limitation here is the fact that few Christian biblical scholars are adept with postbiblical Hebrew. This is a problem that should be considered more carefully in the design of graduate programs of study. In the meantime, enough seminal materials are readily available in translation that it is not difficult for anyone with interest to gain a rudimentary knowledge.

21. As noted in Thesis 4, discernment of the multivalence of Scripture is also a part of Christian tradition.

22. An excellent introduction to these texts is provided by John Lowden, *The Making of the Bibles Moralisées* (University Park, Pa.: Pennsylvania State University Press, 2000).

dangerous, even deadly, to Jews. As Fowl and Jones have insightfully shown, bad biblical interpretation proceeds not just from ignorance but from sin.[23] Therefore, part of the hermeneutical challenge to contemporary Christians is to repent of our millennia-long hardness of heart. The task facing us is to learn again to read Scripture faithfully, in light of the tragic history between church and synagogue, and with a genuine desire to learn from those with whom we still disagree on significant matters.[24] I believe that the most fruitful form our repentance can take is for us actively to seek and cultivate theological friendships with Jews.

Something like a friendship can be formed through books, by reading Jewish interpretation both ancient and modern, but it is far better to befriend people we can meet face to face, with whom we can read "the texts that divide us." It is important to understand, however, that real theological friendship between Jews and Christians does not consist in either side's downplaying its own "right" to interpret. My experience is that Jews are not impressed when Christians genially forfeit our claim to a stake in the texts — as, for instance, in Paul van Buren's well-known characterization of the church's reading of the Old Testament as "reading someone else's mail."[25] Friendship means being forthright and at the same time respectful about our different viewpoints and interpretations.

The most positive outcome I know to such a friendship is the recognition that we do not have to figure out which one of us is wrong; indeed, that concept may not even apply. By ordinary logic, if two people or groups disagree, then one is wrong — or it is all relative and does not much matter anyway. But the basis for both disagreement and friendship is something that is neither strictly logical nor entirely relative. Rather, the basis for theological friendship between Christians and Jews is a mystery — the word Paul rightly uses (Rom 11:25; cf. 11:33) as he struggles with this most painful new fact of salvation history, the separation of Jews and Gentiles within the household of Israel's faith. The mystery has only deepened over time, as the two communities have over a period of two thousand years sustained an allegiance to the God to whom Israel's Scriptures bear witness, and likewise have experienced the faithfulness of that God to them. This prolonged duality is something neither Paul nor anyone else in the first century anticipated. At the very least, it

---

23. Stephen E. Fowl and L. Gregory Jones, *Reading in Communion: Scripture and Ethics in Christian Life* (Grand Rapids: Eerdmans, 1991), pp. 35-44.

24. See the questions for ongoing discussion following Thesis 8.

25. Paul van Buren, "On Reading Someone Else's Mail: The Church and Israel's Scriptures," in *Die Hebräische Bibel und ihre zweifache Nachgeschichte*, ed. Erhard Blum et al. (FS Rolf Rendtorff; Neukirchen-Vluyn: Neukirchener, 1990), pp. 595-606.

should caution us all to modesty in our theological assertions. Both Christians and Jews speak with some authority about the nature of God and what it means to worship God truly, authority that comes out of their willingness to study, to pray, and to suffer for what they understand to be true. On both sides that understanding is partial, so both Christians and Jews could well learn modesty in their assertions of "the Truth."

Modesty may enhance dialogue, but there is reason for excitement as well: the Holy Spirit may even now be doing something new in our midst. Within the last two or three decades, groups of religious Jews and Christians, in the United States and Europe and Israel, have begun to study Bible and theology together, taking an interest in learning how "the other" reads the Scriptures. While the number involved may be small, this is not (as in centuries past) the activity of a few individual scholars. For the first time in the history of the world, not only scholars but also the ordinary ranks of faithful Jews and Christians have an opportunity to grow in their faith as they read and learn together. Perhaps we are standing at a new juncture in the history of the two households that call themselves Israel.

Scripture's Authority in the Church

Robert W. Jenson

Much of what I have to say on this subject is elsewhere in print.[1] In this essay I will take certain points I have made elsewhere but will use them in a particular way: I will occupy them as *view*points, from which perhaps a new perspective may open on the whole matter of scriptural authority.

I

First perspectival point. The title of this essay contains a redundancy if "Scripture" means the unitary book we call the Bible. For outside the church, no such entity as the Christian Bible has any reason to exist. It is not merely that exegesis of the Bible is likely to be mistaken in one way or another when done outside the church; interpretation of the Bible outside the church must be arbitrary, uncontrollable, and finally moot.

The volume we call the Bible, or Scripture, is, to belabor a platitude, a *collection* of documents. These documents are extremely diverse — literarily, religiously, culturally, and theologically — and they derive from a long stretch of ancient Near Eastern and Mediterranean political and religious history. What Christians call the Bible, or Scripture, exists as a single entity because — and only because — the church gathered these documents for her specific purpose: to aid in preserving her peculiar message, to aid in maintaining across time, from the apostles to the End, the self-identity of her message that the God of Israel has raised his servant Jesus from the dead. Outside the com-

---

1. Most especially in my *Systematic Theology,* 2 vols. (New York: Oxford University Press, 1997-99), 1:25-33, 57-59; 2:272-84.

munity with this purpose, binding these particular documents into one volume would be pointless. Outside the community with this purpose, there is no reason to treat all and only these documents as making any kind of whole or to read any of them as a part of a whole.

And indeed, as academic exegesis has alienated itself from the church, Scripture has in fact fragmented for it. The Old Testament, once linked by that name with a New Testament, becomes "Hebrew Scripture," to be interpreted by itself. This entity does not then quite so obviously disintegrate, since the documents so designated have an external unity, being much of what is preserved of ancient Hebrew literature; but little follows from that for their interpretation. They have also an internal unity as a canon of Scripture antecedent to both rabbinic Judaism and Christianity, but this of course is as fragile outside rabbinic Judaism and the church as are the full Jewish or Christian canons themselves.

As for the New Testament, why *not* include a gnostic gospel or two, from more or less the same period? Why not favorites of mine, the letters of Ignatius, in my view rather more interesting and profound than some in the canon? Or, in the other direction, why not discern a "canon within the canon" and read the documents thus elected without material reference to the rest — as, indeed, professional New Testament scholars and denominationally bound preachers alike have done, for unlike reasons?

If for some reason academics outside the church choose to study any or all of the pieces into which Scripture falls in their hands, they are of course at liberty to do so. They are even at liberty to take the whole canon, as this odd collection the Christians once put together, and investigate why the church might have done that, what arbitrary sense she might have been imposing on the collected bits. And the church may happily receive any and all insights such investigations stumble across or information they make available. But such activity is not and cannot be *exegesis* of texts from the volume we call the Bible.

Of course, the problem is not limited to nonbelievers. It bothers us, too, in our secularized personae. We, too, have questions: What justifies specifically churchly exegesis of Scripture? Can church doctrine guide our reading? Why should it? Why should we interpret the story of Abraham and Isaac by the passion of Jesus? The answer is bluntly simple: What justifies churchly reading of Scripture is that there is no other way to read it, since "it" dissolves under other regimes.

Thus a hermeneutical exhortation from this first perspective. Be entirely blatant and unabashed in reading Scripture for the church's purposes and within the context of Christian faith and practice. Indeed, guide your reading by church doctrine. For if, say, the doctrine of Trinity and Matthew's construal of the passion do not fit each other, then the church lost its diachronic self in the early fourth century at the latest, and the whole enterprise of Bible reading is moot. The question, after all, is not whether churchly reading of Scripture is justified; the question is, what could possibly justify any other?

II

Second perspectival point. The message of Jesus' resurrection, the gospel, is a message about an event and so itself has the form of a narrative. Therefore, when the church sets out to read Scripture as a whole, the *kind* of unity by which she construes this whole is narrative unity. The church reads her Scripture as a single plotted succession of events, stretching from creation to consummation, plotted around exodus and resurrection.

We should pause here to note that the church included in her collection a subcollection, the Old Testament, that in some form antedated her existence. There is of course a way to read that subcollection that differs from the church's way. The church has a sibling in her claim to canonical Israel's Scripture — rabbinic Judaism.

Rabbinic Judaism and the Jesus community carried on from the destruction of ancient Israel in parallel fashion. The church added to Israel's Scripture a narrative supplement, the "New Testament," while rabbinic Judaism added not a new narrative but a new Torah, the oral Torah recorded in Mishnah and Talmud. Both church and synagogue thus have a double Scripture.

In accordance with the nature of its supplement, rabbinic Judaism reads the Tanakh as fundamentally Torah, divine guidance for life, identified as divine by the narrative included within it. The narrative thus has a supporting role and does not itself constitute the unity either of the Tanakh or of rabbinic Judaism's total Scripture, the twofold Torah. The church reads Israel's Scripture as what comes, and must come, before the Gospels and so reads the whole of her Scripture as fundamentally narrative; here Torah plays the supporting role, providing the moral structure that any narrative must have to be intelligible.

A hermeneutical exhortation from this second perspective. In the church any passage of Scripture is to be read for its contribution to the telling of Scripture's whole story. A piece of "wisdom," for example, is not properly interpreted if it is examined simply as a floating piece of advice, nor is an etiological narrative if it is read only as an interesting, or even true, explanation of some phenomenon.

III

Third perspectival point, for which the previous was a necessary foundation. Not only is Scripture within the church, but we, the church, are within Scripture — that is, our common life is located *inside* the story Scripture tells. The Bible is not about some other folk, and not even the very beginning steps of biblical exegesis may suppose that it is. Send not to know for whom the shofar sounds, or who will experience what the prophet foretells: *tua res agitur* — it is your thing that is at issue.

The canon itself establishes the continuation of its story to include us. It does so, first, simply by existing. The canonizing act is, after all, an act of republication. The church's canonizing act brought together a selection of documents written originally for other purposes and put them out as a collection for one new purpose. That is, the church republished them for a future group of readers, her own future self. The documents here in question were once directed within old Israel and the primal churches; by the act of canonization, they were redirected to the future church.

Materially, moreover, the New Testament includes a history of the community from which its documents come, the book of Acts. This history breaks off without conclusion, yet Luke shows no consciousness of stylistic failure; he is simply telling a story he expects to continue. And perhaps most telling, the canon includes the book of Revelation, a universal version of its narrative.

Now if we are *in* the story that Scripture tells us, certain ways of construing scriptural authority — which have perhaps been particularly exemplified in Protestantism — cannot be right. I will dwell with these negations for a time.

For a first such prohibition, it cannot be the purpose of Scripture to provide us with certified information about some entity *outside* its story about us, whether that third entity be God or certain classical religious experiences or the theological history of Israel and the primal church or whatever. Since we and Scripture and what Scripture talks about are not external to one another, since Scripture tells a story about God and us that we are even now living, there is no position from which such exchanges could be conducted — perhaps not even God has such an Archimedean point. This observation kills two historically instantiated errors with one stone.

On the one hand, whether or not Protestant high scholastics meant to teach such a hermeneutic, their modern appropriators certainly give the impression that Scripture is a sort of reference volume about God. On the other hand, many of those most eager to denounce such doctrine simply offer a modernist mirror of it. For whether the third entity about which Scripture is supposed to inform us is God or (what is very popular again) a tradition of religious experience or a normative stretch of religious history — and again the list of possibilities is long — the error is the same. Between the dubious aspect of the old-Protestant doctrine of inspiration and the position of many of its most adamant critics there is, in the matter of the actual misstep, no difference at all. Since we are *in* the story, all procedures that read Scripture for information about some third entity are wrong.

For a second negative consequence, a key assumption of historical-critical exegesis, as mostly practiced, cannot be right. We were all taught — and, I fear, I myself have taught — that before we "apply" a passage to ourselves, we first have to grasp it insofar as it is *not* about ourselves. We first have to understand a proposition of Paul's or a story about Samson in *its* community, specified precisely as *not our* community.

The first part of that last sentence is true; the second is false. For the community from which Scripture comes is not in fact "not our community"; the church to which Paul belonged is the very same, diachronically continuous church to which we belong. Paul's Antioch and his Athens and his Rome may have receded to be mere items in the past's dead grip, but his church has not. And if the church's claim to continue Israel is true, then the people of God who told Samson-stories are the very community to which Jews now belong by birth and into which baptized Gentiles have been grafted; the Philistines may be history in the sense of Emerson or Henry Ford, but Samson and his people are not.

This does not mean that historical-critical labors are futile or unnecessary. The story told by Scripture has been in progress for millennia, and *within* it there are historical distances in plenty, and so, in the narrative of this history, hermeneutical gaps in plenty. I do indeed need to build exegetical bridges between, say, Moses and Paul or between Paul and myself. But there is no gap to be bridged between the unitary community of interpretation from which these documents come and in which we now work at reading them, since these are not two communities of interpretation but only one.

Every community, after all, is actual only diachronically, only as it transcends the possible divisions of some stretch of time; a community exists only as it lasts for a while. The earthly *civitas dei*, if it exists at all, lasts from Adam to the eschaton.

For a third and last possibility excluded by the perspective we are currently occupying, if we are not outside the story told by Scripture, we have no leverage for a certain kind of modernist reading. This is the kind that tries to *salvage* something from Scripture, from what we are likely to call, when engaged in this archaeology, the "scriptural tradition."

Reading this way, we start with some antecedent body of convictions — liberating experience or some branch of "theory" or the demands *der deutschen Stunde* or "what science tells us" — and then look in Scripture for what can be construed as coherent with that set of convictions. If we stood outside the story told by Scripture, we could perhaps do this; but since we stand inside the scriptural story, we are bound instead to work just the other way around, to salvage from other bodies of convictions what can be made coherent with Scripture. Indeed, much of what we can plausibly mean by saying that Scripture is "authoritative" is that we are not to read Scripture in this particular modernist way or in any of its premodern analogues.

If we are in and not out of the story Scripture tells, certain ways of construing scriptural authority cannot be right. But what way *is* right? It seems fairly obvious, once one ponders the actual situation as I have tried so far to describe it: Scripture constrains our lives and thinking the way a play or novel constrains the lives and thinking of the characters.

Note that this is so precisely *before* the play or novel is finished. Not every conceivable set of events can be the third act of a play, the first two acts of which are already written — or at least this is true of plays that do not belong to the theater of the absurd. Let us say: Scripture is authoritative for us, as characters in the story that it tells, somewhat as the existing transcript of an unfinished play is determinative of what can be true and right for its characters in the part that remains to be written.

If there were not God, we could not of course exclude the theater of the absurd from the analogy; our situation would be precisely that of characters in a sequence with no outcome and therefore no plot. But the drama we inhabit is not absurd: it has an author with intentions. The author of our play has not written the third act, but when he does, he will do it as the same author who wrote the first two.

So now let us think of the characters in an unfinished play as being aware of their situation — as of course some modernist playwrights have done. In this case the constraint of the play as it has come so far will be actual in a particular way, as the characters pose questions to themselves: What are the author's intentions for us? What does he consider proper and improper for us to do and to suffer? Where is he going with this thing? The characters will try to answer such questions by discerning the plot of their doings and sufferings to this point. And if some "sides," as actors call them, are available, or even a director's notes, or perhaps a light-script or a prop list, they will study and restudy them.

The analogy has to become even more complicated, in a way again exemplified by some modernist plays and novels. For the story of God with his people as it is actually told in Scripture is not only the story of the characters created by the author but is also the story of the author — indeed, of the author as a character in his own play. The story is told not just as our story but fundamentally as God's story. The drama we inhabit with this omnipotent author constitutes his life as it affects ours.

We have come to the doctrine of Trinity, that is, to the church's encompassing hermeneutic. The persons who appear in Scripture as the characters of the divine story — Father, Son, and Spirit — and the plotlines between them simply *are* Scripture's God. The persons Father, Son, and Spirit are the doers not only of our life but of God's; and the plotlines of this action between Father, Son, and Spirit — the Father's finding himself in the Son or the Spirit's liberation of both to love each other — constitute the drama of God not just with us but for himself.

According to Nicene faith, the divine action in which we are involved is God's own being. Therefore, our questioning — Where is he going with us? — does not have to be what normal religion supposes it to be, an attempt to reason our way to knowledge of a distant God from clues other than God. As is demonstrated to satiety by the history of religion, this attempt, which constitutes normal religion's questing and journeying, is at once too arrogant and too unrewarding. It is arrogant in that it presumes that we *can* start with what is other than God and, by taking thought, even if with prayer and fasting, elevate ourselves to his presence. And it is unrewarding in that it ends in profound uncertainty. God, after all, is very different from even the most mysterious created entity. Even with a black hole or distant galaxy or short-lived particle, ingenuity can devise ways to check our reasonings by experience, by deriving from them predictions of new and previously unreckoned experience. How would we do that with God? Agnosticism is thus the natural condition of religion.

Specifying for our matter, Scripture is not a set of clues *from* which to figure out God, for the story it tells *is itself* the truth of God. The negative consequences of this observation are decisive. I will cite just one, of immediate relevance to our topic.

The dominant heresy of our time might be described as a cheapjack form of Arianism, as pop-Feuerbach. We are supposed to be on a quest for God, and the mode of our questing is projection. It seems so reasonable: God dwells in unapproachable light; our ability to see through to him, even if he in some sense reveals himself, must therefore be very limited and fragmentary, a matter of glimpses; and since we thus can have no embracing conceptual structure within which to communicate our glimpses, we can speak only with such metaphorical projections as experience may suggest. It seems so reasonable — but if the gospel is true, it is all wrong.

A hermeneutical exhortation from this third, lengthily occupied, perspective. Scripture's story is not a part of some larger narrative; it is itself the larger narrative of which all other true narratives are parts. Biblical exegesis is reading sides and prop lists and so forth for the drama that God and his universe are now living together. Do not when reading Scripture try to figure out how what you are reading fits into some larger story; there *is* no larger story. Try instead to figure out how American history or scientists' predictions of the universe's future course or the travail of a family in your congregation fit into Scripture's story.

IV

Fourth perspectival point. Since we now live the story Scripture tells, Scripture does not merely inform us about the course of this story, for persons live historically by discourse, by address and response to one another. Thus Scripture is not merely a record of divine-human history but a proclaiming of it, not merely an account of God's life with us to date but a voice in that life. When we read Scripture in the church, someone addresses us. And by the unanimous tradition of the church, this voice is the Word of God, the Logos, the second identity of the Trinity.

Moreover, by the teaching of those who have reflected most profoundly on this mystery — Irenaeus, Athanasius, Cyril, Maximus, Luther, Edwards, Barth — the Logos who speaks is not merely some posited metaphysical extra entity but the *actual* Logos, that is, the *incarnate* Word, the Word that God speaks as Jesus the crucified and risen Christ. Pastors sometimes introduce the reading of Scripture by saying, "Listen for the word of God." When Irenaeus or Athanasius listened for the Word of God in their Scripture, it was their Lord Christ they listened to hear, whether the text at hand came from Matthew or Isaiah or Moses or David. The *religiously* vital preexistence of Christ was, for them, precisely his preexistence in the Old Testament as the voice that speaks there, just as the New Testament was the voice of his continuing prophetic activity.

But is it not absurd to think of the Word as in any sense incarnate before the flesh existed, before Jesus was born? So that it could be the incarnate Word who spoke to Moses on the mountain or who cried out to his Father in many psalms? Or is it not absurd to think of the writing and collecting and reading and interpreting of the New Testament as this same Word's actual speech to us, who, as the angel said, is not here but risen?

The claim that the incarnate Christ speaks in all Scripture sounds preposterous, I suggest, only because we unthinkingly make an (in itself rather naive) assumption about time: that it glumly marches on, that someone born in 4 B.C. could not have spoken to and through Jeremiah or that someone who died in A.D. 30 could not have spoken through, say, the seer John. But time, in any construal adequate to the gospel, does not in fact march in this wooden fashion. Time, as we see it framing biblical narrative, is neither linear nor cyclical but perhaps more like a helix, and what it spirals around is the risen Christ. Thus John, having said in his prologue that the Word "became" flesh, presumably when Jesus was born, presents us with this enfleshed Word, in a context that makes his human enfleshment as obtrusive and, indeed, offensive as possible, and has him say, "Before Abraham was, I am." Which, then, comes first, the incarnation or Abraham? It depends entirely on which chapter of John you are in; that is, it depends on the discursive context.

So Luther's dictum that in the Psalms we find the prayer of Christ and all the saints is not the imposition on these texts of an alien "Christian" interpretation. If the gospel is true, it is simply the fact of the matter. Or — to stay with Luther — his exhortation to take Aaron as Christ, the great high priest (and so on for all the characters of the exodus story), and thus to read sections of the Pentateuch as something like another Gospel is simply a pointer to Exodus's plain sense.

The unity of Scripture is much tighter than we in modernity have dared to think. If the Word of the Lord that came to Second Isaiah and made him a prophet was Jesus Christ, then the vision of Christ that the church has derived from this prophet, of a "man of sorrows and acquainted with grief," is not a mere allowable trope but is in fact a product of Christ's own testimony to his own character, given by the mouth of his prophet. If the Word of the Lord, to whomever it comes, is Jesus, then we can indeed find out about the historical Jesus Christ from Isaiah or Zechariah or David, and about what Isaiah or Zechariah really meant from Jesus' teaching and story.

At the end of this stretch of my argument, another hermeneutical word. Do not be intimidated by the dogma that properly "historical" exegesis will not find Jesus in the Old Testament or discover Paul's intent by reading, say, Leviticus. This dogma is a mere metaphysical prejudice, which, as such, may of course be right — but then again may not be. Properly *biblical* reading of the Bible must, I suggest, proceed on the assumption that it is a false prejudice.

V

Last perspectival point. The first and primary way in which Scripture is authoritative in the church is simply that this collection of documents is privileged in the *life* of the church and, indeed, privileged in such a way as fundamentally to shape that life.

What gives a *liturgy* its plot? A liturgy is always a sort of drama, that is, an intentional sequence of events, however simple or simply done, that has a plot. At St. Vitus in the Exurb on a Sunday morning, what determines that plot? The supposed needs of "seekers" or of "the youth" or the "story" the pastor feels like telling — or the plot of the Bible?

Consider, for how it ought to be, the plot of the ancient service of Easter night. Light *follows* darkness, resurrection follows death, exodus and the Christian Pasch are told together, and the whole biblical narrative of salvation is recited around this transfer. Participants in *this* service *live* the authority of Scripture, in that they participate in a drama with Scripture's plot. If the Easter service is shaped by what we take to be the needs of the instant occasion, it is unlikely that any such event will occur, and the congregation will to that extent be deprived of biblical authority's actuality.

Do we, the congregation, as we sit there, witness the preacher struggling to say what the text says and doing so whether or not he or she personally likes the text? If texts are not determined by a lectionary, do we witness the preacher sometimes choosing a text we know must be difficult for him or her? If we do — and, indeed, perhaps most impressively, if we witness the preacher trying yet failing — then we experience the authority of Scripture.

Do we, in our public and private devotion, simply hear and read and pray a lot of Scripture, so that its phrases and tropes and patterns of argument and odd stories come to furnish our minds? When somebody says that so-and-so "pulled the pillars down on his own head," do recent graduates of church school get the point? When prayers or hymns are to be chosen or, at times, composed, what makes up our repertoire for the purpose? It is on such considerations that the authority of Scripture for faith turns.

A final hermeneutical word. To experience the authority of Scripture, this is the chief thing to do: Hang out with Scripture, on a particular corner, the corner where there is a little crowd gathered around someone telling about the resurrection.

I cannot finish by putting it all together, because that has already been done. The young Karl Barth, laboring between his identification with the oppressed workers of his congregation, the spectacle of liberal Europe's self-destruction, and his obligation to preach and preach and keep on preaching, and to do it from the Bible, discovered that the Bible opens into a world of its own and that, however surprising and upsetting the discovery, *that* is the *real* world.

Reading Scripture as a Coherent Story

Richard Bauckham

The church's reading of Scripture has usually presupposed its narrative unity, that is, that the whole of the Bible — or the Bible read as a whole — tells a coherent story. Any part of Scripture contributes to or illuminates in some way this one story, which is the story of God's purpose for the world. If Scripture does indeed tell the story of God's purpose for the world, then we should certainly expect to find unity and coherence in it. But the idea of reading Scripture as a unified narrative seems problematic from at least two very different perspectives: (1) that of biblical scholars for whom the great diversity of the biblical texts makes the claim of unity inconsistent with the nature of the Bible and (2) that of postmodern critics for whom a unified narrative would establish Christianity as the oppressive metanarrative that historically it has very often been.[1] This essay begins with a section that responds mainly to the first perspective. The argument about the Bible is then interrupted by a critical consideration of the second perspective (the postmodern critique of metanarratives) in order to resume, in the third section, a discussion of the biblical story with some conceptual tools provided by the postmodern approach.

I. The Biblical Story — Unity and Diversity

We should first be clear about the senses in which Scripture is clearly not a unified narrative. First, not all Scripture is narrative. Those books that are in

---

1. There is a third perspective the essay does not address: that of Jews for whom the Christian reading of the two Testaments as a unified narrative is problematic.

narrative form sometimes contain nonnarrative material within the narrative context (e.g., law in Exodus–Deuteronomy). Some books contain no narrative material at all, but it is not difficult to see that the canon implicitly gives some nonnarrative books (e.g., Psalms, Lamentations) a narrative setting within the story told by the narrative books. In a sense, this is true of the largest category of nonnarrative works in each Testament: prophecy and apostolic letters. (The Hebrew Bible explicitly signals the narrative context of prophecy by calling the historical books from Joshua to 2 Kings the Former Prophets and the prophetic books the Latter Prophets.) Prophecy and apostolic letters are intrinsically related to the biblical story, to which they constantly refer, even summarizing and retelling parts of it. The biblical narrative of God, his people, and the world structures their theology and is presupposed in the way they address the present and the future. The apocalypses, Daniel and Revelation, like parts of the Prophets, presuppose "the story so far" in envisioning its eschatological conclusion. Thus, while not all Scripture is generically narrative, it can reasonably be claimed that the story Scripture tells, from creation to new creation, is the unifying element that holds literature of other genres together with narrative in an intelligible whole.

However, there are a few books of which this is more difficult to say: Song of Songs, Proverbs, Ecclesiastes. Association with Solomon links them extrinsically to the story of Israel, but they seem to lack intrinsic connection with it.[2] The presence of these books in the canon might suggest that Scripture finds its unity not in the story it tells but in the God about whom it speaks (though the problem of a book that does not speak of God at all — Song of Songs — would still remain). But this is not a convincing distinction, since Scripture in general knows who God is from the story it tells of God, his people, and the world. The solution surely lies in recognizing that, although this story focuses on the particularity of God's activity in history, it also, especially in its beginning (Gen 1–11), recognizes God's general relationship as sovereign Creator to the whole creation and all people. In any case, it is important to note, with the trend of scholarship since the demise of the biblical theology movement, that the shape of the canon is distorted if biblical theology focuses on salvation history at the expense of either the wisdom literature of the Old Testament or the significance of creation throughout the canon.

There is also a second sense in which Scripture is not a unified narrative. The Bible does not tell a single story in the way that either a novel or a

2. But note the way Ellen Davis finds that the imagery of the Song of Songs links it with significant parts of the Old Testament story in Ellen F. Davis, *Proverbs, Ecclesiastes, and the Song of Songs* (Louisville: Westminster/John Knox, 2000).

modern work of historiography by a single author might. Whatever unity it has is not the kind of coherence that a single author might give to his or her work. The narrative books in fact adopt a wide variety of kinds of storytelling and historiography, while the future completion of the story can naturally be indicated only by narrative means quite different from those that tell, in whatever way, a story set in the past. Moreover, no one before the final editors or compilers of the New Testament canon even planned the assembling of precisely this collection of works. Of course, Christians believe that God's Spirit inspired these books and God's providence guided their collection, but this does not warrant our supposing that the Bible must have the kind of unity a human author might give to a work. God's inspiration has evidently not suppressed the diversity of the many human minds and circumstances that, at the human level, have made Scripture the collection of widely varied materials that it is. Perhaps we could appeal to Mikhail Bakhtin's notion of the polyphonic novel, in which the voices of the various characters and even the narrator are autonomous and equal.[3] The unity of such a novel consists in the dialogue of conflicting voices. The relation of the author to a polyphonic novel might constitute a kind of analogy for the relation of God to Scripture, but it would remain an analogy. Scripture has neither the *kind* of diversity nor the *kind* of unity a polyphonic novel does.

While the Bible does not have the kind of unity and coherence a single human author might give a literary work, there is nevertheless a remarkable extent to which the biblical texts themselves recognize and assert, in a necessarily cumulative manner, the unity of the story they tell. The books from Genesis to 2 Kings constitute a single edited history from creation to the exile, though the editors, especially of the Pentateuch, were evidently content to let stand a good deal of variety in the traditions they incorporated. In this they serve as something of a model for the compilers of the canon itself. The books of 1-2 Chronicles span the same period as Genesis–2 Kings, employing genealogy in the first eight chapters as a sophisticated means of representing the history from Adam to David. Although Ezra-Nehemiah is not placed after 1-2 Chronicles in the Hebrew canon, the editorial replication of the opening verses of Ezra at the end of 2 Chronicles does create a link, indicating the continuation of the same story. As well as these two parallel narratives, stretching from creation to, in one case, the exile, and in the other, the reconstitution af-

---

3. See Sue Vice, *Introducing Bakhtin* (Manchester: Manchester University Press, 1997), ch. 3. One of Bakhtin's major examples of the polyphonic novel was Dostoevsky's *The Brothers Karamazov,* but whether he was correct in regarding the various voices in the novel as equal is debatable. The issue bears some resemblance to debates about unity and diversity in the Bible.

ter the exile, the Old Testament contains three short stories: Ruth, Esther, and Jonah.[4] Each gives a perspective significantly different from those represented within the two major narrative sequences, but this is possible only because each is explicitly linked to the larger story of Israel (Ruth 1:1; 4:17-22; Esth 2:5-6; Jonah 1:1 with 2 Kgs 14:25).

The one biblical book that, in its way, matches the span of the whole canon is the Gospel of John, which begins with a deliberate echo of the opening words of Genesis and ends with a reference to the parousia (John 21:23, "until I come," Jesus' last words and the last words of the Gospel before the colophon), a reference that corresponds to the prayer with which Revelation concludes (Rev 22:20, "Come, Lord Jesus!"). The Gospel of Matthew opens with a genealogy that recapitulates the whole Old Testament history from Abraham onward, at the same time evoking the promises to Abraham and David, and closes with a reference to "the end of the age" (Matt 28:20). (It is worth noting that, whereas the biblical narratives in general leave a chronological gap between Old and New Testament stories — even if the deuterocanonical books of Maccabees are taken into account — the two genealogies of Matthew and Luke do create a kind of narrative link across the gap.) Throughout the New Testament, of course, the story of Jesus is treated as the continuation of the story of Israel and as initiating the fulfillment of the prophetic promises to Israel.

A sense of the unity of the biblical story is also given by a number of summaries to be found in both Testaments, though there is no summary of the whole story from creation to new creation. There are several summaries, of varying scope, of the story of Israel:

Deut 6:20-24 (exodus to occupation of the land);
Deut 26:5-9 (settlement in Egypt to occupation of the land);
Josh 24:2-13 (Abraham to occupation of the land);
Neh 9:6-37 (creation + Abraham to return from exile);
Ps 78 (exodus to David);
Ps 105 (Abraham to occupation of the land) and 106 (exodus to exile), cf. 1 Chr 16:8-36;
Ps 135:8-12 (exodus to occupation of the land);
Ps 136 (creation + exodus to occupation of the land);
Acts 7:2-50 (Abraham to Solomon).

---

4. The book of Jonah appears among the Twelve prophets in all canonical orders, but it clearly differs generically from the other components of the Twelve.

As different in focus and intent as these various summaries are, they tend to highlight the same major landmarks of the story. Just one of them virtually summarizes the whole Old Testament story: Neh 9:6-37, placed at the chronological end of that story, recapitulates the whole story from creation to its own time. Rather surprisingly, the Bible contains only one summary of the Old and New Testament stories as one: Acts 13:17-41 begins with the patriarchs and ends with the resurrection of Jesus and the preaching of the apostolic message. The New Testament contains many, mostly very short, summaries of the story of Jesus, some of which, like the later creeds of the church, project the story to its future end at his parousia (e.g., Acts 10:36-43). Despite such anticipations of the end of the story, it is important to notice that all these summaries are *situated* within the biblical story. Scripture does not and could not summarize its story from a standpoint outside the story, which is unfinished. The summaries are themselves part of the story and even contribute to the story's own development.

Another way in which the canonical texts themselves assert their unity is found in the book of Revelation. I have elsewhere described Revelation as "the climax of prophecy,"[5] because it presents itself as the summation of the whole biblical tradition of prophecy, not least in its prolific allusion to a broad range of Old Testament prophetic texts whose continuing surplus of eschatological reference it affirms and interprets. As a prophetic text, Revelation offers in some sense an overview of the story from the perspective of its end, but even here the end is anticipated from within the still-continuing story.

In these and other ways, we can see that it is not alien to the biblical texts themselves, read as a cumulative whole, to seek a unitary story that encompasses the whole. For warrant to do this, we do not need to rely solely on the mere existence of the canon or the church's tradition of reading it,[6] nor need we make a simply arbitrary decision to read Scripture in this way, but we can appeal to significant features of the texts in themselves. At the same time, however, we must recognize that the unity of the story cannot be a simple one handed to us on a canonical plate. The narratives are told from various junctures within the story and from a variety of perspectives. In the Old Testament, we have something like a master version of the main story up to the

---

5. Richard Bauckham, *The Climax of Prophecy: Studies on the Book of Revelation* (Edinburgh: T. & T. Clark, 1993).

6. I am less happy than Loughlin to rely on the church's "traditional reading rules" (doctrines) for reading Scripture as a unity without also seeking what there is about Scripture that makes such rules appropriate. See Gerard Loughlin, *Telling God's Story* (Cambridge: Cambridge University Press, 1996), pp. 46-51.

exile (Genesis–2 Kings), but we also have diverse rereadings of it and interactions with it in the Prophets, a significantly different retelling of it in 1-2 Chronicles, tangential narratives that seem to offer corrective angles on it (Ruth, Esther, Jonah), and books that challenge essential features of its theology (Job, Ecclesiastes). In the New Testament, we have fresh and diverse rereadings of the Old Testament story (e.g., Paul and James on Abraham), while the story of Jesus is told in no less than four different versions in the Gospels, along with comment and interpretation in Paul, Hebrews, 1 Peter, and Revelation. The fourfold Gospel is the most obvious and telling example of diverse renderings of the biblical story, but the other instances we have mentioned show that this feature is not unique to Jesus' story but of a piece with the general character of Scripture.

At this point it may be helpful to remember the distinction that the narratologist Gérard Genette makes between story and narrative.[7] A literary narrative may differ in many ways from the story it tells (regardless of whether the story is construed as fictional or true). For example, the order in which events are narrated may differ from the order in which they occur in the story. A narrative need not tell all the events of the story, while it may recount some events a number of times — from different points of view (whether of characters or narrators), from different temporal junctures within the story, conveying different information, highlighting different aspects of significance. This important distinction between story and narrative may help us see that the plurality of narratives in Scripture — many of which recount the same events differently and none of which tells the whole story — is not in principle an obstacle to seeking in the Bible a single coherent story, which all the narratives together tell and each partially tells.

It is important also to recognize that the diversity of biblical renderings of the biblical story is distinctly limited. This is evident through comparison with, for example, other versions of the Old Testament story in texts among the Dead Sea Scrolls or the versions of the gospel story to be found in the gnostic gospels from Nag Hammadi. The Gospel of John tells recognizably the same story as the Synoptics, whereas the gnostic gospels do not. In part because of specialization and the narrowing of horizons that it entails, much recent scholarship has tended to exaggerate biblical diversity.

Nevertheless, the diversity is such that readers of Scripture have their own work to do in discerning the unity of the story. Moreover, the diversity of different versions of the story is not the only feature of Scripture that requires

---

7. Loughlin, *Telling God's Story,* pp. 52-62, summarizing the account in Gérard Genette, *Narrative Discourse,* trans. J. E. Lewin (Oxford: Blackwell, 1980).

such work. There is the sheer profusion of narrative material in Scripture, the narrative directions left unfinished, the narrative hints that enlist readers' imagination, the ambiguity of stories that leave their meaning open, the narrative fragments of the stories of prophets in their books or of writers and churches in the apostolic letters, the very different kinds of narrative that resist division into simple alternatives such as "history" and "myth," or "fiction," the references to stories external to Scripture. Such features, even apart from the bearing of the nonnarrative literature on the narrative, make any sort of finality in summarizing the biblical story inconceivable. Summaries are more or less essential, which is why we find them, as we have seen, in Scripture itself and why the creeds of the early church feature them prominently, but in neither case does just one summary emerge preeminent. Essential elements in a summary would not be hard to list. But the summaries cannot replace what they summarize; the story they summarize resists closure. The church must be constantly retelling the story, never losing sight of the landmark events, never losing touch with the main lines of theological meaning in Scripture's own tellings and commentaries, always remaining open to the never exhausted potential of the texts in their resonances with contemporary life.

There are perhaps two ways of understanding what is going on in retellings of the story, both within and beyond Scripture. One, located at the fashionable confluence of midrash and the postmodern, would understand it in terms of intertextuality. Texts are constantly being reinterpreted. There is obvious truth in this, but if it is the whole truth, if there is nothing outside the texts, the story risks being subject to the interests and designs — or mere intellectual playfulness — of its interpreters. Another approach (consistent with Genette's distinction between story and narrative) is to recognize that, while the telling of a story can be true, it can never be adequate to or exhaustive of the reality it renders. In this case, the fact that versions and interpretations multiply — especially in the case of the story of Jesus — is testimony to the importance of not reducing his reality to the limitations of a single rendering. The existence of the four Gospels, not to mention commentary in the apostolic letters, keeps readers aware that Jesus is neither captured in the text nor existent only as a textual construction but that he had and has his own reality to which the texts witness.

The considerations in this essay have largely concerned formal characteristics of the biblical texts rather than their material content. We have barely touched on what sort of a story it is that the Bible tells. To discuss the coherence of the biblical story in terms of the content of its narratives requires a biblical theology, which obviously cannot be undertaken here. But some significant features of the biblical story will be discussed in the third section of the essay, where they will be required to distinguish the biblical story from oppressive metanarratives of the kind that have suffered the critique of postmodern thinkers — a critique to which we now turn our attention.

II. The Postmodern Critique of Metanarratives

The French philosopher Jean-François Lyotard[8] (d. 1998), in his *La condition postmoderne* (1979), famously and influentially defined the postmodern as "incredulity towards grand narratives" (or metanarratives — the terms are interchangeable).[9] A metanarrative is a totalizing theory that aims to subsume all events, all perspectives, and all forms of knowledge in a comprehensive explanation. Lyotard's parade examples were the systems of Hegel and Marx. He later thought *La condition postmoderne* put too much emphasis on the narrative form, since his target was comprehensive systems of explanation that do not necessarily take that form. Nevertheless, it is noteworthy that most such systems in the modern period do have a narrative character. Along with Hegel and Marx, these would include other versions of the idea of progress and scientistic accounts, such as the currently popular elevation of Darwinism into a comprehensive explanation of human as well as other life. Even Platonism had a metanarrative; the term surely remains appropriate. Lyotard also later recognized that his own story of the obsolescence of all metanarratives in postmodernity was paradoxically itself a kind of metanarrative, at least in its absolutist claim to be the truth about history, and he sought to avoid the idea of a historical succession of modernity followed by postmodernity. Whether he successfully resolved the paradox (arguably, it is a version of the kind of paradox that relativism cannot avoid) is relatively unimportant, since that paradox has remained characteristic of much postmodern thinking that follows him in repudiating metanarratives.

Lyotard's rejection of grand narratives does not bear directly on the biblical or Christian story, though a consideration of the latter can certainly profit from attending to Lyotard's critique. It does not bear directly on the

---

8. My account of Lyotard on metanarratives is indebted to Steven Connor, *Postmodernist Culture: An Introduction to Theories of the Contemporary*, 2nd ed. (Oxford: Blackwell, 1997), pp. 23-43; Gary K. Browning, *Lyotard and the End of Grand Narratives* (Cardiff: University of Wales Press, 2000).

9. Jean-François Lyotard, *The Postmodern Condition*, trans. G. Bennington and B. Massumi (Minneapolis: University of Minnesota Press, 1984), p. xxiv.

biblical or Christian story because Lyotard's target is the project of modern reason that aspires to a comprehensive explanation of reality, including the human condition, and seeks rationally based universal criteria by which to order society and to liberate humanity through technology.

This modern project presumes that reality, both nature and human history, is fundamentally comprehensible to reason. Lyotard's opposition to it involves a skeptical epistemology, which stresses the opacity of reality to reason, and a radical espousal of pluralism and heterogeneity against universality and unity. The contingency of events and the intractability of "difference" resist any totalizing theory. Metanarratives are necessarily authoritarian and oppressive, since they can subsume difference only by suppressing it. Lyotard's affirmation of difference is extreme. He opposes any universal values in theory and any attempt to reach consensus in society for the sake of a social order. The diverse language games of postmodern society are incommensurable, and so plurality is irreducible. Order is always false and so oppressive. The centralized organization of society and cultural homogenization are features of the modern project and to be opposed. The only liberating kind of politics is agonistic, intensifying difference and so constantly resisting closure. The valorization of diversity and experimentation seems the only value, and the right of the different to be heard, the only justice.

The alleged incredulity toward metanarratives has a certain plausibility in contemporary Western society, but it can distract attention from the very powerful, late-modern grand narrative of consumerist individualism and free-market globalization, which aims to subsume precisely postmodern plurality. It appears liberating in its valorization of consumer lifestyle choices but is oppressive in the much more realistic sense that affluent postmodern theorists are liable to ignore: it enriches the rich while leaving the poor poor, and it destroys the environment. In this way it continues the kind of oppression that the modern metanarratives of progress have always legitimated. It is hard to acquit much postmodern theory of unintentional or intentional collusion with this metanarrative. Postmodern relativism offers no cogent resistance to this metanarrative, which is not threatened by diversity so long as its overarching framework of alleged economic reality goes unchallenged.[10] Rather than the postmodern story that proclaims the end of metanarratives, we need a story that once again affirms universal values while resisting their co-option by the forces of domination. Terry Eagleton attempts a case for Marxism in

---

10. Cf. Loughlin, *Telling God's Story*, pp. 30-32. "The delirium of free-market consumerism is made possible by the iron fist of capitalist technoscience that brooks no dissenters" (p. 31).

this respect.[11] A case for the Christian story, which has been at least equally compromised by oppressive distortions and collusion with the modern myth of progress, may depend on a retrieval of aspects of the biblical story that resist its ideological distortions. Lyotard's extreme epistemological skepticism and indiscriminate valorization of difference as such are hardly attractive from a Christian perspective, but his critique of the modern grand narratives can still be instructive.

We do not have to go to Lyotard's extreme to see that the dream of modern reason — that it could fully capture and articulate reality — was an illusion. Theories of universal history that explain it in terms of a unidirectional movement of progress stand exposed as legitimations of the modern West's domination of the world.[12] Lyotard is right to stress the contingency of historical events and the intractability of reality to fully rational explanation and control. The present global warming tragically illustrates the hugely powerful unintended consequences of the modern overconfidence in human mastery of nature and history. Auschwitz, of which Lyotard memorably said, "We wanted the progress of the mind, we got its shit,"[13] has rightly acquired the representative role of the surd that defeats any attempt at rational explanation of history. Totalizing metanarratives that entail closure do seem all too friendly to totalitarian politics.

III. The Biblical Story as a Nonmodern Metanarrative

The biblical story is not a metanarrative by Lyotard's definition, which limits the concept to a characteristically modern phenomenon, but I am not the first to extend the meaning, and it seems useful to do so. We might properly call the biblical story a premodern metanarrative were this not to appear to buy into the same sort of metanarrative about metanarratives that Lyotard himself sees lurking in the postmodern talk of the end of metanarratives.

11. Terry Eagleton, *The Illusions of Postmodernism* (Oxford: Blackwell, 1996).

12. Fernández-Armesto's magnificent world history, *Civilizations,* shows by contrast how there is no single unifying and progressive story of civilization, such as was embodied by the modern Eurocentric narratives. Felipe Fernández-Armesto, *Civilizations* (London: Macmillan, 2000). Of course, this does not mean that stories about the development of civilizations can no longer be told. History does not dissolve into a merely random succession of change, as some postmodernism suggests. Fernández-Armesto speaks of process rather than progress (pp. 20-22). Experience is almost inescapably narrative, and we are bound to try to understand the past, as we do the present, by narrativizing it.

13. Quoted in Browning, *Lyotard,* p. 68.

Such a meta-metanarrative remains in thrall to the modern metanarratives of progress, for which the label premodern is equivalent to obsolescent. But from the biblical story's own perspective, its premodern origin is no bar to its contemporary truth or relevance. By calling the biblical story a nonmodern metanarrative, I distinguish it from the modern metanarratives that Lyotard opposes. Consideration of the ways in which it is and is not what Lyotard defines and deplores will help illuminate its character. This route to clarifying its character is particularly useful because there is a sense in which modern metanarratives are indebted to the Christian tradition and because the biblical story has been widely confused with them and their myth of progress in the modern period.[14]

(1) What justifies the term metanarrative is that the biblical story is a story about the meaning of the whole of reality. Just as surely as it must be disentangled from the modern metanarratives of human rational mastery of nature and history, so it cannot be reduced to an unpretentious local language game in the pluralism of postmodernity. It makes a thoroughly universal claim, which combines the universality of the one Creator and Lord of all things with the particularity of this God's identification of himself as the God of Israel and of Jesus Christ. The particularity of the claim is offensive to the modern metanarratives of universal reason; the universality, even more offensive to postmodern relativism. The combination explains the way the biblical story combines "mythical," or symbolic, narrative, especially and necessarily at its beginning and end, with particular historical narrative (which is not modern historiography but historiography of one sort or another nevertheless). But even in this light, a remarkable regard for the particular is evident in the way the main plot emerges from and often risks submersion or dissipation in the apparently redundant superfluity of little stories, as well as the already mentioned complexity and ambiguity the story entails.

(2) Unlike the modern metanarratives, the biblical story accounts for history not in terms of immanent reason or human mastery but in terms of the freedom and purpose of God and of human freedom to obey or to resist God. There is a feature of typically modern narratives of all kinds (novels, films, etc.) that coheres strikingly with the modern metanarratives: they are primarily about human achievement. Things happen to people — there is contingency and coincidence and meaningless tragedy — but on the whole, the point lies in what people can make of these, how they can surmount disaster and achieve their freely chosen goals. These are the little stories that the metanarratives of rational mastery subsume without difficulty. By contrast,

---

14. The most fervent believers in the idea of progress I meet are often Christians.

the protagonists of traditional stories (fairy stories, for example) are typically much more accepting of what happens to them, and they win (for, of course, they do win) by means of the assistance of nature or the favor of supernatural powers or just wildly improbable luck. Their world is more mysterious than comprehensible, and they do not expect to master it. In the biblical stories, events are comprehensible insofar as God reveals his purposes and fulfills them. Human agency, of course, is important and is celebrated where appropriate, but its success follows divine initiative and requires divine concurrence.

(3) In the biblical story, there is therefore ample recognition of contingency in history in the sense that much, perhaps most, that occurs is not the intended result of human activity. The carefully plotted stories of Joseph and Esther show how the providence of God prevails through chance, coincidence, and the unintended results of human activity (cf. Gen 50:20) as much as through the obedient activity of servants of God. The biblical portrayal of divine providence cannot be equated with the immanent reason of history because it is contingent on the freedom of God and not open to rational calculation. So it invites trust, not mastery. God is to be trusted to be faithful to his promises, yet he remains free in his fulfillment of them.

(4) While the biblical storytellers recognize the hand of God in the contingency of history, some aspects of history remain intractable to comprehension in these terms. There is a tension between the divine moral order and incomprehensible evil. (This is surely the most dialectical aspect of biblical theology.) In the Old Testament histories and Prophets, there is a strong tendency to recognize moral order in the world over which God is sovereign. Rulers and nations get what they deserve, and although the God who is merciful as well as just may restrain his anger and remit punishment, the opposite is not equally true — that is, righteousness is not normally rewarded with suffering. What the historical books and the Prophets, from a salvation-historical perspective, assert about the fortunes of political societies, Proverbs, from a creational perspective, asserts about individual lives. In that sense Job's case is "countertestimony"[15] against both Deuteronomistic history and so-called conventional wisdom. The trouble with Job's friends is not so much that they endorse the tradition of observing moral order in God's

---

15. The term is Brueggemann's, which he uses to characterize a variety of Old Testament texts that seem to oppose Israel's "core testimony" to YHWH. Walter Brueggemann, *Theology of the Old Testament* (Minneapolis: Fortress, 1997), pt. 2. I do not find all the material he adduces very convincingly placed in this category, but the dialectical model of a legal dispute involving testimony and countertestimony helps show how texts such as Job and Ecclesiastes make an essential contribution without overturning the "core testimony."

world but rather that they do so in a spirit of dogmatic rationalism that cannot admit to a baffling exception, however obvious it might be. They exhibit the possible distortion of the biblical metanarrative into a rationalistic imposition of order that suppresses the real intractability of the evils of history. Job receives no explanation, only the assurance that God, because he is God, must in the end defeat evil, while Job, because he is human, cannot.[16] The mastery of nature and history remains the more certainly in God's hands, but the inscrutability of his ways, for which he will not be answerable to Job, is majestically asserted against the all too knowing dogmatism of the friends. Within the Old Testament, it is Job above all that ensures that the biblical story is not a comprehensive explanation of reality, even a divinely revealed one. Meaningless innocent suffering is the intractable surd in the story. The canon's inclusion of Job is matched by the Psalter's inclusion of the utterly bleak Psalm 88, with its painfully unanswered complaint.[17]

Though Psalm 88 is the bleakest of the psalms of complaint, evincing scarcely any hope, others also voice the silence and absence of God in questions and complaints that remain unresolved. They entertain even the terrible possibility that God has abrogated his covenant and will not be faithful to his promises (Ps 89:39; cf. Lam 5:22). These psalms by no means contradict the testimony of the biblical story that God does act on behalf of the righteous. They presuppose it; it is only because of the belief that God does characteristically so act that they complain that he has not acted in their own case and insist that he must.[18] These psalms, therefore — and all who are encouraged, by their inclusion in the Psalter, to pray them — live in dialectical tension with the testimony of Israel's story. This is perhaps a clue to the way the dying Jesus, in Matthew and Mark, makes his own the cry of desolation from the first verse of Psalm 22. The question arises precisely because God has so signally acted in the ministry of Jesus and promised the deliverance of his people through him.

The lack of a "literature of dissent" in the New Testament comparable to Job, Ecclesiastes, and the psalms of complaint might be understood by observing that the dialectic created by such material within the Old Testament acquires centrality in the New Testament story through the Matthean and Markan rendering of the cross. But what does this imply for the continuing openness of the biblical story to unassimilable evil? The cross and resurrec-

---

16. I read Job 41 in this sense.

17. Note also, with Brueggemann, the texts Phyllis Trible calls "texts of terror." Walter Brueggemann, *Abiding Astonishment: Psalms, Modernity, and the Making of History* (Louisville: Westminster/John Knox, 1991), pp. 49-50.

18. So Brueggemann, *Abiding Astonishment,* p. 52.

tion of Jesus have sometimes been understood as an answer to the Old Testament's question of theodicy, such that the psalms of complaint should no longer be prayed and Job's protest becomes redundant. In that case the biblical story, at its climax in Jesus, would achieve closure, and the intractable evils of history and experience would be overcome. However, the resurrection only anticipates eschatological closure. It bursts open the constraints of nature and history, promising an overwhelming good of a kind that will not, like any immanent theodicy, leave out the dead, the victims of history whose fate can never be justified by any product of history. Closure — meaning a finally satisfactory resolution of the problem of God's goodness in the world — is found in trust and hope, not in some explanation of the world that makes sense of evil, and still less in the claim of human power to eradicate the evil that human reason has understood.

(5) Although the matter cannot be explored here, we may note that, as well as the major dialectic within Scripture concerning moral order and incomprehensible evil, there are three other dialectics that the three Old Testament short stories open up within the metanarrative: between androcentric and gynocentric perspectives on the story (Ruth),[19] between the evident activity of YHWH and his hidden providence (Esther), and between Israel's privilege and YHWH's concern for the nations (Jonah).

(6) In the Bible, Israel's story is rarely portrayed as the dominant metanarrative but rather as a story of resistance, up against the dominant narratives of the great empires from Pharaoh to Rome. Characteristically, these narratives proclaim their eternity (Isa 47:7-8; Rev 18:7) and celebrate their divine achievement of universal rule (Isa 14:13-14; Dan 4:30; Rev 13:5-8). They are certainly narratives of closure, justifying oppression and suppressing all dissent. It is against these dominant narratives that the biblical metanarrative takes on its most imperial and militant colors, especially in the visions of Daniel and Revelation, which assert the transcendent power of God over all would-be divine rulers on earth and foresee their destruction and supersession by the rule of God triumphant over all evil. These visions empower nonviolent resistance to oppression, enabling God's people to continue to refute the finality and divinity of the empires. They suggest, not that the kingdom of God is merely a more powerful or more successful version of the imperial powers, but that it is an altogether different kind of rule. The tragic irony of Christian history has been that so often Christian empires have taken over the symbol of the kingdom of God to justify the same kind of rule

---

19. See Richard Bauckham, *Gospel Women: Studies of the Named Women in the Gospels* (Grand Rapids: Eerdmans; Edinburgh: T. & T. Clark, 2002), ch. 1.

as that of the empires it was forged to oppose. What has happened in these cases is that the biblical metanarrative has been transformed into a metanarrative much more like those Lyotard rejects, that is, a metanarrative that functions to legitimate existing structures of power.

(7) Not only is the biblical metanarrative a story of God's repeated choice of the dominated and the wretched, the powerless and the marginal; it also breaks the cycle by which the oppressed become oppressors in their turn. This is the effect of the memory of exodus in Israel's laws (e.g., Lev 19:34). The cross is the event in which the cycle is definitively broken. The christological passage in Phil 2 means that Jesus' obedience to the point of identification with the human condition at its most wretched and degraded, the death of the slave or the criminal, is what qualifies him to exercise the divine rule from the cosmic throne of God. Only the human who has thus identified himself irrevocably with the lowest of the low can be entrusted with the power that God exercises characteristically on their behalf. Distortion of the biblical story into an ideology of oppression has to suppress the biblical meaning of the cross.

(8) While these characteristics of the biblical metanarrative make it a story uniquely unsuited to being an instrument of oppression in the usual senses of that term, postmodernism has invented a new sort of oppression or injustice that consists in any claim to universal truth, whatever the character of that claim. Disillusioned by the failure of the modern hope of the emancipatory power of reason, postmodernism has decided that, far from setting free, truth oppresses because it delegitimizes difference.[20] This claim must simply be contested. For a start, there is the relativist paradox: the need to insist that there is one truth — the truth that there is no truth — and one justice — the right of every voice to equal status. If the postmodern relativist claim is fully embraced, then the incommensurability of language games makes it impossible to persuade others of the need to respect difference. Agonistic politics becomes nothing more than a power struggle between the competing interests of the heterogeneous groups. By contrast, a perspective that recognizes and claims truth can be genuinely open to dialogue and the

20. William Placher gives an illuminating example: "In writing about the Spanish invasion of the Americas, Tzvetan Todorov compares Pedro de Alvarado, who murdered native Americans, with Bartolomé de Las Casas who, as a Christian, loved them, opposed violence, and sought to convert them. Todorov finds little enough difference: 'Is there not already a violence in the conviction that one possesses the truth oneself, whereas this is not the case for others . . . ?'" William C. Placher, *Narratives of a Vulnerable God* (Louisville: Westminster/John Knox, 1994), pp. 120-21. Quotation from Tzvetan Todorov, *The Conquest of America*, trans. R. Howard (New York: Harper & Row, 1987), p. 169.

truth of the other. Presumably, a metanarrative that really claims comprehensive understanding of reality and to have already subsumed all other narratives cannot be open to other truth, but it is fair to ask, with Eagleton, whether such a metanarrative[21] is not now in any case something of a straw man. The threat of totalitarianism should not be neglected, but the fact that relativism appears to be its polar opposite does not make relativism the most effective safeguard against that threat. To the totalitarianism of twentieth-century regimes the biblical metanarrative has more effectively inspired resistance than has anything resembling postmodernism. The challenge to the church in the postmodern context is to reclaim the biblical story in a way that expresses its noncoercive claim to truth without imposing premature eschatological closure.

21. More precisely, teleological history. See Eagleton, *Illusions of Postmodernism*, pp. 45, 104-5.

Uncovering a Second Narrative: Detective Fiction and the Construction of Historical Method

David C. Steinmetz

An important difference between historical-critical exegesis of the Bible and the church's traditional exegesis is that traditional exegesis is quite willing to read earlier parts of the Bible in the light of later developments, while historical criticism is very reluctant to do anything of the kind. Historical criticism attempts to set texts in their own place and time. It can do this properly only if it avoids anachronism, that is, reading back into earlier texts the views and assumptions of texts from a much later period. Traditional exegesis, on the other hand, was written by people who were convinced that no one can properly understand earlier developments in the biblical story unless one reads them in the light of later. How the story ends makes a difference for the beginning and middle of the story as well as for its conclusion. From the perspective of historical criticism, traditional exegesis seems hopelessly anachronistic, while from the perspective of traditional exegesis, historical criticism seems needlessly disoriented and fragmentary.

I

Reading a story from its conclusion is not such a strange activity when one leaves the Bible to one side and considers other forms of literature. Mystery stories, a genre of literature to which I am particularly addicted, provide a useful analogy. The mystery story in its classical form is often an enormous puzzle that is slowly put together, bit by bit, until at the end all of the small parts fall together into an intelligible pattern that makes sense of the whole.

This kind of mystery story has two narratives. The first is a sprawling, ramshackle narrative that does not seem to be leading any place in particular.

It is filled with clues, false leads, imaginative hypotheses, and characters who frequently seem overmatched by what appear to be quite ordinary criminal minds. The authorities must sometimes contend with reckless behavior by potential victims who carry the seeds of their own destruction. No one knows for certain where this apparently rudderless ship is drifting, not even (for several chapters, at least) the persons charged with bringing the ship safely to harbor. The principal characters, like the readers of the story (of whom they are oblivious), are often in deep puzzlement. Of course, one must concede that Sherlock Holmes at his most baffled is never as confused as Dr. Watson.

There is a second narrative, one that is invariably recited by the principal investigator in the last or nearly last chapter. This narrative is crisp and clear and explains in considerable detail what was really occurring while the larger narrative was unfolding. The cogency of this narrative is not in the least undermined by the fact that none of the characters except the perpetrator of the crime and, until the very end of the story, the principal investigator himself or herself had any clear notion what the story was really about. Almost invariably, the final recitation of the second, shorter narrative is accompanied by a brief period of intellectual stump-removal in which Miss Marple or Inspector Dalgliesh answers the objections of the characters who have not committed the crime and are not yet completely persuaded by the cogency and finality of the second, concluding narrative.

It is important to understand that this second narrative is not a subplot, even though it is short. It is the disclosure of the architectonic structure of the whole story. Therefore, the second narrative quickly overpowers the first in the mind of the reader, who can no longer read the story as though ignorant of its plot and form. The second narrative is identical in substance to the first and therefore replaces it, not as an extraneous addition superimposed on the story or read back into it, but as a compelling and persuasive disclosure of what the story was about all along.

This also means that alternative plots must be discarded. Both the characters in the story and readers attempting to understand the story have suggested with varying degrees of plausibility alternative plots and endings. Indeed, one of the pleasures of reading mystery stories is the pleasure of resolving its puzzles for oneself. In the end, however, all alternative explanations must be abandoned. Just as the final narrative cannot be subverted by alternative theories proposed at any earlier stage of the story, so can no alternative theories reasonably be maintained after the ending of the story is known. The final narrative corrects all earlier narratives. It does not adjust to them.

The effect of all this on the reader is, of course, enormous. Casual conversations between characters that seemed on first reading to be of no very great significance now appear to be charged with unmistakable importance. How could I, the reader wonders, have overlooked the Irish wool cap in the closet, the old newspapers on the front steps, the half-smoked cigar in the ashtray, or the chipped vase on the side table? Why did I put so much faith in the clever theory of Inspector Morse and so little in the astute observations of Detective Sergeant Lewis? The sprawling, ramshackle narrative of events as lived by the characters is sprawling and ramshackle no more. What appeared on first reading to have been an almost random succession of events now proves to have been nothing of the kind. If one reads the last chapter first, one discovers a complex and intelligible narrative guided unerringly to its destined end by the secret hand of its author. Under the circumstances, reading backwards is not merely a preferred reading strategy; it is the only sensible course of action for a reasonable person.

II

Traditional Christian exegesis reads the Bible very much in this way — not exactly in this way, of course, but close enough to provide useful points of comparison. Early Christians believed that what had occurred in the life, death, and resurrection of Jesus Christ was of such importance that it had transformed the entire story of Israel and, through Israel, of the world. The long, ramshackle narrative of Israel with its promising starts and unexpected twists, with its ecstasies and its betrayals, its laws, its learning, its wisdom, its martyred prophets — this long narrative is retold and reevaluated in the light of what early Christians regarded as the concluding chapter God had written in Jesus Christ.

The New Testament is full of what we might call second-narrative moments, short retellings of Old Testament stories in the light of Christ.[1] These second-narrative moments are not regarded as subplots or additions tacked on to an otherwise complete story. They are believed by the speaker to uncover the plot in a literature that seems to be insufficiently plotted. They disclose at the end the structure of the whole from the beginning. It is, in fact, failure to discern the plot so disclosed, failure to read backwards from Christ to Abraham and Moses, that has left heretics in some difficulty — or at least so Irenaeus and Tertullian thought.

---

1. Some very obvious instances of such second narratives can be found in Acts 2:14-36; Acts 7:2-53; and Heb 11.

The developing patristic argument against heresy had three elements in it. Tertullian put the first point forcefully in his *De praescriptione hereticorum.* Heretics ought not to be allowed to use the Bible because it is not their book.[2] Gnostics who wanted to talk about the origins of the world as a great, unintended cosmic accident or Marcionites who posited the existence of two Gods should write their own inspired books, since the Christian Bible teaches nothing of the kind. Heretics who use the Bible are like beggars who wear garments that do not fit them and in which they appear to the discerning observer more than a little ridiculous.

In the second place, heretics ought not to be allowed to use the Bible because they do not understand it.[3] A myriad of quotations from the Bible does not make biblical the arguments of the theologian who quotes it. Heretics are like witty guests who entertain at parties by constructing on the spot new poems from old. They quote well-loved lines from the works of established poets. Every line in the new poem is from Virgil, and yet Virgil did not write it. The words are Virgil's, but the architectonic structure is not. Heretics, lost in the sprawling narrative of the Bible and ignorant of the second narrative that ties it together, have constructed a second narrative of their own. The words are from the Bible, but the argument is not biblical. Heretics have got the second narrative wrong and are therefore as clueless about the meaning of the Bible as are the characters in an Agatha Christie novel about the significance of the events in which they find themselves embroiled.

The second narrative that the early Fathers had in mind was the expanded baptismal confession.[4] When Christians confessed that they believed in God the Father Almighty, Maker of heaven and earth, they were reciting the second narrative that unlocked for them the meaning of the first and excluded all alternative narratives. One could not confess that God the Father is the Maker of heaven and earth without relegating Marcion's narrative of two Gods to the exegetical dustbin. Like the second narrative of Hercule Poirot, the second narrative of the early Fathers rendered all alternative narratives redundant. Their second narrative, like his, was believed by them to be identical in substance to the first and therefore replaced it, not as an extraneous addition superimposed on the story or read back into it, but as a compelling and persuasive disclosure of what the story was about all along.

But why were Irenaeus and Tertullian confident that they had the correct second narrative? The third element in the early Christian campaign

---

2. Tertullian, *De praescriptione hereticorum* 19.

3. *De praescriptione hereticorum* 16.

4. *De praescriptione hereticorum* 15-19.

against heresy was an appeal to a succession of bishops stretching back over two centuries — not a terribly long time in the great scheme of things — to the age of the apostles.[5] The current orthodox bishop had been taught by a bishop who had been taught by a bishop who had been taught by a bishop who had been taught by an apostle. Lists of these bishops could be produced on demand. In other words, the church in the third century believed it had not only received the Septuagint from Jewish translators and a New Testament from the circles of the apostles; it had also received a second narrative that unlocked the mysteries of both. To be sure, the bishops were not the only people who had transmitted this second narrative from generation to generation, but they served as the public guarantors that the correct narrative had been transmitted.

One does not have to agree with the account of ancient Christian history offered by the early Fathers to appreciate the force of their argument. Nor should one focus on these three elements to the exclusion of other important themes in early Christian writings. I have pointed out elsewhere the importance of what the Jesuits call discernment, the kind of insight that comes from disciplined prayer and long formation in the practices and habits of thought important to Christianity. When Athanasius argued that anyone who wants to understand the minds of the saints must first imitate their lives, he was touching on a theme no less important to the early Christian understanding of the Bible than apostolic succession and what I have called the distinction of first from second narratives.[6]

III

It might be objected that, while the analogy I have drawn with a mystery story may cast some light on the mindset of interpreters who wrote premodern exegesis, it casts very little light on historical method or on the kind of exegesis that should be written by commentators who wish to interpret the Bible historically. But first appearances may be deceiving. In 1951 a well-known mystery writer, Josephine Tey, wrote a novel entitled *The Daughter of Time*.[7] In her story, Alan Grant of Scotland Yard, who was convalescing in a London hospital because of injuries he had suffered while in hot pursuit of a criminal, became

5. On this subject see particularly the third book of *Adversus haereses* by Irenaeus.

6. For the English translation, see Athanasius, "On the Incarnation of the Word," in *Christology of the Later Fathers*, ed. Edward R. Hardy, LCC 3 (Philadelphia: Westminster, 1954), pp. 55-110, esp. 110.

7. Josephine Tey, *The Daughter of Time* (New York: Macmillan, 1951).

fascinated with the question whether Richard III had actually murdered his nephews to secure his claim to the English throne. With the aid of a friend, the actress Marta Hallard, he conducted a full-scale criminal investigation from his sickbed. In the end he concluded that Richard was falsely accused, a verdict agreeable to the Richard III Society but contested by some later historians who believe they have unearthed additional evidence against Richard since 1951. What is important to note, however, is not whether the conclusion Grant reached was correct but how similar were the investigative methods he used to the methods used by professional historians. Both detectives and historians are charged with reconstructing a probable sequence of events on the basis of evidence that is frequently fragmentary and ambiguous.

For example, like detectives, historians have good reason to be suspicious of narratives in which too many coincidences occur. Too many coincidences, like too many clues, suggest that someone may have tampered with the evidence. Yet history is full of surprises, and "too many" coincidences do in fact sometimes occur. The French medievalist Marc Bloch pointed to one such set of circumstances in his book *The Historian's Craft:*

> As Father Delehaye writes, in substance, anyone reading that the church observes a holiday for two of its servants both of whom died in Italy on the very same day, that the conversion of each was brought about by the reading of the Lives of the Saints, that each founded a religious order dedicated to the same patron, and finally that both of these orders were suppressed by popes bearing the same name — anyone reading all this would be tempted to assert that a single individual, duplicated through error, had been entered in the martyrology under two different names. Nevertheless, it is quite true that, similarly converted to the religious life by the example of saintly biographies, St. John Colombini established the Order of the Jesuates and Ignatius Loyola that of the Jesuits; that both of them died on July 31, the former near Siena in 1367, the latter at Rome in 1556; that the Jesuates were dissolved by Pope Clement IX and the Jesuits by Clement XIV. If the example is stimulating, it is certainly not unique.[8]

The difficulty of the task of reconstruction is compounded when, as is sometimes the case in biblical studies, there is little or no corroborating evidence outside the literary evidence of the biblical documents themselves. In such cases scholars may be forced to rely on literary evidence alone to recreate the historical setting of the document they have chosen for study. But literary evidence alone can mislead investigators attempting to reconstruct the past.

8. Marc Bloch, *The Historian's Craft* (New York: Vintage, 1953), p. 123.

The story of John Eck, the Catholic controversialist who taught at the University of Ingolstadt during the early years of the Reformation, may be taken as a case in point. Eck had debated with Luther and Carlstadt in a famous exchange at the University of Leipzig in 1519. In 1529 he published the *Enchiridion of Commonplaces against Luther and Other Enemies of the Church*, a fiercely polemical handbook that attacked early Protestant teaching and the biblical exegesis that underlay it.[9] By turns witty, acerbic, and informative, the book was enormously popular with Catholic readers and went through multiple editions. It was in its own way a masterpiece of partisan writing.

In 1542 Eck lectured for the last time at Ingolstadt on the First Book of the *Sentences* of Peter Lombard.[10] Not only were the lectures not polemical; they made no reference whatever to what Eck regarded as dangerous Lutheran theological errors, though Luther himself was still alive. Rather than attack heretics, Eck discussed placidly the nature and scope of theology, the doctrine of the Trinity, the problem of the divine ideas, and the issue of predestination. In form and content, the lectures provide an excellent example of late scholastic discourse, which is almost by definition nonpolemical. Eck cited Thomas, Scotus, and Ockham, but not Luther, Zwingli, or Bucer. Had we no other evidence for the dating of the *Enchiridion* and the lectures than their literary form and content, we would have been wholly justified in assuming that the nonpolemical lectures were an early work and the fiercely polemical *Enchiridion* a late one. But, of course, we would have been wrong. Even a tough-minded controversialist can turn his mind to other things.

Historians and detectives are similar in one other respect not explicitly mentioned by Josephine Tey, though the similarity would not, I think, have surprised her. Both construct second narratives. Sooner or later, historians, like their fictional counterparts in Tey's novel, must sort out the relevant evidence from the great picaresque narrative of history and say as briefly and clearly as they can what they think the evidence means. Of course, historians are not usually participants in the events they describe and in that important respect differ from Hercule Poirot and Sherlock Holmes. In a good detective story, the investigator often arrives on the scene before the plot has completely run its course. More victims may die. The narrative may take fresh twists and turns, baffling the reader and even furrowing the brows of the nearly omniscient Poirot and Holmes.

9. Johannes Eck, *Enchiridion locorum communium adversus Lutherum et alios hostes ecclesiae (1525-1543)*, ed. Pierre Fraenkel, CCath 34 (Münster: Aschendorffsche Verlagsbuchhandlung, 1979), pp. 97-98.

10. Walter L. Moore, ed., *In Primum Librum Sententiarum Annotatiunculae D. Iohannes Eckio Praelectore*, SMRT 13 (Leiden: Brill, 1976).

But historians who work, as I do, in late medieval and early modern sources always arrive on the scene too late, after all the actors are dead and all the trails are cold, to unravel a mystery for which there is too little evidence or far too much. Historians cannot sit quietly in the corner of a café and simply watch suspects as they go about their daily duties. In that respect criminal investigators have an advantage that historians can only approximate through a vigorous use of their imaginations.

However, historians have one advantage denied to even the most astute detective. They know from the very beginning how things will turn out. They know because they live on this side of the events. They may engage in a teleological suspension of this knowledge in order to write, say, a history of France after Napoleon's return from his first exile in Elba. Indeed, they must suppress their knowledge if they ever hope to recreate the unsettled and excited atmosphere in Paris prior to the battle of Waterloo. No one present at the time in Paris, London, or Berlin knew how things would turn out in the end, even if some predictions were correct. But historians know. They cannot not know. Daniel Patrick Moynihan once observed that "everyone is entitled to his own opinion, but not to his own facts." Historians know that Wellington and Blücher defeated Napoleon and terminated his brief restoration to power. Napoleon's contemporaries may have been surprised by his defeat, but historians cannot be. They know the outcome before they pull their chairs up to their desks. They are therefore professionally obligated to write a second narrative that takes that inescapable and, perhaps at times, even personally disagreeable knowledge into account.

It would, of course, be anachronistic to ascribe to the characters in the original historical setting a knowledge they did not have at the time or to assume too readily a necessary and inevitable connection between early events and their later resolution. But resolution there was. Because of Waterloo my great-grandfather, who emigrated from Düsseldorf in the late nineteenth century, cheerfully announced to my mother that he was Prussian. He was Prussian because of the French defeat at Waterloo and the subsequent decision of the victors to give the Rhineland, in which Düsseldorf is located, to Prussia.

It is not the task of historians to recreate the entire narrative of the past, even if such a recreation were possible. Telling everything that happened is the task of chroniclers, not historians. Nor is it, taken by itself, an anachronistic act to reassess the past in the light of its immediate and longer-term consequences. Historians write second, not first, narratives that make sense of the past by keeping in mind how things turned out. The old ideal of Benjamin Jowett, that "Scripture has one meaning — the meaning which it had to the mind of the Prophet or Evangelist who first uttered or wrote, to the hearers or readers who first received it," is therefore insufficiently historical.[11] Aside from the absurdity of an argument that assumes the complete passivity of the first hearers and their amazing unanimity in discerning the mind of the prophet or evangelist (an illusion easily refuted by anyone who has ever lectured or preached), Jowett omits altogether from the historian's task the historian's knowledge of how things ended. But just as the defeat of Napoleon had consequences that provide an indispensable framework for a historical evaluation of his life and times, so, too, does the prophesying of the prophets and the preaching of the apostles. Historians, no less than early Christian Fathers, worry about how things turn out.

If Jowett were correct, the only thing that would matter in American constitutional history would be the original debates at the Constitutional Convention. All questions of meaning should be referred to the events of that time. But the American Constitution was drafted against the background of centuries of English case and statutory law, to say nothing of English political history, from King John to George III. Since then it has been the fundamental legal charter of an energetic society. It must therefore now be read by scholars in the light of two centuries of American judicial precedents and legislation. Equal protection under the law, for example, has taken on meanings that were assuredly not in the minds of the original drafters but are fully consonant with the principles they embraced. Constitutional history is therefore not an exercise in the phenomenology of constitutional conventions, nor can history be reduced to the search for original intentions, important as that study may be. The history of the Constitution is the story of the origins, development, and consequences of the fundamental law of the United States. All of it, and not some part of it, belongs to the historian's task.

IV

I do not want to suggest, by pointing out similarities in the work of criminal investigators and professional historians, that I fail to see the differences between them. Mystery stories, after all, have one conclusion, whereas the Bible has two. A good mystery ends shortly after the principal investigator recites his or her second narrative, whereas the great, ramshackle narrative of history does not. This is true — especially — of the story of the early church, which blundered on after the apostles offered their second narrative as though noth-

---

11. Benjamin Jowett, "On the Interpretation of Scripture," in *Essays and Reviews*, 7th ed. (London: Longman, Green, Longman & Roberts, 1861), p. 378.

ing much had been resolved. Things, of course, had changed. Gentiles in large numbers were incorporated into the long narrative of Israel's history with its God. Unlike the second narrative of mystery writers, the second narrative of the early church was directed toward both the past and the future. It not only clarified what had happened but also cast light on the unfinished narrative. But the story itself did not stop, even though the apostles thought it would do so very shortly. It kept on as before, stretching into what appeared to be an indeterminate future.

Nor do I want to suggest that either the New Testament writers or the early Christian Fathers were engaged in the writing of critical history. "The appeal of Christianity to history," as Father Georges Florovsky once remarked in class, "is not necessarily an appeal to historians." Yet all three — investigators, historians, and theologians — are confronted from time to time with the task of taming into submission a large and sprawling narrative that seems to lack any unity or cohesion. Each constructs in such circumstances a second narrative that purports to explain briefly what has actually been going on in the larger story. This second narrative must take into account how things have turned out in the end as well as how they began and developed over time. If the second narrative is convincingly constructed, it displaces all rival narratives and provides the indispensable framework for understanding and evaluating all prior events.

But a second narrative, because it purports to make sense of things, must itself make sense. What makes a second narrative convincing, whether on the lips of detectives like Inspector Morse or historians like Eamon Duffy, is that it "saves the appearances"; that is to say, it accounts for all the relevant evidence. It is pointless to accuse the butler of poisoning the Founder's Reserve Port if at the time it was opened he was on holiday in Brighton. It may prove incorrect to suggest that J. R. R. Tolkien had the discovery of atomic energy in mind when he wrote *The Lord of the Rings* if it is true (as C. S. Lewis, who was in an especially good position to know, has pointed out) that the plot of Tolkien's trilogy of novels had been developed prior to the production of the first atomic bomb. Hypotheses, however plausible, can nevertheless prove false. In the end, explanations must really explain. Second narratives must account for the big narrative that spawned them, or they are useless.

V

No analogy is perfect, and I can well understand if some objections to the analogy I have used in this essay have already occurred in the minds of readers otherwise sympathetic to my line of argument. Mystery stories, however ramshackle their first narratives, are generally written in a limited period of time by one author, whereas the Bible was written over a long period of time by many authors, most of whom did not know each other. Furthermore, the relationship between first and second narratives, which I use to characterize the relationship between the Old and New Testaments, is in fact internal to each as well. The prophets offer their own second narratives to make sense of the earlier traditions they inherited, and the apostles are not altogether certain what the coming of Christ means for the future of Israel. Reevaluating what happened earlier in the light of subsequent events is characteristic of the Bible as such and not merely of the relationship between the Testaments.

In the end, all an analogy can do is to compare an aspect of A with an aspect of B in order to clarify something about A that might not otherwise be noticed. A good analogy can stimulate readers to fresh thinking by showing that two things that are not usually thought of together may in some respects be surprisingly similar. The comparison is bound to break down once the reader moves past the limited point the analogy seeks to make. Analogy depends for its force on difference as well as similarity. A is to B as C is to D, but A and B are not C and D and never will be.

I have argued in this essay two simple propositions and want to conclude with a third. The first proposition is that the analogy with detective fiction provides a useful way for approaching premodern biblical exegesis. There is a similarity between the kerygmatic retelling of the larger biblical story in the New Testament and the crisp retelling of the mystery narrative by the principal investigator in a novel by P. D. James or Agatha Christie. The kerygmatic retelling is summarized in the early church in the rule of faith, an equally crisp second narrative that purports to be key to the larger whole. There are, of course, differences between them. The second narrative of the mystery novelist is the product of rational reflection on a wide range of evidence, a good deal of which was present in the beginning for anyone who had eyes to see it. The second narrative of the early Christian church was based primarily on later events — that is to say, on what early Christians thought had happened in the life, death, and resurrection of Jesus Christ. But in both cases, once the second narrative is in place, it is impossible to understand earlier events apart from it. In the order of being, the second narrative comes last. In the order of knowing, it comes first. That is why both mystery stories and the biblical documents are best understood by reading the last chapter first.

My second proposition is that historians, too, are involved in the writing of second narratives in which the knowledge of the way things turned out plays a significant role. It would, of course, be anachronistic to ascribe to the characters in the story a knowledge of how things would turn out as the events themselves were unfolding. But it is not anachronistic for historians to write history in the light of their knowledge, not only of how it unfolded, but also of how it ended. Unlike the work of detectives and apostles, historians rarely feel confident that their second narratives are definitive and incapable of further improvement. But it is also true that historians attempt to write their second narratives as though they were definitive, neglecting no relevant category of evidence. Sooner or later all historians, including biblical scholars, succumb to the almost irresistible urge to imitate Miss Marple or Inspector Morse. They will invite a circle of concerned friends into the drawing room (or, more likely, classroom or seminar) to hear the second narrative they have pieced together to make sense of the evidence they have discovered. Every historian, like every successful investigator, has a second narrative to offer. It is, after all, what the craft of history is about.

My third proposition is fairly modest. I am inclined to think that biblical scholars who are also Christian theologians should worry less about anachronism and more about the quality of the second narratives they have constructed. I can well understand why biblical scholars are wary of a traditional exegesis that ascribes to characters in the Bible, especially characters in the Old Testament, an explicit knowledge of the finer points of Christian theology. Such explicit knowledge would have been impossible for them at the time. But I do not have to believe that Second Isaiah had an explicit knowledge of the crucifixion of Jesus of Nazareth to believe that he was part of a larger narrative that finds its final, though not its sole, meaning in Christ. Like many of the characters in a mystery novel, Isaiah had something else on his mind. But the meaning of his work cannot be limited to the narrow boundaries of his explicit intention. Viewed from the perspective of the way things turned out, his oracles were revealed to have added dimensions of significance that no one could have guessed at the time. It is not anachronistic to believe such added dimensions of meaning exist. It is only good exegesis.

A LIVING TRADITION

Is Patristic Exegesis Still Usable? Some Reflections on Early Christian Interpretation of the Psalms

Brian E. Daley, SJ

Patristic exegesis has become almost fashionable again. After centuries of ne-glect, even hostile dismissal, on the part of Christian preachers and scholars of virtually every hue and stripe, the efforts of early Christian writers to inter-pret the Bible have recently been watered into life again by a small but swell-ing stream of conferences, scholarly books,[1] and doctoral dissertations. Part of this trend, undoubtedly, is due to a growing sense among biblical scholars and theologians — especially those under forty — that the dominant post-Enlightenment approach to identifying the meaning of scriptural texts has begun to lose some of its energy, that it has less that is new and substantial to say than once it did to those who want to spend their time reading the Chris-tian Bible: the members, by and large, of the Christian churches. Part of it, too, seems to belong to a new, romantic enthusiasm — drawn on, no doubt, by postmodern hermeneutics in its various forms — for finding meaning in texts from other times and cultures in ways that are less rationalistic than de-tached historical analysis. Whatever the reasons, a significant number of Christian theologians and biblical scholars are turning with interest and even

---

1. Scholars who wish to do further research in the area of patristic exegesis should con-sult the more fully footnoted version of this essay in *Communio.* In addition, scholars might wish to note two recent, substantial books that draw on patristic exegetical practice as a stimu-lus for new engagement with figural scriptural interpretation: Christopher R. Seitz, *Figured Out: Typology and Providence in Christian Scripture* (Louisville: Westminster/John Knox, 2001), and John David Dawson, *Christian Figural Reading and the Fashioning of Identity* (Berkeley: Univer-sity of California Press, 2002).

An earlier and longer version of this essay, somewhat different in emphasis, appeared in *Communio: International Catholic Review* 29 (2002): 185-216.

respect to the exegetical efforts of the patristic era in the hope of finding there models for new ways of reading the Bible with both scholarly sophistication and a reverent, orthodox faith.

In this present volume, we have attempted, from a variety of perspectives, to confront the pressing theological and pastoral issue of how contemporary Christians, conscious of all the historical and theoretical questions raised by modern scriptural study, might still hear the Bible in an attitude of faithful receptiveness — might hear it as God's word and not simply as a collection of problematic ancient religious texts, some of which are more helpful than others for the religious person today. What I would like to do in this essay is, first of all, to reflect briefly on some of the main similarities and differences between modern and ancient approaches to interpreting the Christian Bible, and then, by way of example, to consider some of the particular exegetical problems and possibilities raised by the book of Psalms for the ancients and for us. Finally, I would like to reflect briefly on how, and how much, a renewed contact with patristic exegesis might help us develop our own ways of interpreting the Bible theologically, as a normative canonical whole still capable of nourishing and challenging our life of faith.

I. Exegesis, Ancient and Modern

"We shall pass in swift review many centuries of exegesis," wrote Frederic W. Farrar in the first of his Oxford Bampton Lectures of 1885 on the history of biblical interpretation, "and shall be compelled to see that they were, in the main, centuries during which the interpretation of Scripture has been dominated by unproven theories, and overladen by untenable results."[2] Making what he seems to have intended as generous allowances for the patristic interpreters' cultural and educational limitations — in contrast to the fierce attacks of such eloquent, earlier critics as John Milton — he nevertheless observed: "There are but few of them whose pages are not rife with errors — errors of method, errors of fact, errors of history, of grammar, and even of doctrine."[3]

Although twentieth-century scholars have tended to express themselves more modestly, their judgment of the value of classical biblical exegesis has been, in general, equally negative. The main focus of modern criticism has been that patristic and medieval exegesis relied so heavily on figural, or alle-

2. Frederic W. Farrar, *History of Interpretation* (London: Macmillan, 1886), p. 8.
3. Farrar, *History of Interpretation*, pp. 162-63.

gorical, interpretation — on taking texts, especially Old Testament texts, not simply in their "plain sense" but as pointing to Christ, to Christian salvation, and to the spiritual growth of Christian believers — that the authentic meaning of the Bible was swallowed up in arbitrarily pious or pedantic fantasy. To take one example from the 1950s, the great Irish patristic scholar R. P. C. Hanson, in his early study of Origen's exegesis, *Allegory and Event*, paints a consistently negative picture of the Alexandrian's figural interpretation.[4] The reason for Hanson's discomfort with allegory as Origen practiced it is that, in his view, it disregarded the significance, and even the reality, of *history* — by which Hanson seems to mean not the discovery or reconstruction of past events by the modern researcher so much as those events themselves, seen by the biblical writers as "*par excellence* the field of God's revelation of himself."[5] In Hanson's reading, Origen was simply blind to this biblical sense of the reality of events in time:

> The critical subject upon which Origen never accepted the biblical viewpoint was the significance of history. . . . In his view history, if it is to have any significance at all, can be no more than an acted parable, a charade for showing forth eternal truths about God; it is not, as it is in the prophets, the place where through tension and uncertainty and danger and faith men encounter God as active towards them.[6]

Apart from the issue of whether Hanson's judgment of Origen is fair — and most scholars today would probably agree that it is not — his work betrays the unmistakable assumption that the events of the past have a reality, independent of the interpreting and narrating subject, that is essentially still accessible to later hearers and readers: history has a significance and an intelligibility contained simply within itself, and God's action in history, although for us an object of faith, is essentially to be considered on the same level of cause and effect as human and natural events.

Yet there is a certain inner tension, even a contradiction, in this view of "salvation history." Behind such evaluative judgments on the quality and seriousness of ancient exegesis, after all, lies a peculiarly modern understanding of what historical reality is, of the truth value of historical narrative, and of the way historical research is conducted. For the post-Enlightenment mind con-

---

4. R. P. C. Hanson, *Allegory and Event: A Study of the Sources and Significance of Origen's Interpretation of Scripture* (London: SCM, 1959). Hanson takes a more measured approach to Origen's exegesis in some of his later works.

5. Hanson, *Allegory and Event*, p. 363.

6. Hanson, *Allegory and Event*, p. 364.

templating the human past, history is understood to be the object of scientific study, conducted as far as possible under the same standards of evidence and verifiability as those used in the laboratory; historical reality — like physical reality — is assumed to be in itself something objective, at least in the sense that it consists in *events* independent of the interests and preconceptions of the scholar or narrator, accessible through the disciplined, methodologically rigorous analysis of present evidence such as texts, artifacts, and human remains. For this reason, the establishment and interpretation of texts from earlier ages, like the study of material archaeological evidence, is understood to be an inductive process governed by the rules of logic, the recognition of natural cause and effect, the assignment of probability based on common human experience. As a result, modern historical criticism — including the criticism of biblical texts — is *methodologically* atheistic, even if what it studies is some form or facet of religious belief, and even if it is practiced by believers. Only "natural," innerworldly explanations of why or how things happen, explanations that could be acceptable to believers and unbelievers alike, are taken as historically admissible. So God is not normally understood to count as an actor on the stage of history, to operate as a historical cause; God's providence in history, the divine inspiration of scriptural authors and texts, even the miracles narrated in the Bible are assumed to be private human interpretations of events, interior and nondemonstrable, rather than events or historical forces in themselves.

Along with this "atheistic," or naturalistic, understanding of history, modern critical interpretation of texts has tended to focus its attention on trying to rediscover what the human author may have intended by the words he or she uttered or wrote and what the original hearers or readers would have understood by them, on the assumption that such original intent is the main constituent of the text's single, inherent *meaning*. This has been especially true of modern historical-critical study of the Bible, which has labored hard at the complex task of unraveling the layers of text and redaction, tradition and reception in the various parts of the biblical canon in the dual hope of producing a diachronic model of the Bible's evolution to its present form and determining — within the context of the life and religious concerns of the communities in which the texts were produced — how the various parts and books of the present Bible may have *originally* been understood. Even interpreters who do regard the biblical text as conveying the word of God to later ages now generally begin their exegetical work with this assumption. The Second Vatican Council's constitution on divine revelation, *Dei verbum*, for instance, intended as a strong theological affirmation of the importance of modern biblical scholarship for the life of the church, begins its description of the process of biblical interpretation in these terms: "Since God speaks in Sacred

Scripture through human beings, in a human fashion, the interpreter of Sacred Scripture, in order to see clearly what God wanted to communicate to us, should carefully investigate what meaning the sacred writers really intended, and what God wanted to manifest by means of their words."[7] To know how a scriptural text reveals God to us, in other words, we must search for the single significance of its words as intended for those who originally spoke, wrote, and heard those words; that original message is assumed to be the main message God still wants to convey to the church that receives the text as part of its Bible. The *meaning* of the text is "what the author meant."

Today, of course, in the wake of various critiques of this approach to texts and their meaning — critiques that style themselves by the catch-all term "postmodern" — we are generally more aware that understanding words from the past is not nearly so simple. Many postmodern hermeneutical theorists would agree with the New Critics of the 1920s that texts possess an independence that continues to challenge later readers to search anew for their meaning and that their legitimate meaning — their literary, social, or religious value, what they have to say to us — can never be simply confined to what the author had in mind. Following Gadamer, most theorists of interpretation today would also agree that a reader's understanding of a text will always, necessarily, be largely conditioned by the reader's own interests and prior experience — by the horizon of understanding he or she brings to the act of engaging the words of another. *Understanding* a text is precisely the event of the interpenetration of horizons: the author's and the reader's, along with the entire set of cultural and community assumptions, intellectual models, and religious value systems through which each comes to participate in the world of intelligent discourse. It can never be a simple matter of the recovery of objective, "original" meaning through a scientific historical criticism that is free of the concerns and commitments of the later reader.

This widespread change in our sense of what it means to read and understand a text, particularly a text whose origin is in a culture remote from our own, may well lie behind the lively new interest in early Christian biblical exegesis. Such premodern exegesis is generally free from the judgments about how to find the Bible's authentic meaning that seem so constricting, so theologically inhibited and inhibiting, to many modern religious readers. Although a great deal could be said about the assumptions and practical strategies of ancient Christian (as well as Jewish and Hellenistic) exegesis, the next sections will summarize briefly what I see as its main features.

---

7. *Dei verbum* 12, in *The Documents of Vatican II,* trans. and ed. Walter M. Abbott and Joseph Gallagher (New York: America Press, 1966), p. 120.

1. *Conviction of the Present Reality of God*

In common with practically everyone else in the ancient world, early Christian interpreters of the Bible took it for granted that a supreme, transcendent, utterly beneficent Being lies at the heart of all reality and that that Being plays an active role in the shaping of human affairs. Just *how* the Christian believer may hope to encounter God in this present life was conceived in different ways; that, in fact, seems to have been the underlying difference between the schools of Antioch and Alexandria in their Christology, their sacramental theology, and their eschatology, as well as in their approach to exegesis. But for all ancient Christian exegetes, God's providence and God's overarching, efficacious plan to save humanity from its endemic disease of sin were assumed to be central realities of history, as Christians experienced and told that history; interpreting the story of the Bible correctly meant taking God's saving involvement seriously in explaining the significance of any person or event, as well as the origin and nature of the Bible itself.

2. *Presumption of a Unified Narrative*

From the first stages of Christian biblical interpretation, evident in the New Testament writings themselves, early Christian exegetes approached individual passages against the assumed background of a single story of God's work in the world to give and to restore life — beginning with God's creation of the material cosmos and the world of intelligent beings and continuing through the story of human alienation from God through sin, God's call of a particular people to be the vehicle of his revelation and blessing, and the climax of this saving, reconciling work in the person, teaching, death, and resurrection of Jesus of Nazareth. This sense of a continuous, overarching narrative of faith is not, of course, peculiar to Christianity; the formation of the Hebrew canon of Scriptures through the centuries relied on the continuous reassimilation of traditional stories and texts into new, larger contexts of interpretation that reflected the sense, on the part of Israel's preachers and scribes, of an ever unfolding sacred narrative that began with ancient memories of a saving and judging God and that included *them.* So the driving theological impulse behind the Christian Gospels, as well as the Letters of Paul, seems to have been not simply the conviction that Jesus, who was crucified, now lives in the midst of the community as Lord but that he must be recognized by the community as *Messiah,* as one promised by Israel's Scriptures and pointed to as "coming" by the Law and the Prophets.[8] The confession of Jesus as "Lord and Christ" (Acts 2:36) is, in a sense, the first act of Christian figural interpretation of the Hebrew Scriptures — the continuation of a pattern of reception and reinterpretation, of seeing new meaning in old texts, that had gone on throughout the formation of Israel's own biblical canon and had given that canon its shape.

3. The Rule of Faith

For Christian writers from the late second century on — from the time when the Christian community had begun to form its own defined sense of a Christian canon of normative Scriptures in the face of gnostic written and oral traditions — the overall shape of this sacred narrative was summarized in familiar catechetical or liturgical formulae known by such names as *regula fidei* or *regula pietatis,* the "norm" or "measuring stick" of devout faith. Origen gives us a sense of the importance of such a summary narrative in the opening lines of the preface to his work *On First Principles:* "All who believe and are convinced that 'grace and truth have come through Jesus Christ' (John 1:17), and who know that Christ is the Truth (cf. John 14:6) . . . , receive the knowledge that calls the human race to live well and happily from no other source than from the very words and teaching of Christ."[9] The whole of what Christians recognize as Scripture, in fact, is in Origen's view a witness to this saving revelation of God in Christ, the Word, a communication that has reached its fulfillment in the incarnation. But because "many of those who profess to believe in Christ" — gnostic Christian sects, especially — have substantially different conceptions of what this revelation actually means, "it therefore seems to be necessary first to establish a sure guideline and a clear rule on these details, and then to continue our investigations on other subjects."[10]

When Origen comes to summarizing the content of the "rule of piety" that governs Christian scriptural interpretation, it sounds very much like

---

8. Examples of this abound in the New Testament. One might, for instance, point to the interpretive use of passages from the Psalms and the prophetic books in the Synoptic passion narratives; to the formulaic assertion that Jesus' death and resurrection were "according to the scriptures" in 1 Cor 15:3-4; to the interpretation of Israel's sacrificial liturgy as a copy of the eternally efficacious, heavenly liturgy performed by Christ in his death and entry into glory in Heb 1–10; to the interpretation of Christian baptism as corresponding to the story of Noah, because of its own figural connection with the death and resurrection of Christ, in 1 Pet 3:18-22; and many other passages.

9. Origen, *De principiis* pref. 1.

10. *De principiis* pref. 2.

what would soon be formulated in the various familiar baptismal creeds: there is one God who created all things; one Son, eternally begotten but recently incarnate as Jesus Christ; one Holy Spirit, who has inspired "all the holy ones, whether prophets or apostles"; there are also real, intelligent, self-determining human spirits, as well as other intellectual powers that surreptitiously affect human thoughts and actions, and a real and good visible world that had a beginning in time and will have a temporal end; the Scriptures have been composed through the Spirit of God and "contain not only that meaning which is obvious, but also a certain other meaning which is hidden from most people."[11] This outline of the basic Christian message (which includes the mysterious character of the Bible itself) serves as the chief guide, in Origen's view, to discovering the possible meaning of individual passages; beyond this, the Bible's contents remain invitingly open to the thoughtful investigation of faithful researchers.[12]

4. Scripture as a Diverse yet Unified Whole

Because the canon of Jewish and Christian Scriptures had been received within the Christian community as telling the single story of a faithful, creative, redeeming God, early Christian interpreters approached the Bible with the assumption that individual passages within that canon could not substantially contradict each other in the message they offered to the believing reader. Origen, again, was convinced that it was precisely the task of the exegete to discover the internal coherence of the Scriptures and to make it clear to others. Commenting on Matthew 5:9, "Blessed are the peacemakers," he applies this text to "the one who shows that what seems to others to be a conflict in the Scriptures is not conflict at all, but who proves their harmony and accord — whether it is of the Old with the New, or of the law with the prophets, or of Gospels with Gospels, or apostolic writings with apostolic writings."[13] Just as it takes a musical person to hear the harmony between the different notes played by a lyre's strings, so the "reader who is trained in God's music" will be able to hear and even to reproduce himself the coherence of the whole Bible, "for he knows that the whole of Scripture is one perfect and harmonious instrument of God, producing a single saving melody out of dif-

11. *De principiis* pref. 4-10.
12. *De principiis* pref. 3.
13. Fragment of *Commentary on Matthew* 2, *Philocalia of Origen* 6, ed. J. Armitage Robinson (Cambridge: Cambridge University Press, 1893), 49.9-15.

ferent voices, for those who wish to learn it."[14] This underlying unity in the message of the Bible, definitively revealed to the Christian in the gospel, was generally understood by patristic and medieval interpreters to produce, not a flat uniformity of doctrine, but a new richness and variety, a kind of unquenchable fountain whose scattered drops all reflect the one Mystery of Christ.

5. Scripture as Historical yet Meant for Us

Early Christian interpretation of the Bible generally assumed that the meaning of any given passage is not some self-contained intelligible entity, some intellectual content placed in it by its author or redactor, but that it also involves *us* — the reader, the hearer, the commentator or preacher, the church — precisely as the community that receives it not simply as a historical document but as a revelation of God's will to heal and transform the hearer. Put another way, because the Bible is not just a book of texts but is *Holy Scripture,* the concern of the ancient exegete was not simply, or even primarily, to reconstruct the *Sitz im Leben* of the text being studied but to elucidate its *Sitz in unserem Leben,* its situation in *our* life; the hearers' faith is the living context in which its scriptural meaning — its meaning for our salvation — is to be found.

This is not to say that early Christian interpreters were generally as careless of questions of authorship, textual intelligibility, or original context as is often supposed. Diodore of Tarsus, the founder of the school of Antioch, for instance, and his followers Theodore of Mopsuestia and Theodoret of Cyrus laid particular stress on situating each text of the Old Testament on which they commented within the story of Israel's history as they understood it; it was this narrative context, as well as the "plain sense" of the text itself, in all its mundane details, that had to serve as the basis for any "higher," prophetic, reference to Christ or human salvation that the text might be providentially ordained to bear, and they made full use of the traditional tools of the ancient grammarian to find and explicate that plain sense.[15] Origen, too — although

---

14. *Philocalia of Origen* 6 (ed. Robinson 50.2-3, 9-12).

15. Diodore makes this clear in a celebrated passage in the prologue to his *Commentary on the Psalms.* Assuming that the Psalms were written by David, who was an inspired prophet, and assuming that clues in the title or text of each psalm enable the exegete to identify a particular situation within the story of Israel to which the psalm as a whole refers, Diodore makes it an axiom of his interpretive method that this situation, and only this, determines both the primary meaning of the psalm and any "higher," figural, references it may have. "For historical narra-

less confident than the later Antiochenes that all the texts in the biblical canon actually *have* a plain sense that can carry out the Bible's role of edifying and nourishing the reader — still insisted that one must not assume that nothing in the Bible is to be taken at face value. In fact, Origen's own exegetical practice shows constant concern for the smallest details of text and narrative and often an unexpected willingness to accept biblical passages as meaning what they say.[16]

Nevertheless, patristic exegesis was primarily concerned with pointing out the meaning of scriptural passages for the hearers and for the present life of the church, not just as a homiletic "application" distinct from the text's original meaning, but as what one might call the text's authentic *biblical* meaning: its meaning as an organic part of the whole received complex of the word of God. Explaining *what the text means in itself* was not seen as separate from explaining *what it has to say to the church,* precisely because the narrative contained in the Bible was not seen as a closed unit, epistemologically distant from the life of its readers and hearers, who receive it as God's word. The narrative of God's work of salvation — the real content of the Bible — was a single, universally significant story, an unfinished story. The biblical scholar's task, as well as the preacher's, was to illumine the cohesion and the continuing relevance of all of its details.

6. Scripture as Mystery

As a result, early Christian biblical exegetes often used words that strike us as hopelessly unscientific when justifying their interpretations of particular texts, arguing that one or another way of interpreting a disputed passage is more "reverent" (εὐσεβής, *eusebēs*) or more "appropriate to God" (θεοπρεπής, *theoprepēs*) than another — terms that were also frequently used in arguments about doctrinal orthodoxy. It might be possible, in fact, to char-

---

tive," he adds, "is not opposed to finding a higher interpretation; on the contrary, it is quite clearly the base and foundation of such interpretations. One must simply be on one's guard against one thing: interpretation (θεωρία, *theōria*) should never appear to overthrow the underlying sense." Diodore, *Commentary on the Psalms* (CCSG 6.7.124-32).

16. After explaining his "rule of thumb," that apparent inconsistencies or unintelligible details in the biblical text are clues to the reader to seek a "deeper" meaning, Origen remarks: "But no one should suppose that we have said this as a universal principle, implying that there is no historical narrative [in the Bible], because this or that reported event did not happen. . . . [T]he passages that are true in their historical sense are far more numerous than those purely spiritual passages that are woven in with them." *De principiis* 4.3.4.

acterize the dominant procedure of scriptural interpretation in the early church as a "hermeneutic of piety": a sense that the ultimate test of the adequacy of any explanation of a biblical passage's meaning is the degree to which that explanation fits with Christian "religion," with the church's traditional understanding of the holiness and uniqueness of the God who is revealed in the biblical story and the holiness to which all the story's hearers are called in response. The consequence of this approach to the text is not simply a preference for certain doctrinal themes but a sense that the text of the Bible, which radiates God's holiness, is itself therefore worthy of enormous reverence.

In the opening paragraph of his *Homily on Psalm 13 (14)*, for example, Hilary of Poitiers offers us a glimpse of his own self-understanding as a biblical preacher, which reflects this widespread attitude toward the text:

> The Apostle, who instructs us on many things, also teaches us that the word of God must be treated with the greatest reverence, saying "whoever speaks, [let him speak] as uttering the oracles of God" (1 Pet 4:11). For we ought not to treat Scripture with a vulgar familiarity, as we do in our ordinary speech; rather, when we speak of what we have learned and read we should give honor to the author by our care for the way we express ourselves. . . . Preachers, then, must think that they are not speaking to a human audience, and hearers must know that it is not human words that are being offered to them, but that they are God's words, God's decrees, God's laws. For both roles, the utmost reverence is fitting.[17]

Sixteen centuries later, John Keble, defending patristic exegesis from the charge of "mysticism" — which, in nineteenth-century English-speaking Protestantism, seems to have suggested superstitious credulity and irrationality rather than its older sense of a graced union with God — suggests that his own contemporaries might benefit from sharing in this ancient Christian sense of awe before the biblical text:

> As we train ourselves, so also, according to our means, should we endeavour to prepare others, for the right study of the Bible. He who looks no deeper than the letter, may simply recommend candour, and patient investigation, and freedom from sensual and other disturbing thoughts: but he who knows beforehand, that the Personal Word is everywhere in the written Word, could we but discern Him, will feel it an awful thing to open his Bible; fasting, and prayer, and scrupulous self-denial,

---

17. Hilary of Poitiers, *Tractatus super Psalmum 13.1* (CCSL 61.76.1-6, 21-24).

and all the ways by which the flesh is tamed to the Spirit, will seem to him no more than natural, when he is to sanctify himself, and draw near, with Moses, to the darkness where God is. And this so much the more, the more that darkness is mingled with evangelical light; for so much the more he may hope to see of God; and we know Who it is, that has inseparably connected seeing God with purity of heart.[18]

Important for both Hilary and Keble is not simply the sense that holy things are held before us by the books of Scripture but also that the discovery of these holy things — which are Scripture's actual *content* and *meaning* — require from the reader a process of purification and an attitude of reverence that are not simply the product of academic learning but belong to the life of worship and faith. The key to this attitude, for both authors, seems to lie in the sense that it is God who speaks through the biblical author and text and that our own engagement with the text is nothing less than a personal encounter with the Divine Mystery.

II. Patristic Exegesis of the Psalms

My own interest in early Christian exegesis began in teaching and scholarly research on the way early Christian biblical interpreters approached the book of Psalms. In many ways, patristic psalm exegesis is unique in its goals and its assumptions about the biblical text; still, familiarity with this area of early Christian exegesis can make us aware of the distinctive cast of mind in which patristic preachers and expositors approached the conundrums and cruces of the whole canon of Scripture.

For the early church, the book of Psalms was clearly one of the most important and familiar books of the Bible. Early Christian commentaries on the Psalms easily exceed in number those on any other book of the Old or New Testament; we still possess partial or complete sets of homilies or scholarly commentaries on the Psalms — in some cases, more than one set — by at least twenty-one Latin or Greek patristic authors, and this interest did not abate in the medieval church. The main reason, undoubtedly, was the fact that by the late fourth century, at least, the Psalms were in constant use, both in public worship and in more private forms of prayer and meditation. How the Christian liturgical use of the biblical psalms began remains a matter of

18. John Keble, "On the Mysticism Attributed to the Early Fathers of the Church," *Tracts for the Times*, no. 89 (London: Rivington, 1841; reprint, New York: AMS, 1969), pp. 134-35.

scholarly debate. Sometime in the mid-fourth century, a synod at Laodicea in Phrygia could lay down as a canon "It is not permitted that privately composed psalms or non-canonical books be read out in Church, but only the canonical books of the New and Old Testament."[19]

With the meteoric rise of monasticism and ascetical piety during the fourth century, the recitation and chanting of the Psalms grew to be the mainstay of Christian daily prayer, both private and communal, in the churches of the Mediterranean world;[20] meditation — the quiet, ruminative "chewing" on the words of the Psalms — was recommended by many spiritual guides as the most effective spiritual weapon against inner demons, a medicine for diseased thoughts.[21] The desert monks seem to have learned large portions of the Psalter (in some cases, even the whole of it) by heart and to have prayed the Psalms constantly as they worked. Epiphanius of Salamis, the pugnacious defender of orthodoxy of the late fourth century, is said to have chided a Palestinian abbot for allowing his monks to restrict their psalmody to three canonical hours, "for the true monk should have prayer and psalmody in his heart with no interruption."[22]

Basil of Caesarea prefaced his homily on Psalm 1 — which was probably conceived as the beginning of a continuous series — with a celebrated encomium on the powers of the Psalter to change the human heart and shape Christian community. In Basil's view, it is the poetry and music inherent in the Psalms that gives them their distinctive power and makes their teaching — which they share with the rest of the Bible — uniquely accessible:

> When, indeed, the Holy Spirit saw that the human race was guided only with difficulty toward virtue, and that, because of our inclination toward pleasure, we were neglectful of an upright life, what did he do? The delight of melody he mingled with the doctrines, so that by the pleasantness

19. Canon 59; see E. J. Jonkers, ed., *Acta et Symbola Conciliorum quae saeculo quarto habita sunt* (Leiden: Brill, 1954), p. 96. Jonkers dates this synod, about which little is known, between 341 and 381.

20. It is interesting to note that the Syrian churches seem to have maintained the tradition of using Christian hymns and versified homilies in monastic and public worship throughout the patristic period and that, consequently, the biblical psalms seem to have played a much less dominant role in their worship and exegetical activity than among Greek, Latin, and Coptic Christians.

21. The fifth-century Latin writer John Cassian insists that the apex of prayer — and, indeed, of the human spiritual journey — is to be united to God in a total, wordless concentration of mind and heart, free from all material images and concepts. John Cassian, *Conference* 10.5-6.

22. *Sayings of the Desert Fathers,* Alphabetical Collection 198, French trans. L. Régnault (Sablé-sur-Sarthe: Solesmes, 1981), p. 83.

" canon as criterion"

and softness of the sound heard we might receive without perceiving it the benefit of the words, just as wise physicians who, when giving the fastidious rather bitter drugs to drink, frequently smear the cup with honey.[23]

The fullest and most original ancient Christian explanation of the peculiar character of the Psalter among the books of the Bible is undoubtedly Athanasius's *Letter to Marcellinus on the Interpretation of the Psalms,* a work so highly valued in antiquity that it was included in the early-fifth-century Codex Alexandrinus of the Greek Bible as the introduction to the book of Psalms. Athanasius presents his essay as embodying the teaching he received from "a scholarly old man," a γέρων *(gerōn)* — presumably meant to be an *abba* from the Egyptian desert.[24] By this device, he situates his own explanation of the peculiar character and "grace" of the Psalter within the thought world of monasticism. Athanasius begins by suggesting, as Basil would soon do, that the actual thematic content of the Psalms is not different from that of the other books but rather "contains in itself what is found in all of them, like a garden, and expresses them in song."[25] Whatever the rest of the Bible has to offer — narratives of God's great deeds of the past, prophetic warnings, moral teachings, even foreshadowings of Christ — can be found, in poetic form, in the book of Psalms. What is distinctive about the Psalter in relation to other books is its more personal, emotional element, which allows the reader to identify the message with him or herself: "[I]t contains within itself the movements of each soul, their changes and adjustments, written out and thoroughly portrayed, so that if someone should wish to grasp himself from it, as from an image, and to understand on that basis how to shape himself, it is written there." The point of portraying the whole range of human spiritual "movements," or emotions, Athanasius goes on to explain, is not simply poetic imitation, mimesis, but *therapy;* the person who recognizes his own inner state in the Psalms "can possess from this, once again, the image contained in the words, so that he does not simply hear them and move on, but learns what one must say and do to heal one's disordered feelings." The Psalms, in other words, do not simply command us to repent of our sins, to bear suffering patiently, or to praise God for his gifts; they actually give us the words by which we can say and do these things for ourselves.[26]

23. Basil of Caesarea, *Homily on Psalm* 1.1, trans. Agnes Clare Way, FC 46 (Washington, D.C.: Catholic University of America Press, 1963), p. 152.
24. Athanasius, *Epistula ad Marcellinum* 1 (PG 27.12).
25. *Epistula ad Marcellinum* 2 (PG 27.12).
26. *Epistula ad Marcellinum* 10 (PG 27.20-21).

For this, once again, is the curious thing about the Psalms: that in reading the other books lectors tend to proclaim the sayings of the holy authors, whatever subjects they are talking about, as concerning those about whom the books are written, and listeners understand that they themselves are different people from those dealt with in the text. . . . But while the person who takes up this book will certainly marvel, in the same way as in other books, at the prophecies concerning the Savior, and will make an act of adoration and read on, still he will read out the rest of the Psalms as if they are his own words; and the one who hears them will be deeply moved, as if he himself were speaking, and will be affected by the words of these songs as if they were his own.[27]

Athanasius's argument in this central section of his work is that in becoming "like a mirror to the one singing them," the Psalms not only lead us to deeper knowledge of ourselves but change us in the process, acting as a providential corrective to the imbalance of our desires and emotions. In hearing and singing them as our own prayers, in recognizing our present needs and deepest longings in them, we allow them subtly to reshape our inner life to conform to God's own Word; "for what Psalm-singers express in words can become forms and models of ourselves."[28] And Athanasius recognizes in this mimetic, modeling role of the Psalms an anticipation of the incarnation: just as the Word, in becoming one of us, not only taught us how to live by his words but "did what he taught," providing us with a living image of "perfect virtue" in his own life, "for the same reason, even before his life among us, he made this resound from the lips of those who sing the Psalms. Just as he revealed the model of the earthly and the heavenly human being in himself, so also anyone who wishes can learn in the Psalms about the motions and conditions of souls, and can find in them the remedy and corrective measure for each of these motions."[29] Toward the end of the treatise, Athanasius draws on Hellenistic music theory to argue that the reason the Psalms are sung and not simply read — besides the fact that this adds "breadth" and solemnity to our praise of God — is to enable them to create a harmony and order in our inner selves that parallels the harmony the Logos, as Creator and Sustainer, perpetually secures in the universe. "For just as we recognize the thoughts of the

---

27. *Epistula ad Marcellinum* 11 (PG 27.21). Athanasius is thinking of the liturgical chanting of the Psalms by a cantor.

28. *Epistula ad Marcellinum* 12 (PG 27.24). For a study of the longer Christian tradition of regarding the Psalms as "spiritual exercises," a training ground for godly affections, see Günter Bader, *Psalterium affectuum palaestra* (Tübingen: Mohr/Siebeck, 1996).

29. *Epistula ad Marcellinum* 12 (PG 27.25).

soul, and signify them through the words [of the Psalms] we utter, so the Lord wishes that the song that springs forth from the words should be a symbol of spiritual harmony in the soul, and has decreed that the Odes be sung to melodies, and the Psalms also be chanted musically."[30]

Athanasius's treatment of the Psalms — as a God-given means of restoring the vital inner balance of the human person through images of both the diseased and the reformed self, assimilated by means of words, ideas, and music — remains largely concerned with their effect on the individual, especially on the individual monk living in a community of prayer, introspection, and ascetic struggle. In Augustine's *Enarrationes in Psalmos,* on the other hand, we find ourselves in a more diverse and more explicitly ecclesial context. Although Augustine himself lived virtually the rest of his life after his baptism in a community — first with other *servi Dei,* later with his own clergy — his interpretation of the Psalms, like that of Hilary and probably that of Ambrose, was offered mainly in the context of liturgical preaching, before "ordinary" Christian congregations: his own, at Hippo Regius, and others to which he was often invited, especially that of the provincial basilica at Carthage. The psalms on which he preached seem to have been at times part of a seasonal lectionary cycle and at times specifically chosen, individually or as a series, as occasional texts.

Augustine's own spiritual vocabulary, in fact, seems to have been shaped by the Psalter from his earliest days as a committed Christian. The Psalms provide many of the themes and phrases that form the complex literary tissue of the *Confessions,* for instance; Henry Chadwick, in the perceptive introduction to his translation of the work, remarks that from the first paragraph on, "Augustine can express Neoplatonic themes in language which sounds like a pastiche of the Psalter."[31] In describing his own spiritual transformation during his withdrawal at Cassiciacum in the months before his baptism, Augustine reflects on the new, ardent voice the Psalms provided for his own "burning" conversations with God and calls them "songs of faith, sounds of devotion that banished heaviness of spirit."[32] One of the results of his decision to enroll for baptism, he seems to suggest, was his new sensitivity to the consoling effects of the Psalms and to their ability to heal the "swelling tumor of pride" in a way that Neoplatonic philosophy, for all its speculative power, had never been able

---

30. *Epistula ad Marcellinum* 27-28 (PG 27.40). Athanasius seems here to be referring to the "Odes," or canticles, contained in other books of the Bible as a separate, musically more elaborate category of sung liturgical text.

31. Henry Chadwick, introduction to *Confessions,* trans. Henry Chadwick (Oxford: Oxford University Press, 1992), p. xxii.

32. "Cantica fidelia, sonos pietatis excludentes turgidum spiritum." *Confessions* 9.4.8.

to do. Yet this highly personal relationship to the Psalms generally yields place, in the verse-by-verse commentaries Augustine wrote or preached as bishop, to a public, collective reading that consistently focuses the audience's attention on a more complex understanding of the *speaker* of the Psalms: as Christ, key to all Christian understanding of the Scriptures, and as the church, his body, in whom and for whom he continues to pray.

Augustine developed, in fact, a hermeneutical principle of hearing more than one "voice" speaking in Scripture that was to remain dominant in later Western interpretation of the Psalms through the time of the Reformation, a principle that was rooted in the central Christian doctrine of the incarnation. The speaker of these scriptural prayers — providentially given to us by the Spirit to be the language by which we speak to God — is at once the "original" author (David or some other biblical figure), the anguished or exultant private user, the church as a unified liturgical subject, and Christ Jesus, the Word made flesh, who has himself cried out to God in abandonment (Mark 15:34, citing Ps 22:1) and who now stands gloriously in the presence of God as our intercessor and in the midst of the church as its Lord (Heb 9:24). As both prophecy and prayer — God's word to us and ours to God — constantly in use by Christians for both private, meditative reading and the public liturgy, the Psalms were traditionally seen in the West, from Augustine to Luther and beyond, as peculiarly open to, even necessitating, such multilayered interpretation.

III. Can We Use Patristic Exegesis?

In a recent article discussing John Keble's defense of patristic exegesis, Ephraim Radner suggests that in our own postmodern age, with its professed love of diversity and its unquenchable thirst for religious or "spiritual" experience, the Fathers' figural mode of scriptural interpretation, like early Christian ascetical practices, may be less controversial to us than it was to Keble's Victorian contemporaries, with their historically informed commitment to literal meaning. The issue for us, rather, is how important, how relevant to the present life and faith of all the Christian churches, such scriptural interpretation still is. Radner pointedly asks whether we can maintain a vision of God's reality, of God's presence and activity in the world, *without* centering our faith on a sense of God's providence and a figural approach to the Bible essentially akin to those of the Fathers.[33]

33. Ephraim Radner, "The Discrepancies of Two Ages: Thoughts on Keble's 'Mysticism of the Fathers,'" *The Anglican* 43 (2000): 10-15.

Clearly, this suggestion raises disturbing questions for the contemporary believer. Despite the vogue of postmodern theories, most of us still cannot think of the world and of the human community except in radically historical terms; we cannot prescind from our knowledge of what is involved in natural and human causality, our sense of the cultural conditioning of language and thought, our assumption of the perspectival character of the perception and communication of truth. Unless we choose to approach the Bible as fundamentalists, we cannot escape being aware that the texts that constitute our scriptural canon have undergone a complex evolution to reach their present form and arrangement and that the meaning any given passage may have had for its original hearers may be very distant from the meaning we find in it today as Christians. Our sense of what a passage may originally have meant always involves, to some degree, a process of hypothetical reconstruction, yet unless we attempt it, we run the risk of simply subjecting the text to our own religious and cultural prejudices. At the same time, however, we are becoming more and more aware that the interpretation of the Bible simply on the basis of religiously neutral historical scholarship offers relatively little interest or promise to the community of faith. If we are to receive the Bible as more than a collection of documents on ancient Near Eastern religion, if we are still to take it as *Scripture* — in fact, as a single "Bible," or *book*, of Scripture, which as such is normative for our faith — then historical exegesis must somehow be united more firmly and continuously with theology (the reflective attempt to make sense of the worshiping community's rule of faith) in a single interpretive practice. In addition, as we become more aware that a credible faith presupposes real unity among Christians, as we become more conscious of the theological misuse of scriptural texts in the past to shore up sectarian interests, we can hardly escape concluding that Christian exegesis must become not only more theological but more theologically ecumenical if it is to nourish those who continue to read the Bible in faith.

In this quest, historical criticism will obviously continue to play an indispensable role in any sophisticated modern interpretation of biblical texts. That role, first of all, must be to free readers from the same destructive literalism that Origen recognized as the basis of most false interpretation of the Bible[34] — taking the apparent face value of a biblical text so seriously, so much in isolation from the rest of the canon, that we invest it with a meaning

---

34. See *De principiis* 4.2.2: "The cause, in all the cases we have mentioned, of false opinions and impious or simple-minded assertions seems to be nothing else but that Scripture has not been understood according to its spiritual meaning, but is taken according to the mere letter."

at odds with both its probable original sense and its traditional Christian application. Second, historical criticism can help free us from the narrowly polemical readings of certain texts — Matt 16:18 in Catholic-Protestant debates about the papacy, for instance, or John 15:26 in Orthodox-Western controversy about the origin of the Holy Spirit — that overload their contextual meaning with interpretive histories that only perpetuate Christian division. But beyond the liberating effect of returning *ad fontes* on any discussion of Christian reform, some sense of the historical trajectory of meaning borne by a biblical passage — from its reconstructed "original" form and content, through its various stages of redaction and interpretation, to the life of the present church — seems to be an indispensable prerequisite for any honest, intellectually plausible treatment of the text. Having a historically sophisticated sense of where a text comes from allows us, in a culture conscious of history, to be appropriately discerning when we read that text in a Christian scriptural perspective. It makes us realize the distance the text has traveled to be God's word to us.

A more positive perception of early Christian exegesis, as not merely premodern but thoroughly and — in many cases, at least — successfully *theological,* can open our eyes to what seems to be the other, less fulfilled, need in biblical interpretation today: the need to recapture an understanding of interpretation's own role within the church and of its centrally theological task as reading, not just texts, but sacred and normative texts, texts that relate to the overarching story of Jewish and Christian faith. As Christians, we need to rediscover the implicit sense of the mutual dependence between theology and biblical interpretation, of the fluid and often imperceptible border between them, that characterized the patristic era. We need to recognize that theology, in all its forms, is really always a remote preparation for preaching — that is what distinguishes it, after all, from the philosophy or the phenomenology or the history of religion — and that Christian preaching has traditionally been chiefly a matter of expounding biblical texts for the present life of the church. We need not only to approach the text of Scripture with a sense of its historical origin and of the historical context of all meaning; we need also to approach history with the conviction that God is present and active within it as its fundamentally real, although fundamentally transcendent, ground and source: that although God is not, in an ontological sense, "historical," he is constantly to be found in history as the condition of its intelligibility. We need to become more conscious of the fact that the church has always received the Bible as the book about Christ, because it was only reference to the Jewish biblical canon that enabled the disciples of Jesus to interpret his death and resurrection as being "for our sins, in accordance with the Scriptures"

(1 Cor 15:3) and because it is only the church's faith in the risen Jesus as the Christ that has permitted it to receive and recognize this hodgepodge of texts as a "Bible" at all. We need, perhaps most of all, to recover a "hermeneutic of piety" for our exegesis, in a mode appropriate to our own life of Christian faith. We need a way of approaching biblical texts that has its roots in our commitment to the faith of the worshiping Christian community, that is nourished by the continuous word of the centuries in which that faith has been preached, that asks of any proposed new application of the biblical message, Does this seem appropriate to what we know of God? Does this fit with the full mystery of our salvation in Christ, as we have received and experienced it in the church? Does this help us lead a holy life?

Early Christian interpretation, grounded in its strong sense of God's long involvement with humanity, can offer us at least parallels and models for reviving our exegetical imagination. It seems unlikely that many modern Christians will find that simply turning to patristic commentaries and homilies will supply all their needs for a more theological style of exegesis. Still, a greater familiarity with early Christian interpretation may lead modern Christian scholarly readers to reflect more radically on the hermeneutical conditions for reappropriating the Bible as the book of the church and may thus stimulate them to develop new strategies for reading it in a Christian — and thus, in some sense, a figural — way, in a historically minded age.

Christ Was like St. Francis

James C. Howell

G. K. Chesterton, noting how Francis of Assisi sought to fashion himself after Christ, how Francis was "a most sublime approximation to his Master," "a splendid and yet a merciful Mirror of Christ," shrewdly suggested that

> if St. Francis was like Christ, Christ was to that extent like St. Francis. And my present point is that it is really very enlightening to realise that Christ was like St. Francis. What I mean is this; that if men find certain riddles and hard sayings in the story of Galilee, and if they find the answers to those riddles in the story of Assisi, it really does show that a secret has been handed down in one religious tradition and no other. It shows that the casket that was locked in Palestine can be unlocked in Umbria; for the Church is the keeper of the keys.
>
> Now in truth while it has always seemed natural to explain St. Francis in the light of Christ, it has not occurred to many people to explain Christ in the light of St. Francis. . . . St. Francis is the mirror of Christ rather as the moon is the mirror of the sun. The moon is much smaller than the sun, but it is also much nearer to us; and being less vivid it is more visible. Exactly in the same sense St. Francis is nearer to us, and being a mere man like ourselves is in that sense more imaginable.[1]

Beyond question, hagiographers were consumed by their zeal to polish Francis's life into such a mirror. But as we fathom their desire to hold up this mirror, and as we delve into even the less fantastic details of what transpired in Assisi at the turn of the thirteenth century, we may find ourselves exploring a hermeneutical principle regarding how to read the Bible.

---

1. G. K. Chesterton, *St. Francis of Assisi* (Garden City, N.Y.: Image, 1957), pp. 117-18.

Imitatio Christi

Francis's early biographers were at pains not just to legitimize a particular mode of being a Franciscan but also to demonstrate the conformity of the saint's life to the life of Christ. To read the *Fioretti*, the charming and at times tedious collection of stories gathered at the remove of two generations from Francis's death, is to see another Jesus walking the hills of Umbria. Its first sentence exposes the *Fioretti*'s agenda: "Let us begin by considering the conformity of the glorious St. Francis, in all the acts of his life, to Christ."[2] And later we read: "Because the true servant of Christ, St. Francis, was in some things almost a second Christ given to the world for the salvation of the people, God the Father made him in many of his acts conform to His Son Jesus Christ. . . ."[3] Francis, like Christ, chose twelve companions, one of whom, Giovanni della Cappella, apostatized and hanged himself. Francis sent his companions out two by two to preach and heal. Francis fasted for forty days (although he did break the fast by eating a half loaf of bread on the thirty-ninth day, so as to avoid vainglory). Water was turned into wine. The blind, the demon-possessed, and the lame were healed. So noteworthy were his miracles that crowds pressed toward him, grasping for the hem of his garment. When he entered a city, crowds clapped and rejoiced, tearing branches from trees to wave. One tradition fixed his birth, not in the five-room house whose traces figure in today's tours of Assisi, but in a stable. The late fourteenth century saw Bartholomew of Pisa's writing of *De conformitate vitae Beati Francisci ad vitam Domini Iesu (Concerning the Conformity of the Life of St. Francis to the Life of the Lord Jesus)*, a lengthy tome on the subject of Francis as an *alter Christus* that strains credulity.

In part, these hagiographers share in a larger tradition of the *imitatio Christi* as a mode of commitment in the life of the church. In the Church Fathers, the imitation of Christ meant participation in his resurrection, receiving a share in Christ's divinity. Giles Constable, among others, has detected a subtle trend throughout the Middle Ages: over time, the focus was less exclusively on joining oneself to the glory of Christ in the resurrection, with increasingly stronger voices urging the faithful to imitate Christ's earthly life, talk, behavior. The *imitatio Christi*

> took on new meanings without entirely losing its old ones. . . . More and more Christians took an interest in Christ's earthly life, surrounded every

---

2. *Fioretti* 1, in *The Little Flowers, Legends, and Lauds*, ed. Otto Karrer, trans. N. Wydenbruck (London: Sheed & Ward, 1947), p. 174.

3. *Fioretti* 7, in *Little Flowers, Legends, and Lauds*, p. 183.

aspect of it with special devotions, and modelled their own lives on His with a degree of literalism which would have surprised and perhaps shocked people in the early Middle Ages; but they did not lose their concern for Christ's divinity, or for His role in securing eternal life. . . .

. . . It was in the course of the Middle Ages, and above all the twelfth century, that Christ was brought to earth as an example for everyday life and that the desire to imitate Him centered on His earthly life and character.[4]

4. Giles Constable, *Three Studies in Medieval Religious and Social Thought* (Cambridge: Cambridge University Press, 1995), pp. 169-70, 248. For centuries the dominant melody was that Christ was our Savior, not so much our exemplar. Ignatius of Antioch could speak of "being conformed to the true image of God which is the Son Himself who becomes incarnate for our restoration." Not surprisingly, the ultimate "imitators" of Christ were the martyrs, those who "completed the sufferings of Christ" (Col 1:24; 2 Cor 4:10). Leo the Great exalted the martyrs "who beyond all men are so close to our Lord Jesus Christ both in the imitation of love and in the likeness of the passion." The shift in focus Constable portrays was not to something previously unnoticed. Irenaeus of Lyons could speak of obedience as imitating Christ's earthly life. Origen, along with others, construed the imitation of Christ as a reclamation of our lost status by the copying of Christ's virtues, especially his humility, poverty, and suffering. And Chrysostom told his congregation in Antioch that "Christ gave thee also power to become like Him, so far as thy ability extends. Be not afraid at hearing this. The fear is not to be like Him." Further: "Teach thy soul to frame thee a mouth like to Christ's mouth. . . . Speak then after His manner, and thou art become in this respect such as He, so far as it is possible for one who is a man to become so." In *Cur Deus homo,* Anselm claimed that Christ "presented himself as an example" and taught us "not to draw back from justice on account of injuries or insults or sufferings or death." The divinity theme was hardly muted. Bernard of Clairvaux was riveted to the notion of the imitation of Christ, but for him that entailed not so much an altered style of participation in this world as a road out of this world, an ascent heavenward in the wake of Christ's resurrection and ascension. The theme of imitation reached a climax with Ignatius Loyola. He mandated that Thomas à Kempis be read, and he relied on it heavily himself. Thomas, born in 1380, was not a creative thinker so much as a collator, a gatherer of the thoughts of many on the devotional life, especially Gerard Groote. *The Imitation of Christ,* its sales solid at the remove of more than six centuries, declares its intention to be true to its title: "'He who follows Me shall not walk in darkness,' says Our Lord. In these words Christ counsels us to follow His life and way if we desire true enlightenment and freedom from all blindness of heart. Let the life of Jesus Christ, then, be our first consideration. . . . Whoever desires to understand and take delight in the words of Christ must strive to conform his whole life to Him." Thomas à Kempis, *The Imitation of Christ,* trans. Leo Sherley-Price (New York: Penguin, 1952), p. 27. The balance of the book, however, as full of wisdom and spirituality as it may be, pays little attention to the actual words of Christ or to actual behaviors or events from Christ's life. That task would be pursued more diligently in the following century by Ignatius Loyola himself. Like Francis, Ignatius was wounded as a soldier, and during his convalescence he weighed carefully the life of Christ and his response to that life. Disposing of his worldly possessions, he donned sackcloth and straightaway wrote *The Spiritual Exercises* (another perennial bestseller). Ignatius prescribed a regimen that would discipline the imagination to an intimate

Inevitably, the notion of imitation is burdened by negative connotations (as it was in the Middle Ages), bearing within itself the seeds of approximation yet failure, or even caricature. Mimicry is hardly a faithful copy, or even a desirable posture. I can hear my son filing suit against his sister from the back of the van: "Daddy, she's copying me!" And yet, for precisely that reason, the notion of imitation is helpful. We can muster no better than a failed approximation of Christ, in laughable, faltering ways.

The Literal Sense Surpasses Allegory

Despite the extravagances of the hagiographers, there can be no doubt that the "real" Francis, the man who lived in space and time with such sanctity that he was canonized a mere two years after his death, quite intentionally patterned his life after the life of Christ with the kind of surprising, and perhaps shocking, literalism Constable has suggested. The narrative of Christ was not merely something in which he believed; that narrative functioned as the script for his life. He read that script with a startling naiveté. Henri d'Avranches, writing just six years after Francis's death, captured this approach to Scripture in verse:

> Nor will he gloss over anything, but follow the text and faithfully cling
> To every word. Allegory may in much prevail; but the literal sense
> Surpasses it, when no metaphor cloaks the author's mind
> And his words mean what they say.
> Having listened therefore to everything demanded of him,
> As his own interpreter he knows better than to be of the word
> A hearer only and not a doer. He says: "What Christ commands
> I must now do. This is my wish, my vow, what my whole soul desires."[5]

---

acquaintance with the life of Christ. Loyola's mode of apprehending Christ ("with interior eyes") is contrasted with Luther's ("with open ears") by David C. Steinmetz in "Luther and Loyola," *Interpretation* 47 (1993): 5-14. We may picture Jesus' walking, the movement of the water and trees, the villages, the house where Jesus lived with Mary, the winding of the road to Nazareth, Christ's bodily sensations of hunger, thirst, heat, and cold. But this regimen is not for voyeurs. We are to imitate Christ, to embrace his poverty and his humility, to bear ridicule and rejection as did he, to shed tears and even to die as did he.

5. Henri d'Avranches, *The Versified Life of Saint Francis* 5, in *Francis of Assisi: Early Documents*, 3 vols., ed. Regis J. Armstrong, J. A. Wayne Hellman, and Wm. J. Short (New York: New City, 1999-2001), 1:459-60. Francis may be a shining example of Alasdair MacIntyre's "Augustinian" reader, who "has to have inculcated into him or herself certain attitudes and dispositions, certain virtues, *before* he or she can know why these are to be accounted virtues. So a prerational

We will look at examples of how the literal sense surpasses the allegorical in the biography by Thomas of Celano, a work commissioned by Francis's friend Pope Gregory IX in connection with ceremonies of canonization in 1228. To this *Vita prima* Thomas added another biography, probably twenty years later; the *Vita secunda,* while drawing on more stories from Leo, Rufino, and Angelo, is more idealized, exhibiting institutional concerns effected by the debate over the future of the order. Both works are clear about the theme of Francis's life:

> His highest aim, foremost desire, and greatest intention was to pay heed to the holy gospel in all things and through all things, to follow the teaching of our Lord Jesus Christ and to retrace His footsteps completely.[6]

Vestigii Christi

Not long after his conversion, Francis went to the Portiuncula for Mass at Santa Maria degli Angeli. In the service he heard Matt 10:9-10, where Jesus told his disciples that they should have neither gold nor coats, shoes, or staves for their journey. Glossing over nothing in this text, Francis became a doer, forsaking fashion and finery, donning a rough garment girded with a rope instead of a belt (now fashionable among the clergy as alb and cincture), and going barefoot (or, as we now say, discalced).

Bernard of Quintavalle, intrigued, invited Francis to his home. After the evening meal, they retired. Francis pretended to sleep; Bernard also pretended to sleep, even feigning a snore. Francis rose and then knelt, praying over and over, all night long, "My God, my all." Bernard was touched; he asked Francis the next morning how to become a servant of God.

The two of them went to a church called San Niccolo, where Francis

---

reordering of the self has to occur. . . . This reordering requires obedient trust." Alasdair MacIntyre, *Three Rival Versions of Moral Enquiry* (Notre Dame: University of Notre Dame Press, 1990), p. 82.

6. Thomas of Celano, *Vita prima* 30, in *Early Documents,* 1:254. Or see *Vita secunda* 9, in *Early Documents,* 1:283:

> He was always with Jesus:
> Jesus in his heart,
> Jesus in his mouth,
> Jesus in his ears,
> Jesus in his eyes,
> Jesus in his hands,
> he bore Jesus always in his whole body.

asked that the Bible be opened three times. The resulting three verses are utterly familiar, yet most of us never take them seriously: "Sell all you have and give it to the poor" (Matt 19:21); "Take nothing for your journey" (Luke 9:3); and "If any man would come after me, let him deny himself" (Matt 16:24). Bernard did as the rich young ruler had not done: he sold everything and gave it to the poor, as did other young men (Giles, Masseo, Leo), and even women (especially Clare). Imitating Christ, the friars became itinerants with no place to lay their heads (Matt 8:20). When Francis had his audience with Innocent III in 1210, he asked for approval for his first *regula,* whose first chapter mandates that the friars are

> "to live in obedience, in chastity, and without anything of their own," and to follow the teaching and footprints of our Lord Jesus Christ, Who says: "If you wish to be perfect, go, sell everything you have and give it to the poor, and you will have treasure in heaven; and come, follow me." And: "If anyone wishes to come after me, let him deny himself and take up his cross and follow me." Again: "If anyone wishes to come to me and does not hate father and mother and wife and children and brothers and sisters, and even his own life, he cannot be my disciple."[7]

Francis was interpreting not just a single text but a cluster of texts among which he perceived a common theme, that of apostolic poverty. In a sense, this poverty was in imitation of Christ, who was poor, and simultaneously in obedience to Christ's words to the first disciples, which, granted Francis's literalist bent on Christ's teachings, were therefore words to disciples in the thirteenth century as well.

So, in this instance, is Chesterton right — that it is illuminating to think of Jesus as being like Francis? The church needs sobering reminders of the reality of Jesus' life. Francis's forsaking of his exotic garments and donning of rags, captured in the famous series of frescoes in the Upper Church of San Francesco in Assisi, is vestigial of Jesus, who, though he was rich, became poor (2 Cor 8:9). Francis also reminds us why this Jesus, who had no place to lay his head, told his disciples (and even the Jesus Seminar puts Matt 10:7-10 in red letters) to travel lightly. An interpreter may actually be right, in a technical sense, in treating this radical poverty as what the text meant in the first century. Tertullian was among the first to argue that Jesus' admonitions in Matt 10:7-10 involve a unique moment in the past, not all moments in all

---

7. Francis of Assisi, *The Earlier Rule* 1, in *Early Documents,* 1:63-64. In a letter to Leo near the end of his life, Francis reiterated this theme of following in the footprints *(vestigii)* of Christ.

times. Clement of Alexandria, in his exposition of Jesus' admonition to "sell all and give it to the poor," had argued:

> But well knowing that the Saviour teaches nothing in a merely human way, but teaches all things to His own with divine and mystic wisdom, we must not listen to His utterances carnally. . . .
>
> . . . He does not, as some conceive off-hand, bid him throw away the substance he possessed, and abandon his property; but bids him banish from his soul his notions about wealth, his excitement . . . about it, the anxieties. . . . For it is no great thing . . . to be destitute of wealth. . . .
>
> . . . So let no man destroy wealth, rather than the passions of the soul, which are incompatible with the better use of wealth.[8]

And within a century of Francis's death, John XXII fashioned a clever case that hinged on technicalities of natural law to undermine Francis's intention that his friars live in absolute poverty.[9]

But to see Francis and his followers taking nothing for their journey and going barefoot raises a question: Is there some ironic exegetical advantage won by those who read the text with a naive literalism, by those who (as Henri d'Avranches put it) "will not gloss over anything"? Ulrich Luz poses the issue surrounding the radical poverty of Jesus and his followers:

> Almost never in its history has the church resembled what is here described. . . . The church has not consisted of itinerant radicals; quite the contrary, the radicals, whenever they existed, were considered suspect. . . . Calvin, more than others, stressed that Matthew 10 was not setting up timeless laws but was exclusively intended for the first mission of the disciples.
>
> Such an interpretation of Matthew 10 is not only very popular but also very convenient. Apart from some monastic traditions, the idea of itinerant radicalism disappeared almost entirely. The churches were extremely successful in ignoring it. No wonder: a church that constructs cathedrals

---

8. Clement of Alexandria, "Who Is the Rich Man That Shall Be Saved?" *ANF* 2:592-95.

9. On his deathbed Francis had warned, "I strictly forbid any of my friars, clerics or lay brothers, to interpret the rule or these words, saying, 'This is what they mean!' God inspired me to write the Rule and these words plainly and simply, and so you too must understand them plainly and simply, and live by them, doing good to the last." No more than four years elapsed after his death before Gregory IX, the ex-cardinal Ugolino who knew Francis intimately, issued the bull *Quo elongati,* shearing Francis's last testament of its authority. This incident is discussed well by Chiara Frugoni, *Francis of Assisi: A Life,* trans. John Bowden (New York: Continuum, 1999), p. 156.

and that offers not only food but both houses and cars to its workers cannot appreciate this kind of tradition.[10]

A recent biographer of Francis, Chiara Frugoni, underlines the novelty and significance of Francis's poverty:

> It was not that the church did not help the needy and distressed in his time. But it had never put itself in question as a privileged structure. It had never departed from its certainties or its established positions. By the conditions in which they lived, their culture, the guarantee of a solid well-being, the clergy maintained between themselves and the host of the disinherited a clear frontier which could not be crossed.[11]

Then Frugoni notes that Francis's innovations "derive from a simple concern to follow the gospel to the letter." As we choose between the readings of Francis and John XXII, perhaps a lifestyle preference impinges upon us in ways of which we are unaware. Certainly, this was the case for the pope: we cannot imagine anyone less fit to interpret the Scriptures and settle the dispute between the Spiritual Franciscans and the Conventuals than the grossly materialist John XXII, who developed the sale of indulgences and enriched the papal treasuries. We will say more about lifestyle preference in its modern context below.

Our Father

After selling his horse and giving away his father's fabrics in Foligno, Francis found himself locked up in a dungeon at the hand of his father, who then filed suit against his son in the Palazzo Communale. Francis not only returned his father's money but also cast off all his garments, proclaiming, "Up to now I have called Pietro Bernardone my father, but as I am now resolved to serve God, I give him back the money about which he was so perturbed, as well as the clothes I wore which belonged to him, and from now on I will say: 'Our Father who art in Heaven' instead of 'my father Pietro Bernardone.'"[12]

---

10. Ulrich Luz, *Matthew in History: Interpretation, Influence, and Effects* (Minneapolis: Fortress, 1994), pp. 40, 45.

11. Frugoni, *Francis of Assisi*, p. 46.

12. Giovanni di Ceprano, *The Youth of St. Francis and the Beginnings of His Foundation*, in *Little Flowers, Legends, and Lauds*, p. 12. Bonaventure adds that when Francis disrobed, a hair shirt was revealed, further demonstrating his asceticism. One of Giotto's frescoes shows Guido covering the naked saint with his episcopal mantle, perhaps both for shame and as a sign of ecclesiastical blessing.

The Lord's Prayer has often been interpreted from a doctrinal perspective. Tertullian called it a *breviarum totius Evangelii* (a summary of the whole gospel), and Cyprian saw it as a *coelestis doctrinae compendium* (an abridged form of heavenly doctrine). Luther's Small Catechism enunciates the way many have understood the Our Father: "God wants us to believe he truly is our Father and we are his children. We are therefore to pray with complete confidence, just as children speak to their loving father." But for Francis, the Our Father took on the nuance of a declaration of allegiance, to the exclusion of other, even admirable, allegiances. Does his reading help us understand Christ's own prayer? Certainly, it invites us to contemplate a link between the Lord's Prayer and another text, Luke 14:26: "If anyone comes to me and does not hate his own father . . . he cannot be my disciple." In fact, many early Franciscans argued that total renunciation of parents was a requirement for all friars.

The Ultimate Sign

The *Vita prima* tells how some other riddles from Galilee may find their answer in Assisi. Until his conversion, Francis had endeavored to stay at least two miles from all lepers; when he inadvertently encountered one, he would tightly hold his nostrils. But one day, as he was riding outside Assisi at Rivo Torto, Francis met a leper. Conquering his loathing and revulsion, he gave the leper a coin and kissed him. The *Vita secunda* adds a hagiographic detail: after the kiss, Francis got back on his horse, looked around, and, although the plain was open for miles, could not see the leper anymore! As this leper played such a pivotal role in his conversion, Francis subsequently touched and bandaged many lepers, calling them brothers in Christ.

While still a young troubadour and would-be knight, Francis was surprisingly compassionate and generous. He met a knight, virtually naked, who had fallen into abject poverty; in a flamboyant gesture, captured again by Giotto, Francis gave his own costly garments to the knight. Celano tells us that Francis, "though he was content with a ragged and rough tunic, often wished to divide it with some poor person. . . . When he met poor people burdened with wood or other heavy loads, he would offer his own weak shoulders to help them."[13] As Bonaventure explains, Francis, "the most Christian of poor men, saw the image of Christ in every poor man. . . . He would spare nothing whatever, neither cloak nor tunic nor book, not even vestments or

13. *Vita prima* 28, in *Early Documents*, 1:247-48.

altarcloths."[14] The saint was thus fulfilling Matt 25:31-46 (cf. 5:42), not gloss-ing over any of Jesus' words. The wonderful stories of the robbers at Monte Casale, and of the wolf of Gubbio, and of Francis's strolling unarmed into the camp of the sultan Malik al-Kamil at Damietta show how he took quite liter-ally the dominical mandates "Love your enemies" and "If your enemy is hun-gry, feed him." We could also look to Francis for explication of parables: in the *Vita prima*, Celano compares Francis to the experienced merchant — an apt metaphor, given his background — who sold all he had to secure the pearl of great price.[15]

More complex would be a consideration of Francis's desire for martyr-dom. As a boy in Assisi, Francis learned of the city's martyrs, Sts. Feliciano, Vittorino, Savino, and especially its patron saint, Rufino. He indeed "took up the cross" as the strangest of all knights in the fifth Crusade; the *Vita prima* explains why he was unharmed:

> In all this, however, the Lord did not fulfill his desire,
> reserving for him the prerogative of a unique grace.[16]

His craving to experience Christ's sufferings culminated in an experience on the rocky Mt. Alverno in September 1224. For years Francis had been obsessed with the crucifixion: "Indeed, so thoroughly did . . . the charity of the Passion occupy his memory that he scarcely wanted to think of anything else."[17] Once more employing the device of randomly opening the Bible, this time with Fr. Leo, Francis heard the Fourth Gospel's narrative of Christ's passion. Bonaventure reports:

> The man filled with God understood that, just as he had imitated Christ in the actions of his life, so he should be conformed to him in the afflic-tion and sorrow of his passion, before he would pass out of this world. And although his body was already weakened by the great austerity of his

---

14. Bonaventure, *S. Francisci Assisinatis vita*, in *Little Flowers, Legends, and Lauds*, p. 161.

15. Julian of Speyer, writing in 1232 and depending on Celano, says, "Francis then re-moved himself from the tumult of business and made himself a salesman of the gospel. He sought good pearls, as it were, until he came upon one precious one, and while he was coming to see what was more pleasing to God, he meditatively entered the workshop of various virtues. And when he went away to meditate on the Lord's field, he found there and hid the Lord's hid-den treasure, and, having sold everything, he proposed to buy it along with the field." Julian of Speyer, *The Life of Saint Francis*, in *Early Documents*, 1:372. This explication of Francis's life, on Chesterton's principle, may illuminate for us Jesus and his parable.

16. *Vita prima* 20, in *Early Documents*, 1:231.

17. *Vita prima* 30, in *Early Documents*, 1:254.

past life and his continual carrying of the Lord's cross, he was in no way terrified, but was inspired even more vigorously to endure martyrdom.[18]

The feast of the Exaltation of the Cross had come. Francis prayed intently; the later work *Considerations on the Most Holy Stigmata* bequeaths to us a prayer that may not be far from what the saint uttered:

> My Lord Jesus Christ, two graces I ask of you before I die:
> the first is that in my life I may feel,
>   in my soul and body, as far as possible,
> that sorrow which you, tender Jesus,
> underwent in the hour of your most bitter passion;
> the second is that I may feel in my heart, as far as possible,
> the abundance of love with which you, son of God, were inflamed,
> so as willingly to undergo such a great passion for us sinners.[19]

Bonaventure captured in words what Giotto impressed into the fresco of the upper nave of the basilica: that a seraph nailed to a cross — indeed, Christ himself — flew down and pierced the hands, feet, and side of Francis. The stigmata, praised by Dante as the "ultimate sign,"[20] were observed by friends in the final two years of Francis's life, though he tried to hide them.

Right Understanding of the Scriptures

What does this survey suggest to us about the discipline of biblical interpretation? An interpreter asks, What is the text about? Attacks have been mounted on the historical-critical enterprise for some time, and for good reason, but the heavy smoke from all these cannon blasts may blind us to the achievements of the enterprise, which are many. Robert Jenson has wisely said that "discovery and exploration of the oral and literary processes that eventuated in the Gospels beneficently *complicate* our involvement with the Gospel texts."[21]

---

18. Bonaventure, *The Major Legend*, in *Early Documents*, 2:631.

19. *The Little Flowers of the Glorious St. Francis*, trans. W. Heywood (Assisi: Casa Editrice Francescana, 1982), p. 197.

20. Dante, *Paradise* 11.107. For historical and modern examples of the stigmata, see Ian Wilson, *Stigmata* (San Francisco: Harper & Row, 1989).

21. Robert W. Jenson, *Systematic Theology*, vol. 1, *The Triune God* (New York: Oxford, 1997), p. 173. The complications are not always beneficent. Nicholas Lash wryly suggests that "between the New Testament and the ordinary Christian, who seeks so to read these texts as to

Many commentators are so bold as to extract theological meaning from a given text, tendering a tentative construal of what it "meant," or even a more gutsy construction of what it "means." Meaning, in either sense, exists in a world of thought, something we fashion in our minds, verbalize in a classroom, or peck into a computer for consumption in print. We poke around behind the text to discern the "intention" of the author, or we compare and contrast texts and contemplate how a "tradition" is "used" or "reformulated," or we dare to tease out beliefs or doctrine from ancient texts. Tangible stuff enters the picture, via the archaeologists, but it is always crumbled stones and shards of pottery.

Nicholas Lash, in an essay entitled "Human Experience and the Knowledge of God,"[22] suggests that as the heirs of Descartes, we stand in the room of ourselves, a room that has two, and only two, windows: that of the physical, or tangible, apprehended by sensory perception; and that of the mental, or even spiritual, apprehended in varied but non-sensory ways. Religion comes and goes through the "mental" window or not at all. "God" is not a physical entity but a mental one, a sort of "idea." Which leads to the conclusion that God is *only* an idea. At worst, such a God can be easily dispensed with. At best, such a God can be cornered into bracketed zones, religious districts, where theology is allowed to roam. But if this dichotomy is a grossly wrong manner of construing our world, if I am not something immaterial that dwells in the room of myself, if there are not two windows; but rather, if my thinking, breathing, functioning body is *me*, and if God in turn is not segregated but is present in every district, then interpretation cannot play appropriately on conceptualities that are exclusively mental.

The kind of interpretation practiced by Francis was not merely mental. His reading was embodied, and an embodied reading is perhaps the only kind of reading that is finally appropriate to these texts, which are about, and are intended to provoke, changed lives. We may remember the dictum of Athanasius:

> For the searching and right understanding of the Scriptures there is need of a good life and a pure soul, and for Christian virtue to guide the mind to grasp, so far as human nature can, the truth concerning God the Word. One cannot possibly understand the teaching of the saints unless one has

---

hear in them the Word of Life, there seem to be set up thickets of expertise, insurmountable barriers of scholarship." Nicholas Lash, "Performing the Scriptures," in *Theology on the Way to Emmaus* (London: SCM, 1986), p. 39. Modern interpretation, for all its good service, does not go far enough, and at times it functions as a kind of protective film between the text's claims and the student or interpreter.

22. Nicholas Lash, "Human Experience and the Knowledge of God," in *Theology on the Way to Emmaus*, pp. 141-57.

a pure mind and is trying to imitate their life. Anyone who wishes to understand the mind of the sacred writers must . . . approach the saints by copying their deeds.[23]

But it isn't just that certain holy modes of behavior are prerequisite to comprehending the text. Rather, the text, when properly comprehended, issues in altered patterns of behavior. As Lash put it in another essay, "The fundamental form of the Christian interpretation of scripture is the life, activity and organization of the believing community."[24] These texts are to be "performed," in patterns of human actions that evidence some continuity with the words, life, and death of Jesus. "We talk of 'holy' scripture, and for good reason. And yet it is not, in fact, the *script* that is 'holy,' but the people: the company who perform the script."[25]

In *Biography as Theology*, James Wm. McClendon argues that "the truth of faith is made good in the living of it or not at all."[26] His methodology, applied in interesting ways in the first volume of his systematic theology,[27] is to consider beliefs not as propositions but as living convictions embodied in actual communities. Such theology requires that we speak of exemplars, heroes, saints.

> In or near the community there appear from time to time singular or striking lives, the lives of persons who embody the convictions of the community, but in a new way; who share the vision of the community, but with new scope or power; who exhibit the style of the community, but with significant differences. It is plain that the example of these lives may serve to disclose and perhaps to correct or enlarge the community's moral vision, at the same time arousing impotent wills within the community to a better fulfillment of the vision already acquired.[28]

23. Athanasius, *On the Incarnation* (Crestwood, N.Y.: St. Vladimir's, 1953), p. 96. Or as MacIntyre puts it, "What the reader . . . has to learn about him or herself is that it is only the self as transformed through and by the reading of the texts which will be capable of reading the texts aright." MacIntyre, *Three Rival Versions of Moral Enquiry*, p. 82.

24. Lash, "Performing the Scriptures," p. 42. Or, Gerald Bruns: "For the basic hermeneutical principle of pesher interpretation is that Scripture makes sense, not by opening inwardly to an intention that lies behind the text, but by laying plain (in front of itself or into its future) a possibility which the community takes upon itself to actualize or fulfill in terms of action, that is, in its forms or way of life." Gerald Bruns, "Midrash and Allegory," in *The Literary Guide to the Bible*, ed. Robert Alter and Frank Kermode (Cambridge, Mass.: Harvard University Press, 1987), p. 635.

25. Lash, "Performing the Scriptures," p. 42.

26. James Wm. McClendon, *Biography as Theology: How Life Stories Can Remake Today's Theology*, 2nd ed. (Philadelphia: Trinity Press International, 1990), p. viii.

27. James Wm. McClendon, *Systematic Theology: Ethics* (Nashville: Abingdon, 1986).

28. McClendon, *Biography as Theology*, p. 22.

We might go further and say that there appear from time to time singular or striking lives of persons who embody what *texts* are about, who answer the riddles in ways that not only illustrate but even correct our enshrined interpretations, who even arouse our wills to "go and do likewise."

Such lives, like Francis's, are beautiful models for the task of interpretation. Indeed, the lives of the saints may serve to correct our tendency to gloss over portions of the text — a tendency that can insulate us from the living of it, or perhaps even from Christ himself. If we grasp the church's life as the *totus Christus,* then the lives of the saints, and our tentative toddling along behind them, constitute theologically a chapter in the life of Christ.[29]

The Hermeneutical Gap

As the Franciscan movement spread, the need arose for a theology that would undergird the mission for a reasoned rebuttal of heresy. Francis was reluctant to approve the pursuit of theology, fearing conflict between the demands of study (such as the costs of libraries), and the demands of evangelical poverty. In a letter to Anthony of Padua, he stated conditions for masters and students:

> I am pleased that you teach sacred theology to the brothers providing that, as is contained in the Rule, you "do not extinguish the Spirit of prayer and devotion" during study of this kind.[30]

In modernity, this spirit of prayer and devotion raises questions of truth. Typically, we bracket off two realms of competence: what the text "meant," which, by virtue of training, is within the historian's competence; and truth (and perhaps here we mean Truth, the verities that pertain to God, not just to an ancient writer's view of his God), which is beyond the historian's competence. Yet, as Lash suggests, "the question remains, shall we say, interesting."[31] And not just interesting, but procedurally essential. The texts are all about trust, living, and following. For interpretation to be appropriate to these texts,

---

29. McClendon clarifies: "Theology makes a distinction . . . between the life of Christ (the one who rose and lives in his community, in his world) and the life of Jesus (the man who lived and died in first-century Palestine). The stories of the saints' lives are thus a part of the life of Christ; they are not in the same way a part of the life of Jesus." *Biography as Theology,* p. 167.

30. *Early Documents,* 1:107. Anthony was actually born in Lisbon and was himself canonized just two years after Francis.

31. Nicholas Lash, "What Might Martyrdom Mean?" in *Theology on the Way to Emmaus,* p. 88.

wrestling with faith, with discipleship, prayer, and devotion, with the God who is in fact the subject of these texts, is unavoidable. Lash continues: "Any model of Christian hermeneutics that ignores such questions, or treats them as marginal or merely consequential, is *theoretically* deficient." There is, indeed, a hermeneutical "gap." "But this 'gap' does not lie, in the last resort, between what was once 'meant' and what might be 'meant' today. It lies, rather, between what was once achieved, intended, or 'shown,' and what might be achieved, intended, or 'shown' today."[32]

The Scholarly Task

In exploring the significance of the history of interpretation, David Steinmetz raised a similar question from his perspective:

> Until the historical-critical method becomes critical of its own theoretical foundations and develops a hermeneutical theory adequate to the nature of the text that it is interpreting, it will remain restricted, as it deserves to be, to the guild and the academy, where the question of truth can endlessly be deferred.[33]

The history of interpretation has at times been dubbed "the history of effects," and appropriately so. If interpretation exists for the life of the community, then the most crucial afterlife of the text is not the academic rivalry the text might instigate but rather faithful living, even in imitation of Christ.

The disciplines of biblical interpretation and theology, therefore, should incorporate biography (and even hagiography) in order to illuminate ways in which the texts have invited, and continue to invite, transformed lives. Our commentaries (and writing them would probably require collaborative efforts) could bear stories of saints — and not of the whitewashed, pastel-colored variety. The gospel is incarnational, even messy, and we learn as much from the foibles of saints as from their luminous moments of genuine imitation of Christ. We are well served by stories that expose how our own kin, real flesh and blood, have both embodied the faith and misshapen it as well. No nostalgia here: the tradition of the saints excites in us a creative and

---

32. Lash, "What Might Martyrdom Mean?" pp. 89-91. My associate Rev. Andy Baxter suggests that Francis might have called this gap sin.

33. David C. Steinmetz, "The Superiority of Pre-Critical Exegesis," *Theology Today* 37 (1980): 38; reprinted in *Memory and Mission: Theological Reflections on the Christian Past* (Nashville: Abingdon, 1988), p. 163.

risky engagement to embody the text, just as they did, in a manner that is faithful today — certainly *faithful*, but inescapably faithful *today.*

Millard Fuller met a New Testament scholar turned farmer named Clarence Jordan, who urged him toward a naive, literal reading of the Gospels — and a camel slipped through the eye of the needle. Fuller gave away his fortune and has now built nearly one hundred thousand homes for the poor through his clever exegesis that we know as Habitat for Humanity. Thomas à Becket, eschewing the regalia suited to the archbishop of Canterbury, donned a hair shirt and rose early every morning to feed and to wash the feet of poor peasants outside the city. Vernon Johns, Martin Luther King Jr.'s predecessor at Dexter Avenue Baptist Church in Montgomery, Alabama, got hauled off to jail in 1949 for advertising his sermon title "Segregation after Death" on the church marquee. His text? The parable of Dives and Lazarus (Luke 16:19-31). Under interrogation, Johns was required to preach the sermon to the police. Dives, gazing across the great gulf of prejudice, is blind to the humanity he shares with Lazarus; he thinks of him still as a servant, demanding that Abraham "send" Lazarus with water. Dives has been condemned by his insistence on segregation, which he perversely maintains even after death. Johns not only draws our attention to the disdain in Dives's assumption that Lazarus is at his beck and call, but he also embodies in his own arrest and harassment that very kind of disdain in a modern context.

Dorothy Day wrought a profound interpretation of the gospel from her Fifteenth Street apartment. She read quite literally Jesus' charge to the disciples when faced with the hungry five thousand, "You give them something to eat" (Mark 6:37). Day took on hunger, serving — from the front of her flat — mulligan stew, bread, and coffee to hundreds off the street. But she also took on systemic injustice, particularly in the church, publishing — from the back of her flat — the *Catholic Worker.* Its first edition carried these words from Peter Maurin, Dorothy's partner in the paper: "Christ drove the money-changers out of the Temple. But today nobody dares to drive the money lenders out of the Temple. And nobody dares to drive the money lenders out of the Temple because the money lenders have taken a mortgage on the Temple." The episode in John 2 and Mark 11 is much discussed in terms of the "historical Jesus," but for Day it was an episode to be repeated today and every day, whenever holy precincts become a caricature of themselves.[34]

34. Day illustrates the role of formation in the imitation of Christ. Shortly before her death, she shared the most remarkable thought with Robert Coles: "I try to remember this life that the Lord gave me; the other day I wrote down the words 'a life remembered,' and I was going to try to make a summary for myself, write what mattered most — but I couldn't do it. I just sat there and thought of our Lord, and His visit to us all those centuries ago, and I said to myself

Mother Teresa's entire life was a profound exegesis of Matthew 25:31-46. As she fed the hungry, bandaged lepers, and clothed the naked, many agnostics found it helpful to consider that Jesus was like Mother Teresa. What happens if we receive her words as if they were spoken to the guild of biblical scholars and theologians? "At the end of life we will not be judged by how many diplomas we have received, how much money we have made, how many great things we have done. We will be judged by 'I was hungry and you gave me to eat, I was naked and you clothed me, I was homeless and you took me in.'"[35]

Two Caveats

When we highlight such tangible readings, we need to be wary of false or inappropriate embodiments of the text. Origen's self-mutilation, Francis's own abuse of his body (for which he apologized late in life), and more banal modern tomfoolery (such as "Jesus as CEO") remind us to test embodiments against the balance of Scripture and the wisdom of tradition. We also proceed with the burden that all our reading is impoverished. The imperative to imitate Christ is simultaneously a judgment. Edith Wyschogrod has understood our predicament, and therefore our hope:

> The infinite wisdom, power, and goodness of Christ are not re-presentable even by a spiritual elite. Human nature cannot conform itself to divine perfection. Thus *Imitatio Christi* is an unrealizable imperative because the life of Christ cannot be replicated. The saint's task is to undertake two intersecting lines of endeavor. The first strategy is . . . to reach for what is inherently refractory to representation, a life like that of Jesus. The second strategy, parasitic on the first, is paradoxically, to *"show"* unrepresentability itself.[36]

Just as Barth famously taught us that our inability to speak of God itself gives glory to God, so our inability to imitate Christ can glorify God as well. Thus

---

that my great luck was to have had Him on my mind for so long in my life." Robert Coles, *Dorothy Day: A Radical Devotion* (Reading, Mass.: Addison-Wesley, 1987), p. 16. Perhaps this is the missing ingredient in the current youth craze for WWJD ("What Would Jesus Do?") jewelry; the instinct is good, but many teens who would claim WWJD as their guiding principle are embarrassingly unfamiliar with the Gospel narratives. It is the regular hearing of Scripture and regular prayer, liturgy, and practice that over time forge a faithful imitation.

35. Mother Teresa, *Words to Love By* (Notre Dame: Ave Maria, 1983), p. 80.

36. Edith Wyschogrod, *Saints and Postmodernism: Revisioning Moral Philosophy* (Chicago: University of Chicago Press, 1990), p. 13.

we edge forward, trusting in some holy transformation or utilization of our fumbling replications of a text into which we long to live.

The Instrumental Character of Scripture

A theoretically sound approach to the text involves some grasp of the "instrumental" character of Scripture, even with regard to the life of the interpreter. Steinmetz has said:

> The gospel is spirit when it serves as an instrument of Christ's grace through the power of the Holy Spirit to hammer an opening in the sealed walls of the human heart. . . .
> . . . The Bible as Christian Scripture (that is, the Hebrew Bible joined to the NT rather than to the Talmud) exists to serve as an instrument of the Holy Spirit to reconcile men and women to God through Jesus Christ in the community of the Church. Unless the Bible achieves that goal in the community of the Church, it does not realize its own true nature.[37]

If the interpreter, as we hope, thinks, writes, and speaks from within that community, this very reconciliation must be taking shape in the interpreter's own life. One of Francis's first biographers described his speech as follows:

> Not with enticing words of human wisdom, but in the doctrine and virtue of the Holy Spirit he proclaimed the Kingdom of God with great confidence; as a true preacher . . . he never used flattering words and he despised all blandishments; what he preached to others in words, he had first experienced by deeds, so that he might speak the truth faithfully.[38]

Hugh of St. Cher articulated the principle at stake more harshly: "He who preaches poverty lies, unless he be poorly clad."[39]

I can confess that I am among the company of those who read about the radical nature of Jesus' life, who regale others with legends of Jesus' astonishing likeness in Francis, who delight in the simplicity of Day, Fuller, and Teresa — but are more than happy to juggle those thoughts nimbly in the mental part of ourselves, zealously keeping the reality of the imitation of Christ at

---

37. David C. Steinmetz, "Calvin and the Irrepressible Spirit," *Ex Auditu* 12 (1996): 100, 105.

38. *Youth of St. Francis, in Little Flowers, Legends, and Lauds*, p. 27.

39. Quoted and discussed by Robert Lerner, "Poverty, Preaching, and Eschatology in the Commentaries of 'Hugh of St. Cher,'" in *The Bible in the Medieval World*, ed. Katherine Walsh and Diana Wood (Oxford: Basil Blackwell, 1985), p. 173.

arm's length. It probably is the case that my reading of Scripture is always compromised by my encumbrances, my hefty salary, the prestige of my position, the garnering of my pension, the maintenance of my vita. For that matter, not just my reading but my very discipleship is forever frustrated by my tenacious hold on my hard-won lifestyle. Ancient interpreters knew better. Jerome shivered in Bethlehem. Less than a decade after Francis's death, the distinguished theologian Alexander of Hales renounced his wealth and became a friar in Paris. Origen put it well:

> Like some spark lighting upon our inmost soul, love was kindled and burst into flame within us — a love at once to the Holy Word, the most lovely object of all, who attracts all irresistibly toward Himself. . . . Being most mightily smitten by this love, I was persuaded to give up all those pursuits which seem to us befitting — yea, my very fatherland and relatives. . . .[40]

*   *   *

Our Father. Take nothing for your journey. Two graces. We began with Chesterton's wry suggestion that Jesus was like Francis. Murray Bodo poses the same thought as a challenge:

> It is easier to rationalize and dismiss Jesus than Francis, because Jesus, after all, is divine and so far above us. But Francis is only human like us. What he is, we can become. . . . What is so unique about Francis is that he does what we would like to do, and he does it in such a simple, ingenuous way that we know we could do the same if only we would.[41]

Hidden in this need for embodied reading is a more elusive hermeneutical concern, that of persuasion. Perhaps there was a day when the church could stake out its claim with admittedly true assertions (like "The Bible is the Word of God" or "The Sacraments are means of grace" or "The Church is of God and will be preserved . . ."). But today, to people outside the church, and increasingly to people inside the church, this sounds like so

---

40. Quoted in Henri Crouzel, *Origen* (Edinburgh: T. & T. Clark, 1989), p. 25. For a fuller suggestion of how sin pollutes our reading of the text, see Stephen E. Fowl, *Engaging Scripture: A Model for Theological Interpretation* (Oxford: Blackwell, 1998). More positively, Fowl argues that "it is ultimately through the formation of virtuous interpreters of scripture that Christian communities can combat the temptation to read scripture in ways that underwrite sinful practices" (pp. 86-87).

41. Murray Bodo, *The Way of St. Francis* (New York: Image, 1984), pp. 105-6.

much chest thumping or like some distant rustling of leaves. For such people to be drawn into the church's metanarrative and moved to reimagine the world theologically, perhaps the only hope is that God will call another Francis, another Teresa — men and women who will naively read the Gospel stories and imitate their subject.

Reading the Scriptures Faithfully
in a Postmodern Age

William Stacy Johnson

The Scriptures are our guide, and we, their apprentices. This conviction ought readily to be embraced by all Christians. It is a general and formal claim about the Bible's role as central to the church's canon.[1] What to make of the Scriptures materially, however, engenders more controversy. It is a question that requires continual investigation. Today, in reaction to the widespread loss of biblical meaning, many are advocating a return to understanding the material content of the Bible as a unified narrative.[2] We may think of the Scriptures as telling a coherent story of God — "the God of Israel who called a people out of bondage, gave them the Torah, . . . raised Jesus of Nazareth from the dead, [and] is still at work in the world today." Scripture "tells the story of God's action of creating, judging, and saving the world."[3] This understanding of the Bible as a unified narrative is the focus of many of the essays in this volume.

At the same time, there is no such thing as a "narrative" — whether unified or otherwise — apart from the contingent theological wisdom of those

---

1. By "canon" I mean the organizing framework of the church's life that includes, in addition to the Bible, the normative creeds, liturgies, practices, and offices that are constitutive of what the church is. See William J. Abraham, *Canon and Criterion in Christian Theology: From the Fathers to Feminism* (Oxford: Clarendon, 1998).

2. For a forceful statement of this claim, see Robert W. Jenson, "Scripture's Authority in the Church," in this volume. Although I am in sympathy with Jenson's claim, the truth about biblical narrative is a bit more complex and in need of nuance. See, for example, Paul Ricoeur, "Toward a Narrative Theology: Its Necessity, Its Resources, Its Difficulties," in Ricoeur, *Figuring the Sacred: Religion, Narrative, and Imagination,* trans. David Pellauer, ed. Mark I. Wallace (Minneapolis: Fortress, 1995), pp. 236-48.

3. See Thesis 1, "Nine Theses on the Interpretation of Scripture."

who are doing the narrating. The narrative is not just a given but must be constructed and reconstructed in the life of the community of faith over time. In addition, the biblical narrative must be supplemented and interrogated by the biblical genre of wisdom:[4] the reflections of the wisdom literature of Scripture challenge the all-inclusiveness and tendencies to triumphalism of narrative.[5]

Today in the community of faith, we undertake the constructive and re-constructive reading of the Scriptures in what many are calling a postmodern time. It is a time in which both modern and premodern ways of thinking — particularly, certain modern and premodern versions of what is real, mean-ingful, and true — have been called radically into question. By questioning traditional notions of objective truth, pointing out the fallibility and contex-tual limits of all our knowing, and seeking to move beyond self-evident "foundations" for belief, postmodernity has prompted us to rethink the very meaning of meaning itself.[6]

While this rethinking has often seemed hostile to religious faith, I want to identify a threefold movement within postmodern thought that may well provide Christian theology a strategic opportunity to understand its own sub-ject matter — the gospel of Jesus Christ — in a fresh way. We may think of this as a movement beyond foundations, beyond totality, and toward the Other.

I. Beyond Foundations

For some time now, a consensus has been developing that the modern objectivist attempt to base all our ideas, institutions, and initiatives upon uni-versal all-encompassing, self-evident, and self-legitimating foundations is self-defeating.[7] The reason is that we have no ready access to these supposedly self-evident foundations — not, at least, apart from a tradition of reflection and criticism that helps legitimate all that we take to be foundational in the first place. Our knowing is built up not so much from discrete and fixed foundations as from a web of interdependent and self-correcting beliefs. To conceive rationality as relying upon foundations that are "self-evident" is to ignore the contingent and situated character of all our knowing.

4. Ricoeur, "Biblical Time," in *Figuring the Sacred*, pp. 167-80.

5. Mark I. Wallace, introduction to *Figuring the Sacred*, p. 27.

6. For a brief introduction to postmodernity, see Paul Lakeland, *Postmodernity: Christian Identity in a Fragmented Age*, GTI (Minneapolis: Fortress, 1997).

7. For a summary of the literature on this subject, see John E. Thiel, *Nonfoundationalism*, GTI (Minneapolis: Fortress, 1994).

The movement beyond foundations, then, reflects a transformation in the status of knowledge. Throughout much of the modern period, Western views of rationality have oscillated between such self-defeating and opposing dualities as absolutism versus skepticism, realism versus idealism, emphasis on the subject versus fixation on the object, and so forth. In response to this, Richard J. Bernstein has helpfully characterized the emerging postmodern rationality as a movement "beyond objectivism and relativism."[8] On the one hand, objectivism is the view that insists on "some permanent, ahistorical matrix or framework to which we can ultimately appeal in determining the nature of rationality, knowledge, truth, reality, goodness, or rightness."[9] Objectivism is usually tied to classical foundationalism, namely, the attempt to secure our lives through the assertion of certain self-evident, incorrigible, and universal truths upon which the edifice of knowledge must be erected. On the other hand, there is relativism, with its denial that there is any access to an objective truth as universally grounded. Apart from the language and culture in which a claim to truth is immersed, says relativism, speaking about "truth" would have no meaning for us. We have no access to truth apart from our own situatedness.

Bernstein has argued, persuasively I think, that a new postmodern form of rationality is emerging, one in which the warfare between objectivism and relativism is unmasked as posing a false dichotomy. On the one hand, this new rationality is historically situated, hermeneutically aware, and rooted in tradition, as relativism insists; on the other hand, it does not believe that we are left with nothing more than an incessant conflict of traditions. The boundaries that separate different traditions are not absolute and incommensurate, which means that there is still the possibility of making common cause in knowing and choosing to do what is right, in seeking justice, and in holding ourselves and others morally accountable. Moving beyond objectivism need not entail the embrace of the sort of relativism that leads us to despair. For as H. Richard Niebuhr put it in his classic book *The Meaning*

8. Richard J. Bernstein, *Beyond Objectivism and Relativism: Science, Hermeneutics, Praxis* (Philadelphia: University of Pennsylvania Press, 1988). Note that Bernstein sharpens this dichotomy by describing it as one between a fallibilistic form of objectivism and a nonsubjective form of relativism. A fallibilistic objectivism is different from a now obsolete absolutism that presumes to have arrived at a truth that is immune from criticism. Similarly, the forms of relativism advanced today are not subjectivist, since they do not necessarily situate the origin of knowledge in the knowing subject. All that is necessary to be a relativist, in Bernstein's sense, is a denial of overarching frameworks of meaning and the belief that all knowledge is situated in particularistic conceptual schemes.

9. Bernstein, *Beyond Objectivism and Relativism*, p. 8.

of Revelation, the recognition of the fallibility that attends the *way* we see need not lead us to doubt the reality of *what* we see.[10]

Nevertheless, this new mode of postmodern rationality is frightening to some Christians. They find it frightening because they have completely succumbed to a one-sided objectivism out of a deep-seated fear of the dangers of relativism. Without an objective and infallible source of meaning, so their reasoning goes, the truth claims of the gospel seem to be undermined. Hence, their response is to ground Christian belief in an infallible text, an infallible experience, or an infallible magisterium.

It is time that we recognized this foundationalist way of thinking for what it is. In its Christian guise, it represents not the strength of faith but the result of a faith that has lost its nerve. The Christian Scriptures set themselves up not so much as truth claims to be defended by philosophical foundations but as witnesses to the transforming power that no truth claim itself can contain. The gospel is not a "foundation" to render our traditional notions of rationality secure but a remaking of everything, including rationality itself.

As a response to the movement beyond foundations, some contemporary theologians have emphasized the need to return to biblical narrative, understanding the church's theological task as an exercise in conceptual redescription of that narrative. For example, Hans Frei advised theologians to consider the conceptual world of the Bible as though it were a thoroughly realistic narrative that "means what it says." Building on aspects of the later work of Karl Barth, Frei spoke of "a sort of *literary* or conceptual-analytical reading of the biblical text rather than either a *historical* or religious-experiential one."[11] In this view, the literary "what" of Christianity takes priority over the experiential "how."[12] Theology becomes a self-descriptive rendering of the biblical story designed to lead modern readers back into a world long forgotten. It accomplishes this feat by appealing only to criteria that are already embedded within the Christian faith itself.

Christian theology, on Frei's reading, is a species of what philosophers

---

10. "It is not evident that the man who is forced to confess that his view of things is conditioned by the standpoint he occupies must doubt the reality of what he sees. It is not apparent that one who knows that his concepts are not universal must also doubt that they are concepts of the universal, or that one who understands how all his experience is historically mediated must believe that nothing is mediated through history." H. Richard Niebuhr, *The Meaning of Revelation* (New York: Macmillan, 1941), pp. 18-19. (In the 1967 Collier-Macmillan paperback edition, the citation is to p. 13.)

11. Hans Frei, *Types of Christian Theology* (New Haven and London: Yale University Press, 1994), p. 81.

12. Frei, *Types of Christian Theology,* p. 43.

today would call holistic justification.[13] Justifying Christian belief, to use Charles Sanders Peirce's metaphor, proceeds less like a single chain of argument and more like a strong cable composed of numerous fibers. Its persuasiveness rests in the totality of the fibers taken together rather than in the cogency of any single strand.[14] Moreover, because the criteria for theology are said to be internal, resting solely within the network of beliefs distinctive to Christianity, Frei's form of Barthian theology has little use for apologetic extrabiblical appeals to make its case, except on what might be called an ad hoc basis.[15] And it purportedly makes no appeals to any "foundations" for knowing, at least not to any such foundations existing outside the language and commitments of the Christian community.[16]

This contemporary narrative approach to biblical religion resonates with the historic Christian reliance upon the rule of faith, or *regula fidei*. Formally, the rule of faith is an affirmation that the faith of the church is the same yesterday, today, and always. Materially, the rule of faith consists in the various creedal summaries and confessional statements that have guided the church in its theological reflection through the centuries.

There is much to be said for recovering the guidance of the rule of faith in the life of the church. Yet this recovery is not just a descriptive endeavor, as Frei and his colleagues insist; it is a constructive theological task. To say that theology is constructive is not to claim that it is just making things up as it goes along. It does mean that it cannot be based on self-evident foundations. Theology responds to revelation, but in so doing, it recognizes that at every turn it proceeds from fallible human constructs and undertakes always to "begin again at the beginning," as Barth put it, under the demands of the contemporary situation. It always acknowledges that truth — above all, the truth of revelation — is not simply a given but a goal. Identifying the truth is an open-ended task at which we must constantly work along the way.

The movement beyond foundations is important not just to our interpretation of the Scriptures but also to our understanding of that to which they bear witness. Neither the Scriptures nor the God to whom they bear witness — in their varying and sometimes conflicting ways — can be reduced to a manip-

13. Frei, *Types of Christian Theology*, chs. 3 and 4; app. C.

14. Charles Sanders Peirce, "Some Consequences of Four Incapacities," in *Collected Papers of Charles Sanders Peirce*, 6 vols. (Cambridge, Mass.: Harvard University Press, 1978), 5:157.

15. See Frei, *Types of Christian Theology*, ch. 6; William Werpehowski, "Ad Hoc Apologetics," *Journal of Religion* 66 (1986): 282-301.

16. The most sophisticated extension of Frei's argument about holistic narrative into constructive theology is that of Ronald F. Thiemann, *Revelation and Theology: The Gospel as Narrated Promise* (Notre Dame: University of Notre Dame Press, 1985).

ulable "foundation." Theology's substantive task today is to gauge the demise of certain classical (e.g., Plato, Aristotle, Plotinus) and modern (e.g., Descartes, Kant, Hegel) portraits of God that — despite their many differences — had a common tendency to reduce God to an accessible basis on which our world was thought to rest. Theology, in both its classical and modern forms, has had a difficult time freeing itself from pagan antiquity's assumption that divinity is an abstract aseity, a fixed *archē*, or beginning, whose essence is to remain forever as it was in the beginning.[17] Eberhard Jüngel has called this the metaphysical concept of God, or the God of theism.[18] Martin Heidegger termed it the God of "onto-theology."[19] It is the "God" whom we reduce to some sort of "supreme being" — the perfectly timeless, impassible, self-satisfied, self-caused cause upon which the world is thought to rest. Beguiled by this assumption, Western Christian theology has become an inadvertent effort to protect this "God" from the vagaries of finitude and surprise — an effort to free God from any of the attributes or experiences we would ordinarily associate with the ability to have meaningful relationships with others.[20] Throughout the career of Western theology, it seems that the God who says, "Behold, I am doing a new thing" has continued to recede from view.

If, on the contrary, we refuse to reduce to a mere foundation for belief the God who is *for* and *with* human beings in Jesus Christ by the Spirit's power, we must take the Bible, and the peculiarities of its form, more seriously. First, we must wrestle with what it means theologically that the truth about God is told in Scripture in the form of a story. It is not enough to point to the biblical narrative and say, in effect, "Look, here is our story; take it or leave it." Rather, a theology that moves beyond foundations must engage a collection of Scriptures that renders a congeries of stories — stories that are not always saying quite the same thing. The testimony of this passage of Scripture is juxtaposed with the "countertestimony" of that passage of Scripture, and so on.[21] Sometimes the stories are disrupting and strange, portray-

17. William Stacy Johnson, "Barth and Beyond," *Christian Century* 118 (2001): 19.

18. Eberhard Jüngel, *God as the Mystery of the World: On the Foundations of the Theology of the Crucified One in the Dispute between Theism and Atheism,* trans. Darrell L. Guder (Grand Rapids: Eerdmans, 1983), p. 182.

19. Martin Heidegger, *Identity and Difference* (New York: Harper & Row, 1960).

20. Johnson, "Barth and Beyond," p. 19. Of course, the postmodern interest in rethinking the dynamic relationality of God is not without precedent, as, for example, in the reflections of nineteenth-century idealists such as Fichte and Hegel.

21. While Walter Brueggemann's dichotomy between "testimony" and "countertestimony" is perhaps too simple, it does help point up the polyvalence and ambiguity in the biblical witness. See Walter Brueggemann, *Theology of the Old Testament: Testimony, Dispute, Advocacy* (Minneapolis: Fortress, 1997).

ing God, the main character, in provocative and counterintuitive ways. In addition, the stories are accompanied by other materials that reflect upon them, problematize them, and use them in fascinating and creative ways, as we see, for example, in Ecclesiastes and the Song of Songs.[22] If the Scriptures do not reduce God to a single perspective, then neither can theology.

Second, seeing beyond the God of simple foundations requires us to come to grips theologically with the fact that something grand and glorious is at stake in these stories. They contain real action, real drama, and real players. Something is at stake in these stories, such that had they gone a different way, the relationship between God and humanity would certainly have been different. What if Moses had renounced his calling? What if Jesus of Nazareth had chosen a different path in the garden of Gethsemane? These questions may seem overly speculative, but they make a difference if the dramatic character of the Bible is taken seriously.[23] Moreover, from the standpoint of Christian faith, it is in the continued telling of these stories that people of faith come to know actually, really, and in ever new ways who God is. That is to say, the stories are not fixed but dynamic, accomplishing new things in new settings. The biblical stories tell us not merely about the *nature* of God in the past; they constantly reveal to us in new ways the *identity* of God in the present. The stories, in other words, are not merely illustrative; they are constitutive of who God is. They mark out the essence of God's very own life, and therefore, when they are read in faith, we see to our amazement that the life of God is still unfolding in humanity's midst.

Nowhere is this more true than in God's identification with the Crucified One, Jesus of Nazareth. By identifying with Jesus of Nazareth, God has determined to bring about something amazing, something that the tradition calls grace, God's self-giving engagement to be *for* and *with* us. By becoming one with humanity in Jesus of Nazareth, God has determined not to be God without us. In other words, there is something real and vital at stake as these stories unfold — something at stake not only for the human beings who play a role in the stories but also for the identity of God.[24]

22. On the way the Song of Songs reflects on earlier parts of the biblical tradition, see the contrasting hermeneutical proposals of André LaCocque, *Romance, She Wrote: A Hermeneutical Essay on Song of Songs* (Harrisburg, Pa.: Trinity Press International, 1998), and Ellen F. Davis, *Proverbs, Ecclesiastes, and the Song of Songs* (Louisville: Westminster/John Knox, 2000).

23. The presupposition that something is dramatically at stake for God in the biblical narrative is worked out systematically in Robert W. Jenson, *Systematic Theology,* vol. 1, *The Triune God* (New York: Oxford University Press, 1997).

24. The theological proposal that best exemplifies this notion, in my view, is Robert W. Jenson, *Systematic Theology,* 2 vols. (New York: Oxford University Press, 1997-99).

Third, we must grapple with what it means theologically that the reality to which these stories bear witness belongs not just to the past but to something that is still unfolding today. The stories of Scripture bear witness to a larger story that is living and not yet finished. Hence, theological interpretation must push beyond viewing the Scriptures as projecting a self-enclosed, already accomplished totality of meaning. What is most important are not the past meanings the stories are thought to contain but the present meanings they continually provoke in the community of faith. At the heart and soul of reading the Scriptures faithfully is the constant rehearing of stories — and also of sayings, commandments, prophecies, and other materials — whose repetition helps kindle and inflame, right here, at this very moment, the "new thing" that the God who is for us in Jesus Christ is calling into being.

II. Beyond Totality

Biblical faithfulness is more than just nailing down the meaning of a text. It is putting oneself in a position — by engaging the text — to recognize what God has done in the past as well as to discern what God is making possible for, and requiring of, us in the present. To that extent, we read the Scriptures not only with a rule of faith but also with a rule of hope. We read with a perspective that hopes, in relationship to the text, to see beyond the limitations and even the evils that may have been lurking in our previous takes on the whole. This leads to a second postmodern movement that may help us in discerning the revelatory dimensions of the Scriptures: the movement beyond totality.

One of the features of postmodern literary theory that may better enable us to imagine this movement beyond totality and, in particular, to appreciate the open-endedness of the Scriptures — their diverse meanings and the way they provoke new meaning and new responses over time — is the controversial approach to texts called deconstruction. If postmodern theology is constructive in that it cannot be based on self-evident foundations, it is also deconstructive in that it recognizes the complex and multivalent way in which the structures of theological meaning are conveyed. To "deconstruct," or "deconstrue," is simply to look at the component parts of a structure. If all meaning is at some level constructive in character, then it is also capable of being deconstructed.

"Deconstruction" is one of those buzzwords on the American scene that has been sometimes misused and often misunderstood, mostly because of misreadings or failures to read carefully the writings of Jacques Derrida, the one who first wrote about deconstruction, in 1967.[25] The deconstruction spoken of by Derrida — despite his often strange and recondite prose — does not maintain, as is often claimed, that texts can mean just anything.[26] Rather, it is a way of seeing how every text, by its very nature of being a text, provokes multiple possibilities of meaning. It is not that deconstruction wants to destroy meaning; instead, deconstruction works as a systematic resistance to arriving at a single totality of meaning. It looks to investigate and uncover the complexity of meaning in the intricacies of its component parts, including the conflicts and tensions to which all meaning inevitably gives rise. Above all, at least in Derrida's later writings, it is a way of reading texts, and especially religious texts, with an eye toward what leaving them open-ended might prompt us to do.[27]

Deconstruction arose in part as a reaction to, but also as a continuation of, certain insights of the approach to literary theory called structuralism.[28] The focus on textual structure showed how the organic relationship between language and its referent is a matter of humanly made convention rather than a mirror of what is supposed to be true for all time.[29] Language does not partake of some permanent, eternal realm that is lying out there waiting to be retrieved but is itself a complex reality that is rooted in difference, that is, in a set of relationships. Individual parts of language have no intrinsic meaning in isolation from other parts. Structuralism, through its radical relativizing of the subject, or self, opposed philosophies of consciousness, such as phenomenology, existentialism, and psychoanalysis. The consequence was to relativize the vantage point of the author and focus on the structure of the

25. See Jacques Derrida, *L'écriture et la différence* (Paris: Éditions du Seuil, 1967), ET *Writing and Difference,* trans. Alan Bass (Chicago and London: University of Chicago Press, 1978); *De la grammatologie* (Paris: Éditions de Minuit, 1967), ET *Of Grammatology,* trans. Gayatri Chakravorty Spivak (Baltimore and London: Johns Hopkins University Press, 1974; corrected edition, 1997); *La voix et le phénomène* (Paris: PUF, 1967), ET *Speech and Phenomena, and Other Essays on Husserl's Theory of Signs,* trans. David B. Allison (Evanston, Ill.: Northwestern University Press, 1973).

26. See Jacques Derrida, "Afterword: Toward an Ethic of Discussion," in *Limited Inc.* (Evanston, Ill.: Northwestern University Press, 1988), pp. 111-54.

27. For the best introduction to the later writings of Derrida from a religious point of view, see John D. Caputo, *The Prayers and Tears of Jacques Derrida: Religion without Religion* (Bloomington and Indianapolis: Indiana University Press, 1997).

28. For a concise introduction, see Terrence Hawkes, *Structuralism and Semiotics* (Berkeley and Los Angeles: University of California Press, 1977).

29. Ferdinand de Saussure, *Cours de linguistique générale* (1915), ed. Tullio de Mauro (Paris: Pavot, 1973), ET *Course in General Linguistics,* trans. Roy Harris (London: Duckworth, 1983; LaSalle, Ill.: Open Court, 1986).

text or other object under investigation. "The death of the author," or the rejection of what is sometimes called the intentional fallacy, has become a main plank in postmodern interpretation. The meaning of texts is not tied to the original intention of an author, for such a thing is no longer available to us. Once in written form, texts take on a life of their own.

Building on — but also moving beyond — the insights of structuralism, Derrida's deconstruction tried to show that the textual "whole" is not without the tensions and contradictions that are built into the way all meaning is structured. The Western way of thinking operates with a foundational *archē* and *telos* that grounds a sense of meaning that seeks to be univocal. This is evidenced in the way it makes use of polar terms (presence/absence, nature/culture, literal/figural, speech/writing) and transmutes them into binary oppositions, giving one side of the hierarchy a place of privilege to the detriment of the other.

According to Derrida, all this stems from a deep-seated Western longing after pure presence. His point is not, as some claim, to deny the reality of presence or to destroy the cogency of meaning. Nor is it simply to invert the binary oppositions so that, for example, he can create a reverse hierarchy, elevating writing over speech or absence over presence. His aim, rather, is to show how meaning is constituted by difference, one meaning pitted against another. Derrida gives "difference" itself a twofold meaning that encompasses the notions of differing and deferring.[30] Meaning depends on difference, but it also functions according to what in theological terms we would call an eschatology. The final meaning — if there is such a thing — is continually deferred.

Some are inclined to dismiss the deconstructive reading of religious texts as simply irreverent or, worse, nihilistic. Perhaps in the hands of some practitioners of deconstruction, it is exactly that. Yet the deconstruction of textual meaning can also serve the religious conviction that there is something elusive and holy in life that can be neither manipulated nor controlled. Deconstructive readings harbor the suspicion that the aim of much modernist interpretation has been actually to do away with the ongoing labor of reading. That is to say, on modernist grounds, once we arrive at an authoritative interpretation, we can file the text away and move on to something else.

This tendency has certainly been evident in modes of modern biblical exegesis. Modern biblical exegesis, in keeping with modern rationality itself, has tended to see Scripture as an object with a single, objectively determined

---

30. In French, while the verb *différer* can mean either "to differ" or "to defer," the noun *différence* means only "difference." Derrida coins a new word, *différance,* to insinuate both.

meaning. It need not detract from the tremendous light modern critical exegesis has shed on what is going on in the texts of Scripture to challenge this same exegesis for the way it reduces the biblical text to a "thing," or object, to be interpreted. The innovations in understanding provided by text criticism, source criticism, redaction criticism, and so forth notwithstanding (including the awareness they have brought of complex layers of linguistic, historical, and intertextual meaning), the ultimate point of these modern critical investigations has been to probe the text for a singular, determinate meaning. Under this reductionistic way of thinking, once the singular meaning of Scripture has been discovered, there is really nothing more to be learned. It matters little from a methodological point of view whether the one who is reading the text is a believer or unbeliever — the same meaning is there to be had by all, at least by all who have acquired the tools of historical investigation. Primacy is placed on the critical imagination, the function of which is to understand and explain — and the net effect of which is to treat revelation as something to be first explicated and then applied.

This approach trades on what is often referred to as the container theory of meaning. It assumes that meaning is a property the text possesses. This assumption depends, moreover, upon the positing of a fundamental split between the critical scrutiny of an autonomous subject or group of subjects and the accessible content of a passive object. According to this subject/object split, the goal is to ascertain the ideal content — the "message" — which may then be communicated either doctrinally, as in the five points of Calvinism or the five points of fundamentalism, or experientially, as in the "love of God and love of neighbor" espoused by liberalism. Either way, revelation is more an abstract object of investigation than a concrete, living subject that speaks, and continues to speak, in the church's life.

Under the pressures of this narrow epistemological framework, the modern church has tried to make its canonical Scriptures carry more probative freight than they can possibly bear. At least since the advent of modernity and perhaps even before that, the church has tended to transmute its Scriptures from interpretive framework — or canon — into an epistemological criterion for truth.[31] Today we see interpreters straining to force the Scriptures to produce precise answers to questions that the biblical authors themselves could never have imagined.

By contrast, deconstruction conceives of its investigation as a ceaseless, open-ended task, for to arrive at a final totality of meaning in the text would, by definition, exclude the need for further reading and reflection. Language is

---

31. Abraham, *Canon and Criterion.*

not ours to wield or control, and texts often operate to disrupt our sense of self-possessive ownership. Deconstruction is not an arbitrary act of the interpreter; rather, its questions are provoked by the texts themselves.

In addition, the purpose of Derrida's analysis is not just theoretical but also practical. The point is that the reader should return again and again to the text and that such returning makes authentic moral action possible. To be open to more than one possibility, according to Derrida, is the precondition of justice.[32] It is the plumbing of alternative meanings that leads to understanding, and the elimination of alternative meanings, to violence. In short, the movement beyond totality represented by the deconstructive moment in postmodern thought is not meant necessarily to eviscerate religion and morality but to give them their necessary orientation and direction. To be faithfully engaged requires a loyalty to something beyond the confines of a self-enclosed totality. So then, a deconstructive approach to meaning begins by inquiring into what our various construals of meaning may have left hidden or excluded. At all events, a deconstructive reading resists any premature totality of meaning.

Just as with the movement beyond foundations, so also the movement beyond totality can be deeply unsettling, and it likewise engenders real resistance among some Christians. Much of modern theology, in fact, has been a sustained effort precisely to exclude anything beyond totality. This reflects the fact that one of the features of a certain type of modernity is the belief that all reality is thought to cohere, that it constitutes an ascertainable totality. And if so, then this whole ought to be subject to description under the tutelage of a single, self-consistent body of knowledge. Included in this monolithic passion for totality, however, is a zeal to eliminate all that is thought not to cohere with truth, to do away with anything that does not fit or conform.

In the world of modernity, this passion for totality has reached a new and obsessive intensity that sometimes defies common sense.[33] It can lead to hegemonies of every sort, from the pretense of scientism to the absurdities of fundamentalism. And, when modulated into a theological key, this aim for completeness can lead to the view that the whole — the totality — is but one grand system of God. In one sense, this is the vision that the tradition of sys-

---

32. Cf. Jacques Derrida, *Force de loi: Le 'fondement mystique de l'autorité'* (Paris: Éditions Galilée, 1987), ET "Force of Law: The 'Mystical Foundation of Authority,'" trans. Mary Quaintance, in *Deconstruction and the Possibility of Justice*, ed. Drucilla Cornell, Michel Rosenfeld, and David Gray Carlson (New York and London: Routledge, 1992), pp. 3-67.

33. Perhaps the chief exemplar of this drive for totality has been Hegel, who summed up the whole of history. In contemporary theology its chief exponent, no doubt, is Wolfhart Pannenberg, though the tendency is found in many theologians.

tematic theology from the nineteenth century forward has tried to achieve. The things of salvation — incarnation, atonement, the reign of God — are all seen as features of the divine self-realization in history. That history, in turn, is comprehensible and discloses a certain pattern of intelligibility, a pattern that the enlightened mind can discern, if only by the light of revelation. Yet it is revelation that makes possible the coherence of a complete rational system.

And this, I think, is the key point. Revelation in modern perspective comes to be construed, not as the disruption of all humanly conceived totalities, nor as the calling into question of our premature "take" on the whole, but as an enlightenment by which we believe we can finally make sense of the encompassing all.

This predilection for an all-embracing totality is by no means the only way to interpret the world. The drive for totality in the modern world is a powerful one, but it has led to an ironic result. In his 1979 book *The Postmodern Condition: A Report on Knowledge,* Jean-François Lyotard argues that the key change brought about by postmodernity is the reluctance of people today to give credence to the overarching and monolithic perspectives of modern rationality.[34] The result is a pervasive cynicism toward the institutions, values, and lofty goals bequeathed to us from the past. We are living in an age marked by what Lyotard calls "an incredulity toward metanarratives." Put more colloquially, the age in which we are living is the age of "Whatever . . ."

The "metanarratives" of which Lyotard speaks are the grand, self-legitimating interpretive frameworks according to which we modern people seek to define our world as complete and whole. A metanarrative is the omnicompetent rationale according to which all individual narratives are thought to find their larger meaning and purpose. Prior to the onset of modernity, it was our very own Christian story of creation, reconciliation, and redemption that provided orientation to Western thought. The modern world did not simply abolish this metanarrative but began retelling it in its own way. Even as it increasingly distanced itself from the master story of Christianity, modernity generated alternative interpretive stories, each seeking to trump the rest: capitalism, Marxism, liberalism, socialism, Freudianism, scientism, and so on. Yet none of these modern metanarratives, according to Lyotard, can be said to embrace the one objective truth, for each turns out to be just one more competing form of discourse.

The paradoxical result is that the more modernity sought to redescribe

---

34. Jean-François Lyotard, *The Postmodern Condition: A Report on Knowledge,* trans. Geoff Bennington and Brian Massumi, THL 10 (Minneapolis: University of Minnesota Press, 1984), p. xxiv.

the whole, the more it prompted the proliferation of knowledge into multiple subdisciplines, each with its own language game, each with its own rules for the determination of meaning. The more metanarratives there are, the more they lose their power not only to explain but to persuade. To the extent that postmodern experience becomes a shifting back and forth between a set of incommensurable language games, each designed to accommodate a different human need, knowledge itself becomes a subject for manipulation, a commodity to be used, recycled, and then used again. The net result is a lapse into the incredulity that Lyotard believes now defines the postmodern age.

In a way, postmodernity is the recognition that all the many "ism's" of modernity have only a relative validity — not that they have no validity, but that they can have no overarching and hegemonic validity. It is against this backdrop that the theological challenge to move beyond foundations and beyond totality must be interpreted. Moving beyond foundations means thinking through the narrative of Christian faith without reducing it to just one more "ism" of modernity. Moving beyond totality means rediscovering the premodern Christian tradition's recognition that the story we are telling is multivalent and open-ended.[35] Only if we move beyond foundations and beyond totality might we be enabled to break out of the confines of any particular "ism" in order to embrace the Other.

III. Toward the Other

If the faithful reading of Scripture has traditionally required a rule of faith, together with a rule of hope, it needs also to employ a rule of love. The injunction to move beyond foundations and beyond totality must be completed in a movement toward the Other. This emphasis on otherness is one of the most promising in the postmodern repertoire, and it is a theme that finds its most prominent voice in the Jewish philosopher Emmanuel Levinas.[36] Levinas's philosophy is a relentless critique of all totalizing forms of reason that make no place for the Other.[37]

35. See David C. Steinmetz, "Uncovering a Second Narrative," Brian E. Daley, SJ, "Is Patristic Exegesis Still Usable?" and Gary A. Anderson, "Joseph and the Passion of Our Lord," in this volume.

36. For a treatment of Levinas's contribution to interpretation, see Richard A. Cohen, *Ethics, Exegesis, and Philosophy: Interpretation after Levinas* (Cambridge: Cambridge University Press, 2001).

37. This is nowhere better captured than in Levinas's magnum opus: Emmanuel Levinas, *Totalité et infini: Essai sur l'extériorité* (The Hague: Martinus Nijhoff, 1961), ET *Totality and Infinity: An Essay on Exteriority,* trans. Alphonso Lingis (Pittsburgh: Duquesne University Press, 1969).

This primacy of otherness has three distinct connotations. First, there is the philosophical meaning. The Other can be understood as anything or anyone that falls outside one's own categories. The realm of one's own selfhood, or what Levinas calls the "same," is constantly confronted by that which is other. The challenge is to refrain from violation by reducing the Other to this self-enclosed realm of the same.

Second, there is the ethical meaning. Ethically speaking, the (capitalized) Other is the poor, the oppressed, the weak, the widow, the orphan, the stranger in our midst — a familiar usage with deep biblical resonance. We are all too familiar with the "othering" that takes place in human life in which some person or group is vilified or turned into an outcast. Levinas turns this around and claims that to confront the Other is to find oneself on hallowed ground. Understood as the stranger or neighbor near at hand, the Other makes a moral claim upon my sensibility and compassion, a claim that exerts itself not from within my own subjectivity and consciousness but from without.

Third, there is the temporal meaning, which for Levinas has an explicitly messianic and political connotation. The Other is that which is to come, and specifically the liberating state of affairs that is yet to come, the future that is still awaited as a realm of justice and peace. This third sense is deeply resonant with the Jewish yearning for the Messiah. In his resolutely ethical version of philosophy, Levinas can speak of a messianic vocation incumbent upon each person in realizing his or her election. There is a way in which each person has a vocation to respond right here, at this very moment, to the specific "Other" for whom that person is uniquely responsible.

In some ways, this third dimension is the most important for biblical hermeneutics. It is now generally agreed that the reader always comes to the biblical text with a certain preunderstanding, including certain questions and expectations. One of these questions is, What are we waiting or hoping for? Different versions of postmodernity come to the text with different answers. For some nihilistic postmodernists, the answer is clear: We are waiting for nothing. For Christians and Jews, the answer is a different one: We come to the text waiting for the Redeemer to show us the way into the reign of God.

In all three of its connotations — philosophical, ethical, and temporal-political — the "Other" is not a projection of my own interiority but an exteriority that shatters the protective totality I have constructed around myself. The Other marks an infinity "beyond being" and "beyond totality" that claims me and will not let me go, giving me my unique vocation of responsibility to this need, right here, at this very moment. I must move beyond the foundations of my own selfhood, beyond the limitations of my own version of the totality of meaning and truth, and toward the Other who claims me from on high. To read the Scriptures with this in mind and act accordingly is to experience the God who is not only *for* us and *with* us but also already at work *among* us.

Conclusion

It has often been argued that biblical interpreters need a larger theological framework within which to think if biblical meaning is rightly to be discerned.[38] If so, then the task set before us here is one of understanding that framework in a more open-ended and eschatological way. While some of what a postmodern way of thinking seems to demand may strike us as overly technical and far removed from the task of gaining purchase on biblical meaning, there are ways in which the movement beyond foundations, beyond totality, and toward the Other has a certain resonance with what Christians have always wanted to claim. First, God is *for* us in a way that transcends every humanly conceived foundation for knowing. Second, in the concreteness of Jesus' suffering on the cross, God is *with* us in a self-donation that no premature totality can contain. Third, in the power of the Spirit, God is at work *among* us, beckoning us as well to be for and with the Other. This confession — God for us, Christ with us, and the Spirit among us — sets the framework for all faithful reading of the Scriptures.

38. A classical example is that of John Calvin. See "Subject Matter of the Present Work," from the French edition of 1560 of Calvin, *Institutes of the Christian Religion*, trans. Ford Lewis Battles, LCC (Philadelphia: Westminster, 1960), p. 6.

Preaching Scripture Faithfully in a Post-Christendom Church

Christine McSpadden

As a small study community of fifteen scholars and pastors, the authors of this volume embarked on a project to "recover the church's rich heritage of biblical interpretation" as it might speak to the church today — a church that finds itself in a post-Christendom era, seeking to communicate with a postmodern world. We came to nine central affirmations, or theses, about the interpretation of Scripture. Throughout this volume, we have sought to clarify, describe, illustrate, and flesh out what it might look like to read Scripture "theologically," in light of these affirmations.

This essay now turns to the question, very live for the foreseeable future, of how to communicate faithfully and effectively the gospel of Jesus Christ as portrayed in the biblical witness of the Old and New Testaments. More specifically, this essay explores the challenges of preaching in the contemporary mainline church environment and suggests ideas and strategies for preaching faithful, scriptural sermons in the post-Christendom church.

Dynamics of the Post-Christendom Church

Since the eighteenth century, Christianity has been losing ground as the great Western culture-religion. With a rising emphasis on human reason, the reading of Scripture has become a discipline modeled more on the sciences than on the humanities. Increasingly, science has replaced theology as a way of apprehending reality and of understanding our relationship with the world. At the same time, an increased secularization of society, a greater awareness of the plurality of religions, and an erosion of institutional authority in general have all weakened Christianity's stronghold.

This is by no means the first time that Christianity as a universal proclamation has lost ground while society fragments. St. Augustine found himself speaking to diverse communities, many of them pagan, and most of them quite anxious, after the sack of Rome. Thomas Aquinas found himself speaking in a time of intellectual ferment as Islam challenged the predominant religion of Europe. Islam, gaining momentum from the seventh century, had a great impact on European theology and philosophy by introducing a challenging monotheism and by reintroducing Aristotelian thought — philosophical thought that had been largely lost in the West. In both these instances, Christian proclamation had to reckon with a plurality of societal voices. Consequently, Christianity's confessional bases had to be rigorously reconsidered and reclaimed, and new strategies for delivering the gospel devised, so that the gospel could be heard in a convincing and compelling way.[1]

At the turn of the third millennium, Christianity once again finds itself with something valuable to say but uncertain about how best to do the talking. As an upside to this situation, Christianity has been released from much of its cultural baggage. Where once the "nomenclature 'Christian' was obliged to stand for all sorts of dispositions extraneous or tangential in relation to biblical faith," the clutter of associated and often random moral codes, affectations, and sentiments are falling away from the root *corpus Christianum*. In other words, as Christianity becomes disentangled from its host culture, it is thrust "back on its rudimentary confessional basis."[2]

Released from its cultural baggage, the faith tradition that claims Jesus Christ as Lord and Savior has the opportunity to be heard anew, in a new age. In many ways, Christianity sits poised to recapture the force of its apostolic witness, its original urgency, and to recapture the sense of "goodness" and "newness" of the good news. At this time in history, how we preach the good news, tell the Christian story, and reclaim the biblical witness for the faith community is of utmost importance.

1. See Thesis 7, "Nine Theses on the Interpretation of Scripture."

2. Douglas John Hall, "Confessing Christ in a Post-Christendom Context" (address to the 1999 Covenant Conference, Covenant Network of Presbyterians, Atlanta, Ga., 5 November 1999). Hall is Emeritus Professor of Christian Theology at McGill University, Montreal.

Preaching the Biblical Story in the Post-Christendom Church: An Opportunity to Be Seized

Within the life of the church community, the sermon commonly serves as the most far-reaching, numerically influential form of teaching. Generally, a single sermon can teach and minister to more souls, in less time, than any other pastoral activity. Therefore, the way in which preachers "read, mark, learn, and inwardly digest"[3] the scriptural witness in preparation for their sermons, and then the way in which they shape those sermons and deliver them, may have great impact on the inclinations, attitudes, and aptitudes of the hearers.

A valuable adage for preaching in the post-Christendom church is this: Never assume. While preachers could once assume familiarity with the grand metanarrative of Christian faith — namely, that the Ultimate chose to disclose divine identity and purposes through historical events that culminated (though by no means terminated) in the life, death, resurrection, and ascension of the God-man Jesus — that assumption is no longer valid. Even when a vague, passing apprehension of such a story does exist, foundational theological categories like salvation, atonement, sin, redemption, sanctification, and eschatological hope carry diminished force and meaning.

These fundamental theological categories have lost traction because post-Christendom churchgoers — those in the pulpit as well as in the pews — have a shrinking biblical literacy. We know less about the Bible — its stories, its diverse forms, its presentation of anthropological and theological truths. Consequently, we are less able to engage the biblical witness and to make sense of scriptural categories in an integrated, theological way. With this shrinking literacy comes a waning trust in Scripture as the authority for faith and life. Thus the downward spiral: We know less about Scripture, which therefore seems less relevant for our lives and therefore not authoritative for our lives, and which therefore — with all those "weird" stories — we don't really need to pay that much attention to anyway.

It seems particularly difficult to engender trust in scriptural authority when the prevailing cultural attitude within the Western milieu remains one of suspicion. Foundational institutions have seen their bedrock status crumbling. Organized religion, politics, education, and science have all come under highly critical scrutiny. Concurrently, the proliferation of — and easier access to — mass media has yielded a host of "authorities." The gap between Scripture's claims and its claim on believers' lives thus widens.

---

3. Cf. the propers for the Season after Pentecost, *The Book of Common Prayer* of the Episcopal Church, USA (1979), p. 236.

The formidable task of bridging this gap falls to preachers. The gap needs to be bridged because the Christian faith depends on the biblical witness to reveal the nature and purposes of God and requires trust in the authority of that witness. Jesus the living Christ, the person, reveals the nature and purposes of God, yes, but the New Testament offers the only historical witness to his life, death, and resurrection, events that were remembered and understood in the context of the "Old Testament." And as much as some scholars might like to repristinate a persona for Jesus independent of the Bible, such a project soon reaches limits, because the accounts by which we have any information about Jesus were compiled within the very faith community that proclaims him as Lord and Savior. Therefore, the quest for the historical Jesus tends to circularity.

The question of how to bridge the gap in order to communicate the gospel effectively in a post-Christendom church is a further challenge to preachers. While there is no single answer, this essay will explore some preaching strategies and suggest some sermon preparation exercises designed to help the biblical witness speak powerfully by sparking new awareness and imagination.

These suggestions come out of my own experience as a priest serving a large congregation in midtown Manhattan — a hotbed of competing voices, both secular and sacred. In that congregation I never knew who would be listening to my sermons: the audience ranged from completely unchurched seekers and persons of other faith traditions to seasoned theologians and bishops! I learned quickly that I needed to be cautious when making assumptions about them. At times I was confounded by the dearth of biblical literacy — my own included. How could I invoke this great story when no one knew it anymore? Nonetheless, I was encouraged by parishioners' appetite to explore and their great hunger to know more. I was privileged to find myself in a place where, in contrast to many other settings in which religion or the Bible might be discussed, people came predisposed to faith. By entering the church doors and joining the life of a worshiping community, they acted upon a desire to hear and believe.

Preaching the Biblical Story: Strategies and Suggestions

1. Preach the basics.

As more previously unchurched people and those who consider themselves seekers[4] find their way into churches, an old story is often heard for the first

---

4. My use of the term "seekers" follows that of the so-called church-growth movement. While it has no formal definition, the term's usage encompasses a broad range of attitudes and

time. Where the culture once commingled with Christianity, the current, broader culture now acts as the new mission field for the good news to be news again. Remarkably, the story once grayed by familiarity gains vibrant color and interest with its new unfamiliarity.

This desire to hear the basic story can be tracked in the success of a mushrooming industry of programs that teach Christian basics. For example, the Alpha course — so called because it begins with "A," the first letter of the Greek/Christian alphabet — has seen wild success. This ten-week program assumes no prior knowledge of Christianity and deals with fundamental questions like, Who is Jesus? Why did he die? What do Christians believe? The program addresses these questions thoughtfully and unflinchingly because the great population of seekers — unchurched and dechurched — needs to start with these basic explanations.

Amid the myriad questions that might be asked, the great underlying question of the age, often posed with bored, less-than-hopeful malaise, seems to be, So what? And once the question is asked, most people will stick around for only a short time, maybe no more than a couple of minutes, to see if a compelling answer is forthcoming. Preaching in the post-Christendom church, then, does well to recover a sense of apologetic — articulating the fundamentals of the faith clearly, simply, and hospitably to an audience no longer predisposed to assimilate the Christian story readily. In a fast-paced, message-bombarding, consumerist milieu, the sound bite reigns. In response, preachers are challenged to undertake theologically rigorous personal study to hone their own beliefs, as well as their understanding of the beliefs of the church, so that they can articulate those beliefs in crisp, clear ways that invite further discussion and deeper engagement.

Preaching benefits from study of the text with an ear toward the basic confessional affirmations of the church, most explicitly stated in the creeds. The compilation of biblical texts acknowledged by the church as its canon of Holy Scripture was shaped and authenticated by the church's rule of faith, which was itself created and implemented by that same faith community. Reciprocally, the rule of faith was shaped and authenticated by inchoate Scripture. The two — this loose confederation of faith claims and this growing col-

---

inclinations. Typically, the (Christian) seeker is one who is in the process of exploring Christianity, the church, or a particular faith community with a genuine interest in what is taught, practiced, and believed. Seekers may have prior experience with the church or Christianity — may even be baptized — but are exploring Christianity anew from a more critical, evaluative stance. Seekers are often characterized as consumers because their exploration resembles shopping; many seekers remain consumers, dilettantes in their involvement. But some become disciples, and this potential "conversion" fuels the church's incentive to attract and welcome them.

lection of authoritative and inspired texts — were simultaneous shaping forces in the development of the *ekklēsia*.

In other words, Scripture existed from the beginning as writings of the church for the church. The historical-critical method arose, in part, as an effort to gain hermeneutical leverage against this symbiotic relationship. At its most noble, the historical-critical method has sought to build contextual boundaries for interpretation and check misappropriations of the text. It has raised important issues, invited reconsideration, and, for that reason, gained great prominence as an interpretive method (and as a parent to derivative methods) in the academy. It has brought a new kind of rigor to biblical studies. Nevertheless, its shortcomings are showing as its usage continues over time. And while I am not advocating an anti- or uncritical stance, I am advocating a recognition of the method's limits; it is but one tool in the interpreter's toolbox.

Scripture, then, is rightly understood in light of the church's rule of faith.[5] Scripture's intent was never to prove scientifically the existence of God or to argue rationally for the event of the incarnation. Scripture simply makes these claims as fact, as the kerygma — that Jesus, Son of God, is Lord and Savior. This kerygma remains the foundation of all preaching through the ages.

Christian preaching calls to conversion on the basis of the kerygma. Announcing the event of salvation, it is designed to deliver, not a mere moralizing exhortation, but a call to conversion — to change of mind or heart, repentance, *metanoia* — as well as a way through to that conversion. Because the event of incarnation has happened, we can live a new kind of life. Or, to back up for a moment, because the event has happened, we can begin to imagine a new way of being, and through that imagination, our hearts, minds, souls, and strength are laid open for transfiguration.

"Imagination" as used in this essay articulates that moment when presuppositions, expectations, and worldviews are broken open — broken open so forcefully and expansively that individuals find themselves in a surprising place, beyond that which was theretofore conceived. Perceptions shift so radically that a "third way" is seen through dilemma, or a new whole exceeds the sum of its parts, or a transcendent vision is gained, albeit fleetingly. "Imagination" describes the capacity for self-transcendence when hearts are opened to hear the word of God.

As you consider your own contribution to the proclamation of the kerygma, it may be helpful to enlist the aid of sermon preparation exercises in

---

5. See Thesis 2; see also Robert W. Jenson, "Scripture's Authority in the Church," in this volume.

order to raise self-awareness about — and to gain critical distance from — your own preaching. The following exercise is proposed to help you incorporate the suggestion to preach the basics:

→ As you read through the text to be preached, and as you gather your thoughts on ways in which it might be preached, think about what creedal affirmation correlates with your ideas. Whether it is a point of the Nicene Creed, the Apostles' Creed, or the Westminster Confession, think about how it supports and directs your explication. Simultaneously, think about how the biblical text gives dimension to, illustrates, and makes sense of the creedal affirmation.

This exercise may sound pedantic, and you may worry about boring your more seasoned congregants, but I am continually amazed at how refreshing it is to hear a robust, cohesive explanation of even the most fundamental points of Christian faith when those points are drawn out of Scripture with a passion for showing their interrelatedness and mutuality.

2. Conceive of the sermon as an "environment" for wondering, rumination, and imagination.

Those who find their way into the post-Christendom church — believers and unbelievers alike — need a hospitable environment in which to ask questions. Those questions, which often spring from deep, existential concerns, must be taken seriously if God's saving word is to be heard in a convincing and compelling way. An environment that treats questions hospitably, as the starting point of conversation, becomes a place for wondering, rumination, and imagination. In such an environment, a variety of answers can be weighed and considered; the meaning that thus unfolds carries authenticity for having been personally integrated rather than adopted by rote.

Indeed, the sermon may itself be conceived as a hospitable environment for those who find their way into the pews. Understood as environment, the sermon is released from the flattened realm of explanation, explication, moral directive, or, indeed, any "thing" to be communicated. Rather, understood as environment, the sermon achieves a kind of spatial quality, becomes a safe space in which hearers can contemplate something foreign and desire its becoming familiar, can approach something threatening and welcome its challenge, can chance upon something unexpected and delight in its turning of the mind. The sermon as hospitable environment for wondering, rumination, and imagination encourages growth and change out of desire and delight.

Preachers aim to create such an environment, one in which hearts can be opened and found willing, one in which the transfiguring word of God can be heard. At its best, the sermon will minister to preacher as well as hearers; at its best, it will be engaging, stimulating, and inspiring. But the crucial point is that these things are possible because the biblical witness itself is potent, engaging, stimulating, and inspiring. Above all, the biblical story is one of realized and eschatological hope. The sermon provides a window through the fear, anxiety, fragmentation, and alienation, drawing the hearers' desire and delight toward the vision of God's reconciling, saving, steadfast work in the world today.[6] Therefore, the sermon that has been fundamentally shaped by the biblical witness can embody the sacramental character of proclamation and act as a vehicle for God's saving word.

Preaching that takes its origin in Scripture, in the sacramental proclamation, the kerygma, draws on the tried and true tradition of pastoral care.[7] Throughout the ages, the biblical witness has offered guidance for living, for modulating the emotions, for healing the soul, for forming the will. Athanasius, in his *Letter to Marcellinus,* describes how a person might gain healing, behavioral guidance, peace of mind, and self-control through the appropriation of Holy Scripture — in particular, the Psalter, which he views as a microcosm of the Bible.[8] "[I]n the Book of Psalms," writes Athanasius, "the one who hears . . . also comprehends and is taught in it the emotions of the soul, and, consequently, on the basis of that which affects him and by which he is constrained, he also is enabled by this book to possess the image [of Christ] deriving from the words" (p. 108). The Psalms can transform the person who hears Scripture in this way:

> [Their] words become like a mirror to the person singing them, so that he might perceive himself and the emotions of his soul, and thus affected, he might recite them. For in fact he who hears the one reading receives the song that is recited as being about him. . . . And these words, as his own, he chants to the Lord. And so, on the whole, each psalm is both spoken

6. See Thesis 1.

7. My use of the term "pastoral care" here is in no way limited to the common, contemporary usage that connotes a kind of parapsychotherapeutic activity practiced by clergy and other pastoral caregivers. Rather, it represents the most expansive understanding of the term, including, but not limited to, activities of preaching, teaching, mentoring, and spiritual direction. "Pastoral care," as I am using it, refers to all those activities that cultivate growth of the heart and enable healing and wholeness of body, mind, and soul.

8. Athanasius, *Letter to Marcellinus,* in *Athanasius: The Life of Antony and the Letter to Marcellinus,* trans. Robert C. Gregg, CWS (New York: Paulist, 1980).

and composed by the Spirit so that in these same words, as was said earlier, the stirrings of our souls might be grasped, and all of them be said as
concerning us, and the same issue from us as our own words, for a remembrance of the emotions in us, and a chastening of our life. (p. 111)

According to Athanasius, the Psalms have this power because, like all
Scripture, they are inspired by the Holy Spirit (p. 101; cf. 107, 111) and because
they possess the image of Christ, for ". . . just as [Jesus] provided the model of
the earthly and heavenly man in his own person, so also from the Psalms he
who wants to do so can learn the emotions and dispositions of the souls, finding in them also the therapy and correction suited for each emotion" (p. 112).

Athanasius presents Marcellinus, and anyone who reads this letter, with a
method for understanding the Psalms (for that is his first project, in response
to Marcellinus's request); he also presents a method for submitting thoughts
and behavior to be coerced by the Psalms, thereby bringing the whole self to
stand under them. This is his explanation of how such a method works:

> But when they chant . . . so that the melody of the phrases is brought
> forth from the soul's good order and from the concord with the Spirit,
> such people sing with the tongue, but singing also with the mind they
> greatly benefit not only themselves but even those willing to hear
> them. . . . Therefore the Psalms are not recited with melodies because of a
> desire for pleasant sounds. Rather, this is a sure sign of the harmony of
> the soul's reflections. Indeed, the melodic reading is a symbol of the
> mind's well-ordered and undisturbed condition. . . . And gaining its com-
> posure by the singing of phrases, it becomes forgetful of the passions and,
> while rejoicing, sees in accordance with the mind of Christ, conceiving
> the most excellent thoughts. (pp. 125-26)

Athanasius trusted in Scripture's power to effect change and growth
when a soul could open itself, could allow a space for the Holy Spirit to come
in and work, and could imagine ("image for one's self") the image of Christ.
Ephrem, Athanasius, Origen, and so many of the ancients understood the in-
valuable project of creating an environment for wondering, rumination, and
imagination in which the word of God, proclaimed and heard, becomes the
event for transfiguration.

These ancient saints of the church model helpful methods for incorporating the use of Scripture into pastoral care. As you imagine your own sermons becoming an environment for wondering, rumination, and imagination in which the transfiguring word of God might best be heard, you may
wish to experiment with these exercises:

→ Imagine how you would preach a given sermon without words. What medium would you use to communicate your message? Visual images? Movement? Music? Community service?

→ Ignatian spirituality draws on all the senses, involving them in the theological contemplation of Scripture. Imagine yourself in the biblical story, or hearing the story told for the first time. What does it feel like, look like, sound like, taste like, smell like? Which senses are awakened, and what imagery comes forward? What new insight might be gleaned from placing yourself in the story?

The theme common to these exercises is an attempt to embody the biblical text for our own lives. Hearers will be looking for evidence of a changed life in those who purport to preach one. In a quotation attributed to St. Francis, it is said: "At all times preach; and sometimes use words." James Howell, in his essay "Christ Was like St. Francis," commends the kind of scriptural reading and interpretation practiced by Francis: "His reading was embodied, and an embodied reading is perhaps the only kind of reading that is finally appropriate to these texts, which are about, and intended to provoke, changed lives." Howell continues: "[Scriptural] texts are to be 'performed,' in patterns of human actions that evidence some continuity with the words, life, and death of Jesus."[9] The life of St. Francis and, indeed, the lives of all the saints who sought to embody the gospel preach forcefully through word and deed. Their lives, as testaments to the impact of the gospel, present model sermons in an age that longs for authenticity and meaning above all else.[10]

The sermon that is an environment hospitable to questions — an environment for wondering, rumination, and imagination — will most likely spark more questions. Resisting oversimplification, such a sermon will raise the hearers' comfort level with complexity and with not knowing, will privilege the pursuit of wisdom over running after knowledge.

3. Preach the multifoliate self-disclosure of God represented in the biblical witness of the Old and New Testaments.

As is noted in the previous section, preaching — the proclamation of the kerygma — is a sacramental act that communicates visibly, audibly, and contemporarily the mystery and grace of I AM. The project of preaching must draw, then, from the whole of the kerygma in order to represent God most

---

9. James C. Howell, "Christ Was like St. Francis," pp. 100, 101 in this volume.

10. For a compelling analysis that arrives at this observation, see Tom Beaudoin, *Virtual Faith: The Irreverent Spiritual Quest of Generation X* (San Francisco: Jossey-Bass, 1998).

faithfully. It must take into account the entire biblical witness, Old Testament and New, because the entire canon tells the story of one and the same God enmeshed in the lives of faithful (and unfaithful) people across generations.

Reading the biblical witness as a living text acknowledges that passages of Scripture do not have a single meaning limited to the intent of the original author but are constantly open to new reading and understanding.[11] The authors and editors of the canonical texts repeatedly gave new contexts and senses to earlier traditions; they read from new perspectives and with new hermeneutics, hearing new things and attending different nuances. Within the biblical witness itself, "[t]he growth of the larger composition has often been shaped by the use of a conscious resonance with a previous core of oral or written texts . . . , [revealing] how the editors conceived of their task as forming a chorus of different voices and fresh interpretations, but all addressing in different ways, different issues, and different ages a part of the selfsame, truthful witness to God's salvific purpose for his people."[12] Likewise, meaning continues to unfold as new hearts enter Scripture's perpetual dialogue. Layers of meaning allow the text to be a living conversation. The Old Testament opens meaning in the New, and the New Testament illuminates the Old. "The relation of the synchronic and diachronic dimensions is an extremely subtle one in the Bible and both aspects must be retained."[13]

While no individual sermon can wholly represent God, preaching from the canonical breadth of the Bible, from the great variety of biblical texts, Old Testament and New, will render a fuller portrayal. In this endeavor, preachers will be challenged to wrestle with less attractive sides of God and texts that elicit confusion, resistance, or offense. For the whole of Scripture presents God as simultaneously immanent and transcendent, as near and far, the same and other, vulnerable and impassible, passionate and steadfast, fully human and fully divine, destructive and constructive, beginning and end. This dialectical depiction makes for an undomesticable deity. Allowing the biblical texts to speak a fuller — and sometimes uncomplimentary — picture of God lets them breathe, lets them be the living word that they are. It allows them to make a claim on our lives.

When God and God's ways are not portrayed in this fuller way, the religion to which we subscribe may bear little relation to Christianity. To state the problem more tendentiously, anyone can read the Bible hardened to its proclamation and power. But to read and preach the Bible as Scripture and

---

11. See Theses 4 and 9.

12. Brevard Childs, *Isaiah*, OTL (Louisville: Westminster/John Knox, 2001), p. 4.

13. Childs, *Isaiah*, p. 4.

proclamation, to read and preach it as God's word and as the Word of God, enjoins us to embrace the difficulties, choosing authenticity over comfort. Embracing the difficulties may not resolve them, but it leads to engagement with the text, which means that our hearts and minds remain open to its meaning.

So how might we remain faithfully engaged with the biblical text?

Approaching textual difficulties from a place of faith (or from a desire to be faithful) shifts the "burden of proof" from the text to the one seeking its wisdom. This is not to say that no critical perspective should be brought to the reading of difficult texts, but it is to say that our own prejudices, shortcomings, limitations, and blind spots should be considered first. It shifts the burden from what's wrong with the text to what may be wanting in our own hearts. To paraphrase loosely, Augustine stated the charitable approach to reading Scripture in this way: If all of God's word is meant for good, and all of God's word is true, then any rogue interpretation results from the human interpreter's own frailty and fallenness.

Inevitably, preachers encounter texts that will elicit resistance. Yet that resistance can lead to valuable insight. Resistance highlights places of cognitive dissonance within ourselves. It highlights places where the text confronts and criticizes behavior, values, priorities, and choices (our own and those of the larger society). It flags places where we are scandalized or repelled. Again, while some texts may seem unpreachable (a topic for another essay!), self-exploration leads to insight into why they are so difficult, scandalous, and offensive and thus to the very reason why they may need to be preached.

For example, the story of Jephthah's daughter makes us bristle, for it highlights the same oppressive gender dynamics that are evident in various forms in our world today. A woman is victimized because of her father's unnecessary and foolish vow to make a burnt offering of "what should come out from the doors of my house to meet me when I come back safe from the Ammonites" (Judg 11:31). However, since the story appears within the context of the Bible, a preacher is led to ask whether there is a difference between a (mere) victim and a martyr. The martyr is always the victim of human evil, and yet at the same time she transcends the passive agony we generally associate with victimization, bearing powerful witness to God even in the midst of death-dealing circumstances. Although Jephthah's (unnamed) daughter demands two months to "weep over her virginity" with her female companions, she chooses not to run away. She is willing to die for God, even though the religious demand remains rationally incomprehensible. Early Jewish interpreters saw in Jephthah's daughter a female counterpart to Isaac on Mount Moriah (Gen 22); medieval Christians often saw in Isaac a type of Christ.

Maybe the innovation of modern Christian preachers could be to suggest that this nameless woman — in her life, death, and perpetual remembrance (Judg 11:40) — anticipates even more fully the significance of the passion.

So embracing difficulties can lead to more profound engagement with the biblical witness. As another example, the picture of God in Gen 22 might suggest to us a heartless, bloodthirsty, child-abusing demon who relishes manipulation and testing. But to read the story in that way would be to impose categories upon the text that lie outside the larger canonical witness, outside the interpretive tradition, and outside the rule of faith — three hermeneutical controls that guide the faithful reading of Scripture.[14] Ellen Davis's "Vulnerability, the Condition of Covenant: Three Meditations on Genesis 22" grows out of a reading that employs these three hermeneutical controls.[15] The imaginative insight that she extracts illustrates how faithful readings of difficult texts speak powerfully of God and of God's ways to an expectant world today.

We encounter inevitable resistance in the human heart when we strive to stand under Scripture. And while we may employ methods of charitable reading — admit our own shortcomings, shortsightedness, and limits; challenge our own preconceptions, values, and attitudes; seek continuing engagement with God's word — still, preaching through the difficulties found in Scripture requires an attitude of prayer. Apostolic proclamation grew out of prayer and the gift of the Holy Spirit; faithful preaching has the same points of origin.

In *Jesus and the Word,* Rudolf Bultmann describes the requisite disposition shaped by the words that Christ has taught us, and which "we are bold to say,"[16] "thy will be done." Notes Bultmann: "Obedience can be attained only by [our] confessing [our] wishes before God, recounting them to Him, as in prayer of petition — not indeed presenting them as a claim, but always accompanied by 'Not as I will, but as Thou wilt.'" And further: "[Jesus' own] belief in prayer involves the paradox of the union of trustful petition with the will to surrender."[17] Praying shapes believing, and believing directs being.

For preachers, this means starting any reading or preparation from a place of prayer. It means being willing to have our presuppositions challenged

14. Indeed, it was not until the twentieth century that the image of God as child abuser could be proposed. (No such interpretation exists within the previous tradition.) Such a view can gain currency now because the authority of Scripture and tradition has eroded, because there is a lack of canonical fluency, and because a post-Christendom amnesia has set in.

15. See Ellen F. Davis, "Vulnerability, the Condition of Covenant," in this volume.

16. Cf. the liturgical introduction to the Lord's Prayer, *Book of Common Prayer,* p. 363.

17. Rudolf Bultmann, *Jesus and the Word* (New York: Scribner, 1958), pp. 187-88.

and our expectations foiled. It means approaching sermon preparation as an exercise of exegesis, not eisegesis — not imposing our own ideas upon the text, knowing what we want to say and then tailoring the text (or reading into it) to make our point. The dichotomy between objective and subjective readings is not always so pronounced; we often hear a certain resonance within a text because we come to it with an a priori concern. Yet the discipline of exegesis helps guard against misrepresentations of the biblical witness and invites us to encounter the word of God as "other." That is the point! In the crucible of these two entities interacting, clashing, combining, reacting, the wonderful alchemy of sermon-creating occurs. Creator meets creation in the differences, and something new and valuable emerges.

When confronted with a text that elicits resistance, you may wish to reflect on the following questions to spark a deeper awareness of possible meanings:

→ Examine why the text makes you bristle. What does it challenge, criticize, or propose that might be offensive? Is there an underlying, existential issue related to your own resistance that might connect with a similar resistance in your hearers?

→ What insight can you gain from applying the three hermeneutical controls outlined above, namely, the larger canonical narrative, the interpretive tradition, and the rule of faith?

→ How might the passage be illumined by reading back through it in light of the "end of the story"?[18]

As described in this essay, the biblical witness challenges us to imagine God, a world, relationships beyond our presuppositions and expectations. Ideally, the passage to be preached, and the resulting sermon, will elicit surprise, will stimulate previously unconsidered ways of thinking. Try the following exercise to see if it helps bring forth something previously unconsidered:

→ As you read through the passage, cross out the things on which you could preach a sermon at first glance. Consider what is left.

My own experience illustrates what might happen: I was faced with preaching the slaughter of the innocents following on Yuletide festivities.[19] The material

18. See Richard B. Hays, "Reading Scripture in Light of the Resurrection," and David C. Steinmetz, "Uncovering a Second Narrative," in this volume.

19. The Episcopal Sunday Lectionary (from which I normally preach) in effect "crosses out" this passage from the second chapter of Matthew. The verses appointed for reading on the Second Sunday after Christmas (vv. 13-15, 19-23) bracket it on either side.

seemed utterly unpromising and out of step with the mood of the season. My own desire to avoid this horrid piece of the nativity story reflects a perennial tendency among believers to wish to tailor God to our liking, to create God in our own image. We may be offended by a God who seems to be impotent in the face of the worst human brutality or a God who allows "his own boy" to escape safe and secure to Egypt while so many others die in Judea. We may be disappointed that the gospel does not at this point remove the scandal of innocent suffering, on which so many would-be believers have stumbled. No, what the gospel does instead is point to how inextricably the mystery of salvation is bound up with the mystery of human evil. Probing that connection, we may come to see that this piece of the story is not optional for preachers; indeed, it may be the most important part of the story. For it reveals that the incarnation is about God consenting to love us in the most tragic way imaginable. God lives and dwells among us, right in the middle and mess of things, *without* overriding our decisions and actions — no matter how inimical to God's purposes they may be. Putting it another way, God enters our reality not to obliterate evil (for it would not be possible to obliterate evil alone) but to transfigure it for the eyes of faith, to open "the door of hope" (Hos 2:17 Heb) and light the way of salvation for us who are still "sitting in darkness and the shadow of death, to guide our feet into the way of peace" (Luke 1:79).

4. Engage the multiplicity of voices from the surrounding culture.

Our world hosts a plurality of voices both secular and sacred, some of whom claim their authority deservedly; others, through self-authentication (just about anyone who can set up a Web site can become an authority). Often, it is hard to tell the difference between the two, to know whom to trust. Although we may feel a desire to ignore them, open engagement with these voices proves a better strategy for preaching in the postmodern milieu.[20] Familiarity with what they are saying allows preachers to present the gospel within the hearers' cultural context, within their frame of reference. Preaching benefits from being in conversation with other traditions, with other philosophies, and with the prevailing cultural symbols, icons, anxieties, and perspectives.[21] Such practice has a long, successful history in the church. After all, Christianity emerged within a pluralistic world, has flourished within a pluralistic world, and has something distinctive to say within a pluralistic world.

20. For a cohesive explanation of postmodernism, see William Stacy Johnson, "Reading the Scriptures Faithfully in a Postmodern Age," in this volume.

21. See Thesis 8.

Preachers can clarify what Christianity distinctively says, but such clarification is most effectively made with the humility that comes from having heard — and honored — what other voices distinctively say. More often, in the postmodern milieu, our attitude is one of tolerance rather than humility. There is an important difference between the two. Tolerance can keep its distance: Competing ideas can be relativized, promoting polite agreements like "You have your view and I have mine, and both are of equal value." Differences can be shrugged off, allowing misleading generalizations like "All religions are saying the same thing anyway." Common ground thus gained rests on artificial supports and pleasantries; it cannot withstand the give-and-take of real exchange. Humility, however, requires engagement: One view is held in relation to another. Conversants hold a stake in a point of view for which they are willing to argue. Conversation goes back and forth; there is an exchange. With this exchange, viewpoints are challenged and honed. A robust teasing out of meaning comes through difference, engagement, and a willingness to have views revised.[22] An attitude of humility requires a willingness to explore competing ideologies and to identify the fault lines and shortcomings of our own beliefs as well as those of others.

In this age, as in others in which Christianity's credibility has been questioned, the faith tradition has something compelling, valuable, and transfiguring to communicate in response to the signs of the times. Christianity has always been a religion that grounds itself in this world, refusing to retreat from the world but instead situating itself in the midst of unfolding history. Its distinguishing narrative — that the Son of God, the second person of God's triune Self, became human and dwelt on this earth, in real time — asserts that this God enmeshes divine being in the most intimate and mundane details of human existence. Far from eschewing this world, God stands behind creation as good, delights in it, and goes to the extent of becoming incarnate in that creation to preserve the relationship God so desires. In the midst of competing voices, the Christian witness declares in word and deed the faithful, incarnational commitment of a God who is with us — Emmanuel — creating, judging, and saving the world.[23]

As an exercise for engaging with other voices, try the following:

→ Review past sermons, asking the question, What have I said that gives Christianity a compelling voice in conversation with other voices in our culture or the larger world? Consider how someone listening to your

22. See Thesis 9.
23. See Thesis 1.

sermons would gain tools of discernment for parsing the plurality of voices within the cultural milieu.

5. Preach so that your hearers want to hear more about the Bible.
Today's hearers have little experience with the thoughtful reading of Scripture; every sermon is an opportunity to cultivate a desire to know more about the biblical witness. Given the statistics on church attendance, the trends in church consumerism, and the growing number of unchurched and dechurched in the pews, every sermon presents an opportunity — maybe *the* opportunity — to spark the hearers' interest and imagination, enticing them to come back to hear more. Over time, by engendering a sense of wonder, approaching and better apprehending a scriptural world, providing a map through a well-traveled yet foreign-feeling landscape, and offering a warm hand as a fellow traveler on a transfiguring journey, preachers break down perceived barriers between the world of the Bible and the world in which its texts are heard. Those "weird" stories thus gain meaning and force once again.

The following exercise is designed to help you track your improvement at incorporating this principle:

→ A week or so after you have preached, ask a few people in the congregation if they can remember the text on which you preached.
  Here's how to score your result:
  • If they remember the text and have thought about what it means in their own lives, or if they remember the text and have gone home and looked it up, give yourself 10 points.
  • If they remember the text but it has had no impact, give yourself 5 points. Who knows what the Holy Spirit will do?
  • If they do not remember the text but do remember the cute anecdote in your sermon, deduct 10 points.

Conclusion

In the traditional shape of the divine liturgy, the constituent parts serve the purpose of gathering the community; collecting the prayers; recounting the distinguishing narrative; seeking repentance and making supplication in response to that narrative; remembering, and thus making real again, the events from which a transfigured existence proceeds; giving thanks *(eucharistia);* blessing; and sending. Come and see. Go and tell. Come back and regroup. Go.

The sermon finds its place within the order of these activities. And more expansively, it finds its place within the entire life of the church, integrated with the biblical witness; within the church's hymnody, iconography, art, ethics, and theology; within its servant ministry and its response to current events and trends. The sermon connects premodern wisdom with a postmodern world fraught with anxiety, flux, fragmentation, alienation, and perennial human sin. It connects the community's ancient narrative with its contemporary story. This connection can happen because the same God who animated everything visible and invisible continues to give life and relate to that life in the world today. This connection can happen because the Word through whom all was created, who spoke through the prophets, who was made known to us in the Son, continues as the head of the body of the risen Christ in the world. It can happen because the Spirit who moved over the deep and formless void, who prays in us with sighs too deep for words, continues to dwell wherever two or three may be gathered together in God's name. It can happen because the one, holy, and living God has chosen to be intimately involved in the lives of mortals, to make us mortals part of God's own history and being.

Through its preaching, the church lets the world know about God's history and being. Thus preparing and delivering a sermon is a holy act, one set aside by God from all other kinds of public speaking for the purpose of serving God's mission and ends. The written and spoken word of God has the power to topple kingdoms and move mountains; it upends the status quo, turns expectations inside out, and gives voice to the voiceless. In seeking to understand and proclaim God's word, we must agree to stand under it.

Preaching this reality in a post-Christendom church has its challenges; at the same time, it presents the rare historical opportunity to communicate good news that is heard as good and as news once again. The saints through the ages have faced similarly perplexing situations. Yet God continually raises up artists, musicians, theologians, and orators who can speak with force and faith to their time and place. The strategies outlined in this essay are intended to help preachers navigate the vicissitudes of our time and place as they strive to restore trust in the authority of Scripture, to cultivate desire to better understand the Bible, and to engender willingness and even eagerness to stand under and embrace the good news revealed within the scriptural witness to what God in Christ has done, is doing, and will do.

Embodying Scripture in the Community of Faith

L. Gregory Jones

The seminary students had been anxiously awaiting the posting of the list that would assign each student in the homiletics class a biblical text. Each was to write an exegesis paper, and then a sermon, on his or her text. The students were anxious because, while some would undoubtedly get the Prodigal Son or another favorite text, many feared that they would get a passage from 1 or 2 Chronicles or, even worse, the story of Balaam's ass. A crowd gathered as soon as the list went up. A third-year seminary student, nearing graduation, was distressed when he saw his text. "Darn it," he said. "Mine is from Hebrews. I really wanted a New Testament text."

I have often wondered what that student's ministry has been like in the parishes to which he has been appointed. More broadly, though, the lack of familiarity with Scripture that his story illustrates has become an increasing problem among clergy and laity across the Christian traditions. I showed a group of sixty undergraduates, almost all of whom identified themselves as (at least nominal) Christians, a video of Martin Luther King Jr.'s "I Have a Dream" speech from 1963. After watching the video, I observed to the students that at a pivotal point in the speech, King said, "Let justice roll down like waters, and righteousness like an ever-flowing stream." Where, I asked the students, did that phrase come from? After an awkward silence, one student suggested that King was such a good orator, he had probably coined the phrase himself. Another student hazarded a guess that King had gotten it from the Bible or from Shakespeare. But not one student knew that it was

Portions of this essay appeared as "The Word That Journeys with Us: Bible, Character Formation, and Christian Community," *Theology Today* 55 (1998): 69-76.

from the Bible or, more specifically, from the Prophets — much less from Amos. Yet King, just thirty-five years ago, did not think he needed to say, "As the prophet Amos said, in the Old Testament of the Christian Bible . . ." He presumed, I think rightly, that no matter how poor Christian embodiment of the Scriptures might have been in the United States, the vast majority of his listeners would hear those words as Amos's critique of people who worship God without practicing justice.

Yet this familiarity with biblical texts has diminished in recent decades. There are complex reasons that account for the loss. However, the key point in this context is that we have lost a sense of the Bible as a (or the) central text in the formation of Christian character and identity. That is not to say whether our interpretations of the Bible have been excellent or poor, constructive or destructive. It is to say that, rather than struggling to provide wise readings and performances of the biblical texts, we in the United States have largely marginalized those texts in Christian community and Christian life. In so doing, we have lost a clear sense of the ways in which Scripture's words (and the Word) shape both our minds and our lives.

There is an obvious objection to this claim: Who is "we"? After all, large numbers of people in the United States gather in small groups on a regular basis for "Bible study." Indeed, according to Robert Wuthnow, perhaps as many as two-thirds of all small groups in America gather specifically as "Bible study" groups.[1] Surely such groups stand as a crucial counterexample to my claim. Yet what Wuthnow and his associates discovered was that these groups are actually far more focused on providing personal support to one another than on learning the Bible. Indeed, he found that such groups often produce wooden interpretations of the Bible with little increase in knowledge of the Bible's content (e.g., one person commented, quite bizarrely, "The Bible helped me get a job; therefore, it must be true").

A more decisive objection is that the claim's "we" refers only to people from middle-class, white (and perhaps Protestant) America. After all, King's own practice was nourished in the black church; surely the rich patterns of biblical interpretation in black preaching and black music provide important counterexamples to my claim. This is a significant point, and I will return below to the black church as a resource for a richer conception of the importance of embodying Scripture in the community of faith. At this point, however, I would simply observe that, while the black church is in better shape on these matters than most Euro-American churches, my im-

---

1. See Robert Wuthnow, *Sharing the Journey: Support Groups and America's New Quest for Community* (New York: Free Press, 1994).

pression is that these issues are becoming more and more pressing even in that setting.

The heart of my concern is that American Christians have largely lost a rich familiarity with ruled patterns for reading and embodying Scripture, the kind of familiarity that shapes people's lives and, at its best, enlivens a scriptural imagination. Indeed, this loss of familiarity is at least in part a consequence of an increasing preoccupation with questions of biblical method and biblical authority. As Christians in modernity have increasingly argued about the appropriate method or methods for biblical study as well as the perceived status of Scripture's authority, we have failed to attend adequately to the task of actually reading and embodying the texts themselves. This is a particular problem within predominantly white, mainline Protestant churches in the United States, but it has become an increasing problem across the traditions and across the theological spectrum. Even evangelicals who have a very high view of the Bible's authority often have a rather low competence in reading and embodying Scripture.

Our loss of familiarity with Scripture, besides being a consequence, is at the same time a cause of our preoccupation with biblical method and biblical authority. The less familiar we are with the texts of Scripture in all their diversity and complexity, the easier it is for us to remain at a more generalized level of argument about whether Scripture has authority — or, more accurately, what kind of authority diverse people are willing to ascribe to it.

Perhaps most importantly, our loss of familiarity with Scripture is morally convenient. As United Methodist Bishop Kenneth Carder has suggested: "[I]t is much easier to argue about evolution and creation than it is to live as though this is God's world. Or, debating whether a 'great fish' really swallowed Jonah is far less costly and risky than acknowledging that God loves our enemies as much as God loves us."[2] Carder's point hits home autobiographically, for as I have begun to absorb the significance of Jonah's message with respect to some of my own attitudes, I simultaneously have discovered that I prefer debates about its historicity. Such debates do not put my own character at risk, whereas the force of the story is to challenge my refusal to be personally open to God's work of transformation.

I have also discovered that Jonah has significance for challenging even how we articulate our disagreements about biblical method, biblical authority, and biblical texts with fellow Christians. We construct these people as enemies to be defeated, not as fellow children of God with whom we ought to

2. Bishop Kenneth L. Carder, "Bible's True Authority Lies in Power to Change" (United Methodist News Service commentary, 2 June 1999).

engage, hoping that they will be converted, *and* recognizing that *we also* need to be converted.

To be sure, we cannot evade questions of method or authority simply by immersing ourselves once again in Scripture. The questions are unavoidable, particularly on this side of modernity's understandings and challenges. But I am suggesting that we can make an important difference in addressing these questions by developing habits of effective and faithful reading and embodiment of Scripture. These habits are essential to a lively scriptural imagination. In such an imagination, people know and live the stories and convictions embedded in Scripture in ways that then provide the freedom for creatively (and faithfully) "imagining the world that Scripture imagines."[3]

In order to cultivate such a scriptural imagination, we need to rediscover Scripture as the "word that journeys with us" in Christian living. I borrow this phrase from the Roman Catholic theologian Hans Urs von Balthasar in order to suggest the sense in which we need to learn to live with, and embody, the texts of Scripture throughout our lives.[4] Each of our project's theses is crucial to learning how to have Scripture journey with us. In this essay, I focus on Theses 6 and 7, namely, what it means to read and embody Scripture in the community of faith and to allow saintly interpreters to guide that reading and embodiment.

In the next section of the essay, I briefly explore the importance of communities and saintly interpreters. Communities and saintly interpreters are crucial to embodying Scripture faithfully, but we need to be clear about the respects in which they do and do not matter. Saintly interpreters arise out of, and are made possible by, the wider community of faith.

I then turn to an exploration of the tasks of engagement with Scripture by arguing that learning to live with, and immerse ourselves in, Scripture occurs in three distinct but overlapping contexts: in catechesis, in critical study, and in witness. I briefly identify how each context provides vital opportunities for reenlivening Scripture as a word that journeys with us. Throughout the discussion, I point to two persons who are saintly exemplars of the kind of practice I am suggesting: Augustine of Hippo and Martin Luther King Jr.

In the final section of the essay, I explore the implications of these contexts and these saintly exemplars for understanding the tasks of our own interpretation and embodiment of Scripture. Despite the obvious differences

---

3. This phrase comes from the title of an essay by Luke Timothy Johnson, "Imagining the World Scripture Imagines," *Modern Theology* 14 (1998): 165-80.

4. See Hans Urs von Balthasar, *Theo-Drama*, vol. 2, trans. Graham Harrison (San Francisco: Ignatius, 1990), pp. 102ff.

between the premodern Augustine and the modern Martin Luther King Jr. — differences in time, culture, denominational presumptions, and method of biblical interpretation — I suggest that they have a great deal in common because of their commitment to Scripture as the word that journeys with us.

Throughout, I suggest that reclaiming a rich familiarity with Scripture, nurtured through habits of reading and practices of discipleship better than those we typically exercise, will provide us with greater resources for challenging unfaithful readings of Scripture and for discovering afresh Scripture's formative and transformative power.

I. Communities and Saintly Interpreters

The notion of reading and embodying Scripture in the community of faith means that we are participants in a company that includes all people who have sought to read and embody Scripture faithfully through the ages — for us as Christians, the church of Jesus Christ. To be sure, this notion is complicated by the sinful tragedy of a divided church, making it difficult for us to define even what we mean by Scripture (does it include the books of the Apocrypha?), much less what it means to read in company with those with whom we are not formally in communion. Nevertheless, for Christians, the gospel is mediated through the community of faith, the church, as nurturing mother.

Of course, in the complex, mobile worlds of the twenty-first century, especially in the West, many Christians do not actually live in any one "community" — ecclesial or otherwise. In fact, a more appropriate description of our reading and embodiment of Scripture would be to say that it is done in and through *overlapping* communities of faith, so that questions of accountability and nurture are even more complicated. Moreover, our reading and embodiment occurs in diverse contexts (catechesis, critical study, and witness). Despite the daunting complexity of the task, we should not seek to valorize any one context or community as the *only* or even *primary* setting of interpretation. Rather, we should read in company with many other Christians to whom we are accountable and from whom we can gain insight and encouragement. The texts of Scripture both presuppose and are ordered to communities of faith, in all their concreteness, richness, and messiness.

At the same time, however, there are crucial roles for individual readings and performances of Scripture. Individual saintly interpreters are neither independent of the community nor wholly determined by it. They are people whose wisdom, insights, and lives shed particular light on the gospel that bears witness to, and for, the wider community of faith. By "saintly interpreters" I do not mean only those saints officially recognized by the church; I include also the "great cloud of witnesses" acknowledged by believers across time and traditions.[5]

Identifying who these saintly interpreters are is a matter of discernment, debate, and even abiding disagreement. We have a tendency to presume too superficial and wooden a conception of "saints." Yet in a variety of ways, we can see the grace and holiness of God working in and through their fallible, often conflicted lives to shed specific light on our own readings and embodiments of Scripture. We depend on public, saintly interpreters who call forth our own patterns of discipleship. There is no room, methodologically or substantively, for individualistic readings or embodiments of Scripture; there *is* room — indeed, there is great need — for individual readings and embodiments that arise from and are ordered to the community of faith.

In the next two sections, I will draw on two such saintly interpreters to help illumine the tasks of reading and embodying Scripture in the community of faith: Augustine of Hippo, one of those saintly interpreters officially recognized by the church, and Martin Luther King Jr., a twentieth-century African American whose leadership of the black church and whose witness in the United States became a beacon of light until he was assassinated. Neither of them lived a superficial or wooden life, and neither was immune from personal sin and failure. These two saints represent contrasting yet complementary examples of interpreters whose preaching, reading, and witness were made possible by the community of faith and who bore extraordinary witness for the community of faith. Moreover, these saintly interpreters drew from and contributed to the diverse contexts in which Christians engage in scriptural interpretation.

II. Contexts for Engaging Scripture

Christians need to reclaim the centrality of catechesis if Scripture is to be formative for our character and our communal life. Most basically, we need to learn the stories — to have Moses and Deborah, Amos and Paul, Mary and John become people we know. My colleague Willie J. Jennings, raised in the African American Christian tradition, says his parents talked so much about biblical characters that when he was young, he really thought that

---

5. See Thesis 7, "Nine Theses on the Interpretation of Scripture."

people such as Ruth and Naomi were members of his extended family. Such stories are crucial for forming a Christian understanding of, and desire for, God.

Even more, we need to locate the practice of learning and interpreting Scripture within the context of other practices of Christian living, both personally and as communities. This was at the heart of one of the most powerful examples of catechesis, the ancient catechumenate.[6] In the early church, there was a commitment to Scripture as the word that journeys with us; that commitment shaped and directed the Christian life. Wherever they occur, such "dramatic" interpretations of Scripture immerse people in the actual texts of Scripture and offer more complex and more imaginative sets of practices for dealing with difficult texts than we tend to employ in modernity. In so doing, they produce embodied readings — we would do well to recall the monastic metaphors of "consuming" the text — making the words and stories part of the fabric of the interpreters' very being and identity.

St. Augustine was integrally involved with catechumenal practices, and he modeled exemplary catechetical engagements with Scripture. As William Harmless has documented, Augustine's preaching and theological reflection were often shaped by concerns for his congregation's developing relationships with Scripture and with various practices of Christian living. Augustine thought a long period for catechesis (typically, two years for adults) was necessary in order to "hear what the faith and pattern of Christian life should be."[7] One can hear in Augustine's preaching the rich resonances of a life for which Scripture was a word journeying with the community. He told catechumens:

> Your sins will be like the Egyptians following the Israelites, pursuing you only up to the Red Sea. What does up to the Red Sea mean? Up to the font, consecrated by the cross and blood of Christ. For, because that font is red, it reddens [the water]. . . . Baptism is signified by the sign of the cross, that is, by the water in which you are immersed and through which you pass, as it were, in the Red Sea. Your sins are your enemies. They follow you, but only up to the Red Sea. When you have entered, you will es-

6. The convictions and practices of the ancient catechumenate are being reclaimed in such contemporary contexts as the Roman Catholic Rite of Christian Initiation of Adults. Even so, the RCIA has not been as intentional in reshaping engagement with Scripture as I am suggesting needs to be done — in part because it has not really confronted the crises of ecclesial biblical interpretation.

7. Augustine, *De fide et operibus* 6.9, cited in William Harmless, *Augustine and the Catechumenate* (Collegeville, Minn.: Liturgical Press, 1995), p. 156.

cape; they will be destroyed, just as the Egyptians were engulfed by the waters while the Israelites escaped on dry land.[8]

Augustine's complex imagery is intelligible only to people who have become familiar with the story of the exodus, the Gospels, and the baptismal covenant.

Similarly, Martin Luther King Jr. was nurtured in practices of interpreting Scripture, fostered both through preaching and through the rich biblical allusions and performances of spirituals and other black church music. His life and the power of his witness do not make sense apart from an extraordinary scriptural imagination learned through catechetical practices of the church. Richard Lischer's study *The Preacher King: Martin Luther King Jr. and the Word That Moved America* wonderfully displays the tapestry of King's engagements with Scripture. As Lischer puts it, King's formation in the African-Baptist Church

> prepared him to be the public advocate of God's justice for black people in America, which in the African-American tradition meant that he would take a church and preach. From this environment he absorbed key theological strategies for dealing with injustice that he would never relinquish. He learned more from the Negro preacher's methods of sustaining a people and readying it for action than from any of his courses in graduate school; he absorbed more from his own church's identification with the Suffering Servant than from anything he read in Gandhi. What came earliest to him remained longest and enabled him to put a distinctively Christian seal on the struggle for civil rights in the United States.[9]

Note, for example, one sentence in which King evoked a complex set of biblical images. At Holt Street Baptist Church in Montgomery, King interpreted the unfolding events of the bus boycott in the following way: "'We, the disinherited of this land,' he cried, 'we who have been oppressed so long, are tired of going through the long night of captivity.'"[10] Here King located the black struggle for freedom in the context of Israel's longing for deliverance. King's preaching actually sounded like the Bible, and the similarity ran deeper than the surface verbal texture of his sermons. The words of Scripture significantly shaped King's practice as well as his rhetoric.

8. Augustine, *Sermon* 213.8, cited in Harmless, *Augustine and the Catechumenate*, p. 282.

9. Richard Lischer, *The Preacher King: Martin Luther King Jr. and the Word That Moved America* (Oxford: Oxford University Press, 1995), p. 6.

10. Cited in Lischer, *The Preacher King*, p. 198.

Even so, both Augustine and King knew that engagement with Scripture must also include critical study — a second context of our journey with the text. Of course, what we mean by "critical" is a contestable issue that involves interpretive debates about the methods of "higher criticism," methods that were, of course, unavailable in Augustine's time. My point here is a more modest one. Anyone who journeys with Scripture for very long will discover issues and perplexities that will undoubtedly lead to struggle. Perhaps it is the diverse and difficult textual variants of Job, or the gaps in the Gospels, or the fact that different Gospels tell the "same" story differently. Or perhaps it is because there are passages that seem to defy understanding in relation to other fields of inquiry, or passages that bear striking similarity to other stories from the ancient Near East, or because there are passages that we simply find difficult to understand or to accept.

Critical study of such difficulties may occur through formal education at degree-granting institutions, but it need not. It may occur through the sorts of practices we associate with the ancient rabbis, or studying Talmud among contemporary Jews. However we practice it, and in whatever setting, we need to be schooled in critical engagement with Scripture. Augustine described Scripture — or, more accurately, the church in which Scripture is primarily read — as a "school," and those who come to hear Scripture read as "students of divine letters." Notably, he did not hesitate to acknowledge that there were texts he did not understand and avoided speaking about (e.g., Matt 12:31-32, on the sin against the Holy Spirit), although he did not stop "seeking, asking, knocking" concerning them.[11] He also turned to the philosophical tools of Neoplatonism to help him understand issues that seemed perplexing in Scripture, issues that had been obscured for him by popular philosophical understandings incompatible with Scripture (e.g., Manichaean dualisms).

Similarly, King engaged in scholarly study of Scripture throughout his formal education at Morehouse College, in seminary at Crozer, and in the graduate program at Boston University. His engagements with Scripture were informed by the liberal theological tradition that helped shape his social activism. His acquired language of liberal theology became a means by which his scriptural imagination was unfolded in his preaching and teaching. Interestingly, although historical criticism of the Bible played an important role in the development of liberal theology, King's formal education in historical criticism did not seem to influence him directly; his own interpretations of

---

11. See Augustine's discussion in *Sermon* 71.7-8. I am indebted to John Cavadini for directing me to this sermon.

Scripture were shaped far more by the sophisticated patterns of allegory and typology that were characteristic of scholarly study of the Bible in premodern periods. In this, King was truly a person of the black church. For the black church's engagement with critical study has more closely resembled premodern patterns of allegory and typology than historical-critical readings. This is so even for difficult texts, and for those texts *made* difficult by ideologically oppressive white readings (e.g., the "curse of Ham" in nineteenth- and early-twentieth-century America).[12]

Both Augustine and King used diverse historical, philological, philosophical, literary, and rhetorical tools to develop rich and faithful interpretations of Scripture. They used different critical methods, but both drew on their formal education to undertake scholarly, critical readings of Scripture in deep and penetrating ways. We may disagree with their readings of particular texts, but the scriptural imaginations of both men were shaped by powerful, ongoing subtle interpretations of Scripture that transformed their own lives as well as the lives of those to whom they preached and with whom they read.

A third context in which Scripture journeys with us is witness — our patterns of engagement with the world. This context comes to life in communities as diverse as Wesleyan class meetings in the eighteenth century and Latin American base communities in the late twentieth century. Common to such communities is the struggle to imagine with Scripture in the wake of particular experiences of joy and grief, triumph and suffering, blessing and oppression. Such struggle may produce difficulty in understanding or accepting what the text seems to be saying and may pose significant interpretive obstacles for a variety of reasons. But such struggle may also produce a deep engagement with the texts and with the God who Christians believe is revealed through them.

Augustine reflected in quite provocative ways on the divisions and vices he saw within his world. He knew that a lack of forgiveness was a local vice, and so he focused on it in his reflections. For example, he noted in a sermon that people tended to bring their fierce resentments and their desires for revenge to prayer: "Each day, people come, bend their knees, touch the earth with their foreheads, sometimes moistening their faces with tears, and in all this great humility and distress say: 'Lord, avenge me. Kill my enemy.'" Reflecting on this situation in light of Matt 6:14-15, he insisted that they recognize their enemies as children of God and that, when praying for those ene-

---

12. For an instructive discussion of this passage in the context of African American biblical interpretation, see Michael G. Cartwright, "Ideology and the Interpretation of the Bible in the African-American Christian Tradition," *Modern Theology* 9 (1993): 141-58.

mies, they let their prayer be "against the malice of your enemy; may his malice die, but may he live. . . . If his malice should die, then you would have lost an enemy and gained a friend."[13]

King's reflections were tested in the crucible of fire that was the American civil rights movement. King transposed biblical themes of love, suffering, deliverance, and justice into the great social and political debates of the day. His sermons and speeches show the power, and the interpretive freedom, of one whose scriptural imagination was so fertile that he could "move America" through the power of the word — even when he did not explicitly appeal to any biblical or theological language. Lischer nicely summarizes the power of King's witness in the context of social engagements:

> The black church not only sought to locate truth *in* the Bible, in order to derive lessons from it, but also extended the Bible into its own worldly experience. King found the ancient methods of interpretation useful in his effort to enroll the Civil Rights Movement in the saga of divine revelation. These techniques he joined to the black church's practice of "performing" the Scripture in its music, its rhythmic pattern of call and response, and a variety of rhetorical adornments — all of which he exported from the church's Sunday worship to political mass meetings around the country.[14]

I have been suggesting that if we want to understand the ways Scripture should be read in and through Christian communities, we need to see Scripture as the word that journeys with us through the diverse contexts of our lives. We need more intensive schooling in catechesis, in critical study, and in witness. While these contexts are distinct, they require rich interrelations for character formation and transformation. These are the sources that fund scriptural imagination and shape habits of thought and life.

There is, of course, much more to be said, and many issues and objections that would need to be addressed in order to develop my proposal more fully. After all, I am well aware that the devil is adept at quoting Scripture. Nevertheless, I think Augustine and King display the transformative possibilities of scriptural imagination. My proposal does not foreclose counterarguments, nor does it guarantee that our readings will be formative (much less transformative) rather than malformative. But it does suggest a much better and more life-giving set of options than are offered by our current arguments about the Bible, and our ignorance of it.

13. Augustine, *Sermons* 56.13-14 and 211.6, cited in Harmless, *Augustine and the Catechumenate*, pp. 290-91.

14. Lischer, *The Preacher King*, p. 7.

Indeed, as our nine theses suggest, we need to develop and reclaim habits of wise and faithful readings and embodiments of Scripture within the community of faith. How might we be guided in this task by the examples of Augustine and King?

III. Embodying Scripture

I can only sketch here the contours of an answer that would require a much longer and more extended analysis. Even so, there are several guiding judgments that are crucial to understanding the task of embodying Scripture in the community of faith, judgments that would be shared by Augustine and King (as well as by many other exemplary readers of Scripture) despite other methodological and substantive disagreements and divergences.

First, a primary way in which we adjudicate what constitutes wisdom and faithfulness in the embodiment of Scripture is whether it bears appropriate witness to the God of Jesus Christ. As Augustine put it in *De doctrina christiana,* all Scripture, when correctly interpreted, is conducive to the knowledge and love of God and neighbor. He emphasized that in this light, "correct" interpretation requires an understanding of the multiple senses of Scripture. Augustine wrote: "[W]hatever appears in the divine Word that does not literally pertain to virtuous behavior or to the truth of faith you must take to be figurative. Virtuous behavior pertains to the love of God and of one's neighbor; the truth of faith pertains to a knowledge of God and of one's neighbor."[15] This criterion, which underlies several of our theses, establishes the organic continuity between our contemporary communities of interpretation and the communities from which we received the Bible. Put more bluntly, despite their many differences, Augustine and King shared a fundamental commitment, namely, that wise interpretation and faithful discipleship converge in appropriate witness to the God of Jesus Christ. Interpreting Scripture presupposes the continuity of the communities of faith; when practiced faithfully and with an ongoing vigilance against sinful readings and practices, interpreting Scripture also sustains and transforms those communities in their faith.

Because of this continuity in our understanding of diverse Christian

---

15. Augustine, *On Christian Doctrine* 3.10.14, trans. D. W. Robertson Jr., LLA 80 (New York: Macmillan, 1958), p. 88. To be sure, this criterion of love of God and neighbor raises important substantive questions about how to interpret the moral sense of Scripture. There are clearly a number of passages in Scripture that are not straightforwardly conducive to the love of God and neighbor.

communities, a second guiding judgment is that we need to cultivate an expansive notion of the "us" that Scripture journeys with throughout life. The "community of faith" assumes a communal focus for interpretation rather than an individualistic one; we are called to interpret and embody Scripture in company with others seeking to live faithfully before God. Once again, Augustine offers an eloquent testimony. He proposes that we are all joint inquirers, with Christ as our ultimate Teacher:

> Your graces know that all of us have one Teacher, and that under him we are fellow disciples, fellow pupils. And the fact that we bishops speak to you from a higher place does not make us your teachers; but it's the one who dwells in all of us that is the Teacher of us all. He was talking to all of us just now in the gospel, and saying to us what I am also saying to you; he says it, though about us, about both me and you: *If you remain in my word* — not mine, of course, not Augustine's, now speaking, but his, who was speaking just now from the gospel. . . .[16]

This notion of joint inquiry reminds us of the importance of including as fellow inquirers brothers and sisters throughout the history of the Christian tradition. They not only offer illumination that expands our interpretive horizons and sheds light on difficult passages; they also offer challenges to our tendencies toward malformation and ideological paralysis. For example, Augustine's interpretation of the parting of the Red Sea in relation to the cross and baptism challenges our modern tendency to read the Old Testament in isolation from the New or from any Christian practices. He, like King and many other interpreters, also engages the multiple senses of Scripture in a way that challenges the dominance of historical criticism in biblical studies. King regularly wove together biblical types and allusions in order to illumine God's work in the contemporary plight of African Americans. Further, King's critique of American worship that is severed from justice has challenged Christians to see how clearly the prophetic critique of Israel's injustice toward the poor also indicts systemic dimensions of sin inside and outside the church. Hence, we need to read Scripture in the midst of a wide company of interpreters who both nurture and challenge us. In this sense, we need to read, hear, and perform Scripture "in communion" with the whole company of disciples of Jesus Christ — understood both diachronically through time and synchronically around the world.

Yet even as we seek to interpret and embody Scripture within the com-

---

16. Augustine, *Sermon* 134.1, cited in John Cavadini, "Simplifying Augustine," unpublished paper.

munity of faith, we need also to be attentive to conversations with diverse others outside the church.[17] Their challenges and objections offer important opportunities for us to recognize our capacity for blindness and ideological distortion, even as we also offer challenges and objections to them.[18] There is no special "insider knowledge" that precludes insightful readings by those outside the Christian faith; nevertheless, we recognize a crucial difference between their readings and ours. The difference is found in what the reading is ordered to — for Christians, it is ordered to faithful discipleship in service to the triune God of Scripture.

A third guiding judgment is that saintly exemplars offer guidance in the interpretation and embodiment of Scripture. This is true in several respects: the imitation of saintly exemplars helps us prepare ourselves to see and understand Scripture more deeply; their lives illumine for us key passages of Scripture; and their readings help us grasp the centrality of such interpretive virtues as receptivity, humility, truthfulness, courage, charity, and imagination.

The imitation of saintly exemplars helps us begin to unlearn patterns of sin and to learn patterns of holy living. This is important not only with respect to morality; it is central to interpretation as well. As Athanasius put it:

> For the searching and right understanding of the Scriptures there is need of a good life and a pure soul, and for Christian virtue to guide the mind to grasp, so far as human nature can, the truth concerning God the Word. One cannot possibly understand the teaching of the saints unless one has a pure mind and is trying to imitate their life. Anyone who wants to look at sunlight naturally wipes his eye clear first, in order to make at any rate some approximation to the purity of that on which he looks; and a person wishing to see a city or country goes to the place in order to do so. Similarly, anyone who wishes to understand the mind of the sacred writers must first cleanse his own life, and approach the saints by copying their deeds.[19]

A contemporary illustration of this insight was provided by an Old Testament professor who was asked by a student, dissatisfied with his grade on an exegesis paper, how he might improve the grade. "Become a deeper person," the professor replied. We tend to think that interpretation is a technique to be

17. See Thesis 8.

18. See the longer argument in Stephen E. Fowl and L. Gregory Jones, *Reading in Communion: Scripture and Ethics in Christian Life* (Grand Rapids: Eerdmans, 1991), esp. ch. 5.

19. Athanasius, *The Incarnation of the Word of God* (New York: Macmillan, 1946), p. 96.

improved by diligence or cleverness; rather, it is a habit to be cultivated through wisdom and holiness.

In addition, saintly exemplars illumine key passages of Scripture through the examples of their lives. Hans Urs von Balthasar has noted that often a saint's whole life can be seen as living out just one verse or story of Scripture. For example, Augustine embodied the great twofold commandment of love of God and neighbor, manifested through his teaching, his preaching, and his leadership of the Christian community. King embodied Amos's injunction to "let justice roll down like waters, and righteousness like an ever-flowing stream." St. Therese of Lisieux, in her life's gentle simplicity, embodied the beatitude "Blessed are the pure in heart, for they shall see God." Mother Teresa of Calcutta powerfully embodied Matt 25:31-46 in her focus on reaching out to "the least of these." The life and witness of Dietrich Bonhoeffer was shaped by two particular sayings of Jesus: "He that is not with me is against me" (Matt 12:30) and "He that is not against us is for us" (Mark 9:40). The former led to his disciplined focus on Christian community in *Life Together* and *The Cost of Discipleship*. The latter led to an expansive sense of the Christian's involvement in the world, expressed in his *Ethics* and *Letters and Papers from Prison;* it led also to his joining with non-Christian allies in a plot to assassinate Hitler.

Hence, we are not called to copy all of the saints' deeds; nor could any individual (other than Christ) begin to embody the fullness of Scripture. Rather, we are called to be the body of Christ as the community of faith, learning with and from each other through friendships and the practices of the Christian life. What we may learn together is the holiness that enables us to serve as ministers of reconciliation. Stephen Fowl, describing the dynamics of this life together, notes that our recognition of ourselves as sinners draws us

> into a collection of practices designed to restore, reconcile, and subsequently deepen [our] communion with God and others. As a result, Christians will find themselves transformed by the Spirit to conform more nearly to the image of Christ (cf. 2 Cor. 3:18). Traditionally, this transformation has been (and still is) characterized as growth in virtue. As one might expect, growth in virtue will demonstrate itself in scriptural interpretation as well.[20]

---

20. Stephen E. Fowl, *Engaging Scripture: A Model for Theological Interpretation* (Oxford: Blackwell, 1999), p. 86. Fowl draws on the exemplary readings of Bernard of Clairvaux in his *Homilies on the Song of Songs* to illustrate this claim.

Saintly exemplars, through their holy living, cultivate virtues conducive to wise interpretation. No individual embodies all the virtues; Augustine and King, no less than ordinary interpreters in local congregations, lived as people for whom the virtues remained an eschatological goal as much as a present reality. Even so, saintly patterns of interpretation typically reflect a convergence of key virtues. Receptivity and humility are linked to the recognition that Christ is the only true Teacher and that sin has both epistemological and moral effects. Likewise, truthfulness and courage are linked to a willingness to embody Scripture wherever its wisdom leads us, even at risk to ourselves. Part of the power of Augustine's and King's interpretations, and their lives, lies in their imaginative rendering of the world Scripture imagines, including — as the previous examples suggest — their remarkable capacity to read intertextually to illumine passages in new ways.

I have already indicated how wise interpretation of Scripture is conducive to charity, in that Augustine emphasized that the truth of Scripture is manifested in the love of God and neighbor. But the virtue of charity is also conducive to wise interpretation, especially in the midst of disputes about how best to construe the message of Scripture. A charitable interpreter will seek to find places of overlap and agreement with interlocutors. The presumption, as Stephen Fowl argues, is that "by illuminating points of agreement and by minimizing ascriptions of irrationality one can better account for the words and deeds of others, not that one has to agree with them."[21]

King exemplified this virtue in his recurring attempt to interpret charitably the actions and convictions of white Christians. He was particularly powerful in his capacity to exemplify interpretive charity through his engagement with Jesus' call to "love your enemies and pray for those who persecute you." Fowl sees evidence of Augustine's interpretive charity in a rather unlikely place: Augustine's sermons on John that articulate his disagreements with the Donatists over baptism. Augustine interpreted the Donatists more charitably than would have been expected, thus opening a way for their reincorporation into the body of faith.[22]

As I indicated at the outset, we cannot resolve contemporary disputes about biblical method and biblical authority simply by refamiliarizing ourselves with Scripture. Even so, we can make significant progress if, following such examples as Augustine and King — in all the complexity of their interpretations and the fallibility of their own lives — we cultivate a scriptural imagination, rediscovering Scripture as the word that journeys with us

21. Fowl, *Engaging Scripture*, p. 91.
22. Fowl, *Engaging Scripture*, pp. 91-95.

through catechesis, critical study, and witness. With Christ as our true teacher, we are called to a lifelong journey of joint inquiry in which we seek to embody Scripture wisely and faithfully in Christian community. After all, even as we apprentice ourselves to Christ and to saintly exemplars before and around us, we are simultaneously called to live in such a way that others will want to apprentice themselves to us.

READING DIFFICULT TEXTS

Critical Traditioning: Seeking an Inner Biblical Hermeneutic

Ellen F. Davis

One of the things that has benefited me most in my study has been the occasional question — posed by a teacher, a student, a colleague — that I could not get out of my mind. Some years ago now, a younger colleague (just completing her doctoral study) posed such a question: "Is there any text you would reject?" I had just presented a paper on the binding of Isaac (Gen 22), a text that many consider to have no revelatory value. Her question was for me the most memorable thing said that evening: "Is there, then, *any* text you would reject?" A question that simple has the potential for being haunting; and indeed, it has recurred to me periodically since, whenever I have come up against an uncongenial, even repellant, text. The beauty of the question is that it is confrontational in the best sense. It poses with inescapable simplicity the most basic ethical question of biblical hermeneutics: What should we in the church do with biblical texts that do not seem to accord with a well-considered understanding of the Christian faith? Can we precisely *as church* increase our understanding through listening to such texts and acknowledging the difficulty? Probably all of us would answer, Yes, of course, up to a point. But beyond that I think we probably differ. I am fairly confident that within this group[1] — as among my students, as among biblical scholars — we would find very different opinions on this further question: Is there a point at

<hr/>

1. The "group" originally addressed was a gathering of the Fellows of the Episcopal Church Foundation — i.e., Anglican scholars of religion and theology active in the United States and Canada. I expect that the same difference of opinion I identify here for that group also exists within the readership of the present volume.

<hr/>

A form of this essay appeared in *Anglican Theological Review* 82 (2000): 733-51. Permission granted.

which we have to give up the struggle and admit that in this case edification is not possible? That this particular biblical text must be repudiated as a potential source of valid theological insight? That it is disqualified for public or authoritative reading in the church?

This seems to be the position taken by Elisabeth Schüssler Fiorenza. While acknowledging that all biblical traditions should be transmitted through teaching, she comments that not all traditions are "meaningful and relevant" to Christian communities today. "In some situations it would be wrong to proclaim certain biblical traditions, and at some time one is not able to do more than keep the traditions of biblical faith. We cannot preach all traditions because we do not understand them or they do not come alive for us." And further: "[B]iblical revelation and truth can today be found only in those texts and traditions that transcend and criticize the patriarchal culture and religion of their times."[2] While I agree with her that the biblical text is not to be simply equated with divine revelation, it seems to me that the criterion she suggests threatens to reduce the scriptural base available for theological reflection to a relatively small "canon within the canon."[3]

So my own bias is to say, No, no biblical text may be safely repudiated as a potential source of edification for the church.[4] When we think we have reached the point of zero edification, then that perception indicates that we are not reading deeply enough; we have not probed the layers of the text with sufficient care. The idea that the biblical text may say quite different things when considered at different levels of interpretation is congruent with Augustine's principle of charity as set forth in *De doctrina christiana*.[5] Invoking Au-

2. Elisabeth Schüssler Fiorenza, *Bread, Not Stone: The Challenge of Feminist Biblical Interpretation* (Boston: Beacon, 1984), pp. 37, 41.

3. See her discussion of this concept, *Bread, Not Stone*, pp. 39-41.

4. Thus Brevard Childs states the [New Testament] interpreter's obligation to make use of the whole biblical text while maintaining an awareness of both the complexity of the text's message(s) and the present community's need for insight: "In my judgment, the entire biblical canon in the sense of the whole New Testament collection must remain the authoritative starting point for all exegesis; however, the interpreter must strive to discern afresh a theological construal which does justice to the variegated texture of biblical thought in its dialectical relation to the modern world of the interpreter." Brevard Childs, *The New Testament as Canon: An Introduction* (Philadelphia: Fortress, 1984), p. 42.

5. Augustine's principle, set forth in *De doctrina christiana*, is based on the understanding that all Scripture, when correctly interpreted, conduces to love of God and neighbor. Whenever a literal interpretation does not serve that end, then another approach is necessary: "[W]hatever appears in the divine Word that does not literally pertain to virtuous behavior or to the truth of faith you must take to be figurative. Virtuous behavior pertains to the love of God and of one's neighbor; the truth of faith pertains to a knowledge of God and of one's neighbor." Augustine, *On Christian Doctrine* 3.10.14, trans. D. W. Robertson Jr., LLA 80 (Indianapolis: Bobbs-Merrill, 1958), p. 88.

gustine would be a good Anglican line of defense, yet if I do not take that approach here, it is because I see our current interpretive dilemma as so grave that I must make my argument directly from the biblical text itself. The Episcopal Church is now living under the suspicion, held by many Anglicans in Asia and Africa, that we do not take the Bible seriously as a guide for faith and life. It would be cavalier to dismiss that suspicion as groundless. There is too much sermonic evidence that corroborates it (to name only the most ubiquitous form of evidence). One does not have to do a lot of church-hopping to know that many Episcopal clergy no longer consider it necessary to speak in careful response to the biblical text rather than out of their own spiritual or ethical musings, be they informed by the *Atlantic Monthly* or by pop culture. Although probably most sermons touch upon the biblical text at some point, it is clear that many preachers no longer feel the steady "pressure of the Church's experience of Scripture"[6] weighing upon their own hearts and words, and so the question whether they approve of the text or agree with it never becomes urgent.

At the same time, there is another group of North American Anglicans — a smaller group, I would guess — who do feel the pressure of the text and yet register it negatively. I am thinking of those who would argue, with Schüssler Fiorenza, that the Bible (or large portions of it) is not fit to serve as such a guide. They would make that argument on the basis of a clear hermeneutical presupposition: The Bible is a cultural artifact, and it emanates from a culture whose ethical presuppositions and dispositions were inferior to the best of our own, a culture that was xenophobic, patriarchal, classist, and bloodthirsty. In other words, if the North American church is under suspicion for not taking the Bible seriously, it is equally true that the Bible is under suspicion in the North American church for not being a trustworthy guide for faith and life, for claiming too many victims through the centuries. This suspicion can be applied in different ways to most of the Old Testament, to the Gospels of Matthew and John, to many of the Pauline and Pastoral Epistles, and to the book of Revelation.

It would be cavalier as well to dismiss this suspicion as groundless. There is too much historical evidence that the Bible has been read in ways that seemed at the time to authorize appalling abuse, even murder, of women, Jews, slaves, colonized peoples, homosexuals. One of the great advances

---

6. The phrase is taken from Andrew Louth, *Discerning the Mystery: An Essay on the Nature of Theology* (Oxford: Clarendon, 1983), p. 129. He comments aptly that when the Anglican Church ceased, for a time at least, to feel this pressure (in the mid-seventeenth century), the sermon "degenerated into a moral discourse."

within critical study of the Bible in our own lifetime is that we now have methods for investigating this history of abuse and means of articulating the problem that are gaining wide acceptance within the church. That is unquestionably a good thing, and I take it seriously in the search for an inner biblical hermeneutic that follows. Yet still I would maintain that there is a more excellent way than outright repudiation or public silencing of texts that repel us and seem to present a threat to the marginalized and powerless.

Negotiating Difficulty within the Tradition

The way I propose here is to consider how the biblical writers themselves dealt with difficult texts, that is, how they handled elements of the tradition that they could no longer accept as ethical or edifying. I think this consideration may point to something fundamental in biblical hermeneutics, for what is hermeneutics but the art of negotiating difficulty within the biblical tradition? One premise of this essay, then, is that the history of biblical hermeneutics began centuries before the closure of the canon, as the people we now call the biblical writers responded to the pressure of the tradition *they* had inherited. The artful negotiation of difficulty was a primary factor in producing the biblical books as we have them, as tradents struggled in faith (I am convinced) to preserve and pass on what they had received as authoritative, while at the same time registering for their own and future generations profound changes in the understandings of faith. Negotiation of difficulty was, moreover, a primary element in the formation of the canon as a whole. As I shall try to show here, the balance between preserving the tradition and articulating change is one significant factor in the interaction between the Old Testament and the New.

Michael Fishbane has written a magisterial study of how the biblical tradents worked with an authoritative tradition that nonetheless remained subject to modification. *Biblical Interpretation in Ancient Israel* is to date the most important study of the process of "inner biblical exegesis," through which the Hebrew Bible assumed its present form. Fishbane uses the term to designate a process of scribal adaptation, reinterpretation, and transformation of "a basically fixed *traditum*."[7] He views as "somewhat artificial" the attempt to demarcate sharply the roles of author, as originator of a text, and scribe, as preserver and tradent. Rather, he proposes that there was an overlap

7. Michael Fishbane, *Biblical Interpretation in Ancient Israel* (Oxford: Clarendon, 1985), p. 7.

between the two roles. Accordingly, there is a complex interaction between the two aspects of tradition: *traditio,* the process of creating, changing, and passing on; and *traditum,* the literary deposit that is received as authoritative, interpreted (i.e., changed), and passed on, still authoritative in its altered form.

Fishbane's comment is worth citing at length here, as it bears at several points on the concept of critical traditioning that I shall discuss in the next section of this essay:

> if scribes and authors are considered to be radically distinct, so that au-
> thors only compose texts and scribes only copy them, the occasional
> emending activities of the scribal *traditio* in the [Masoretic Text] would
> produce a *traditum* with multiple levels of authority. However, in contra-
> distinction, if scribes and authors cannot always or productively be dis-
> tinguished in the Hebrew Bible, an emending *traditio* (whose primary
> concern is — in any event — the faithful transmission of the text) does
> not so much interrupt the *traditum* with material of independent author-
> ity as simply supplement or adjust it. Viewed in this way, the *traditum*
> dominates the *traditio* and conditions its operations. And to the extent
> that the scribal *traditio* makes the *traditum* lexically more accessible,
> theologically more palatable, or materially more comprehensive, its oper-
> ations are intended to reinforce the authority of the *traditum* and to serve
> it. Even those scribal remarks which contradict the manifest *traditum,*
> one might add, confirm the dominating presence of the *traditum* in their
> attempts to provide alternatives to it.[8]

Several points from Fishbane's discussion should be highlighted. First and above all, the central concern of the tradents was "the faithful transmission of the text." I believe that the term "faithful" is here to be understood in the strong sense; that is, tradents were not called to be faithful to some "authorial intention" (to cite a cherished notion of modern hermeneutics),[9] conceived as the human understanding of a previous generation of tradents. As I shall try to demonstrate, the biblical writers felt free to disagree with their predecessors about how God's will and word to Israel were to be interpreted. But there was no disagreement about the fact that God *had* spoken to Israel and that Israel consequently had an obligation to try to render that divine

---

8. Fishbane, *Biblical Interpretation,* pp. 86-87.

9. E. D. Hirsch is a prominent proponent of the view that the only valid interpretation is that which reproduces the author's intention. E. D. Hirsch, *Validity in Interpretation* (New Haven: Yale University Press, 1967).

word "in human language," as the rabbis said,[10] that is, as a comprehensible guide for faith and life. Fishbane's central emphasis here is that the scribal-authorial tradents felt bound by the word received, the *traditum,* although in the process of "serving" it, they necessarily modified it. The inference would seem to be that faithful transmission of authoritative tradition must always be something more than rote repetition. On the contrary, it is just because the tradition is authoritative that it demands interpretation and modification so that it may have fresh power to bind a new generation in the easy yoke of faith.

This sense of obligation to the *traditum,* shared by all the tradents, accounts for the fact that the received tradition does *not* evidence "multiple levels of authority," even though the modifications it has undergone may be profound. It is noteworthy that Fishbane considers the changes worked by the scribe-authors to go far beyond such matters as lexical clarification. They include also the presentation of new theological perspectives as alternatives to views or doctrinal positions that were no longer "palatable." Yet even while working far-reaching changes within the tradition, the scribe-authors managed to produce a text that speaks with a unified authority. One might see in this the strength of their common conviction that the word of God, rightly conveyed, is "smooth to the palate" (Ps 119:103). Moreover, the force of that conviction had a bearing on the literary style of the tradition as we have received it. Elements that seem to be viewed as "unpalatable" from the perspective of the final form of the text were not simply eliminated. Rather, as the following study of the so-called conquest tradition in Joshua will show, undesirable elements were retained and submitted to critique, direct or indirect.

It is sometimes implied that the biblical writers' propensity for retention, evident especially in the Hebrew Bible, was a mindless reflex. The tradents were so burdened by the tradition that it made them clumsy; they did not care (nor perhaps even notice) that the juxtaposition of conflicting views makes for labored reading. Or maybe they were afraid to throw anything away; thus the canon evidences something akin to the neurotic compulsion to stuff the basement with old junk. But it seems to me more likely that the preference for retention reflects the author-scribes' understanding that simply throwing away old ideas, even bad ones, is not the most effective way of handling them. For it is easy enough to discard one ideology and replace it with another one, a new idea system devoid of any history. But what distinguishes a tradition from an ideology is just this sense of history. A tradition earns its authority through long rumination on the past. A living tradition is a potentially courageous

10. Cf. the frequent rabbinic dictum "The words of Torah are in human language." *Sifra Kedoshim* 5; Babylonian Talmud *Nedarim* 3a, *Makkot* 12a, *Baba Metzia* 94b.

form of shared consciousness, because a tradition, in contrast to an ideology, preserves (in some form) our mistakes and atrocities as well as our insights and moral victories. Moreover, with its habit of retention, a tradition preserves side by side the disagreements that are still unresolved in the present. So the price that must be paid by those who are (from a biblical perspective) privileged to live within a tradition is accepting a high degree of inherent tension. The possibility open to them, which is not open to committed ideologues, is repentance, the kind of radical reorientation of thinking that the New Testament writers term *metanoia,* literally, "a change of mind."

The strongest canonical expression of the unified authority of the tradition is found near the end of Torah, as God's word is given the last time through Moses: "You shall not add to the word which I am commanding you, and you shall not take away from it, in order to keep the commandments of YHWH your God which I am commanding you" (Deut 4:2; cf. 13:1 Heb). Here Moses embodies the presence and voice of the tradition, unifying in his own person the many hands and even divergent understandings that produced it. I disagree with Robert Polzin's view that Moses here represents the voice of "authoritarian dogmatism" that would like to ban the whole scribal project of interpretation, a dogmatism that the scribal book of Deuteronomy then proceeds to deconstruct.[11] I find insightful Polzin's general view of the tension within Scripture between "authoritarian dogmatism" and "critical traditionalism"; the distinction between the two is seminal for my thinking in this essay. Yet on this point it seems useful to apply Occam's razor. Polzin sees Moses banning "revision or revitalization of God's word" and then the Deuteronomic scribes opposing that position. But it is simpler to see Moses here speaking *for* the scribal tradition; he is providing guidelines for what Fishbane calls "the faithful transmission of the text." Strong interpretation freshens the tradition without adding extraneous elements or detracting from its essentials. This programmatic statement is then followed by that great example of strong interpretation, the Deuteronomic law code. And in light of Moses' dictum, we are now ready to appreciate it. We now see that this Second (giving of the) Law is not adding to Torah from Sinai or taking away from it, even though the changes the Deuteronomists work in the tradition are in some instances profound and far reaching. Change serves precisely to retain the integrity of the tradition. How could it be otherwise, if God's word is to speak with vital force to a new generation, facing the unprecedented opportunity and challenge of living in the promised land?

11. Robert Polzin, *Moses and the Deuteronomist: A Literary Study of the Deuteronomic History* (New York: Seabury, 1980), p. 65.

In the following section, I point to two instances of the negotiation of deep theological difficulty within biblical tradition — instances, in other words, that evidence a disposition I shall call "critical traditioning." The term denotes the willingness to engage in radical rethinking of a formerly accepted theological position. The first example I discuss shows reworking of a tradition within a single book, namely, the conquest tradition as it is passed on to us by the book of Joshua. The second example shows negotiation between what eventually became the two Testaments.

Critical Traditioning at Work

Certainly for contemporary readers of the Bible, one of the gravest ethical problems posed by the Old Testament is the Deuteronomic party line "The only good Canaanite is a dead Canaanite." This party line is given clear theological justification: "It is not on account of your righteousness or on account of the straightforwardness of your heart that you are coming to take possession of their land; but rather on account of the wickedness of these peoples, YHWH your God is dispossessing them before you, and in order to establish the word which YHWH swore to your ancestors, to Abraham, to Isaac, and to Jacob" (Deut 9:5). The perfidy of the Canaanites is deeply embedded in biblical tradition. Its first unambiguous narrative appearance is Shechem's rape of Jacob's daughter, Dinah (Gen 34). Yet even at that early point, the violent retaliation of Dinah's brothers is called into question, on strategic if not moral grounds: "And Jacob said to Simeon and to Levi, 'You have caused me trouble, by making me stink among the inhabitants of the land, the Canaanite and the Perizzite — and I being few in number! And they will band against me and strike me, and I shall be eliminated, I and my house'" (Gen 34:30).

What I wish to show here is that, although Jacob is the first to perceive that Canaanites cannot be slaughtered with impunity, his is not an isolated response. In fact, viewed in light of the final form of the conquest tradition, Jacob-Israel's response may be seen as paradigmatic for the people that assumes his name. Granted, the official party line on the Canaanites is never directly repudiated, and hints of it appear even in the latest books of the Hebrew Bible.[12] But as the story of the so-called conquest unfolds, the standard Deuteronomic line is undermined by the emergence of another voice, one

---

12. In the book of Esther, Haman, the quintessential persecutor of the Jews, is designated "the Agagite" (Esth 3:1, 10, et passim), i.e., the descendant of Agag, the Amalekite king who is condemned by God for Amalekite harassment of Israel in the wilderness (1 Sam 15).

that suggests a very different way of viewing both Canaanites and Israelites. In other words, in the final form of the text, two views are competing for our vote: hard-line Deuteronomism and its subtle opponent, the perspective here termed critical traditioning.[13]

It is a striking narrative fact, and one too little noted, that the purported "wickedness of these [Canaanite] peoples" (Deut 9:5) is never substantiated within the conquest account. The last wicked Canaanites we see are at Baal-Peor in Transjordan (Num 25), and then it is quite clear that they are a problem only because Israel is so eager to "yoke itself" with them in their sexy cult. But once Israel has crossed the Jordan into the promised land, the portraits of the Canaanites are surprisingly positive. Yes, they fight against the invaders (Josh 9:1-2). Yet it is noteworthy that all the Canaanites who are not faceless — that is, all who have names or any real narrative presence — are in fact "friendlies." The Gibeonites scheme and lie only in order to make covenant alliance with Israel. The terms are humble enough: "And Joshua made them on that day hewers of wood and drawers of water for the congregation and for the altar of YHWH, even to this day . . ." (Josh 9:27). If anyone in all the Hebrew Scriptures exemplifies the psalmist's ideal of perpetual "doorkeeping in the house of [Israel's] God" (Ps 84:11 Heb), it is the Gibeonites.

Similarly, Rahab the Canaanite harlot is the first to confess orthodox Israelite faith within the borders of the promised land — and to an Israelite audience, namely, the two spies whom Joshua sent out "on the sly" (חֶרֶשׁ, *kheresh*, Josh 2:1). The note of secrecy is already mildly jarring, since God seems to have authorized bold entry into the land: "Only be strong and of good courage" (1:6, 7, 9, 18). On the other hand, no divine authorization has been given for a further spy mission. Is it possible that the mission is meant to be a secret from God? Could this be the first hint that even Joshua is not completely confident that adherence to God's Torah is itself sufficient guarantee of Israelite success? Doubts accumulate as the story proceeds. For even if the

---

13. In *Moses and the Deuteronomist* (see n. 11), Robert Polzin comments thus on the function of "critical traditionalism" in Deuteronomy, over against "authoritarian dogmatism," the perspective that I have called the party line: "[T]he ultimate semantic authority of the book is busy 'taking over' these overt positions in the service of a dominating point of view that is ceaselessly a softening, rather than a rejection, of an unconditional covenant between God and Israel, and a diminution, for varying reasons, of the unique status of Israel and of their prophet Moses" (p. 67). I find persuasive the main points of his argument about the concept of critical traditionalism. My modification of his terminology ("traditioning") follows the suggestion of Christopher Duraisingh in his essay "Contextual and Catholic: Conditions for Cross-Cultural Hermeneutics," *Anglican Theological Review* 82 (2000): 679-701. The notion of traditioning better reflects the fact that a process, not a fixed ideology, is at work.

secret mission should itself be legitimate, a brothel in downtown Jericho, which evidently has a hotline to the palace (2:2), is an unpromising place to begin it. Moreover, the spies are cast in a distinctly antiheroic light. At the moment of Rahab's confession, they are hiding under the bundles of flax that are drying on her roof. Despite this unimpressive showing, Rahab, with remarkable prescience, recites the Israelite creed:

> I know that YHWH has given to you the land. . . . For we have heard how YHWH dried up the waters of the Red Sea before your faces, when you set out from Egypt, and what you did to the two kings of the Amorites who are across the Jordan, to Sihon and to Og, whom you put to the ban. We heard, and our hearts melted, and no longer is there spirit left standing in any person because of you. For YHWH your God, he is God in the heavens above and on the earth beneath. (2:9-11)

So the conquest account begins with a sort of ethical and theological inversion. The power of Israel's God is perceived, affirmed, and even celebrated by the "conquered." It is due to the religious perceptiveness of a Canaanite woman and harlot, for God's sake, that the Israelites first gain a toehold in the promised land. In the story of Rahab, the stock notion of Canaanite wickedness is ironized and radically relativized, if not demolished altogether. Moreover, the corresponding notion of Israelite faithfulness is certainly not strengthened. Indeed, in the whole conquest account, the only recorded sins in the promised land are those committed by Israelites.[14] Polzin comments on the inversion thus: "The underlying ideological position of the Rahab story as a preview of the entire Book of Joshua is that some nations (represented by Rahab) will be spared a punishment they deserve, just as Israel (also represented by Rahab) obtains a land they do not deserve."[15]

The seminal story of Rahab is not likely to have been wholly an invention of the "critical traditionalist" who used it to counter classic Deuteronomic dogmatism. If we imagine, following Fishbane, that the Deuteronomistic tradition was reworked by many hands over (probably) centuries,

14. Indeed, in the whole Deuteronomistic History, Jezebel is, I believe, the only Canaanite villain who appears on Israelite soil. Tellingly, her role in engineering the murder of Naboth (1 Kgs 21) and the appropriation of his God-given piece of land is in effect an undoing of the "conquest." But she is the exception who proves the rule established at the outset. Jezebel the Canaanite princess has the opportunity to function as wicked with respect to Israel only because the king of Israel installs her in the royal palace and lets her teach him how to "exercise kingship over Israel" (1 Kgs 21:7). So in the final analysis, her action is merely an extension of the established pattern of Israelite wickedness in the land.

15. Polzin, *Moses and the Deuteronomist*, p. 90.

then the early antecedents of the present conquest account may have been self-congratulatory accounts of whatever Israelite victories there were. Those victory accounts were told with a straight face, or rather, what humor they had was not aimed at showing up Israelites. For example, Rahab's name was probably an old soldiers' joke. The Semitic word means "wide"; in Ugaritic epic literature, it appears as a term for the female genitalia.[16] People heard the name and chuckled; they knew what to make of this "broad," or so they thought. But as the story comes to us now, what we might suppose to have been its early intent has been completely transformed. The literary means by which this ethical and theological transformation has been accomplished are aptly identified by Leslie Brisman, commenting on another reworked tradition, as "the controlled silences and ironies of the author of the passage *qua author*," through which we may hear "a voice of moral reservation that comes like the voice of God."[17]

My second example of the artful negotiation of difficulty is Jesus' reinterpretation of the levitical legislation, as it is represented in the Synoptic Gospels. I choose this example also because I think it touches on ethical, even ecclesiological, matters that are pressing for contemporary Christians. For the church universal has been now for several decades deeply divided over levitical issues: the ordination of women and practicing homosexuals, the blessing of same-sex unions. These are levitical issues because they point to the one great question that is central to the vast amount of levitical — that is, priestly — material found in Torah, namely, What constitutes a holy people? In other words, what is the nature and discipline of a community capable of hosting the presence of God in its midst (cf. Lev 9:6)? For that is what holiness is. It is hospitality toward God, living in such a way that God may feel at home in our midst.

The fact that Christians are arguing about levitical issues shows our debt to and affinity with Judaism. For that kind of interpretive argument has been the very hallmark of rabbinic Judaism from the outset (and as Fishbane shows, it grows out of the interpretive process active within ancient Israel, the process that produced the Bible). It is also a generative factor within the synagogue community no less important than is prayer itself. In other words, Jews characteristically debate about holiness matters, first because decisions on those matters determine how they live together and with God, and second be-

---

16. I am indebted to Frank Spina for pointing out this connection.

17. Leslie Brisman, "Sacred Butchery: Exodus 32:25-29," in *Theological Exegesis: Essays in Honor of Brevard S. Childs,* ed. C. Seitz and K. Greene-McCreight (Grand Rapids: Eerdmans, 1999), p. 181.

cause they differ on those matters. Some degree of difference is tolerable, indeed desirable. Disagreement calls forth new interpretation, and that keeps the tradition alive and authoritative within the community, as we have seen. But sometimes disagreement in matters of interpretation becomes too great to be tolerated within a single community of religious practice. That is what happened with the Jesus movement in the latter part of the first century, and the Gospels trace the beginnings of those ultimately intolerable disagreements to Jesus' own style of reading Scripture.

As the New Testament writers represent it, one of the key points of contention was Jesus' understanding of how Jews are to relate to (or alternatively, how God sees Jews in relation to) Gentiles. It is no coincidence, then, that the evangelists highlight how Jesus read Leviticus. For the purity legislation that is such a prominent element in that book serves to make a Jewish "lifestyle" distinctive in unmistakable ways. In Jesus' time, it had served that function with remarkable success for at least half a millennium.[18] Despite the fact that for most of that time Jews had been a diaspora people, or vassals in their own land, observance of the dietary laws above all proved to have powerful countervalent force against pressure and temptation to assimilate. In other words, the levitical legislation afforded Jews effective daily reminders that they were a people set apart by God.

Understanding how Jesus and his followers were reading Leviticus may begin with the "Summary of the Law," which appears in all three Synoptic Gospels. For our purposes, Luke's version of the encounter with the "legal expert" (νομικός, *nomikos,* Luke 10:25) is especially interesting. Jesus reciprocates his question about how to inherit eternal life with another question: "What is written in the Law? *How do you read?*" (10:26). The expert's answer is unmistakably authentic; early rabbinic sources focus special attention on the commandment "Be loving to your neighbor" (Lev 19:18b). Akiba, the greatest teacher of second-century Judaism, calls this "the great principle of the Torah" *(Sifra).* Thus Rabbi Hillel offers his summary "while standing on one leg": "That which is hateful to you, do not do to your neighbor. That is Torah; all the rest is commentary. Go and study."

But now (in Luke's account) comes the crucial question — "Who is my

---

18. The book of Leviticus probably received its present form sometime early in the exilic period (late sixth century B.C.E.). Much of the material was probably composed in writing a century or two before and is based on earlier oral traditions. However, Leviticus assumes its characteristic accent — "You shall be holy, for I, YHWH your God, am holy" (Lev 19:2 et passim) — in the section commonly termed the Holiness Code (chs. 18–26). The Code appears to be a new synthesis of levitical regulations composed in the exilic period as a response to the unprecedented needs of a community living in vassalage and diaspora.

neighbor?" (10:29) — to which Jesus responds with the parable of the Good Samaritan. The inference clearly to be drawn is that the Jew's best neighbor may turn out to be a non-Jew. Less obviously, the choice of a Samaritan as a role model (10:36) has special interest with respect to the question of interpreting Leviticus. For Samaritans were not just garden-variety Gentiles; they were not like the uncircumcised Greeks, who had no knowledge of Torah. Rather, the Samaritans were in their own way a Torah-observant community, but they read, interpreted, and therefore lived in ways that distinguished them from Jews. It is a sad fact of history that authoritative texts held in common but read differently are less likely to create mutual sympathy than bitter division between religious communities. The mention of the Samaritan here might be seen as a sort of prophecy of where the discussion between Jesus and other Jews about interpretation of the Torah would eventually lead. For the Jewish contempt for Samaritans, on which Jesus' parable trades, foreshadowed (only faintly, to our shame) the theological contempt and religious hatred toward Jews that would perdure in Christian communities for two millennia, culminating in the tragic events of the twentieth century.

"Who is my neighbor?" — Luke somewhat tendentiously supposes that the legal expert is "wanting to justify himself" (10:29) when he asks that question. Since the question is unique to Luke's imaginative rendering of the event and may well originate with him, he is entitled to his own interpretation of his character's motive. But another line of interpretation is possible, one that takes more serious account of the fact that Jesus and the legal expert are talking about how to read Torah. For even if Luke did put the question in the legal expert's mouth, and did so with a certain anti-Pharisaic edge, it is nonetheless an exegetically relevant question with respect to Leviticus. Within that book, which probably assumed final form in response to assimilationist pressure on exilic Israel, the obvious answer would seem to be that it is only the Israelite "neighbor" to whom love can safely be shown. Such an intra-Israelite interpretation is supported both by semantics and by immediate literary context in Leviticus 19. Semantically, the Hebrew word רֵעַ *(reʿa)* indicates something more than someone who lives nearby. Rather, it implies a deep bond and obligation within the context of community life; normally in Torah it means one's fellow Israelite. This interpretation is initially secured by the fact that the immediately preceding lines contain multiple references to "your kin" and "your people."

Yet later in the very same chapter, that intra-Israelite interpretation is destabilized. Leviticus 19:34 has been formulated as an unmistakable echo of this cardinal principle of Torah: "As a native among you shall be to you the sojourner who sojourns with you; *you shall be loving to him as (to) yourself,* for you were sojourners in the land of Egypt." The effect of that echo is to force wide the scope of the love commandment. Through the proximity of these two verses, the resident alien has been redefined as a neighbor to whom is due the covenant obligation of love. So we see that the levitical vision of Israelite distinctiveness and solidarity already contains the mustard seed that will grow to burst the limits of that vision. What happens with Jesus and his followers is that the levitical vision of holiness is burst open in a way that is heavy with historical and theological consequences. Paul's mission to the Gentiles is inconceivable without such a reinterpretation of the levitical understanding of what constitutes covenant community.

To return to the concept I am seeking to elucidate here, Jesus' parable of the Good Samaritan is a work of "critical traditioning." He is working from within the tradition toward a profoundly new understanding of the tradition.[19] Luke is not the only evangelist to portray Jesus thus, and specifically with respect to levitical tradition. Three evangelists give considerable attention to the de-emphasis upon the dietary regulations[20] that is evidenced by Jesus and his followers (Matt 15:1-20; Mark 7:1-23; Acts 11:1-18). But how consequential that reevaluation of purity practice is becomes apparent only with the remarkable story of the "Canaanite woman" (Matt 15:22; cf. Mark 7:26, "a Syrophoenician") that follows immediately in Matthew and Mark. In asking him to heal her demonized daughter, she challenges Jesus to step across the invisible border separating Jew from Gentile. And Jesus hands her a line that makes him sound like an "authoritarian dogmatist" with respect to Jewish-Gentile relations: "It is not fair to take the children's food and throw it to the dogs" (Matt 15:26; cf. Mark 7:27). Without pausing to gasp, she exposes the inadequacy of that position: "Yes sir, and even the dogs eat from the crumbs that fall from their lords' table" (Matt 15:27; cf. Mark 7:28). Jesus accepts the correction; he heals the child. In Matthew and Mark, that act of power both validates his sovereign reinterpretation of Torah with respect to defilement and reveals that the boundary between Jew and Gentile is now blurry indeed. In Matthew and Mark, the incident of the Canaanite or Syrophoenician woman might be seen as parallel to Luke's parable of the Good Samaritan, which forces us to reconsider who is the neighbor to whom covenant love is due.

19. Richard Bauckham argues that "the general halakhic principle which the parable suggests — that the love commandment should always override others in cases of conflict — seems to be unparalleled." Richard Bauckham, "The Scrupulous Priest and the Good Samaritan: Jesus' Parabolic Interpretation of the Law of Moses," *New Testament Studies* 44 (1998): 475.

20. Matthew does not go all the way with Mark in asserting outright that Jesus "declared all foods clean" (Mark 7:19), and Luke sees that definitive move occurring with Peter's vision in Joppa, sometime after Jesus' death.

In both instances, we see Jesus reconceiving the essentially levitical no-tion of holiness. Henceforth, holiness must be demonstrated, not as internal consolidation within the Jewish community, but rather as the power to reach out to the stranger without losing one's own footing in the tradition. The levitical Holiness Code, as we have seen, welcomes the sojourner who immi-grates to the people Israel (Lev 19:34). But Jesus himself becomes an emigrant from Israel, at least for a time, when he travels to the district of Tyre and Sidon. Even more, there he submits to be instructed on no small point of ho-liness by a woman whom Matthew pointedly designates a "Canaanite." This story is the most dramatic illustration in all Scripture of what critical traditioning means. It means exercising profound, even godly, humility, opening oneself to learn something previously unimaginable about the fundaments of life with God — and to learn it from "the least of these."

Critical Charity

This is, or should be, the scandal of every introductory Bible course, in semi-nary and in parish: The Scriptures are chock-full of embarrassing, offensive, and internally contradictory texts, texts we do not wish to live with, let alone live *by*. The burden of this essay is to argue that this is not accidental and maybe not ultimately regrettable, since it is the means by which we are being formed in the disposition I am calling critical traditioning. In other words, we are to see the evident difficulty of the tradition as an invitation to accept re-sponsibility for mediating a tension that abides in any community living in response to an authoritative text. That tension exists between two concerns:[21] one, the traditionalist concern to acknowledge the integrity of the tradition and to preserve it through our interpretations; and two, the critical concern that there be a benefit to the community from its experience of the text. Per-haps an acceptable minimal definition of such benefit would be that a socially and politically heterogeneous community is able to retain a vital religious identity through varying historical circumstances at the same time that it continues to feel what I have previously called the pressure of the text on its faith and practice.

I have given two extended examples of the operation of critical traditioning within the Bible and have characterized in more general terms

21. I believe the elements held in tension are the same regardless of whether the text tra-dition has reached the state of canonical closure (a point on which contemporary faith commu-nities obviously differ from the Israelite tradents of the text-in-formation).

what might be the philosophical base for that hermeneutical disposition. I conclude by identifying four principles of critical traditioning.

First, the text is difficult — that is, it presents ethical difficulties for its interpreters. There is a tension between the integrity of the text and the moral integrity and well-being of the community that lives with it. Yet difficulty in itself is no impediment to the text's authoritative status. On the contrary, it is probably a reliable axiom that the more revered is a textual tradition as it develops over a long period of time, the more likely it is to have been found difficult. And as we have seen, that discovery has the potential for enhancing the tradition through multiple, often divergent, interpretive voices that are passed on within the tradition.[22]

Second, the difficult text is worthy of charity from its interpreters. Interpretive charity does not mean pity but rather something more like generosity and patience toward the text, and it is evidenced largely in the willingness to contend with the recurrent and not wholly resolvable difficulties that attend reliance on this text. Here I am thinking primarily of ethical difficulties, not linguistic or literary difficulties in the narrow sense. However, as I have tried to show, careful attention to words and literary structure is part of the ethical obligation that charity toward the text demands of us. Charitable reading requires considerable effort; it is easier to dispense with the difficult text. Those who regard a text as religiously authoritative are willing to sustain that effort, because they perceive it, in some sense, as a gift from God. They may not see it as a divinely dictated word (although some would), but they see it nonetheless as an earnest of God's blessing for those who seek God in faith. The holy text thus deserves our best. Moshe Halbertal comments perceptively:

> In the case of the Scriptures, there is an *a priori* interpretive commitment to show the text in the best possible light. Conversely, the loss of this sense of obligation to the text is an undeniable sign that it is no longer perceived as holy. Making use of the principle of charity, the following principle can be stipulated: the degree of canonicity of a text corresponds to the amount of charity it receives in its interpretation. The more canonical a text, the more generous its treatment.[23]

---

22. In postbiblical tradition, the outstanding example here would be the Mishnah, whose style Moshe Halbertal represents as "the codification of controversy." Moshe Halbertal, *People of the Book: Canon, Meaning, and Authority* (Cambridge, Mass.: Harvard University Press, 1997), p. 45.

23. Halbertal, *People of the Book*, p. 29. Although these are the only "principles" Halbertal states, in formulating my own principles I have been much instructed by his extended discussion of interpretive charity.

Third, ethical consciousness, informed by prayerful life within the faith community, is a legitimate hermeneutical tool. One might say that charity toward the text must finally prove to be congruent with the operation of charity within the interpretive community. Augustine's principle of charity is an early Christian example of such a search for congruence.[24] An interesting contemporary example is Stephen Fowl's suggestion that the issue of "how and under what circumstances homosexuals are to be recognized and included in the church" be investigated in a manner analogous to the first Jewish Christians' discernment about Gentile inclusion, as recorded in Acts 10–15. The force of the analogy is that discernment in that case involved witnessing, through personal contact and hospitality, the new work of the Spirit active in those new friends. Similarly, Fowl argues that attempts to resolve our divisions about homosexual Christians "will fail as long as the ecclesial practices of forming friendships through acts of hospitality which then enable Christians to testify about the work of the Spirit are in disrepair."[25]

Fourth, the validity of a given interpretation does not depend on the interpreter's proximity to the authorial source, since an authoritative text is one authorized for repeated rereading and reinterpretation within the faith community. Such proximity might be understood temporally, in which case the principle would mean that early interpretations are not necessarily more authentic. Equally, proximity might be understood hermeneutically. In this case, the principle would mean that attempts to reconstruct original authorial intention do not always produce the best interpretation. Therefore, the principle serves to moderate enthusiasm for historical-critical method, yet it argues also against enshrining "pre-critical" exegetical methods and ancient interpretations. In answer to *un*critical enthusiasts of both stripes, critical traditioning offers the possibility that new and excellent interpretations will arise in response to new challenges. Furthermore, as we saw in the case of the "Canaanite" woman, the impetus for these new interpretations may come from those outside the tradition. I believe that something like this is now happening with respect to the ecological crisis, as Christians and Jews begin a more careful examination of biblical and theological traditions in order to understand our relation to nonhuman creation. It is noteworthy that this interest has awakened in response to ecological work being done (largely) by secular physical and social scientists, some of whom accuse the church of silence or even complicity in the depredation of the earth. Yet these critics of

24. See n. 5 above.

25. Stephen E. Fowl, *Engaging Scripture: A Model for Theological Interpretation* (London: Blackwell, 1998), p. 127.

the religious tradition have now become teachers to those within the tradition. With their help, a growing number of theologians, biblical scholars, and congregational leaders are engaged in a process of massive recovery, bringing to light aspects of the Bible that had been wholly neglected for millennia except by a few earthy mystics like Hildegard of Bingen, Francis of Assisi, Thomas Traherne, and Rav (Abraham Isaac) Kook. This is one of many encouraging examples of what critical traditioning aims to achieve: to deepen appreciation of the integrity of the tradition and, at the same time, to enable the community to use its living tradition more creatively in response to the needs of the world.

Living Dangerously: Genesis 22 and the Quest for Good Biblical Interpretation

R. W. L. Moberly

"Do you understand what you are reading?" "How can I, unless someone guides me?" This conversation between Philip and the Ethiopian eunuch (Acts 8:30-31) provides in a nutshell the justification for scholarly biblical study. Scripture is not some kind of esoteric puzzle, and many of its words speak directly to the hearts of many people in many different contexts. Nonetheless, there is much in Scripture that can be more or less puzzling even to a sympathetic and informed reader, and those parts that do not *appear* puzzling are not by that token necessarily more likely to be well understood. Hence the need for the labors of interpretation, and with texts as ancient and as studied as those of Scripture, the resultant literature of interpretation is extensive indeed.

Yet the task that is meant to help and guide the reader quickly creates a new problem: interpreters differ and disagree, and the disagreements can sometimes be fundamental. When guides wish to lead in different directions, one cannot follow them all. Choices must be made, and the choices here, as with most important decisions in life, come down ultimately to a matter of trust: Who can be trusted, and on what basis?

The moving and memorable story of Abraham's journey in the land of Moriah to sacrifice his long-awaited and beloved son, Isaac, in obedience to God — that is, Gen 22[1] — has for both Christians and Jews been a key passage within Scripture, a story where much that is central within Scripture is somehow distilled, compressed, focused. Correspondingly, the literature of interpretation is a lake both broad and deep.[2] The story therefore offers a good

---

1. I will use "Gen 22" as a convenient shorthand for Gen 22:1-19. In Jewish tradition, Gen 22 is called the Akedah ("Binding"); the term is taken from the verb in 22:9.

2. I regret that it is not possible here even to begin to do justice to the richness of the literature, some of which suggestively informed certain of our CTI discussions.

case study for how, at the outset of the twenty-first century, one can engage with an ancient biblical text that raises big and enduring issues and, in so engaging, learn something about how to choose good interpretative guides amid the clamor of surrounding voices.[3]

The Interpretative Debate Surrounding Genesis 22

The vast majority of Jews and Christians down the ages (and also Muslims, though the story takes a distinctive form within Islam),[4] whatever their differences of emphasis, have interpreted the story of Gen 22 positively. For example, in the two places where the New Testament explicitly cites the passage, Abraham is a model of that right responsiveness to God which in Christian vocabulary is designated "faith," whether it takes the form of trusting God for a future as yet unseen (Heb 11:1-2, 17-19; 12:1-2) or of showing that a true response to God must be a total response (Jas 2:18-24). More recently, Gerhard von Rad, one of the outstanding Christian interpreters of the Old Testament in the twentieth century, climaxes his exposition of the text by saying: "Therefore, unfortunately, one can only answer all plaintive scruples about this narrative by saying that it concerns something much more frightful than child sacrifice. It has to do with a road out into Godforsakenness, a road on which Abraham does not know that God is only testing him."[5] The resonances of "road out into Godforsakenness" with Jesus' cry on the cross "My God, my God, why have you forsaken me?" (Matt 27:46; Mark 15:34) indicate that von Rad is interpreting Abraham by analogy with Jesus, as one who embodies the dynamics found supremely in the death of Jesus but also more generally in the life of faith.

Particularly worthy of note is an assessment by Clemens Thoma. Although the context of Thoma's remarks is a study of the impact of Gen 22 within antiquity, what he says characterizes what has tended to be the case in many periods of history, up to and including today, for those, both Jewish and Christian, for whom the story functions as Scripture:

---

3. The following is for the most part a compression of the fuller discussion in my *The Bible, Theology, and Faith: A Study of Abraham and Jesus* (Cambridge: Cambridge University Press, 2000), chs. 3-5. Fuller elaboration and documentation with regard to the positions adopted can be found there.

4. Qur'an, Sura 37:83-113.

5. Gerhard von Rad, *Genesis*, 3rd ed. (London: SCM, 1972; ET from 9th German ed.), p. 244.

The narrative found in Gen 22 had not only a significant religious and spiritual development in late Old Testament times and afterwards, but above all, it affected the history of piety. Many people, finding themselves in difficult situations, were able to sustain themselves on the strength of this account about Abraham who, confidently obeying the God who was "testing" him (Gen 22,1), was prepared to slaughter his only and beloved son, and about Isaac who was willing to be offered as a sacrifice. This expression of obedience by Abraham and submission by Isaac constitutes an example worthy of imitation. The story motivated people to accept obediently and submissively in their lives what seemed incomprehensible, unendurable and contradictory and to reflect upon it. . . .

. . . It is generally accepted then that the adherent of Akedah-spirituality imitates Abraham in a special way when he is threatened with the loss or removal by force of something beloved and dear to him. In contrast, when someone finds himself as a sacrifice on the altar, when rejected, ill or close to death, then Isaac comes into the center of focus. Ultimately the person concerned with Akedah-spirituality concentrates his inner sensibilities neither on Abraham nor on Isaac, nor on the two of them together, but on the God of Abraham, Isaac and other great witnesses of faithful obedience.[6]

Although it is difficult to escape some kind of existential engagement with a text such as Gen 22, the kind of engagement may vary greatly. When the scholarly questions put to the biblical text were predominantly those to do with the history of the religious thought and practice of ancient Israel, as tended to be the case in the nineteenth and twentieth centuries, then existential questions did not disappear (for academic biblical scholars were still overwhelmingly Christian, of one or another form of Protestantism) but tended to be transposed or marginalized. One of the most influential twentieth-century commentators on Genesis, Hermann Gunkel, wanted to rebut Wellhausen's contention that the stories of Genesis were only as old as the date of those who wrote them (the period of the monarchy, ninth to seventh centuries B.C.) by showing that ancient legends *(Sage)* underlie the written text. Thus his prime interest (apart from adducing religio-historical parallels to motifs in the text) is in a history of attitudes to child sacrifice underlying the text. He constructs a form of the story in which it was a "cult

---

6. Clemens Thoma, "Observations on the Concept and the Early Forms of Akedah-Spirituality," in *Standing before God: Studies on Prayer in Scriptures and in Tradition with Essays in Honor of John M. Oesterreicher,* ed. A. Finkel and L. Frizzell (New York: Ktav, 1981), pp. 213-22, quote 213, 215.

legend," a legitimation of the offer of an animal instead of a child at the otherwise obscure sanctuary of Jeruel (a place in the Judean wilderness attested in 2 Chr 20:16).[7] Yet Gunkel still offers an existential engagement that relates to his classification of the material as legend:

> Historiography, which wants to instruct concerning actual events, is by nature prose. Legend, however, is by nature poetry. It seeks to gladden, elevate, inspire, touch. Thus, one who wants to do justice to such old accounts must have sufficient esthetic sensibility to hear an account as it is and as it wants to be. Here, too, it is not a question of reaching an unkind or even skeptical judgment, but rather lovingly to understand the nature of things. Whoever has the heart and the sensitivity must observe, for example, that the narrative of Isaac's sacrifice is not concerned with establishing certain historical facts. Instead, the hearer should feel the heart-rending pain of the father who is to sacrifice his own child with his own hand and, then, his infinite thankfulness and joy when God's grace frees him from this heavy sacrifice. Whoever has recognized the unique poetical charm of these old legends becomes angry at the barbarian — there are also pious barbarians — who thinks that he can only value these accounts if he treats them as prose and history. The judgment that such an account is legend is not meant to diminish it. Instead, it is meant to express the evaluator's sense of something of its literary beauty and his belief that he has thereby understood it. Only ignorance can understand such a judgment as impious. Instead it is the judgment of piety and love.[8]

Many of Gunkel's points, above all his concern to understand the text for what it is, are well taken. The genre of the text is indeed a key issue, and the recognition that it is legend rather than history (though both of these modern categories need careful definition if they are to be useful) is surely correct, as is his assertion that such a judgment need not be "unkind/skeptical" in such a way as to "diminish" the text; the appropriate bearing of judgments of piety/faith upon the text also remains a live issue. Yet his frame of reference is an aesthetic, indeed strongly Romantic, sensibility that is hardly as self-evident as Gunkel seems to suppose. The imaginative engagement with the text whereby one experiences "heartrending pain" and "infinite thankfulness and joy" seems designed to encourage a kind of emotional roller coaster as a part of the reading experience (akin to what is commonly experienced at

---

7. Hermann Gunkel, *Genesis* (Macon, Ga.: Mercer University Press, 1997; ET from 3rd German ed. of 1910), pp. 233-40.

8. Gunkel, *Genesis*, p. xi.

the movies), an emotionalism that is at a considerable remove from a reading that engenders obedient submission to the unendurable, incomprehensible, and contradictory.

For all that Gunkel's proposed aesthetic response to the text differs markedly from that of classic Jewish and Christian spirituality, it can still be classified as broadly "positive" in its stance toward the text. Yet over the last two hundred years there has been a steadily increasing tendency to view the text negatively, as both mistaken in its assumptions and misguided as a reference point for living. A key voice is that of Immanuel Kant at the end of the eighteenth century. Kant polarized philosophy and theology, moral law and religion, always to the advantage of the former:

> In some cases man can be sure that the voice he hears is *not* God's; for if the voice commands him to do something contrary to the moral law, then no matter how majestic the apparition may be, and no matter how it may seem to surpass the whole of nature, he must consider it an illusion. [Here he appends the following as a footnote.] We can use, as an example, the myth of the sacrifice that Abraham was going to make by butchering and burning his only son at God's command (the poor child, without knowing it, even brought the wood for the fire). Abraham should have replied to this supposedly divine voice: "That I ought not to kill my good son is quite certain. But that you, this apparition, are God — of that I am not certain, and never can be, not even if this voice rings down to me from (visible) heaven."[9]

Kant's critique has obvious force, insofar as it is indeed a basic biblical tenet that moral criteria are a fundamental factor in evaluating what should and should not be recognized as coming from God. Yet the critique seeks to overthrow the story as a whole and thereby sets a powerful precedent, which has in one way or another become increasingly attractive to many people in recent years. Clare Amos, for example, in a recent review of Steven Saltzman's *A Small Glimmer of Light: Reflections on the Book of Genesis*, writes:

> I was particularly struck with his comments on the Aqedah — Genesis 22: "Avraham failed the test. He chose God over his son. He chose being God's servant over being his son's father. He loved God more than he loved his own son, and he made the wrong choice" (p. 56).

When I think of the convolutions so many writers, both Christian and

---

9. Immanuel Kant, *The Conflict of the Faculties* (New York: Abaris, 1979; ET from German of 1798), p. 115.

Jewish, get up to in their attempts to "justify" Abraham at this point, I want to give thanks for Saltzman's sanity and say, "three cheers."[10]

Psychoanalyst Alice Miller claims that Gen 22 may have contributed to an atmosphere that makes possible one of the most heinous of contemporary offenses, child abuse.[11] And even biblical scholars who work at close exegesis can see Abraham in general, and Gen 22 in particular, in a thoroughly unfavorable light. David Gunn and Danna Nolan Fewell, for example, in their textbook introduction to narrative criticism, *Narrative in the Hebrew Bible,* offer (with no qualification or alternative interpretation) an account of Abraham as a model of ruthless self-seeking at the expense of others by taking those (on any reckoning, puzzling) stories in which Abraham deceives Pharaoh and Abimelech about Sarah (Gen 12:10-20; 20:1-18) and allows Hagar to be maltreated (16:1-6) as the keys to understanding Abraham's character. They then read Gen 22 in this light:

> Suppose, however, that God is well aware of Abraham's tendency to forfeit his family to danger and uncertainty. What if the test is really designed to see just how far Abraham will go? . . .
>
> . . . Perhaps God needs to see if there is ever a point where Abraham is willing to sacrifice himself rather than his family. He has sacrificed the other members of his household; will he go so far as to sacrifice this son of promise? . . .
>
> What might we have heard from an exemplary Abraham? "Take me! I am old. The boy has his whole life in front of him." Or might we have even heard the Abraham of old (cf. Gen 18:25): "Far be it from you to expect such a thing. . . ." But . . . this Abraham risks nothing for this innocent boy.
>
> Instead, we get nothing but silent obedience. . . . Abraham makes every effort to go through with the sacrifice of his son. Only God's intervention keeps him from murder. . . .
>
> Abraham, ironically, names the place "YHWH will see." . . . But what has YHWH actually seen? On the mountain, YHWH sees a man who fears, a man in need of grace. . . .
>
> Whether or not Abraham has passed the test, we do not know. We fear not.[12]

10. Clare Amos, "Review of S. Saltzman, *A Small Glimmer of Light: Reflections on the Book of Genesis* (Hoboken: Ktav, 1996)," *Expository Times* 108 (1997): 243.

11. Alice Miller, *The Untouched Key: Tracing Childhood Trauma in Creativity and Destructiveness* (New York: Doubleday, 1990), p. 139.

12. David Gunn and Danna Nolan Fewell, *Narrative in the Hebrew Bible* (Oxford: Oxford University Press, 1993), pp. 98, 99, 100.

Does Gen 22 portray a model of true responsiveness to God, to be emulated by others, a source of strength and fortitude when life falls apart? Or does it portray a fundamentally mistaken view of God and an Abraham who is at best misguided and at worst ruthlessly self-seeking? The guides who would help the reader understand the text could hardly disagree more than they do here. Moreover, these interpretative issues are, in important ways, a microcosm of contemporary attitudes toward the Bible (and Christian faith) as a whole. On the one hand, believers have reverenced Scripture as the prime source of light and truth for understanding God and oneself and for living life more wisely and fully and faithfully. On the other hand, many insist that the only honest thing to do with the Bible is to distance oneself from its influence, for it is a sexist, racist, homophobic collection of documents that encourages delusion of oneself and intolerance toward others and justifies it all by the supposedly unimpeachable authority of God.

There are, to be sure, various possible mediating positions. One prevalent option, somewhat à la Gunkel, wants to preserve the Bible as an aesthetic masterpiece, alongside the other literature, art, and music of Western civilization, but to distance it from making any significant difference today to the ways in which one lives, the priorities one holds, or the choices one makes. Yet such a mediating position, where aesthetic response does not accompany but replaces religious response, tends to derive such significance and vitality as it has from its relative proximity to a more traditional assessment of Scripture. For the more the integrity of Scripture is seriously impugned, the less is one likely to take time to find aesthetic delight in its pages or to encourage and enable others to do so. If one seeks aesthetic enrichment, there are so many human artifacts that can be obviously and satisfyingly rewarding that it seems increasingly odd to resort to religious texts that have passed their "use by" date.

The issues at stake, therefore, in the interpretation of Gen 22, especially insofar as they focus the wider question of the status and interpretation of the Bible as a whole, are fundamental.

Some Criteria for Christian Scriptural Interpretation

It is not possible in this context to offer any comprehensive account of how Christians should approach the Old Testament as Christian Scripture or to discuss how the purposes of faith do and do not require those methods and skills and forms of knowledge that have to do with ancient languages and historical understanding, which have their own integrity and disciplines and which have been central to the development of modern biblical criticism. Rather, I wish briefly to set out five principles for the contextualizing of technical skills, principles that I believe to be central to Christian engagement with the Old Testament (though they do *not* represent a general hermeneutical program).

First, the world of the Bible is still in a real sense our world. In saying this I am not discounting the problems posed by the enormous cultural differences between the world of the Bible (itself made up of significantly different cultural contexts) and the urban-oriented, technological, mobile, and individualistic world of today, even though these make problematic any easy formulations of common humanity. Rather, I wish to make two affirmations, without which historic Christian faith can hardly function: (a) human beings now are not fundamentally different from then; both then and now the basic existential realities of life and death and choices of good or evil persist (an assumption we make whenever we seek to understand any great classic from Gilgamesh or Homer onward); and (b) the God of whom the Bible speaks is the only true God, with whom, now no less than then, humanity has to do.

Second, the Bible is our own particular story, as Christians. It is not only that humanity and God are depicted in the Bible but that the particular story of Israel and Jesus is our story. That is, the Bible is the story of how and why there are such people as Jews and Christians in God's world at all. As a child forms his or her identity in large part through absorbing particular cultures, so one way in which we grow as Christians is through absorbing a biblical and Christian pattern of thought and life. This is, of course, a prime reason why regular reading of Scripture, both corporate and individual, so as to "read, mark, learn, and inwardly digest" its content, is a basic spiritual discipline.[13]

Third, we must read the scriptural text with total imaginative seriousness. It is a curious paradox that many people in a contemporary culture that does most of its thinking via stories, either the novel or the film, should find it difficult to recognize that the biblical writers may have operated in a markedly similar way or to allow that they may have done so with the kind of subtlety and sophistication that distinguishes skilled communicators. Questions of textual composition and originating historical context, questions that have loomed large in much modern biblical study, unarguably have their place.

---

13. "Blessed Lord, who hast caused all holy Scriptures to be written for our learning: Grant that we may in such wise hear them, read, mark, learn, and inwardly digest them, that by patience and comfort of thy holy Word, we may embrace and ever hold fast the blessed hope of everlasting life, which thou hast given us in our Saviour Jesus Christ." Collect for the Second Sunday in Advent, *The Book of Common Prayer* of the Church of England. This prayer also appears in *The Book of Common Prayer* of the Episcopal Church, USA (1979), p. 184.

Too often, however, they can function to disable rather than enable serious imaginative engagement with the text, for they tend to direct attention to questions about the text rather than a questioning of what the text is about. There is an analogy in the way we may try to disengage ourselves from uncomfortable suspense in a film by saying, "It's only a film," or, "They're only special effects"; the crunch comes when we know full well all such "only's" but it makes no difference because we find we are hooked anyway. If we will not read the Bible with at least the same degree of imaginative engagement we accord to our favorite novels or soaps, no contemporary account of biblical authority or trustworthiness is likely to be much more than a form of words.

Fourth, Scripture consistently (though not, of course, exclusively) deals with basic and perennial issues of life. Although Christians acknowledge this in principle, in practice the real force of many biblical texts is too easily blunted. On the one hand, we often simply fail to grasp what a story is about and instead content ourselves with focusing on circumstantial details (an abundance of which, usually genuinely interesting, present themselves to anyone who works seriously on the biblical text). On the other hand, we think we see the concern of the text but then either make it sound trite and moralistic or make every biblical writer sound like a certain popular understanding of St. Paul or an exposition of our own favored theological insights. Trivialization of Scripture is so common that we usually do not even recognize when we are doing it.

Fifth, because the enduring issues of life and death are at heart moral and spiritual issues, we become better at engaging with them insofar as we grow in our own moral and spiritual literacy. This, in essence, is what is meant by the historic practice of reading Scripture within the context of the rule of faith, which aims so to guide our thinking and living that we will be more likely to realize, in ourselves and others, the life-giving transformations to which God calls us (though sadly this is not always what happens, for the rule, like anything else, may be misunderstood and misused). We need to relearn the disciplines of genuinely attending to the biblical text, of recognizing how it searchingly probes enduring issues of life and death, and of realizing the positive transformations of life that are thereby made possible through faith. We best do this — indeed, probably *only* do this — as we are willing to open and expose ourselves to God and other people and to live truly and faithfully in the way the Bible envisages.

Preliminary Exegesis and Interpretation of Genesis 22

We turn now to the specifics of the biblical text. The story is introduced by the explicit statement that God "tested" (נִסָּה, *nissah*) Abraham (v. 1) in requiring him to sacrifice his only and beloved son, Isaac, in the land of Moriah (v. 2). The test is unfolded in Abraham's compliance with the divine requirement up to and including the penultimate action of taking the knife for slaughtering his son — at which point the angel of YHWH pronounces that Abraham has thereby demonstrated that he "fears God" (properly, that he is a "God-fearer," יְרֵא אֱלֹהִים, *yere' 'elohim* — that is, a particular type of person, v. 12). Abraham's ensuing sacrifice of the ram in place of Isaac is memorialized in the name Abraham gives to the place, "YHWH sees/provides" (יְהוָה יִרְאֶה, *yhwh yir'eh*, v. 14), and the angel then pronounces emphatic blessing (בָּרֵךְ אֲבָרֶכְךָ, *barekh 'avarekhekha*) upon Abraham (vv. 16-18). These four key verbs provide a good way into the interpretation of the story.

The first point to appreciate is that "fear of God" is the prime category within the Old Testament for depicting appropriate human response to God, and as such, it plays a role within the Old Testament somewhat analogous to that of "faith" within the New Testament.[14] If the purpose of the narrative is to establish that Abraham truly belongs to the category "God-fearer," then its purpose, rephrased in Christian terminology, is to establish that Abraham is truly a "believer" (and the question of who is truly a believer, and on what basis, is a perennial critical issue).

To be "God-fearing" within the Old Testament has little or nothing to do with being frightened of God (say, of the consequences if one is disobedient) or being awed by divine majesty and mystery (though this can be a proper religious experience). Rather, it is a moral and relational term with many different facets. One particularly illuminating narrative, whose affinities with Gen 22 are apparent, is that of Job (Job 1:1–2:10). Job is portrayed as a model of true response to God in various terms, one of which is that he is a God-fearer (1:1). This is taken up by the satan, who does not doubt Job's rectitude on one level but is skeptical about the inner reality, raising the possibility that Job is essentially self-seeking ("Does Job fear God for nothing?" 1:9). When the vast prosperity that Job has is stripped away, Job holds fast to God and so, surely, passes the test (1:21). Yet the satan is unimpressed and suggests that Job is not only self-seeking but ruthless about it too, happy to lose pos-

---

14. "One who fears God" plays a role analogous to that of "a believer/the faithful" in Christian parlance in numerous texts, e.g., Pss 103:11, 13, 17; 112:1; 128:1; Prov 31:30; Isa 50:10; Luke 1:50.

sessions and family as long as he himself is spared (2:4-5; the satan's construal of Job is thus similar to Gunn and Fewell's construal of Abraham noted above). When Job subsequently is so afflicted that absolutely every part of him suffers ("from the sole of his foot to the crown of his head," 2:7), he holds fast to God and explicitly refuses to be a fair-weather friend (2:9-10). Such constancy, independent of circumstance, a constancy "for better, for worse, for richer, for poorer, in sickness and in health," shows that Job's fear of God means integrity of relationship with God and is indeed genuine. Abraham's exemplary fear of God is unlikely to mean something different from that of Job.

The language of divine "testing" (נִסָּה, *nissah*), which in Gen 22 is correlative with, and instrumental of, Abraham's fear of God, is commonly used to depict YHWH's dealings with Israel. Characteristic is the use in Deut 8, where Israel's forty years in the wilderness are construed as a time of testing (נִסָּה). The sense of this testing is clarified in at least six ways. First, it is explicitly "to do you good in the end" (v. 16). Second, it is analogous to the exercise of discipline (v. 5), the whole process of possibly painful but ultimately fruitful character formation that constitutes what a child should receive from its parents.[15] Third, it involves the divine introduction of hardship into the conditions of life, hardship that is then relieved by unprecedented divine provision (v. 3a). Fourth, its goal is the learning of the fundamental principle that human life is constituted not solely in material terms but in obedient reception of what YHWH says and gives (v. 3b). Fifth, this learning is tantamount to observance of the commandments (v. 2b). Sixth, this lesson, which is constitutive of Israel's human well-being and which is learned through hardship, is in danger of being unlearned and forgotten when life becomes easy (vv. 7-16) and replaced by a diminished and purely self-referential account of life (vv. 17-18); it therefore needs constant recollection (to which one might compare the practices designed to ensure that the fundamental relationship between YHWH and Israel, Deut 6:4-5, is constantly molding Israel's awareness, 6:6-9). This exposition of the nature of divine testing greatly illuminates the kind of assumptions implicit in the use of the verb in Gen 22:1.

The combination of divine "testing" (נִסָּה, *nissah*) with a view to human "fear" (יָרֵא, *yare'*), while conceptually common in the Old Testament, occurs in this precise terminology in only one other passage in addition to Gen 22, that is, Exod 20:20. Here Moses interprets to Israel God's giving of the Ten Commandments: "Do not be afraid, for God has come to *test* you so that the *fear* of him may be with you and keep you from sinning." This usage not only

---

15. This receives a definitive Christian exposition in Heb 12:5-11.

underlines the morally demanding and constructive nature of divine testing and human fear of God but also suggests a different kind of interpretation: the story of Abraham and Isaac demonstrates the kind of response to God that should characterize Israel as a whole. That is, Abraham is a model or type or figure of Israel, perhaps especially with regard to the first two commandments, which require Israel to renounce anything that might compromise its loyalty to the true God.

Abraham's words to Isaac that "God will provide" (Gen 22:8) become an enduring affirmation of trust that is memorialized in Abraham's naming of the place where his sacrifice was offered, "YHWH sees/provides" (v. 14a). Strikingly, this particular place-name is not used anywhere else in the Old Testament, yet the writer seems to assume a knowledge of the place in question by his allusive linking of the name to a saying current in his own time of writing (v. 14b). Rabbinic tradition always took for granted that this mysterious yet important place was none other than Jerusalem with its temple, and although modern scholars have tended to discount this identification, there are strong reasons to see it as integral to the text.

A variety of details indicate Jerusalem. The unusual name Moriah occurs in only one other passage in the Old Testament (2 Chr 3:1), where Mount Moriah is said to be the site of Solomon's temple. The name Moriah is probably to be understood as a noun formed from the verbal root רָאָה (ra'ah, "see/provide") and so means "place of seeing"; that is, Moriah carries a similar significance to the name Abraham bestows. The current saying to which the writer refers is about the "mount of YHWH," a term that is elsewhere used only of Jerusalem (Isa 2:3; Zech 8:3), apart from once of Sinai (Num 10:33). The place to which Abraham is told to go is a three days' journey (i.e., a short journey, as distinct from a long, forty days' journey, which is necessary to reach Sinai/Horeb, 1 Kgs 19:3, 8); it must therefore be somewhere central, and Jerusalem fulfills this specification (even though, of course, it is not required by it).

Perhaps most of all, the concerns of the story resonate strongly with those associated elsewhere in the Old Testament with the Jerusalem temple. Abraham is to offer his sacrifice at the place where God directs him (v. 2), just as Israel is to offer its sacrifices in a divinely chosen place (Deut 12:5-6, 13-14), which elsewhere is explicitly identified as Jerusalem (1 Kgs 14:21). Abraham's sacrifice is an outworking of his integrity before God, just as the sacrifice of those who sacrifice in the Jerusalem temple should accompany and represent integrity of living (Pss 15; 24:3-6). Thus Abraham's journey of sacrifice can be seen as a representative picture, or a kind of symbolic transparency, of Israel's coming to sacrifice in the temple in Jerusalem (just as its language also resonates with that of Israel's obedience to the Ten Commandments).

The story is thus naturally read as an interpretation of what the whole practice of sacrifice in the Jerusalem temple means, or should mean (for it could always be abused, as passages such as Jer 7 remind us). Within the context of Gen 22, where the ram sacrificed by Abraham takes the place of Isaac, the point is not a religio-historical concern with animal sacrifice displacing child sacrifice (or variations on that theory) but an interpretative point about the meaning of sacrifice: the whole burnt offering is symbolic of Abraham's effective self-sacrifice as one who, through relinquishing his beloved Isaac, truly fears God; and so for others, too, the "outward" public action of sacrifice should express "inward" personal self-giving to God.

The renewed blessing pronounced upon Abraham in closure of the story is strikingly emphatic (vv. 16a, 17a). It is closely related to, indeed pronounced because of, Abraham's exemplary responsiveness to God (vv. 16b, 18b). The divine promise of blessing structures Abraham's story from the outset (12:1-3), and its restatement here, in the last direct address of God to Abraham, suggests that it has climactic significance in at least three ways.

First, Abraham's fear of God has in some sense been incorporated into the terms of reference of God's will to bless Abraham's descendants; God's will to bless is no longer grounded solely in his own purposes but also in his responsiveness to Abraham (in a way analogous to how human repentance or faithful intercession matter to God and can elicit responsiveness within God, Jer 18:7-10; Exod 32:11-14). Faithful human action is dignified with enduring significance in God's purposes.

Second, Abraham's implicit understanding of the existing promise of blessing is confirmed. That is, Abraham has not appealed to YHWH's promise of descendants through Isaac (17:15-19; cf. 18:18) as a reason for not doing what YHWH requires of him. He has not said, "I cannot sacrifice my son, because he is the destined channel of your promise," but rather has trusted God ("God will provide," 22:8), even when God's requirement seems to contradict God's own purposes; thereby the nature of true trust is starkly revealed.

Third, the final element of the blessing, "all the peoples of the earth shall pronounce blessing by your descendants," similar to the conclusion of God's initial promise of blessing (12:3b), envisages Israel as a focus of respect and emulation among other peoples. Yet if other peoples will say, "May God make you like Israel," Israel must remember that they are the descendants of Abraham who showed the true meaning of fear of God; that is, the regard of the nations is not an encouragement of vanity or complacency but rather a reminder that Israel is significant for others only as it lives out for itself the responsiveness to God of its ancestor.

The Significance of Genesis 22

On the basis of this outline exegesis, some of the problems of interpretation can be more fully addressed. First, the genre of the text. The way in which the portrayal of Abraham has been worded and shaped so as to resonate with Israel's obedience to God's gift of Torah at Sinai and with Israel's pilgrimages to worship in Jerusalem is highly indicative for the genre of the material. However much it may be possible to see in the patriarchal narratives as a whole a pattern of religious thought and practice that is different from that of Mosaic Yahwism and to argue on that basis for the currently unfashionable position that some very ancient history is preserved within the text,[16] the quest for the "historical Abraham" cannot be other than tenuous and interpretatively unfruitful. The significant Abraham is Abraham as interpreted by Mosaic Yahwism, that is, as construed within a frame of reference different from that of his own pre-Mosaic-Yahwistic narrative context. Abraham has been remembered and preserved because of the continuing vitality of that story at whose outset he stands and because he was able to be construed in the developing categories of that continuing story. Terminologically, therefore, the story is probably best depicted as a legend, in the sense of a story that has certain givens but that develops over time and is capable of different kinds of retelling by those who cherish and preserve it. In a religious context, the retelling can incorporate the deepest insights into identity and life that have arisen in the course of its development. Genesis 22 is that version of the story of Abraham and Isaac which has been accepted by Jews and Christians as constitutive of their identity.

The legendary nature of the text accords well with the nature of religious language as metaphorical; that is, it encourages analogical thinking of various and subtle kinds between the text and the situations of those who hear or read it. It also accords well with the actual usage of the text in numerous ways by Jews and Christians alike through many centuries. It may be appropriate, therefore, to comment on the regrettably enduring tendency on the part of both believers and debunkers to insist that a biblical story can be true only if it relates "what actually happened." This leads to the sad spectacle of unwarranted claims that the text "really is historical" being countered by debunking demonstrations that "it ain't necessarily so." What tends to charac-

---

16. I have argued this in my *The Old Testament of the Old Testament: Patriarchal Narratives and Mosaic Yahwism*, OBT (Minneapolis: Fortress, 1992), pp. 79-104, 191-202. The tendency at present, however, is to see the "unorthodox" nature of patriarchal religion as indicative of marginal, perhaps familial, patterns *within* Yahwism rather than as the preservation of material *antecedent to* Yahwism.

terize such disputes is the imposition of one's own preconceptions and pre-conditions upon the text instead of an attentive openness to it for what it actually is (as Gunkel well put it, "lovingly to understand the nature of things"). Total imaginative seriousness need in no way prejudge the relation-ship between literary text and the context of life that gave rise to it, nor should a reasonable concern with what may be known historically be reduced to a naive and wooden historicism. To recognize that Gen 22 in historical terms tells one more about the religious norms of post-Solomonic Judah than about Israel's ancestors in the second millennium B.C. is not to transpose bib-lical faith into some kind of ahistorical gnosticism but rather to recognize that the peculiar mixture of event, memory, narrative, creative retelling, iden-tity formation, community construction, moral seriousness, and religious principle that have gone into making Gen 22 has value in its own terms. In-deed, legends of various kinds are common in all cultures, and they can be the most enduring and engaging and identity-forming kind of story in the popular mind.[17] If this is a significant mode of human communication, its presence within Israel's Scripture (its validation by the Spirit, in theological terms) should in no way be a problem.

What, then, of a hermeneutic of suspicion that sees Gen 22 as problem-atic and any emulation of Abraham as objectionable? One must certainly al-low that the suspicion that taking the story seriously might encourage some-one to abuse or kill a child has a certain prima facie plausibility — but only of the same order as the wooden insistence that "if the text says so, then it must have happened like that." For in the extensive history of interpretation and use of Gen 22 up to modern times, there is *no* recorded example of Jews or Christians using the text to justify their own abuse or killing of a child. This means that the metaphorical significance of the text was always (until re-cently) taken for granted, because it was read within a wider scriptural and communal context that provided guidelines and constraints for understand-ing and appropriating the story (in the kind of way outlined by Thoma) in ac-cordance with the story's intrinsic character. To take the story in isolation from the context that enabled its meaningful appropriation and then pro-claim it a problem in terms of its apparent face value is to be confronted by a problem of one's own making; analysis of parts in separation from their con-textual whole can sometimes enable understanding, but can also impede it.

Of course, suspicion can take other forms, as, for example, a sociopolitical questioning, which looks past the letter of the text so as to focus

---

17. In Britain one thinks of the historic and still lingering impact of the stories of Arthur and of Robin Hood.

on its presuppositions. If Gen 22 privileges worship in Jerusalem, then is this not at heart a manipulative (by invoking the illustrious Abraham) claim to power (and the material resources that worshipers bring) by the religious establishment in Jerusalem, at the expense of other places within Israel? On any reckoning the significance of Jerusalem was much contested within Israel's history — though the Old Testament's own perspective is that the contesting of Jerusalem is, even if understandable (as when Rehoboam alienates Jeroboam and Israel, 1 Kgs 12), nonetheless fundamentally mistaken. Yet to suggest that the story is *really* about promoting subservience to a self-seeking religious hierarchy is precisely to ignore what the story is actually about — that true religion entails a costly self-dispossession that relinquishes what is most precious in trustful hope in a demanding but gracious God.

Conclusion

It is dismaying that one and the same text can be interpreted in diametrically opposite ways, that self-giving can be construed as self-will, that trust can be construed as manipulation. Even if, in the complexity of life, it is often the case that motives and actions are mixed, it is hard to imagine that Gen 22 genuinely bears both interpretations. Our exegesis and interpretation have suggested that characteristic negative construals of Gen 22, while understandable, are nonetheless poor readings of the text.

To be sure, the sense that Gen 22 is a "dangerous" text could be shared by those who otherwise differ, for Jewish and Christian faiths have always recognized that the call of the true God must constitute the supreme allegiance and so cut across and relativize all other loyalties and priorities. The more important the truth of God is, the more serious are the problems that arise when human ignorance or self-will distorts that truth. Yet that danger looks different according to where one stands. To the (would-be) believer, the danger of God's supreme demand is the risk of learning so to die to self that one begins to live fully and without compromise in the light and love of God. This will always be a costly process where there are no guarantees that one may not be seduced by self-will, misunderstanding, disappointment, resentment, fear, or whatever; yet if the way is hard, it is a way into truth and life, and it is correspondingly worthwhile. To many, however, the danger is that Jewish and Christian (and Muslim) language and claims are nothing but elaborately coded human claims, claims that because of their code can justify abuse and atrocity, claims that — even when benign — are still misguided and so better relegated to a private sphere and replaced in public discourse by straightforwardly human accounts that correspond better to the reality of things. The ease with which religious faith can be, and has been, abused may make even believers wish that there were some other way. But there will never be anything of truth and value that cannot be abused.

To return to our initial problem of how one should rightly understand the biblical text and how one can know which of the many clamoring voices to trust, it has become clear that there can be no easy answers. Rigorous exegetical study of the biblical text is necessary, but it is not sufficient. Interpreters, like the curate's egg, may be good in parts. Much depends on context, but the possible contexts both of the biblical text and of its interpreters are many and varied. The (would-be) believer, however, comes to the biblical text not in a vacuum but in the context of a "great cloud of witnesses," those who have lived faithfully in the light of Scripture and have found it to be tested and true. There is a rich interpretative heritage to enter into, even if that heritage needs not only trust but also understanding and sifting.

Christian faith creates a presumption that in Scripture in general, and in Gen 22 in particular, there is truth. This presumption, however, should lead not to any kind of complacency ("we have the answers") or superiority toward others ("we're right, you're wrong") but rather to a willingness on the part of community and individual alike to expose oneself to what the truth, and right worship, of God actually entails: a rigorous, searching, critical, purifying process in which what one holds most dear and God-given may be precisely that which must in some sense be relinquished if faith is to be genuine — and in accordance with the pattern of father Abraham.

Joseph and the Passion of Our Lord

Gary A. Anderson

The stories about the patriarchs in Genesis function at two levels simultaneously. At the simplest level, they are to be read as they appear — that is, as stories about those heroic individuals whom God mysteriously and inscrutably called out of Mesopotamia and brought to the promised land. There, in the land of Canaan, Abraham, Isaac, and Jacob had to bide their time. Some four hundred years would need to pass before the burden of the sins of the current residents would reach its breaking point and God would drive them out.[1] But at a second level, these stories map out a quite different terrain. For what is at stake is hardly the chronicling of those four hundred years as though all that remained in the plot of our story was a restless marking of time. Rather, what we witness in the book of Genesis is the delineation of Israel's character, a character intimately tied to the very identity of God.

The stories thus point beyond themselves and take on, even within the confines of the Jewish Bible, a figural sense.[2] The meaning of the lives of Abraham, Isaac, and Jacob, as well as Jacob's most favored son, Joseph, is not

---

1. "Then the LORD said to Abram, 'Know this for certain, that your offspring shall be aliens in a land that is not theirs, and shall be slaves there, and they shall be oppressed for four hundred years; but I will bring judgment on the nation that they serve, and afterward they shall come out with great possessions. As for yourself, you shall go to your ancestors in peace; you shall be buried in a good old age. And they shall come back here in the fourth generation; for the iniquity of the Amorites is not yet complete" (Gen 15:13-16). Scripture quotations, unless otherwise noted, are from the New Revised Standard Version (NRSV).

2. For a detailed development of this theological notion, see the aptly titled book by R. W. L. Moberly, *The Old Testament of the Old Testament: Patriarchal Narratives and Mosaic Yahwism* (Minneapolis: Fortress, 1992).

exhausted by what happens to them within the narrow contours of Genesis. Part of the narratives' burden is to bequeath the roles played by these individuals to a much larger sodality, the nation Israel.

At the opening of the book of Exodus, when God hears the cries of his people who have been subjected to cruel servitude in Egypt, he calls forth Moses as his prophet to lead his people to freedom. Having appeared to him at the burning bush (Exod 3:1-6), he proceeds to reveal to Moses some crucial details about himself and about what Moses' mission will entail. At the end of that meeting, God brings the discussion to a close with these words:

> When you return to Egypt, see that you perform before Pharaoh all the marvels that I have put within your power. I, however, will stiffen his heart so that he will not let the people go. Then you shall say to Pharaoh, "Thus says the LORD, *Israel is my first-born son.* I have said to you, 'Let My son go, that he may worship Me,' yet you refuse to let him go. Now I will slay your first-born son." (4:21-23 NJPS)

These remarkable lines telescope the next seven chapters of the book of Exodus into just a couple of sentences. The hardening of Pharaoh's heart will lead to the tenth and last plague, the slaying of all the firstborn of Egypt. By providential design, the story points in this direction so that God may lay claim to his true firstborn, the nation Israel. As God's firstborn son, Israel shares in the identity of the firstborn sons of Genesis; indeed, those patriarchal heroes prefigure Israel.

But for the Christian reader, there is even more at stake, for the designation of God's firstborn does not end with the exodus from Egypt. As Paul declares in the Epistle to the Colossians: "[Christ] is the image of the invisible God, the firstborn of all creation. . . . He is the head of the body, the church; he is the beginning, the firstborn from the dead, so that he might come to have first place in everything" (Col 1:15, 18). Christ, the firstborn of all creation, bears a familial resemblance to Israel, God's other explicitly designated firstborn son. To understand one, we must understand the other.

Over the course of this essay, I would like to step back into the thought world of the early church — that is, a church not yet in possession of the New Testament. For those early Christians, the claim of Paul that Jesus died and was raised "in accordance with the scriptures" (1 Cor 15:4) was not just a simple affirmation of faith. It was a challenge to them to pore over the old texts afresh with the goal of laying bare just how and why this is so. If Christ is God's firstborn son, then he must stand in a very tight, figural relationship to God's firstborn son Israel. Jesus does not supplant that earlier figure; rather,

Jesus' identity is deepened by attending to the plain sense of Israel's scriptural witness.[3]

Election and the Old Testament

One path the church has consistently trod on her way to understanding the life of Jesus has been the story of Abraham's election and subsequent command to offer Isaac as a sacrifice (the Akedah). The latter text is regularly read during Holy Week and is intended to be heard as a typological foreshadowing of the crucifixion and resurrection. A significant selection of patristic literature and early Christian art interpret the story in precisely this fashion. Nearly every square inch of this sparse narrative has been traced and retraced in an attempt to map out the identity of God's beloved Son.

But to understand the significance of these interpretive moves, we must step back from the dense, forbidding thicket of Gen 22. We must consider the election of Abraham and the subsequent Akedah as a charter story that expresses in quite concentrated form a theological theme that spills over into much of the remainder of Genesis, that is, the election of the beloved son.[4] In the Akedah we have the barest (and most horrifying) narrative outline of its development; in the stories of the other patriarchs, the details emerge in much more elaborate (and temperate) form.

Let's begin with a consideration of how this literary motif works in the stories of Genesis. It will be convenient to unpack the theme through four defining features: surprise, cost, rivalry, and mystery.

---

3. There is not sufficient room to develop all that is implied in these brief lines. For now, compare the profound reflection on this matter by Michael Wyschogrod: "If we are prepared to take seriously the implanting of Jesus in his people, if the Israel that gave birth to him and whose boundaries (spiritual, geographic, linguistic, intellectual, etc.) he never left is more than just a backdrop to the drama, a backdrop from which Jesus is to be distinguished rather than into which he is to be integrated, if all this is to change, then what is true of Jesus must in some fundamental way also be true of the Jewish people. And that includes the incarnation." And earlier, in order to draw this particular thesis to a very poignant level, he remarks: "It is told that when the man who was to become Pope John XXIII saw the pictures of the bulldozers pushing Jewish corpses into mass graves at the newly liberated Nazi murder camps, he exclaimed: 'There is the body of Christ.'" Michael Wyschogrod, "A Jewish Perspective on the Incarnation," *Modern Theology* 12 (1996): 207, 205.

4. On these points, see Jon D. Levenson, *The Death and Resurrection of the Beloved Son* (New Haven: Yale University Press, 1993), and R. W. L. Moberly, *The Bible, Theology, and Faith: A Study of Abraham and Jesus* (Cambridge: Cambridge University Press, 2000).

The Surprise of Election

In nearly all the stories of Genesis, the designation of the beloved son appears as a *surprise*.[5] For this, we have no better example than the call of Abraham in Gen 12. The second half of Gen 11 consists of a genealogy of the descendants of Shem, ending with Abram (Abraham)[6] — significantly, the *tenth* figure in the list. This genealogy looks very much like the one in Gen 5, which begins with Adam and ends with Noah; both chronicle a succession of righteous descendants that concludes with a climactic flourish in the tenth figure.[7]

Here, as with the story of Noah, our narrator leaves his habit of revealing just the bare minimum about each of the nine previous descendants and tells us something more about this important tenth figure (Gen 11:27-32).[8] But we don't learn too much. We are told that Abraham's father, Terah, has three boys: Abraham, Nahor, and Haran. Haran, the father of Lot, has died in

---

5. See Levenson, *Death and Resurrection,* p. 70: "To some, these unpredictable acts of choosing will be best described as grace and celebrated as proof of the generosity of God. This is the dominant view within both Judaism and Christianity, though Christianity has generally been more comfortable than Judaism with the utter unpredictability of the choices, that is, with the irrelevance of human worthiness to the intention of God. To others, these unpredictable acts of choosing will be best described as arbitrariness and condemned as unworthy of a God of justice. This view, though rejected by the dominant trends in the Jewish and the Christian traditions, is to be detected behind some biblical narratives. That the justice of the God who chooses is broached at all in the Hebrew Bible is eloquent testimony to the challenge that the theology under discussion posed, the challenge of accepting chosenness as a category of ultimate theological meaning."

6. Abram and his wife Sarai are renamed "Abraham" and "Sarah" by God in Gen 17. In accordance with the practice of many interpreters, I will refer to them consistently by the latter names except in quotations of the biblical text.

7. Genesis 5: Adam; Seth; Enosh; Kenan; Mahalalel; Jared; Enoch; Methuselah; Lamech; *Noah.* Genesis 11: Shem; Arpachshad; Shelah; Eber; Peleg; Reu; Serug; Nahor; Terah; *Abram.* I will not consider here the problem of the Greek Bible, which inserts another descendant into the list such that Terah becomes number ten and Abraham is the beginning of a new line. The Greek, in fact, brings Gen 5 and 11 into stronger alignment. Both end with a righteous figure in position ten (Noah/Terah) who, in turn, gives birth to three sons (Shem, Ham, Japheth // Haran, Nahor, Abraham), one of whom will be favored by God (Shem and Abraham).

8. Compare what is said about Enosh in 5:9-11. There we learn how old Enosh was when he gave birth to Kenan, how long he lived afterwards, the fact that he gave birth to other sons and daughters, and the age he was when he died. In 5:32 we learn that Noah was 500 years old when he became the father of Shem, Ham, and Japheth (already a deviation from the established model, as everyone else is said to give birth at a far younger age and only one child is mentioned by name). The intervening story of the flood breaks apart the genealogical rubric (6:1–9:28); we must wait until the close of ch. 9, where we learn Noah's age upon death (9:29), for the conclusion of the formula.

Ur of the Chaldeans prior to Terah's emigration to Aramea. Abraham and Nahor take wives, and Nahor begets children, but Abraham and Sarah remain childless. The section closes with the genealogical notice that Terah was 205 years old when he died in the city of Haran (11:32).

Then, after the curtain goes down on Gen 11 — and with no proper transition — the reader comes face to face with these amazing lines: "Now the LORD said to Abram, 'Go from your country and your kindred and your father's house to the land that I will show you. I will make of you a great nation . . .'" (12:1-2).

Why Abraham? we must ask, as have many interpreters. The history of the Jewish interpretation of these verses is littered with various midrashim as to what Abraham had done to merit this boon.[9] Consider, for example, the book of *Jubilees,* one of our earliest examples of biblical interpretation (second century B.C.E.). It devotes dozens of verses to filling in the textual gap between Gen 11 and 12. By its account, God revealed the secret of monotheism to Abraham in Mesopotamia. In that land of polytheism and idolatry, the doctrine proved to be quite controversial. Abraham's courage to affirm God's oneness in the face of physical danger became the occasion for God's rewarding him with the supreme promise. This interpretive tradition makes for wonderful midrash, but the louder it sounds, the more deafening is the Bible's silence about the same.

The theme of God's unpredictable choices continues throughout the book of Genesis. Consider the preference of God and, in turn, the matriarch Rebekah for Jacob. Esau was the firstborn son, the beloved of his father, Isaac. By the dictates of biblical law, he should have been the heir of his father's blessing and patrimony. But in Genesis, the expected course of events is reversed. "Jacob I have loved and Esau I have hated," Malachi observes (see Mal 1:2-3) — words as surprising to him as they were to the hearers of the original story. As will become even clearer through the figure of Joseph, beloved though the youngest of eleven, and later with the choice of Ephraim over the firstborn Manasseh, birth order does not determine divine preference.

The Cost of Election

The natural human response to election is to assume that it represents a very good deal for the person so chosen. In the cases of Isaac and Jacob, the status

---

9. See James Kugel, *The Bible As It Was* (Cambridge, Mass.: Harvard University Press, 1997), pp. 131-48.

of favored son means an inheritance that will dwarf that of the other siblings. But there is another aspect to being chosen. Election is not a matter simply of a set of benefits to be claimed and enjoyed; election involves a *cost*. Consider the similarity of these two texts:

Genesis 12:1-3	Genesis 22:2, 15-17
[1]Now the LORD said to Abram, "Go from your country and your kindred and your father's house to the land that I will show you."	[2]God said [to Abraham], "Take your son, your only son whom you love, Isaac, and go to the land of Moriah, and offer him there as a burnt offering on one of the mountains that I shall show you." (my translation)
[2-3]"I will make of you a great nation, and I will bless you, and make your name great, so that you will be a blessing. . . ."	[15-17]The angel of the LORD called to Abraham a second time from heaven, and said, "By myself I have sworn, says the LORD: Because you have done this and have not withheld your son, your only son, I will indeed bless you, and will make your offspring as numerous as the stars of heaven. . . ."

The story of the Akedah is told in a way that draws it into comparison with Abraham's original call. Just as Abraham is asked to leave (1) his country, (2) his kindred, and (3) his father's house — each signifying a higher degree of personal attachment — so in Gen 22 he is asked to take (1) his son, (2) his only and beloved son, (3) Isaac by name — each designation likewise marking a higher degree of attachment. And just as Abraham is told to journey to a land unknown that God will show him, so in Gen 22 he is told to venture forth to a mountain that God will show him. And finally, just as the conclusion of Abraham's journey will result in a glorious promise, so the conclusion of the Akedah results in the reaffirmation of the promise.

But despite these parallels, there is one significant variation. Rather than being simply the recipient of an unmerited divine blessing as he is in Gen 12, Abraham, through his willingness to sacrifice his only son, becomes the meritorious possessor of that blessing in Gen 22. What looks like pure gift in Gen 12 becomes a reward for unparalleled human obedience in Gen 22. Abraham has to relinquish the very grounds of the promise in order to receive the promise in full. The cost of divine favor is a sacrifice of immeasurable proportion.

There is a tremendously high cost to be paid by those whom God favors. For us, God's choice of Abraham in Gen 12 or Jacob in Gen 25 may appear as unfair as it did to the biblical characters who were passed over in silence. The burden of the passed-over sibling, such as Esau, is envy. Why Jacob, Esau must wonder, and not me? But the envy that follows naturally from these stories depends on a superficial understanding of election, an understanding that our biblical writer wishes to overturn.[10] Election does not mean living a life of unending blessings; it means being chosen to give up one's all for God, even what one holds most dear. For some ten chapters we wait, along with Abraham, for the news that Sarah has become pregnant and will bear a son. Yet almost immediately after the child is born and weaned, Abraham is asked to give that child up. And according to the logic of the Akedah, only by his willingness to give him up does Abraham merit the enjoyment of the benefits the child will bring.

This is the importance of the Akedah, a tale that makes us recoil in horror, in Israel's grand narrative of election. What we find to be most precious must be given up; the Akedah is the ultimate bulwark against any form of spiritual triumphalism. The election of Abraham does not end with his becoming king over the land of Canaan; its literary apogee is Abraham's call to free himself of what he holds most dear. Calvin once said, "Christ is the Mirror wherein we must, and without self-deception may, contemplate our own election."[11] In light of the patent parallelism between Abraham's sacrifice and that of Christ, perhaps we could slightly rephrase this dictum of Calvin: "Abraham is the mirror wherein we must, and without self-deception may, contemplate our own election."[12]

---

10. Luther learned from the cross that God reveals himself through opposites. What the world takes as glory, God counts as chaff; what the world takes as ignominy, God esteems as honor. The election of Abraham in Gen 12, at first blush, calls to mind the randomness of a state lottery — is the electing hand of God as fickle as the winning number in a game of chance? The author of Genesis, however, takes every opportunity to subvert this understanding.

11. John Calvin, *Institutes of the Christian Religion* 3.24.5.

12. This theme of radical sacrifice adorns the liturgical calendar. Consider the days that are honored immediately after the feast of Christmas: the martyrdom of St. Stephen, the martyrdom of Thomas à Becket, and the slaughter of the holy innocents. Savagery follows on the heels of the birth. Or consider the icons of the nativity among the Orthodox. In a number of images, Mary lays Jesus out on an altar instead of a crib. No sentimental manger scene, this! Or consider those icons in which Jesus' arms stretch wide across Mary's breast while his head leans backward. Is this the pose of a resistant infant or a cruciform man? It is no surprise that retailers and other merchandisers keep this dimension of Christmastide under wraps. To fall under the spell of that baby born in Bethlehem is not always the charmed moment our secular apostles would wish it to be.

The Rivalry between Elect and Nonelect

A third feature of our stories from Genesis concerns the *rivalry* between the elect and nonelect, a rivalry that seeks and moves toward resolution. The notion is absent in the figure of Abraham himself. Though he is one of three brothers, the Bible does not record his family's reaction to his being singled out by God. Instead, the text relates that one brother, Haran, has died prior to that moment and the other brother, Nahor, has evidently been left behind in Ur. Abraham is alone when he hears God's call.[13]

However this might be with Abraham, the situation is quite different with Jacob and Joseph. Both of these sons are clearly favored over their blood brothers, and the act of favoritism becomes a legitimate source of intense anger. Esau schemes to slay Jacob (Gen 27:41), and only his mother's intervention saves the day (27:42-44). Joseph, on the other hand, is not so lucky; his brothers take steps to do him in. Only the last-minute interventions of Reuben and Judah preserve him. But these tales of rivalry do not end on notes of rage or vengeance. The Jacob and Joseph cycles have similar denouements: the reconciliation of the brothers. Both Esau (Gen 33) and Joseph's brothers (Gen 45; 50:15-21) come to terms with their rivals.

The Mystery of Election

The fourth feature — and perhaps the most remarkable one of all — is the *mystery* of election. Although the subject of most of the fifty chapters of Genesis, election is not fully understood, even by the elect. One of the most stunning stories in all of Genesis is found near the end of the book at the deathbed of Jacob (Gen 48:8-22). Joseph has gathered his two sons, Manasseh and Ephraim, to be blessed by their grandfather. In this act, Joseph lays legal claim to the rights of the firstborn even though he was the second-to-last child born to his father. He receives the double portion of his father's blessing through his two sons; his brothers will receive only one blessing each.

Joseph presents the sons to his father, now nearly blind from old age (48:10), in such a fashion that Manasseh, his firstborn, will be blessed by his

13. The figure of Lot, the son of Haran and hence nephew of Abraham, provides some complication here. Lot accompanies Abraham to Canaan but does not receive a promise like that of Abraham. Abraham, however, is extraordinarily gracious, allowing Lot first choice as to where he would like to settle in this promised land. To Lot's consternation — but certainly not outside the umbrella of providence — the land he chooses is rendered uninhabitable by the sins and consequent punishment of Sodom and Gomorrah.

father's right hand. "Joseph took them both, Ephraim in his right hand toward Israel's left, and Manasseh in his left hand toward Israel's right, and brought them near him" (48:13). Clearly, Joseph, like his brothers before him, expects the paternal blessing to follow the normal rules of primogeniture. Yet as Jacob reaches forward, he undoes Joseph's efforts to orchestrate the blessing: "But Israel stretched out his right hand and laid it on the head of Ephraim, who was the younger, and his left hand on the head of Manasseh, *crossing his hands,* for Manasseh was the firstborn" (48:14).

Although this motif of preferring the younger sibling has been appearing and reappearing in the stories of Genesis — including that of Joseph himself — Joseph reacts with astonishment. "When Joseph saw that his father laid his right hand on the head of Ephraim, it displeased him; so he took his father's hand, to remove it from Ephraim's head to Manasseh's head. Joseph said to his father, 'Not so, my father! Since this one is the firstborn, put your right hand on his head'" (48:17-18). In words that recall those of Isaac to Esau, Jacob tells Joseph that, while the firstborn son will become the progenitor of a numerous and mighty people, "his younger brother shall be greater than he" (48:19).

Joseph as Beloved Son

The central thesis of Jon Levenson's recent book on the Akedah is that the near death of Isaac is not some odd, aberrant narrative stuck in the middle of more uplifting tales about the patriarchs. It is, instead, a précis of Genesis in extremely concentrated form. When Levenson comes to Joseph, he writes:

> The story of Joseph in Genesis 37–50 is not only the longest and most intricate Israelite exemplar of the narrative of the death and resurrection of the beloved son, but also the most explicit. In it is concentrated almost every variation of the theme that first appeared in the little tale of Cain and Abel and has been growing and becoming more involved and more complex through the book of Genesis. . . . It is the crescendo to the theme of the beloved son, which it presents in extraordinarily polished form. It is arguably the most sophisticated narrative in the Jewish or Christian Bibles.[14]

It is in the story of Joseph that we find the theme of election and its high cost set in most brilliant relief. Joseph is elevated over his brothers by his fa-

---

14. Levenson, *Death and Resurrection,* p. 142.

ther. This choice is a grand surprise, for Joseph is "the son of his [father's] old age" (37:3). And it is the occasion for a most zealous rivalry, for the choosing of Joseph means the spurning of other, more legitimate claimants. And like the paradigmatic "beloved son," Isaac, Joseph must die as a result of such favor. His death is quite realistic from the perspective of the father; after being sent off to seek his brothers, he comes back in the form of a bloodied garment (37:31-35).

From Joseph's own perspective, the death is more metaphorical. He is dropped into a pit, taken down into Egypt, and sold into slavery (37:22-24, 27-28). The Psalter offers good proof that entrapment in a pit was strongly associated with entering the underworld: "To you, O LORD, I cried, and to the LORD I made supplication. 'What profit is there in my death, *if I go down to the Pit? Will the dust praise you? Will it tell of your faithfulness?*'" (Ps 30:8-9).[15]

While in Egypt, Joseph undergoes a series of elevations and humiliations only to find himself the provisioner not only of his family in Canaan but of the entire known world.[16] During the first wave of hunger that ripples through Canaan, Jacob sends the ten older brothers to Egypt to buy grain (Gen 42:1-5). They return with food — from Joseph's hand — but without Simeon, who has been held as surety for Joseph's demand to see their brother Benjamin (42:29-34). When father and brothers again find themselves near death from famine (43:1-10), Jacob is left with a tragic choice. If the brothers stand any chance of securing food, he must surrender Benjamin, his beloved son in place of Joseph, to accompany them into Egypt (43:3-5). In light of Jacob's experience, the surrender of Benjamin to these brothers is tantamount to sacrifice[17] — recalling, once again, the sacrifice of the Akedah.

When his brothers return to Egypt, Joseph greets them happily and provides them with a sumptuous meal in his own home (43:26-34). Later, as the brothers prepare to depart for Canaan with their newly procured food supplies, Joseph arranges to have his prized divining cup placed in Benjamin's belongings. When Joseph's steward subsequently overtakes the brothers and orders a search of all their goods, the cup is "found" — to the brothers' utter horror — in Benjamin's bag (44:6-13). At that moment the brothers are faced

---

15. On this theme, see Gary A. Anderson, *A Time to Mourn, A Time to Dance* (University Park, Pa.: Pennsylvania State University Press, 1991).

16. He serves as head of the household of Potiphar in Gen 39; chief assistant to the head jailer in chs. 39–40; and, after successfully interpreting Pharaoh's dreams, ruler of Egypt second only to Pharaoh in chs. 41ff.

17. Consider what Jacob says after the brothers' first return from Egypt, without Simeon: "I am the one you have bereaved of children: Joseph is no more, and Simeon is no more, and now you would take Benjamin. All this has happened to me!" (42:36).

with a choice that recalls in a striking way the beginning of the tale. They may once again (this time under external pressure) act to rid themselves of a favored sibling, spurning their father and leaving Benjamin behind in Egypt. But in this case, Judah — who once advocated selling Joseph to the Ishmaelites (37:26-27) — recognizes and chooses an option that requires him to make the supreme sacrifice. He insists on pledging his own life in the adored child's stead. Joseph is moved to tears by Judah's love for the son his father dotes on (45:1-2). The envy of his brothers has dissipated, and Joseph can finally reveal his identity. The brothers are sent back to Canaan to tell their father the news.

Consider well the situation of the father. He sent Joseph out to find the brothers, and only a bloodied robe returned. He sent ten brothers out to buy food, and only nine returned. Now he has sent Benjamin out in the care of the brothers, and he holds no hope that this son will return. Yet Benjamin and the brothers do return — "and [the brothers told Jacob], 'Joseph is alive again! What's more, he is ruler over all of the land of Egypt'" (45:26; my translation).

To catch the sense of surprise here, consider the reaction of the apostles on Easter Sunday. According to the Gospel of Luke, when told what the women have seen at the tomb, the apostles do not believe them; they reckon it "an idle tale" (Luke 24:11). The loss of Joseph is a type of death; his return, as ruler of Egypt, a type of resurrection in glory. Like the apostles, Jacob is dumbfounded.

A twelfth-century Cistercian homily put it this way:

> What I have placed before you, brethren, is like an egg or a nut; break the shell and you will find the food. Beneath the image of Joseph you will find the Paschal Lamb, Jesus, the one for whom you yearn. The great depth at which he is hidden and the diligence necessary in seeking him and the difficulty you will have in finding him will only make him all the sweeter to your taste. . . . And so here is the explanation in a nutshell. If we think with faith and reverence about the meaning of his name (Gen 30:24) and go on to consider that he was more handsome and good-looking than the rest of his brothers (Gen 39:6), that his actions were blameless, that he was prudent in his judgments, that after he had been sold by his own he redeemed his own from death, that he was humbled even to imprisonment, then elevated to a throne, and was rewarded for his work by being given a new name among the nations — the Savior of the World (Gen 41:45)[18] — if we think, I say, about all these things reverently and faith-

---

18. The Vulgate renders his Egyptian name, Zaphenath-paneah (untranslated in the Hebrew), as *Salvatorem mundi.*

fully, we shall surely recognize how truly it was said by the Lord: "Through the Prophets I gave parables" (Hos 12:10).[19]

The association of Joseph's figural death with the death of Christ is magnificently illustrated in the *Biblia pauperum* (Bible of the Poor) of the thirteenth century (see p. 210). In this image, we see the lowering of Joseph into the pit, the laying out of Christ's body after his death, and the tossing of Jonah into the sea. In all these instances, the person facing death will be restored and those who instigated the death will stand to benefit. Consider the plight of Joseph, a man "sold by his own" who "redeemed his own from death." Those who hatefully tried to slay him found their very existence dependent on that rejection.

Forgiveness of the Brothers

And finally, our story takes one more turn and reveals one more denouement. After Jacob dies, the brothers find themselves in a very uncomfortable position. For in giving Joseph up to death, they behaved in a way that is well recognized from the psalms of lament. Our compact text is worth citing in full: "So when Joseph came to his brothers, they stripped him of his robe, the long robe with sleeves that he wore; and they took him and threw him into the pit. The pit was empty; there was no water in it. Then they sat down to eat" (Gen 37:23-25). The account of the angry act of stripping Joseph of his sign of favor is accompanied by two important details. First is the notice that the pit was empty and without water, a sure indicator that murder was the initial intention. Second is the surprising revelation that they promptly sat down to eat. This seemingly inconsequential detail sets the actions of these brothers against a much wider canvas. For in the Psalter, to eat and drink in the presence of the demise of another is to put oneself in the role of the "enemy." Psalm 30, which describes the plight of the lamenter as one who has been lowered into a pit likened to Sheol, implores the Lord to release him so that his foes may not "rejoice over" him (Ps 30:1).[20] Just as Christ is subject to the taunts of the "enemies" while suffering on the cross, so Joseph undergoes a similar fate. If, as the Gospels suggest (Matt 27:34-35, 39, 46, 48, and parallels), Psalms 22 and 69 accurately portray the indignity of the treatment of Jesus, one could argue with some reason that Psalm 30 does the same for Joseph.

19. Guerric of Igny, *Liturgical Sermons [by] Guerric of Igny*, vol. 2, trans. Monks of Mount Saint Bernard Abbey, CF 32 (Spencer, Mass.: Cistercian, 1971), p. 81.

20. On this common trope in the psalms of lament and its relation to eating and drinking, see Anderson, *A Time to Mourn*.

Entombment. Joseph lowered into the well. Jonah. *Biblia pauperum.* Paris, Bibliothèque nationale de France, Xylographes 2, f. g. (Permission granted.)

But the invocation of this psalmic category points even deeper. In many of the psalms of lament, the person who is subject to such hatred invokes the deity to take harshest vengeance on the offending enemies. Consider these words (of prayer!) from Psalm 58:

> O God, break the teeth in their mouths;
>   tear out the fangs of the young lions, O LORD!
> Let them vanish like water that runs away;
>   like grass let them be trodden down and wither. . . .
> The righteous will rejoice when they see vengeance done;
>   they will bathe their feet in the blood of the wicked.
> People will say, "Surely there is a reward for the righteous;
>   surely there is a God who judges on earth."
>
> (Ps 58:6-7, 10-11)

Those who are wronged have every right to expect justice in the end. It is not simply a matter of personal revenge; according to the psalmist, the meting out of vengeance is crucial in showing the world that there is a God who judges moral behavior.

And so the brothers have very good reason to be anxious about what Joseph might do. As the psalms of lament give witness, Joseph would have good grounds to seek vengeance against those who have treated him so unjustly. Indeed, the brothers themselves give explicit testimony to the fact that such punishment for their behavior is in order. When they first appear before Joseph and are thrown into jail for a few days on the false charge that they are spies (Gen 42:6-17), they confess, "Alas, we are paying the penalty for what we did to our brother; we saw his anguish when he pleaded with us, but we would not listen. That is why this anguish has come upon us" (42:21). This honest admission of guilt highlights another aspect of the pain the brothers inflicted: Joseph wept for mercy from the waterless pit while they sat by and enjoyed their meal (cf. 37:24-25).

The brothers have every right to wonder just *who* is the Joseph that now stands before them. Was Joseph earlier restraining a fierce desire for vengeance solely as a courtesy to his father, Jacob? "What if Joseph still bears a grudge against us" the brothers rightfully wonder, "and pays us back in full for all the wrong that we did to him?" (50:15). How does Joseph respond? "Do not be afraid!" — words that call to mind the stirring words of consolation and forgiveness that God often speaks through his prophets[21] — "Am I in the place of God? Even though you intended to do

---

21. Most prominently found in Isaiah; see Isa 35:4; 40:9; 41:10; et passim.

harm to me, God intended it for good, in order to preserve a numerous people" (50:19-20).[22]

The brothers' hatred and envy of Joseph is crucial to the story as a whole. The transformation of Judah into one who will die for Benjamin (44:18-34) loses its profundity if his prior rejection of Joseph is not *complete.* And the beneficence of Joseph, his providing for his family and overlooking the sin of his brothers,[23] loses its gravitas if it is not calibrated against the *expectation of retributive justice* on the part of the brothers.

Who Are the Betrayers of Jesus?

It is precisely this scenario of a group of men who have callously betrayed their brother and now seem anxious about the price they must pay that warrants a shift in our narrative gaze. Indeed, the story of Joseph and his brothers assumes a new tone when set against the backdrop of the Gospels. For as these books record, the disciples of Jesus also abandoned their Lord at the hour he needed them most. Mark is the bleakest here: Jesus dies alone with just an intimation of the resurrection. Only the centurion gets it right: "Truly this man was God's Son!" (Mark 15:39). The disciples (and the *reader*) are left in a position strikingly similar to that of Joseph's brothers: "[The disciples] went out and fled from the tomb, for terror and amazement had seized them; and they said nothing to anyone, *for they were afraid*" (16:8).

As readers, we fill in the gaps of the tale with our post-Easter knowledge from the other Gospels. But let us pause on this bleak Markan moment. If we take our cues from Genesis, I think we can read these lines in a new light. Just *who* is the Jesus that will meet the disciples who spurned him in his most trying hour? The psalms of lament that fill out the events of Good Friday bear elegant witness to the dejection and humiliation of Jesus. But for those who

---

22. The reconciliation between Joseph and his brothers is the subject of a marvelous chapter in Uriel Simon, *Seek Peace and Pursue It* (Tel Aviv: Yediot Aharonot, 2002), pp. 58-85 [Hebrew]. Especially profound is Simon's sensitive attention to how both the brothers and Joseph mature into their respective roles within the story.

23. We would do well, however, not to interpret the scene that closes the tale of Joseph and his brothers (50:15-21) from too sentimental a point of view. It is not at all clear that Joseph and his brothers are fully reconciled. Rather, it seems that Joseph, regardless of whatever personal — and quite human — feelings he may harbor toward his brothers, has determined that any calculated act of vengeance at this time would be an affront to providence. The brothers' intentions notwithstanding, "God intended it for good," Joseph concludes, "in order to preserve a numerous people." In this sense Joseph mediates forgiveness without necessarily owning it. Nevertheless, it is through Joseph, and Joseph alone, that the brothers must seek solace.

have betrayed him, these psalms could hint at an even darker reality. The prayer of Psalm 69 (see Mark 15:36 and parallels) says not only "For my thirst they gave me vinegar to drink" (69:21) but also "Add guilt to their guilt; may they have no acquittal from you. Let them be blotted out of the book of the living" (69:27-28). The disciples must wonder, who is this Jesus that awaits them? Will the encounter be one of wrath or of mercy?

Mark is not alone in the harsh indictment passed on the very men Jesus called to follow him. Matthew, Luke, and John are just as insistent about their perfidy. At the foot of the cross — while Jesus suffers — they are absent. And so, may I suggest, are we. "The chain of these handings-over is forged theologically," Hans Urs von Balthasar concludes; ". . . all of humanity's representatives, considered theologically, are integrated from the outset into guilty responsibility for Jesus' death."[24]

For this insight von Balthasar is indebted to Luther. In Luther's theology of the cross, none of us is innocent. "You must get this through your head," Luther advised his congregants in his understated way,

> and not doubt that you are the one who is torturing Christ thus, for your sins have surely wrought this. In Acts 2 [:36-37] St. Peter frightened the Jews like a peal of thunder when he said to all of them, "You crucified him." Consequently three thousand alarmed and terrified Jews asked the apostles on that one day, "O dear brethren, what shall we do now?" Therefore, when you see the nails piercing Christ's hands, you can be certain that it is your work.[25]

This insight was not lost on Bach, known among Lutherans as "the fifth evangelist." In his recent book on Bach's *St. John Passion*, Michael Marissen has this to say about the death of Jesus:

> The second stanza of no. 11, the Lutheran chorale with its remarkable dissonance on the first syllable of *Sünden* (sins), spells things out the most clearly and forcefully of all, its "I, I" referring to the Lutheran congregants:

---

24. Hans Urs von Balthasar, *Mysterium Paschale: The Mystery of Easter*, trans. Aidan Nichols (Edinburgh: T. & T. Clark, 1990), pp. 113-14.

25. Martin Luther, "A Meditation on the Passion," in *Luther's Works*, vol. 42, *Devotional Writings 1* (Philadelphia: Fortress, 1971), p. 9. Of course, this is not to deny the highly vituperative character of Luther's anti-Semitism as witnessed in other parts of his writings. But it is worth noting that precisely here at the crucifixion, where a diatribe against the Jews would seem most natural, Luther holds back. His theological understanding of the cross requires him to focus the blame on contemporary Christian congregants.

> I, I and my sins,
> which are as numerous as the grains
> of sand on the seashore,
> they have caused you
> the sorrow that strikes you
> and the grievous host of pain.[26]

Bach makes it quite clear that no benefit is gained from reflecting on the question of culpability from a purely *historical* frame of reference. Whether Jew or Roman or both actually slew Christ is not of prime significance. The death of Jesus must be grasped *theologically.* From a theological frame of reference, Jesus' death was made necessary by *our* sin. Through the disciples whom Jesus called, we have spurned his loving advances.[27]

At Passiontide we are absent. We have abandoned Jesus in his most demanding hour. At the foot of the cross, we do not kneel. If we kneel now, in the liturgy, it is only in view of our post-Easter knowledge that he has forgiven us in spite of our spurning him. A hymn of Luther furnishes us our only prayer:

> Our great sin and sore misdeed
> Jesus, the true Son of God, to the cross has nailed.
> Thus you, poor Judas, as well as the host of Jews,
> we may not inimically upbraid; guilt is truly ours.
> Lord, have mercy.[28]

And this is the key to the passion: Like the brothers of Joseph, we reject the Elect One of Israel, but the Elect One does not reject us. And strikingly, it is precisely the *culpability* of the brothers or the disciples that allows them to experience and ponder the miracle of their forgiveness. As Robert Jenson so aptly puts it: "To the question 'Who crucified Jesus?' only the church is able to say, 'We did.' The [human] race in general must, in justice, say, 'We were not there,' and just so go its way."[29]

26. Michael Marissen, *Lutheranism, Anti-Judaism, and Bach's* St. John Passion (New York: Oxford University Press, 1998), p. 34.

27. It is worth noting that the midrash makes a similar move regarding the culpability for Joseph's "death." The guilt continues to haunt Israel, even after the actual brothers have died and vanished from the scene. According to the early Tannaitic midrash, the *Sifra* (ad Lev 9:3), Israel must bring a goat offering at the inauguration of the public cult in order to atone for the sin of selling Joseph into slavery.

28. From the Wittenberg hymnal of 1544; cited in Marissen, *Lutheranism,* p. 26.

29. Robert W. Jenson, *Systematic Theology,* vol. 1, *The Triune God* (Oxford: Oxford Uni-

A Precursor to the Felix Culpa?

If we pause again on the story of Joseph, we may uncover a darker irony. Had the brothers of Joseph not "slain" their brother, would they have survived the famine? And what of the rest of humanity? Their fate as well seems to have depended on what occurred between the brothers: "*[A]ll the world* came to Joseph in Egypt to buy grain, because the famine became severe throughout the world" (Gen 41:57). In other words, is the story of God's people dependent on an act of betrayal? By raising such a question, we call to mind the theme of the *felix culpa* as well as the age-old question whether Christ would have become human apart from the fall. How profoundly the story of Joseph illumines what Luther called the supreme saving act of the cross. God's works are hidden "under the form of their opposite" *(abscondita sub contrario)*. The brothers thought they were putting Joseph to death, but what they really were doing was assuring their own salvation. The brothers, even at the end, worried that such an act would merit harshest vengeance. But Joseph knew differently: "Even though you intended to do harm to me, God intended it for good, in order to preserve a numerous people" (50:20).

I have often thought that the story of Joseph should be read on one's knees. Or, to borrow an image from how we perform the creed — that is, bowing at the moment we come to the mystery of the incarnation — perhaps we should bow periodically during the reading of this story. Let us bow when the brothers lower Joseph into the pit, when Judah offers to give up his life for Benjamin, when Jacob surrenders Benjamin to his other sons, when Jacob hears that Joseph is alive and of royal stature. And let us reserve our deepest and longest bow for when we hear Joseph's words of forgiveness to his brothers: "Do not be afraid!" We are those brothers, and only the Elect One of Israel can speak the words of absolution.

---

versity Press, 1997), p. 192. The irony here is how the classic smear of the Jews as Christ-killers is disarmed. The act of laying the blame outside oneself places one outside the very bounds of grace that the story seeks to establish. Those who have hated the Jews have not been good Christian theologians.

Reading Scripture in Light of the Resurrection

Richard B. Hays

I. The Offense of the Resurrection

On the issue of the resurrection, many preachers and New Testament scholars are unwitting partisans of the Sadducees. Because they deny the truth of Scripture's proclamation that God raised Jesus from the dead — or waffle about it — they leave the church in a state of uncertainty, lacking confidence in its mission, knowing neither the Scriptures nor the power of God.

As we stand on the cusp of postmodernity, many Christians are unsure about how to interpret the Bible and what role to give it within the church. At the same time, there is widespread confusion in the church about the New Testament's resurrection accounts. My proposal in this essay is that these two phenomena are linked: confusion about the resurrection has hindered the church's ability to interpret Scripture, and our ignorance of Scripture has obscured our understanding of the resurrection. Stated positively: *We interpret Scripture rightly only when we read it in light of the resurrection, and we begin to comprehend the resurrection only when we see it as the climax of the scriptural story of God's gracious deliverance of Israel.*

The New Testament's accounts of the resurrection of Jesus have proven particularly problematical for modern interpreters. Stories about the resurrection of a man crucified, dead, and buried contradict everything that orthodox post-Enlightenment historians take to be axiomatic about the nature of history and the reality in which we live. For that reason, the recent history of theology is replete with attempts to reinterpret the meaning of the New Testament's resurrection stories in ways that will not conflict with a modern scientific worldview. John Shelby Spong offers a blunt assessment: "If the resurrection of Jesus cannot be believed except by assenting to the fantastic descriptions included in the Gospels, then Christianity is doomed. For that view of resurrection is not believable, and if that is all there is, then Christianity, which depends on the truth and authenticity of Jesus' resurrection, also is not believable."[1] How, then, is "Christianity" to be salvaged without requiring acceptance of the New Testament's resurrection stories?

The most abidingly influential answer to this question in the twentieth century was given by Rudolf Bultmann, who offered the lapidary explanation that "Jesus rose in the kerygma." According to Bultmann, the New Testament's stories about a bodily resurrection and empty tomb are not in any sense factual descriptions of something that happened to Jesus of Nazareth, who had been put to death; rather, they are to be understood as expressions of the "Easter faith" of the first disciples. They are attempts to express in mythic imagery the early church's conviction that Jesus' life and death were in fact an expression of the unquenchable love and grace of God. In Bultmann's formulation, "The Easter-event as the resurrection of Christ is no historical event. . . . Resurrection faith is nothing other than faith in the cross as salvation-event."[2]

Bultmann's demythologized post-Kantian account of Easter faith continues to prevail in many circles of New Testament scholarship, including the work of Gerd Lüdemann[3] and of the scholars who have marketed themselves as the Jesus Seminar. Some interpreters who follow this line, like Bultmann himself, regard "Easter faith" as spiritually authentic and true, while others, such as Lüdemann, regard it as "only a pious wish" that ultimately has produced deceptive and destructive consequences.[4] Lüdemann and Spong have recently produced speculative accounts of the psychological states and experiences ("mass ecstasy," "grief work," etc.) that might have given rise to "Easter faith."[5]

---

1. John Shelby Spong, *Resurrection: Myth or Reality? A Bishop's Search for the Origins of Christianity* (San Francisco: HarperSanFrancisco, 1994), p. 238.

2. Rudolf Bultmann, "Neues Testament und Mythologie," in *Kerygma und Mythos*, vol. 1, ed. H. W. Bartsch (Hamburg/Bergstedt: Herbert Reich-Evangelischer Verlag, 1960), pp. 46-47; my translation. For a concise, sympathetic exposition of Bultmann's views on this issue, see John Painter, *Theology as Hermeneutics: Rudolf Bultmann's Interpretation of the History of Jesus* (Sheffield: Almond, 1987), pp. 166-68.

3. Gerd Lüdemann, *The Resurrection of Jesus: History, Experience, Theology* (Minneapolis: Fortress, 1994).

4. For Lüdemann's public statement renouncing Christian faith, see his book *The Great Deception: And What Jesus Really Said and Did* (London: SCM, 1998), esp. "A Letter to Jesus," pp. 1-9. The phrase "only a pious wish" appears on p. 3, where Lüdemann asserts that the body of Jesus either rotted in the tomb or "was devoured by vultures and jackals."

5. For an extended imaginative reconstruction, see Spong, *Resurrection*, pp. 242-60.

On the other hand, not all interpreters have been ready to dispense with the notion, however vague, that something really did happen to Jesus, even if that "something" defies historical description. For example, Luke Timothy Johnson, a vehement critic of the methods of the Jesus Seminar, declares that "[t]he Christian claim concerning the resurrection in the strong sense is simply not 'historical.' The problem in this case is, however, not with the reality of the resurrection. The problem lies in history's limited mode of knowing."[6] Johnson enters a plea for historical humility and a sober recognition of the limits of historical knowledge while holding open the claim that the resurrection of Jesus was nonetheless a real event.[7]

Johnson sometimes comes very close, however, to adopting the Bultmannian strategy of describing the resurrection exclusively through the filter of subjective faith experience. Consider the following passage from his book *The Real Jesus:*

> At the very heart of Christianity, therefore, is an experience and a claim. The experience is one of transforming, transcendent, personal power within communities that can be expressed in shorthand as "the gift of the Holy Spirit." The claim is that this power comes from Jesus, who was crucified but now lives by the life of God, and is expressed by the declaration "Jesus is Lord." . . . *Experience and conviction together form the primordial "resurrection experience" that founds the Christian movement and continues to ground it today.* . . . The resurrection experience that founded and grounds the Church is not based on the transitory encounters of a few people on Easter day or for forty days thereafter, but on the experience of power through Jesus by generations of people across the centuries and continuing still today.[8]

This account of resurrection is a textbook instance of a method of theological reflection — classically exemplified by Friedrich Schleiermacher — that

---

6. Luke Timothy Johnson, *The Real Jesus: The Misguided Quest for the Historical Jesus and the Truth of the Traditional Gospels* (San Francisco: HarperSanFrancisco), p. 136.

7. Spong can also make statements in this vein; see, e.g., *Resurrection,* pp. 239, 256. It should always be acknowledged that his project is apologetic in character: he is seeking to affirm belief in "resurrection" (as he redefines it), not to debunk it.

8. Johnson, *Real Jesus,* p. 135; emphasis mine. Here Johnson sounds strikingly like Bultmann: "A merely 'reminiscent' historical account referring to what happened in the past cannot make the salvation-occurrence visible. . . . [T]he salvation-occurrence continues to take place in the proclamation of the word. The salvation-occurrence is eschatological occurrence just in this fact, that it does not become a fact of the past but constantly takes place anew in the present." Rudolf Bultmann, *Theology of the New Testament,* 2 vols. (New York: Scribner, 1951-55), 1:302.

George Lindbeck has characterized as "experiential-expressive": it begins with the religious experiences of believers as the primary data of theology and construes doctrinal claims as attempts to bring such inchoate experiences to expression.[9] There can be no doubt that the New Testament authors do describe the sort of transforming experiences to which Johnson points as an *effect* of the resurrection. It may be questioned, however, whether the narration of such experiences can stand as a fully adequate account of what they *mean* by resurrection. Particularly, it is doubtful that such an account provides an adequate hermeneutical framework for understanding the resurrection narratives we actually find in the Gospels, which speak of an empty tomb and a palpable, embodied risen Jesus who eats fish with his astonished disciples.[10]

Let us consider one final example of an attempt to reshape the understanding of "Christianity" to accommodate modernist epistemology. Robert W. Funk, the founder of the Jesus Seminar, has set forth on his Web site a programmatic manifesto titled "The Coming Radical Reformation: Twenty-One Theses." For purposes of illustration, I shall cite only four of the theses, culminating in Funk's declaration on the resurrection:

1. The God of the metaphysical age is dead. There is not a personal god out there external to human beings and the material world. We must reckon with a deep crisis in God talk and replace it with talk about whether the universe has meaning and whether human life has a purpose.

    . . .

6. We should give Jesus a demotion. It is no longer credible to think of Jesus as divine. Jesus' divinity goes together with the old theistic way of thinking about God.

7. The plot early Christians invented for a divine redeemer figure is as archaic as the mythology in which it is framed. A Jesus who drops down out of heaven, performs some magical act that frees human beings from

---

9. George Lindbeck, *The Nature of Doctrine: Religion and Theology in a Postliberal Age* (Philadelphia: Westminster, 1984), pp. 16-17 et passim. To be fair to Johnson, we must recognize that he writes as a Roman Catholic for whom experience of the risen Lord is constantly mediated through liturgy and sacrament; therefore, the "experience" of which he speaks cannot be dissolved into purely individual subjectivity — the abiding danger of Protestant versions of experiential-expressive theology.

10. All the recent revisionist accounts of the New Testament's witness to the resurrection, of course, discount precisely these features of the New Testament witness as late legendary accretions to a more original and authentic testimony to visionary "experiences" of the resurrection.

the power of sin, rises from the dead, and returns to heaven is simply no longer credible. The notion that he will return at the end of time and sit in cosmic judgment is equally incredible. We must find a new plot for a more credible Jesus.

. . .

10. The resurrection of Jesus did not involve the resuscitation of a corpse. Jesus did not rise from the dead except perhaps in some metaphorical sense. The meaning of the resurrection is that a few of his followers — probably no more than two or three — finally came to understand what he was all about. When the significance of his words and deeds dawned on them, they knew of no other terms in which to express their amazement than to claim that they had seen him alive.[11]

Funk has spelled out aggressively and explicitly what seems to be implicit in the critical work of numerous other New Testament scholars who also do not believe that Jesus rose from the dead "except perhaps in some metaphorical sense." His declaration enables us to reflect clearly on what is at stake in our deliberations on this topic. The resurrection is the climactic element — indeed, the linchpin — of the biblical story of God's redemption of the world. Without it, the story falls apart, and there are, as Funk recognizes, wide-ranging systematic implications for theology. (Perhaps the most surprising feature of Funk's agenda is that he understands himself to be advocating a "reformation" rather than a refutation of Christianity.) The resurrectionless story that Funk envisions differs drastically from the story told by the Bible, and the canonical Scriptures of the Old and New Testaments become for him an obstacle to be overcome ("we must find a new plot") rather than a source of good news and life.

But what if God really did raise Jesus from the dead? What if "resurrection" names not just the transformed self-understanding of Jesus' followers

11. Robert W. Funk, "The Coming Radical Reformation: Twenty-One Theses," found on the Westar/Jesus Seminar Web site (www.westarinstitute.org/periodicals/21Theses/21Theses.html). For a fuller account of Funk's views, see his book *Honest to Jesus: Jesus for a New Millennium* (San Francisco: HarperSanFrancisco, 1996), pp. 257-77. With regard to Funk's condescending suggestion that "they knew of no other terms in which to express their amazement," see the convincing argument of N. T. Wright that Jews in the Second Temple period had many terms and categories for describing visionary or revelatory experiences but that "resurrection" was not one of them. "Resurrection" referred unambiguously to the resurrection of the body, and it was symbolically associated with hopes for God's ultimate restoration and vindication of Israel. N. T. Wright, "Christian Origins and the Resurrection of Jesus: The Resurrection of Jesus as a Historical Problem," *Sewanee Theological Review* 41 (1998): 107-23.

but rather God's mighty act of raising one particular man, who was crucified, dead, and buried, from the grave? Wouldn't that open up a totally different perspective for understanding the world and interpreting the Bible? In the brief scope of this essay, we shall explore this proposal by attending carefully to three Gospel passages that connect resurrection with the reading of Scripture.

II. Three Texts on Reading and Resurrection

John 2:13-22: Remembering Scripture and Jesus' Word

John's account of Jesus' protest action against trade and moneychanging in the temple appears near the beginning of his narrative. Rather than functioning, as it does in the Synoptic Gospels, as the culminating provocation that precipitates Jesus' arrest, it serves for John as a scene of dramatic foreshadowing. The story forges a symbolic identification between the temple and Jesus' own body in Jesus' enigmatic prophecy "Destroy this temple, and in three days I will raise it up."[12] As the passage indicates, the meaning of this prophecy becomes intelligible — and its truth validated — only after the resurrection. Jesus' interlocutors misunderstand his saying because, in the dramatic irony typical of Johannine dialogues, they perceive only the surface literal sense and miss the hidden christological meaning. This meaning, of course, was inaccessible to them in the pre-resurrection situation.

The hermeneutical key to the passage is given explicitly in an authorial voice-over directed to the reader in John 2:21-22: "But he was speaking of the temple of his body. *When, therefore* (ὅτε οὖν, *hote oun*), he was raised from the dead, his disciples remembered that he had said this; and they believed the scripture and the word that Jesus had spoken." The force of John's οὖν (not translated by the NRSV) is elusive, but it seems to mean something like this: "Jesus spoke *figuratively* about the resurrection of his own body; *therefore,* the meaning of his prophecy could be understood only after the resurrection, only after he had embodied its figural sense." It is not too much to suggest that John, early in his narrative, is teaching his readers how to read. Look beyond the literal sense, he whispers, and read for figuration. Read Scripture retrospectively, in light of the resurrection. If you do, you will see the temple as *prefiguring* the truth definitively embodied in Jesus.

---

12. Scripture quotations, unless otherwise noted, are from the New Revised Standard Version (NRSV).

But how does the reference to believing *the scripture* fit into this hermeneutical directive? There is no citation of Scripture in Jesus' saying. We could hypothesize that John is alluding to various uncited biblical passages about restoring the temple after the exile,[13] but there is a more immediate solution at hand in the passage itself. The key is to recognize the structural parallelism between vv. 17a and 22a:

17a: His disciples remembered that it was written. . . .
22a: his disciples remembered that he had said this. . . .

In both cases we find precisely the same wording in the Greek text: ἐμνήσθησαν οἱ μαθηταὶ αὐτοῦ ὅτι *(emnēsthēsan hoi mathētai autou hoti)*. In the first instance, the disciples are said to have remembered a scriptural text (Ps 69:9a: "Zeal for your house . . . has consumed me"); in the second, they are said to have remembered a word of Jesus ("Destroy this temple, and in three days I will raise it up"). Thus when John tells us that they "believed (a) *the scripture* and (b) *the word that Jesus had spoken*" (v. 22b), we should understand this as a summary comment about the whole narrative unit (vv. 13-22a), including the story of driving out the traders and moneychangers. If so — and here is the key point — "the scripture" that they believed was Psalm 69.

What does a reading of Psalm 69 after the resurrection disclose? In what sense can the disciples be said to have believed this scripture in a new way as a result of the resurrection?[14] The most important clue lies in the fact that the post-resurrection reading sketched in John 2 requires us to understand Jesus as the *speaker,* the praying voice of the psalm: "Zeal for your house will consume *me.*" This interpretation opens up the entire psalm, not just one half-verse of it, as a proleptic disclosure of the mystery of Jesus' identity.

13. Particularly interesting is Zech 14:21, the concluding verse of Zechariah's eschatological prophecy: "And there shall no longer be traders in the house of the Lord of hosts on that day."

14. Later in John's Gospel, we learn that the disciples' post-resurrection remembering is to be aided by the Paraclete, the Holy Spirit, who will recall and interpret Jesus' words for the community (John 14:25-26; 16:12-15). At one level, of course, we are to understand that Psalm 69 foreshadowed Jesus' "zeal" for the house of God, as demonstrated in his angry rebuke of the merchants in the temple. At this level, to "believe the scripture" would be to accept the insight that this snippet (Ps 69:9a) was a hidden prophecy about something Jesus was later to do. This reading is facilitated by John's shifting of the verb tense: where Ps 69:9 (=68:10 LXX) reads "Zeal for your house *has consumed* me" (κατέφαγεν, *katephagen,* a 2 aorist form), John "remembers" the text to say ". . . *will consume* me" (καταφάγεται, *kataphagetai,* a future form). The post-resurrection perspective, however, contributes little to this interpretation.

Indeed, from a range of other evidence, we know that the early church did read Psalm 69 in precisely this way: as a passion psalm portraying Jesus as the righteous sufferer.[15] For example, Paul quotes the other half of the same verse that John cites in order to portray Jesus as one who suffers vicariously for the sake of others (Rom 15:3).[16] All four canonical Gospels say that on the cross Jesus was offered vinegar (ὄξος, *oxos*) to drink (Matt 27:48; Mark 15:36; Luke 23:36; John 19:29), a narrative detail whose correspondence with Psalm 69:21 (68:22 LXX) can scarcely have escaped John's notice. Thus a reading of Psalm 69 after the passion and resurrection of Jesus would disclose that the psalm is to be read as a poetic prefiguration of the suffering and vindication of Jesus the Messiah, whose voice "David" anticipated.

This interpretation was perhaps further encouraged by the fact that the Septuagint translated the obscure Hebrew phrase לַמְנַצֵּחַ (*lamnatseakh,* "to the leader"?) in the superscription of Psalm 69 as εἰς τὸ τέλος (*eis to telos,* "for the end"), a phrase that early Christian interpreters could readily have understood as a directive to read the psalm as having eschatological reference.[17] From this perspective, to "believe the scripture" would mean to understand that Jesus is the speaker of the psalm taken as whole — or perhaps even of the Psalter as a whole — and that the sentence "Zeal for your house will consume me" should be read as a pointer to the destruction that came upon Jesus as a result of his zeal and faithfulness to God, a destruction prefigured in the psalm, foreshadowed prophetically by Jesus' own words, and narrated fully in the passion story.

Once one begins to read Psalm 69 from a post-resurrection perspective, the psalm's concluding turn to praise and thanksgiving (vv. 30-36) can also be read as a prefiguration of the resurrection. In that case, it is perhaps not sheerly coincidental that the psalm's final verses speak of God's saving Zion and *(re)building* the cities of Judah — an image that echoes suggestively in counterpoint with Jesus' prophecy that he will raise up the destroyed temple

---

15. C. H. Dodd observes a wide range of different citations of this psalm by various New Testament writers and concludes as follows: "The intention of the New Testament writers is clearly to apply the whole [of Psalm 69] to the sufferings and ultimate triumph of Christ." C. H. Dodd, *According to the Scriptures: The Sub-structure of New Testament Theology* (London: Nisbet, 1952), pp. 57-60, 96-97, quote 97. See also Brian E. Daley, SJ, "Is Patristic Exegesis Still Usable? Some Reflections on Early Christian Interpretation of the Psalms," in this volume.

16. Elsewhere, he also cites vv. 22-23 of the psalm (following the wording of the LXX) as a depiction of the "hardened" Israel that rejects the gospel (Rom 11:9-10).

17. I have made this suggestion previously in Richard B. Hays, "Christ Prays the Psalms: Paul's Use of an Early Christian Exegetical Convention," in *The Future of Christology: Essays in Honor of Leander E. Keck,* ed. A. J. Malherbe and W. A. Meeks (Minneapolis: Fortress, 1993), pp. 122-36. See particularly p. 127.

of his body.[18] One important implication of such a reading is that *the mean-ing of Jesus' resurrection is not to be understood apart from Israel's hope for de-liverance and restoration; the resurrection is not an alternative to such hopes but rather a sign of their consummation.* To be sure, John does not cite these verses of the psalm, but if we follow his implied direction about reading the scrip-ture and the saying of Jesus *together* in light of the resurrection, we belated disciples, long after the resurrection, may find ourselves recalling and under-standing more than we could have imagined. If so, part of what we under-stand will be that Jesus' resurrection and the fate of Israel are inseparable.

Thus in John 2:13-22 the story of Jesus' death and resurrection is posited as the key that unlocks the interpretation of Scripture. Retrospective reading of the Old Testament after the resurrection enables Jesus' disciples to "be-lieve" in a new way both the Scripture and Jesus' teaching and to see how each illuminates the other. Such retrospective reading neither denies nor invali-dates the meaning that the Old Testament text might have had in its original historical setting. Psalm 69 is fully comprehensible as an expression of Israel-ite piety: it is a prayer for deliverance in a time of trouble and suffering. When it is reread, however, in light of the New Testament's story of Jesus' passion and resurrection, it takes on additional resonances beyond those perceptible to its earlier readers. The figural correlation between the psalmist's prayer and the story of Jesus illuminates both in unexpected ways.[19]

Mark 12:18-27: Knowing the Scriptures and the Power of God

In this controversy story, Jesus is challenged by the Sadducees, who seek to discredit the idea of a resurrection of the dead.[20] (The story presupposes that Jesus was generally known to share the Jewish apocalyptic expectation of the resurrection of the dead; otherwise, the challenge from the Sadducees makes

---

18. This is an instance of the rhetorical device of metalepsis. For discussion of this figure, see Richard B. Hays, *Echoes of Scripture in the Letters of Paul* (New Haven: Yale, 1989), p. 20 et passim.

19. This example illustrates what is meant by "figural reading." The retrospective interpre-tation of an Old Testament text as a typological prefiguration of a subsequent person or event does not in any way negate the historical reality of the precursor. Both type and antitype are embraced together as concrete disclosures of God's activity in the world. Therefore, the hermeneutical cur-rent flows in both directions, and the "meaning" of each pole in the typological correlation is en-hanced by its relation to the other. For a helpful discussion of figural reading and typology, see Hans Frei, *The Eclipse of Biblical Narrative* (New Haven: Yale University Press, 1974), pp. 1-37.

20. For Synoptic parallels, see Matt 22:23-33 and Luke 20:27-40.

no sense.) The Sadducees — about whom we know relatively little — were probably an aristocratic party that exercised influence in the political and religious establishment in Jerusalem during the era leading up to the war against Rome (66-70 C.E.). They rejected the doctrine of resurrection of the dead — apparently because it was not to be found in the law of Moses.[21] One suspects, additionally, that they may have found such apocalyptic ideas unsettling because they threatened the status quo of social power and privilege. Proclaiming resurrection turns the world upside down (cf. Acts 17:1-9) and holds out to the poor and lowly the hope of being vindicated while posing a worrisome prospect to those who have already received their consolation in the present life (cf. Luke 6:24).[22] Thus the Sadducees would have had a particular interest in debunking the belief in resurrection that was widely held among other Jews in the first century C.E.[23]

In the story of Mark 12:18-27, the Sadducees conjure up an improbable tale about a woman who, under the provisions of levirate marriage law, is married in succession to seven brothers, all of whom die childless, with the woman being the last to go to the grave. In other circumstances this might provide the plot for a juicy murder mystery (with the woman as the chief suspect; cf. Tob 3:7-9), but the Sadducees have a different interest. They want to inquire how this scenario might inform theological reflection about resurrection: "In the resurrection, whose wife will she be?" The question is intended as a reductio ad absurdum.

Jesus' answer has three components: a put-down of his interlocutors (v. 24), a statement that the life of the resurrection will transcend sexual and marital relations as we know them (v. 25), and a cryptic attempt to demonstrate that the Pentateuch does, after all, provide warrant for the doctrine of resurrection (vv. 26-27). Each of these three components is of some importance for our reflections about reading Scripture in light of the resurrection.

First, the put-down. Jesus not only rejects the Sadducees' argument as silly but diagnoses the source of their error: "Is not this the reason you are wrong, that you know neither *the scriptures* nor *the power of God?*" (v. 24). This opening rebuff frames the other elements of Jesus' response and directs our attention to what is theologically at stake in this controversy. To say that

---

21. Josephus, *Antiquities* 18.16-17; on the Sadducees' rejection of Pharisaic oral traditions, see *Antiquities* 13.297.

22. See Richard Bauckham, "Life, Death, and the Afterlife in Second Temple Judaism," in *Life in the Face of Death: The Resurrection Message of the New Testament*, ed. R. N. Longenecker (Grand Rapids: Eerdmans), p. 82.

23. As Bauckham convincingly argues, belief in resurrection of the dead was not a Pharisaic peculiarity: it was the Sadducees who held a distinctive minority opinion on this question.

the Sadducees do not know the Scriptures is a direct affront to their competence as religious leaders. Presumably, in fact, their rejection of the resurrection rests precisely on appeals to the authority of Scripture: no such belief was taught by Moses, so it should not be accepted. By challenging them at this point, Jesus creates the expectation that he will produce scriptural evidence to discredit their skepticism — an expectation that he will fulfill, albeit in a surprising way, in vv. 26-27. Just as importantly, he implies that knowledge of biblical content is not the same thing as "knowing the Scriptures" in the way that matters. The telling of this controversy story suggests that authentic knowledge of the Scriptures depends on a hermeneutic of resurrection, the ability to discern in Scripture a witness of God's life-giving power.

The reference to "the power of God" (τὴν δύναμιν τοῦ θεοῦ, *tēn dynamin tou theou*) has several possible meanings here. It could allude to the power of God to raise up children to the childless, the general power of God to raise the dead, or — most interestingly — the eschatological manifestation of God's glory at the time when the Son of Man is to be revealed seated at the right hand of *the Power*" (τῆς δυνάμεως, *tēs dynameōs,* Mark 14:62; Matt 26:64). Mark links this eschatological manifestation of God as Power with Daniel's vision of the Son of Man (Dan 7:13-14), which in turn is linked with the expectation of resurrection of the dead (Dan 12:2-3) and the vindication of the elect. Thus Jesus' accusation about the Sadducees' ignorance could be construed as a charge that they are ignorant of this eschatological vision: they are living only in the world of business as usual, heedless of the eschatological power of God that looms over the present. They know in advance what is and is not realistically possible, and so they foreclose the freedom of God to raise the dead.

Second, in v. 25 Jesus asserts that the life of resurrection will not conform to the patterns and categories that we know in the present life: "they neither marry nor are given in marriage, but are like angels in heaven." The Sadducees' derisive question actually reveals a plodding literalism that assumes the life of the world to come — in which they profess disbelief — could be nothing other than an extension of the existence we know now. The belief they reject, however, is a caricature of what Jesus and the New Testament writers mean by "resurrection." Jesus tries to get his adversaries to think outside the box, to conceive of the resurrection as a transformation, not just a continuation, of life as we know it. This is an extremely important point: to read and think in light of the resurrection is to open ourselves to "What no eye has seen, nor ear heard, nor the human heart conceived, what God has prepared for those who love him" (1 Cor 2:9). A hermeneutic of resurrection opens us to eschatological surprises of grace, to blessings that confound our casuistic calculations.

Third, Jesus returns to the issue of what the Scriptures teach about resurrection and adduces a surprising text "in the book of Moses, in the story about the bush" (v. 26). Countering the Sadducean belief that the law does not support the doctrine of resurrection, Jesus goes to the heart of God's self-revelation in the Old Testament, God's appearance to Moses in the burning bush (Exod 3:1-6). How does this text support resurrection? Most New Testament commentators say that the argument turns on a grammatical technicality: because God says "I *am* the God of Abraham, the God of Isaac, and the God of Jacob," not "I *was* the God of Abraham . . . ," it must be inferred that these three patriarchs — who had long since departed earthly life — are to be found among the living, not the dead. It is often suggested, rather loosely, that this is a particularly "rabbinic" mode of argumentation.[24]

One difficulty, however, is that it is not at all clear how the argument, so construed, actually would support *resurrection,* as distinct from immortality of the soul. The Jewish apocalyptic doctrine of resurrection of the body envisioned the resurrection as part of God's comprehensive restoration of justice "on earth as it is in heaven." As long as injustice and suffering persist, as long as the world remains unredeemed, it would be a non sequitur to assert that the continued personal existence of the three great patriarchs in some other spiritual sphere could somehow prove the validity of belief in the resurrection. Generally, interpreters of Mark chalk this up as one of Jesus' weaker arguments and go on to the next passage — the more satisfying declaration of the double love commandment (Mark 12:28-34).

J. Gerald Janzen, however, has shown that the Exodus story reinforces resurrection in a much more theologically compelling way.[25] The God who speaks to Moses using the "three-ancestor formula" is a God who took the initiative to establish covenant relation with the patriarchs and to promise covenant blessings to their descendants. God consistently acted to protect and save them even in the face of the most dire and impossible circumstances. God's faithfulness in securing the future of his chosen people is the sure basis on which the descendants of the patriarchs can continue to hope for the future. Therefore, God's use of the three-ancestor formula in Exod 3:6 implies that there must be an "analogy between the ancestral situations and the situation of the generation of Moses." Just as God delivered and saved the patriarchs, so he will do for his people

24. See, however, the rebuttal to this claim by D. M. Cohn-Sherbok, "Jesus' Defence of the Resurrection of the Dead," *Journal for the Study of the New Testament* 11 (1981): 64-73.

25. J. Gerald Janzen, "Resurrection and Hermeneutics: On Exodus 3:6 in Mark 12:26," *Journal for the Study of the New Testament* 23 (1985): 43-58. Janzen's argument builds on the earlier work of F. Dreyfus, "L'argument scripturaire de Jésus en faveur de le résurrection des morts (Marc XII, vv. 26-27)," *Revue biblique* 66 (1959): 213-24.

in their plight in Egypt. Furthermore, if God acted to deliver his people from the "death" of slavery in Egypt, surely he will do so again in the future — not in precisely the same way, but in ways that are recognizably analogous. Consequently, Jesus' use of Exod 3:6 in support of the resurrection — the claim that God will finally save his beloved people from death — is nothing other than a metaphorical extension of the Exodus theophany's claim about God's identity. In other words, a "resurrectionist textual hermeneutics"[26] is already implicitly present in the book of Exodus, and Jesus' appeal to that book makes more explicit what is already there for those who have eyes to see.

Janzen offers yet one more turn in this provocative argument. The three-ancestor formula is a singularly appropriate rejoinder to the Sadducees' test-story about the woman whose seven successive husbands fail to *raise up seed* (cf. Gen 38:8) for the first one (i.e., to perpetuate his line).[27] This failure corresponds symbolically to their denial that God will *raise up* the dead. The Sadducees' story is a story about historical existence ordered toward death, under death's reign. As Janzen notes, the stories of Abraham, Isaac, and Jacob are also stories of sterility despite divine promise and long-deferred hope; nonetheless, when read in full, they are stories of "ancestral sterility overcome by divine action." The story told by Genesis and Exodus is a story about God "who gives life to the dead and calls into existence the things that do not exist" — Paul's summary of the meaning of the Abraham story (Rom 4:17).[28] The story of God's life-giving power is evoked by Jesus' appeal to "the God of Abraham, the God of Isaac, and the God of Jacob." Once we know God as the God revealed in the patriarchal narratives, we perceive that giving life to the dead is not far-fetched but fundamentally in keeping with his character.[29] God's self-revelation from the burning bush, therefore, may indeed be understood as a witness to the resurrection.

Here — as in other passages where New Testament writers cite the Old Testament — the allusive ripples spread out widely from brief explicit cita-

---

26. Janzen, "Resurrection and Hermeneutics," p. 43.

27. The parallel in Matt 22:24 makes the link to the dispute about resurrection even more overt by using the verb ἀναστήσει (*anastēsei*, "raise up"), which is elsewhere used of resurrection. In Mark 12:19, the verb is ἐξαναστήσῃ (*exanastēsē*, literally "raise up out of").

28. Janzen, "Resurrection and Hermeneutics," pp. 50-55. Janzen also notes Heb 11:11-12 as a significant reading of the story along similar lines.

29. Jon Levenson has recently argued in a similar fashion that the Torah supports the later rabbinic understanding of resurrection because its stories of God's miraculous intervention to ensure the continuance of the line of Abraham's seed are the "functional equivalent" of bringing life out of death. Jon D. Levenson, "Resurrection in the Torah? A Second Look" (2002 Palmer Lecture, Center of Theological Inquiry, Princeton, N.J., 21 March 2002).

tions to evoke larger narrative patterns. When these larger narrative patterns of the Old Testament are brought into conjunction with the story of Jesus' death and resurrection, we are enabled to read Scripture with new eyes and to see Jesus as carrying forward the story of God's gracious life-giving power. To know the Scriptures and the power of God is to discern in Israel's story the working of the same God who raised Jesus from the dead.

Luke 24:13-35: Opening the Scriptures

The final passage we shall consider is Luke's account of the risen Jesus' encounter with two disciples on the road to Emmaus (Luke 24:13-35). In this episode Luke highlights Jesus' role as exegete of the biblical story: the risen Lord becomes the definitive interpreter of "the things about himself in all the scriptures" (v. 27).

Cleopas and his anonymous companion on the road to Emmaus are well acquainted with all the stories and traditions about Jesus' life, including the report of the empty tomb and the angelic proclamation of the resurrection (vv. 19-24). Nonetheless, they are departing Jerusalem in a state of gloomy disappointment: "But we had hoped that he was the one to redeem Israel" (v. 21a). This is a moment of wrenching irony: Jesus, the Redeemer of Israel, stands before them, yet they fail to recognize him.

Jesus scolds them for their failure to believe *the prophets*[30] (interestingly, not for their failure to believe Jesus' own predictions of his death and resurrection) and begins to instruct them all over again: "Then beginning with Moses and all the prophets, he interpreted to them the things about himself in all the scriptures." As Walter Moberly has observed, the risen Jesus offers no new visions from heaven or mysteries from beyond the grave but instead focuses on patient exposition of Israel's Scripture. The crucial truth lies there, not in some hidden heavenly revelation.[31] Furthermore, Luke's formulation suggests that testimony to Jesus is to be found "in all the scriptures" (ἐν πάσαις ταῖς γραφαῖς, *en pasais tais graphais*), not just in a few isolated proof texts. The whole story of Israel builds to its narrative climax in Jesus, the Messiah who had to suffer before entering into his glory. That is what Jesus tries to teach them on the road.

---

30. I am persuaded by C. F. Evans's suggestion that the rebuke should be translated, "Oh, how foolish you are, and how slow of heart to become believers *on the basis of* all that the prophets had said." C. F. Evans, *Saint Luke*, TPINTC (London: SCM, 1990), p. 910.

31. R. W. L. Moberly, *The Bible, Theology, and Faith: A Study of Abraham and Jesus* (Cambridge: Cambridge University Press, 2000), p. 51.

It is essential to teach them about Scripture because Scripture forms the hermeneutical matrix within which the recent events in Jerusalem become intelligible. Understanding can dawn only when these shattering events are brought into an interpretive dialectic with Israel's story: "[A]s Jesus cannot be understood apart from Jewish scripture, Jewish scripture cannot be understood apart from Jesus; what is needed is an interpretation which relates the two — and it is this that Jesus provides (v. 27)."[32] The puzzled Emmaus disciples have all the facts but lack the pattern, the integrative interpretation, that makes them meaningful. Luke's tantalizingly brief summary of the meaning-pattern is offered in v. 26: "Was it not necessary that the Messiah should suffer these things and then enter into his glory?" (For Luke, entering "into his glory" refers to Jesus' resurrection and ascension.) Somehow, Jesus' exposition of Israel's Scripture will have to show the pervasive presence of this theme — which had never been perceived by anyone in Israel prior to the crucifixion and resurrection.[33]

Luke, as a skillful storyteller, does not yet give away all his secrets. He does not divulge the contents of this privileged exposition of the Bible by the risen Jesus. In order to see what Luke has in mind, we must await his second volume, where his accounts of the apostolic preaching draw heavily on scriptural texts.[34] The apostolic sermons exemplify the sort of readings that (we may suppose) Luke imagines Jesus to have offered on the Emmaus road. For example, Peter's Pentecost sermon finds in Ps 16:8-11 a prefiguration of Jesus' resurrection, and in Ps 110:1 a reference to Jesus' enthronement (Acts 2:22-36). Similarly, Peter's speech before the Jewish council reads Ps 118:22 as a prefiguration of Jesus' rejection, death, and vindication (Acts 4:8-12). To cite just one more example, Philip, in his encounter with the Ethiopian eunuch, finds "the good news about Jesus" in the Isaiah 53 account of the Suffering Servant (Acts 8:26-40).[35] These passages provide clear models for the reading strategy that Luke 24:25-27 articulates in principle.

32. Moberly, *Bible, Theology, and Faith,* p. 51.

33. As Professor Paul Meyer, in a written communication commenting on an earlier draft of this essay, observes, "What is not in doubt is the Messiah's glory. What needs explaining is that the path to this glory lies through the crucifixion."

34. Moberly points out that Luke's portrayal of Jesus' identity throughout his Gospel draws on Old Testament texts, for example, the Spirit-anointed Servant of Isa 61 in Luke 4:16-21. Moberly, *Bible, Theology, and Faith,* pp. 51-52. The point is well taken, but most of the examples offered by Moberly do not clearly demonstrate the pattern of suffering and glorification of which Luke 24:26 speaks. The pattern appears more unambiguously in the Acts material.

35. For an exposition of Acts 8:26-40 in light of Luke's resurrection themes, see J. B. Green, "Witnesses of His Resurrection: Resurrection, Salvation, Discipleship, and Mission in the Acts of the Apostles," in *Life in the Face of Death,* ed. Longenecker, pp. 227-46, esp. 233-35.

Yet strikingly, even Jesus' definitive peripatetic Bible study does not produce understanding and recognition in the Emmaus disciples, at least not immediately. The moment of recognition comes only as they sit at table and Jesus breaks bread with them (vv. 30-32) — an action that recalls Jesus' last supper with his disciples in Jerusalem (22:14-20). This point, too, is significant for understanding the hermeneutics of resurrection. We do not gain a grasp of Scripture's significance solely through lectures on the text; we come to understand the death and resurrection of Jesus as we participate in the shared life of the community, enacted in meals shared at table.[36]

For those who participate in the practices of sharing modeled by Jesus, an "opening" occurs. It is not by accident that Luke uses this word twice in quick succession. When Jesus broke the bread and gave it to them, their eyes *were opened* (διηνοίχθησαν, *diēnoichthēsan,* v. 31) to recognize him, and as they later recall his teaching, they say, "Weren't our hearts burning within us as he was speaking to us on the road, as he *opened* (διήνοιγεν, *diēnoigen*) to us the scriptures?" (v. 32; my translation). The disciples' faculties of perception are opened by God in such a way that they now recognize not only Jesus but also that the Scriptures have been opened by Jesus' interpretations. The same word appears once more in the following account of Jesus' teaching of the disciples in Jerusalem: "Then he opened (διήνοιξεν, *diēnoixen*) their minds to understand the scriptures" (v. 45).[37] Reading in light of the resurrection opens both text and reader to new, previously unimagined, possibilities.

36. Moberly states the point concisely: "Christian understanding is inseparable from a certain kind of 'eucharistic' lifestyle and practice. It is to those who are willing to live and act as Jesus did that the way Jesus understood God and scripture is most likely to make sense." Moberly, *Bible, Theology, and Faith,* p. 66. Moberly intends the term "eucharistic" to refer not just to liturgical ceremonies but to a broad range of practices that are "symbolically suggestive of the kind of action through which Jesus, the Christ, welcomed people and mediated God's kingdom to them" (p. 65).

37. The second part of the story, Jesus' appearance to the gathered disciples (vv. 36-49), continues the motifs we have already seen in the Emmaus narrative while adding an antidocetic emphasis on the physically embodied form of the risen Jesus (vv. 38-43). The theme of Scripture fulfillment resurfaces in vv. 44-47. This time Jesus specifies more fully that there are things written about him in "the law of Moses, the prophets, and the psalms" that must be fulfilled (v. 44). The unusual threefold formula (in place of the more usual "the law and the prophets") may correspond loosely to the tripartite division of the Hebrew canon (Law, Prophets, and Writings), but it also highlights the particular importance of the Psalms, read christologically, in early Christianity. In any case, Jesus declares that the Scriptures are full of foreshadowings of himself. A new element is added in v. 47 — the claim that the mission to all nations is also adumbrated in Scripture. Thus the new resurrection-shaped reading of Scripture also finds in the Old Testament a warrant for the preaching mission to the Gentiles.

All three texts we have examined dramatize the hermeneutical nexus between Scripture and resurrection. Luke 24 proclaims overtly what was hinted by our first two passages, in John 2 and Mark 12: in the new situation created by the resurrection of Jesus, Israel's Scripture is to be comprehensively construed as a witness to the gospel. According to these Gospel texts, those who fail to read the Old Testament this way have not yet understood it, at least not fully, for understanding is rendered possible only after the encounter with the risen Jesus. At the same time, the resurrection of Jesus will remain a mute, uninterpretable puzzle unless it is placed firmly within the Old Testament's story of Israel. The disciples on the way to Emmaus had already heard it reported that Jesus was alive, but because they did not know how to locate this report within Israel's story, it seemed a curious and meaningless claim. Their incomprehension exemplifies the grimly ironic dictum with which Luke's parable of the rich man and Lazarus concludes: "If they do not listen to Moses and the prophets, neither will they be convinced even if someone rises from the dead" (Luke 16:31). The good news of Luke 24, however, is that the story does not end in incomprehension and hermeneutical failure, because the one who rose from the dead teaches us anew how to listen to Moses and the prophets.

III. Implications for Our Practices of Reading

What, then, does it mean to read Scripture in light of the resurrection? What are the *hermeneutical* consequences of standing on this side of the empty tomb? The following observations are preliminary reflections about how we might begin to answer this question.[38]

(1) God is the subject of the crucial verbs in the biblical story. When we read Scripture in light of the resurrection, we read it as a story about the power of the God who gives life to the dead and calls into existence the things that do not exist. It is not a story about self-help, not a story about human wisdom, not a story about shaping our own identity. It is a story about God — a God who has revealed himself definitively through a mighty act beyond all human capacity, raising Jesus from the dead and transforming the cosmos.

---

38. The following nine points are not intended to correspond precisely to the "Nine Theses on the Interpretation of Scripture." The *numerical* correspondence is coincidental. On the other hand, the *material* convergence of these points with the Nine Theses reflects the significant extent to which my own thinking has been influenced by the deliberations of the Scripture Project. The present essay seeks to demonstrate how the interpretive approach recommended in the Nine Theses might inform exegetical practice.

Therefore, anthropocentric readings are at best flattened and truncated accounts of the story.[39]

(2) When we read Scripture in light of the resurrection, we understand Scripture as testimony to the life-giving power of God. The resurrection of Jesus is not an isolated miracle but a disclosure of God's purpose finally to subdue death and to embrace us within the life of the resurrection. "As all die in Adam, so all will be made alive in Christ" (1 Cor 15:22). For that reason, a hermeneutic responsive to the resurrection can never be a hermeneutic of suspicion toward Scripture's word of promise. The God with whom we have to do is a God who wills life and wholeness for us. If we read the biblical story rightly as a story about this God, we will learn to read it in hopeful trust, open to joyous surprises. We will read with hearts open to the divine power disclosed in the resurrection — a power that overthrows all human systems of violence and oppression. (See Eph 1:17-23.)

(3) The New Testament's resurrection accounts teach us to read the Old Testament as Christian Scripture. To read it in this way, as we have noted, does not mean to deny its original historical sense, nor does it preclude responsible historical criticism. Christians have a stake in seeking the most historically careful readings of the Old Testament texts that we can attain. At the same time, however, in light of the New Testament's witness, we cannot confine the meaning of the Old Testament to the literal sense understood by its original authors and readers, for these ancient texts have been taken up into a new story that amplifies and illumines their meaning in unexpected ways. The New Testament writers insist that we are to read Israel's story as a witness to the righteousness of God, climactically disclosed in Jesus Christ. They insist that Israel's Scriptures, understood in the fullest and deepest way, prefigure Jesus. This claim, of course, has important implications for Jewish-Christian dialogue. I would suggest that the goal of such dialogue should be not "tolerance" but respectful controversy between communities that make competing and partly incompatible claims about the meaning of Israel's story. In any case, the stories we have considered here show emphatically that a hermeneutic of resurrection will not treat the Old Testament as superseded or obsolete. It has an indispensable role in bearing witness to the gospel.

(4) Reading in light of the resurrection is figural reading. Because the Old Testament's pointers to the resurrection are indirect and symbolic in character, the resurrection teaches us to read for figuration and latent sense. The Sadducees were literalists, but God seems to have delighted in veiled an-

---

39. This point accords with Brian Daley's observations about the emphasis on divine action in patristic biblical interpretation. See Daley, "Is Patristic Exegesis Still Usable?"

ticipations of the gospel. For that reason, resurrection is the enemy of textual literalism. Or, more precisely, resurrection reconfigures the literal sense of Scripture by catalyzing new readings that destabilize entrenched interpretations: the resurrection stories teach us always to remain alert to analogical possibilities and surprises. Resurrection-informed reading sees the life-giving power of God manifested and prefigured in unexpected ways throughout Scripture. It would therefore be a mistake to catalogue, say, all the explicitly christological readings of Old Testament texts in Luke-Acts and suppose that we had thereby exhausted the hermeneutical possibilities for understanding Scripture's witness to Jesus Christ. On the contrary, the Jesus who taught the disciples on the Emmaus road that *all* the scriptures bore witness to him continues to teach us to discover figural senses of Scripture that are not developed in the New Testament.[40]

(5) To read Scripture in light of the resurrection is to read with emphasis on eschatological hope. The resurrection as a hermeneutical lens brings into focus the Old Testament's propensity to lean forward with eager longing for God to make all things whole. I do not mean simply that texts such as Isa 25:6-8, Ezek 37, and Dan 12:2-3 take on new weight in light of the story of Jesus' resurrection — though of course they do. Rather, I mean that in light of the resurrection, the Old Testament's narrative movement — from sterility to miraculous childbirth, from slavery in Egypt to freedom in the promised land, from exile to return — is to be interpreted as an adumbration of the eschatological hope signified in the New Testament by the resurrection of the dead. The logic of eschatological hope is structurally fundamental to the Old Testament canon.

Reading in light of the resurrection in no way nullifies the cross. In some New Testament scholarship, there has been a tendency to disparage resurrection texts such as Luke 24 as "triumphalistic" in contrast to a Pauline *theologia crucis*. This tendency simply displays a misunderstanding of the way the New Testament's resurrection stories function: by vindicating the crucified Jesus, the resurrection marks the cross as "the decisive, apocalyptic event that makes sense of Israel's story."[41] Furthermore, the New Testament's resurrection stories, no less than the Old Testament's narratives, continue to celebrate God's acts of saving power as proleptic signs of the ultimate triumph of God's righteousness (as, e.g., 1 Cor 15:20-28 clearly indicates). In the time between Jesus' resurrection and parousia, therefore, the church lives under the sign of the cross

40. For an excellent example of this open process of figuration, see the discussion of christological resonances of the Joseph story in Gary A. Anderson, "Joseph and the Passion of Our Lord," in this volume.

41. Paul Meyer, written communication, 26 April 2002.

while awaiting the consummation of God's promises. Thus the New Testament and the Old Testament are closely analogous in their eschatological orientation and in their posture of awaiting God's deliverance in the midst of suffering.

(6) Reading Scripture in light of the resurrection produces an epistemological transformation of the readers. Having encountered the risen Jesus, we are forced — enabled — to revise our perceptual categories and our estimates of what is "real." The epistemological shift is nicely illustrated by Paul's rhetorical question in his speech before Agrippa: "Why is it thought incredible by any of you that God raises the dead?" (Acts 26:8). Paul, already trained as a Pharisee to expect the resurrection, now finds himself living in a world in which the truth of Jesus' resurrection shapes his commonsense view of daily reality. That someone might find resurrection incredible seems as odd to him as it would seem to us today that someone might still believe the earth to be flat. The resurrection produces a "conversion of the imagination" that causes us to understand everything else differently.[42]

Sarah Coakley has drawn attention to this phenomenon of transformed understanding in a fascinating essay, "The Resurrection and the 'Spiritual Senses': On Wittgenstein, Epistemology and the Risen Christ."[43] She explores the claim that the resurrection of Jesus might bring about "a transformation of the believer's actual epistemic *apparatus*."[44] She explains that Origen and Gregory of Nyssa, in their doctrine of the spiritual senses, suggest "how seeking and recognising the resurrected Christ require a *process* of change . . . ; it will involve an initial 'turning-around' morally,[45] then practice in seeing the world differently, then only finally the full intimacy of 'spiritual/sensual' knowledge of Christ. What happens in this process is a transformation of one's actual epistemic capacities through their purgation."[46] The resurrection

42. See Richard B. Hays, "The Conversion of the Imagination: Scripture and Eschatology in 1 Corinthians," *New Testament Studies* 45 (1999): 391-412.

43. Sarah Coakley, *Powers and Submissions: Spirituality, Philosophy, and Gender* (Oxford: Blackwell, 2002), pp. 130-52.

44. Coakley, *Powers and Submissions*, p. 131.

45. By reminding us that the process of epistemic transformation also involves a moral "turning-around," Coakley draws attention to the process of character formation in community as an indispensable preparation for the faithful interpretation of Scripture. On this theme, see especially L. Gregory Jones, "Embodying Scripture in the Community of Faith," and R. W. L. Moberly, "Living Dangerously," in this volume.

46. Coakley, *Powers and Submissions*, pp. 139-40. My remarks here have drawn attention primarily to the second stage of this process, the intellectual transformation through which we see the world differently. This need not necessarily be a long, drawn-out process. As Coakley notes, the New Testament's resurrection appearance stories "seem to involve 'epistemic transformations' much more instantaneous than those described in Origen's schema" (p. 146).

purges the death-bound illusions that previously held us captive and sets us free to perceive the real world of God's life-giving resurrection power.

The Gospel resurrection stories, then, expand our imagination and lead us to discern that God is at work within the sphere of physical time-space reality to transform and restore all things, negating death's power over the body. Our bodies become the vehicles and theaters of God's transforming power. That is why the gospel's epistemology privileges concreteness and anathematizes all docetism, Neoplatonism, and Kantian epistemological dualism. God the Creator raised Jesus from the dead; therefore, "flesh is precious."[47]

(7) The Gospel resurrection stories portray the risen Jesus as both palpable and elusive. A persistent motif of the appearance narratives, not just in Luke 24 but elsewhere as well, is that the disciples do not recognize the risen Lord at once. Furthermore, his presence seems to be oddly fleeting or intermittent. Luke Timothy Johnson, noting these elements of the story, speaks of a "dialectic of absence and presence at the heart of the resurrection faith."[48] This dialectic teaches us that, despite our new epistemological vantage point after the resurrection, we are not ourselves in control of the new knowledge we are given. The risen Christ is present where and when he chooses. Paradoxically, our new understanding depends on an event that we cannot possibly understand. Therefore, we are radically dependent on a God who insists on being known on his terms, not ours: "For my thoughts are not your thoughts, nor are your ways my ways" (Isa 55:8). A hermeneutic of resurrection, then, will teach us epistemic humility.

(8) In Luke 24, we have encountered the hint that resurrection-empowered reading occurs primarily in the context of a shared life in community, in the practice of breaking bread together. But here we must reckon with a hermeneutical circle. In Acts and the Epistles, it becomes abundantly clear that the resurrection is a generative event that creates a new community whose practices embody the message of resurrection. That embodiment, in turn, enables us to perceive the truth of the resurrection in Scripture. To take a single striking example, Luke narrates the sharing of possessions as an identity-defining practice of the early Jerusalem community and links this practice to the resurrection: "With great power the apostles gave their testimony to the resurrection of the Lord Jesus, and great grace was upon them all, *for* (γὰρ, *gar*) there was not a needy person among them, for (γὰρ) as

47. Robert Morgan articulates this insight but curiously tries to integrate it into a Bultmannian hermeneutic that undercuts the point he is seeking to make. Robert Morgan, "Flesh Is Precious: The Significance of Luke 24.36-43," in *Resurrection: Essays in Honour of Leslie Houlden*, ed. S. Barton and G. Stanton (London: SPCK, 1994), pp. 8-20.

48. Luke Timothy Johnson, "Luke 24:1-11," *Interpretation* 46 (1992): 58.

many as owned lands or houses sold them and brought the proceeds of what was sold. They laid it at the apostles' feet, and it was distributed to each as any had need."[49] Thus the hermeneutics of resurrection is intimately linked with practices of discipleship and mission.[50]

(9) Finally, reading Scripture in light of the resurrection will provoke us to rethink our methods for studying the Gospels. New Testament scholars since the Enlightenment have, on the whole, been sympathizers of the Sadducees; that is to say, they have constructed historical accounts of the formation of the Gospel narratives that bracket out the resurrection as a real event in history. The theses of Robert Funk, quoted in the first section of this essay, offer a particularly egregious example, but Funk's proposals are in fact nothing more than extensions of modernist presuppositions that have influenced much mainstream New Testament exegesis for the past two centuries: God does not intervene in the processes of history; incarnation, resurrection, and judgment are mythological conceptions; Jesus could not have prophesied his own death and resurrection; the resurrection narratives are legendary; and so forth.[51] If, however, God did raise the crucified Jesus from his tomb, such critical commonplaces should be among the first elements of the status quo to be overturned. The problem was acutely described in 1909 in a penetrating essay by Adolf Schlatter:

> According to the sceptical position, it is true that the historian explains; he observes the New Testament neutrally. But in reality this is to begin at once with a determined struggle against it. The word with which the New Testament confronts us intends to be believed, and so rules out once and for all any sort of neutral treatment. As soon as the historian sets aside or brackets the question of faith, he is making his concern with the New Testament and his presentation of it into a radical and total polemic against it. . . . If he claims to be an observer, concerned solely with his object, then he is concealing what is really happening. As a matter of fact, he is always in possession of certain convictions, and these determine him not simply

---

49. Acts 4:33-35. The NRSV fails to translate the γὰρ at the beginning of v. 34, thus obscuring the text's claim that the practice of sharing is the warrant that demonstrates the presence of God's grace and resurrection power in the community.

50. Green, "Witnesses of His Resurrection," p. 242; Stephen Barton, "The Hermeneutics of the Gospel Resurrection Narratives," in *Resurrection,* ed. Barton and Stanton, pp. 45-57, esp. 54-55. See also the discussion in Moberly, *Bible, Theology, and Faith,* pp. 65-66.

51. Funk characterizes the views of his fellow participants in the Jesus Seminar as follows: ". . . we all assume, they said, that Jesus' life ended with his crucifixion and death." Funk, *Honest to Jesus,* p. 258.

in the sense that his judgments derive from them, but also in that his perception and observation is molded by them.[52]

What would critical study of the Bible look like if we heeded Schlatter's argument that dogmatics necessarily "permeates the whole course of historical work"[53] and that our location within the community of faith enhances rather than hinders our capacity to understand the past and the historical development of the tradition?[54] What would biblical criticism look like if we sought to develop a consistent critical approach from within the community that knows itself to be given life by the resurrection of Jesus of Nazareth? I do not mean to suggest that it is unheard of for New Testament scholars to be believers, but it is rare for them to ask how the resurrection — if it is true — ought to affect our methods for studying the history of the Synoptic tradition. To pursue this question consistently would be to create a disturbance as troubling to the New Testament guild as Jesus' protest action in the temple must have been to the moneychangers — or, perhaps, as troubling as the report of Jesus' resurrection must have been to the Sadducees.

---

52. Adolf Schlatter, "The Theology of the New Testament and Dogmatics," in *The Nature of New Testament Theology: The Contribution of William Wrede and Adolf Schlatter*, ed. and trans. R. Morgan, SBT 2/25 (Naperville, Ill.: Allenson, 1973), pp. 122-24.

53. Schlatter, "Theology of the New Testament," p. 126.

54. By way of contrast, see the recent assertion of Gerd Lüdemann that "the pursuit of theology as an academic discipline should not be tied to the confession [of faith], and . . . if it is, it is not a true academic discipline." Gerd Lüdemann, *Washington Post*, 6 April 2002, B9.

How Can We Know the Truth?
A Study of John 7:14-18

R. W. L. Moberly

What difference, if any, should belief in the Bible as the revelation of God make to the way in which one studies the Bible? How, if at all, should academic biblical study contribute to growth in faith and the knowledge of God? These are the kinds of questions that tend, in one form or another, to be asked by many students of theology at some time in their studies.

Sandra Schneiders, for example, prefaces her groundbreaking study of biblical interpretation with the following anecdote:

> I found myself increasingly plagued by questions that seemed to have no answers. Once in Paris, in a graduate seminar in Old Testament exegesis, I asked my brilliant and justly famous professor (a man of deep religious conviction) what implication the fact that the Old Testament was inspired had for our interpretation of the text. He replied simply, *"Rien de tout."* I filed this answer in the mental drawer labeled only with a large question mark. I had no idea what the hermeneutical implications of inspiration might be, but it seemed strange that, if the very reason for our interest in this text was that it was somehow "the word of God," this theological fact had no significance for the interpretation of the text.[1]

There are, of course, various tasks within biblical study that need have little direct relation to theological issues — perhaps most obviously, the mastering of the biblical languages, for the rewards of theological insight, though potentially great, come only after the exercise of prolonged self-discipline and patience in the mastering of grammar, syntax, vocabulary, and idiom (though

---

1. Sandra Schneiders, *The Revelatory Text: Interpreting the New Testament as Sacred Scripture,* 2nd ed. (Collegeville, Minn.: Liturgical Press, 1999), p. 2.

of course the qualities required for language learning are a reminder that all academic work, rightly approached, can — indeed, should — be understood as a moral and spiritual discipline).[2]

Nonetheless, the ways in which our initial questions tend to be asked are usually related to the ways in which biblical study has developed in the modern period. For biblical study was able to become a discipline in its own right only by disentangling and distancing itself from the context of Christian theology, where it had previously been located.[3] One of the formative moments (in retrospect) was Johann Gabler's inaugural lecture of 1787, "On the Proper Distinction between Biblical and Dogmatic Theology and the Specific Objectives of Each."[4] Whatever Gabler's own concerns,[5] his title came to be widely seen as articulating a fundamental distinction between biblical and theological study, a distinction that could be expressed in a number of seemingly related antitheses concerning proper biblical scholarship: unfettered historical research vs. the constraints of authoritative dogmatic pronouncements; original meaning vs. ecclesiastical reinterpretation; descriptive accounts vs. normative affirmations. Thus the distinction between biblical and dogmatic theology became primarily not a pragmatic division of labor (though of course it might function thus) but an expression of modernity's fundamental antithesis between scientific reason and Christian faith, an antithesis intended to privilege the former and problematize the latter.

For many reasons this kind of antithesis is seriously flawed.[6] The purpose of this essay is thus to contribute, via a small case study, toward the broad task of reconceiving academic biblical interpretation. The goal is not to

2. For a fascinating account of the spiritual value of academic work, see Simone Weil, "Reflections on the Right Use of School Studies with a View to the Love of God," in *Waiting on God* (London: Fontana, 1959), pp. 66-76.

3. My conventional reference to Christian theology is in fact a shorthand for predominantly Protestant theology. The cumulative transformations of biblical study in the Renaissance, Reformation, and Enlightenment did not have a serious impact on the Roman Catholic Church until well into the twentieth century, and even more recently in Eastern Orthodox contexts. Similar issues have also arisen, mutatis mutandis, in Judaism.

4. See J. Sandys-Wunsch and L. Eldredge, "J. P. Gabler and the Distinction between Biblical and Dogmatic Theology: Translation, Commentary, and Discussion of his Originality," *Scottish Journal of Theology* 33 (1980): 133-58.

5. For Gabler's own context and concerns, see Loren T. Stuckenbruck, "Johann Philipp Gabler and the Delineation of Biblical Theology," *Scottish Journal of Theology* 52 (1999): 139-57.

6. See Schneiders's work (n. 1); also Anthony C. Thiselton, *New Horizons in Hermeneutics* (New York: HarperCollins, 1992). A lucid and compelling work of broader philosophical considerations, which does not discuss Bible or theology but which clarifies the conceptual contexts within which biblical interpretation is done, is Mary Midgley, *Science and Poetry* (London and New York: Routledge, 2001).

say that all biblical study must become theological, for the Bible can legitimately be studied in differing ways according to context and purpose. The concern, rather, is of a different kind: to seek a way of overcoming the antithesis between reason and faith — which is also a dissociation of knowledge from love, of the head from the heart — such that a renewed and more integrated understanding of the academic task becomes possible.

Introduction to John 7:14-18

Our text is a short piece of narrative:

> [14]When the feast was already under way, Jesus went up to the temple courts[7] and taught. [15]The Jews were astonished and said, "How does this man have such learning when he has not formally studied?"[8] [16]Jesus answered them, "My teaching is not mine but his who sent me. [17]If anyone is prepared to do his will, then that person shall know about the teaching — whether it is from God or whether what I say is only my own. [18]The one whose words are only his own seeks his own honor; but the one who seeks the honor of him who sent him — such a one is true and does not deceive [lit., injustice is not in him]."

This little paragraph is not obviously significant. Nothing particularly dramatic is taking place at this point in John's narrative, even though the subsequent exchanges between Jesus and others in the temple precincts become highly charged and include a momentous pronouncement by Jesus (7:37-39). Correspondingly, many commentators find little of special significance in these five verses, often being content mainly to discuss how these verses relate to similar material in 5:31-47 (some relocate 7:15-24 to a position after 5:47), how the question in 7:15 is to be understood, how the train of thought flows from 7:18 to 7:19, and then to offer an interpretative paraphrase to the effect that John understands divine revelation in Jesus to be self-authenticating.

The passage is of course striking in the way in which the dialogue be-

---

7. τὸ ἱερόν *(to hieron)* signifies the temple courts and enclosure as a whole, while ὁ ναός *(ho naos)* is the temple proper (cf. John 2:13-22, where this distinction is observed: ἱερόν in vv. 14, 15; ναός in vv. 19, 20, 21).

8. The point of the text is not astonishment that Jesus is literate, though the language of "knowing letters" could in itself mean this, but rather that he engages in the kind of learned discourse and disputation that would normally presuppose study (being a *mathētēs*) in a rabbinic school (as Paul sat at the feet of Gamaliel, Acts 22:3).

tween Jesus and others both is and is not a dialogue. It is a dialogue in the obvious sense that that is how John presents the material. It is not a dialogue in the sense that the interlocutors are hardly talking to each other. The astonished Jews in v. 15 address their question not to Jesus (i.e., "How do you know . . . ?") but to themselves ("How does he know . . . ?"). Likewise, Jesus moves quickly from answering the specific question raised (v. 16) to dealing with his own (i.e., unasked) question of how one might know when teaching is from God. He handles the question in terms of two general principles, one relating to any would-be hearer (v. 17, not specifically addressed to those present: "If you are prepared . . .") and one relating to any would-be teacher (v. 18, though of course with reference to himself). This suggests that, as so often is the case in John's profound presentation of the mind of the master, Jesus is speaking not only to his interlocutors in his own context but also directly to the reader (or hearer) of the Gospel text.

How should we approach the text? The general convention among modern biblical commentators has been to consider primarily the context(s) of the *origins* of the text — the nature, purpose, and meaning of John's Gospel as a late-first-century/early-second-century text — and to consider only secondarily (if at all) questions about the *use* of the text over the last two millennia (a restriction of labor that has regularly been aligned, at least implicitly, with the polarities between reason/history and faith/dogma sketched above). Of course, even if one wishes to attend both to origins and to use, it often makes sense to start with origins. Yet since in the understanding of a text, knowledge of origins and of use often contribute dialectically, sometimes it may be helpful to approach the text via its use.

Modern writers of commentaries on John sometimes mention, whether or not they engage with, the most famous and influential early Christian commentary on the text (esp. vv. 16-17), that of St. Augustine.[9] For in *Homily 29* of his *Homilies on the Gospel of John*,[10] Augustine uses his exposition of this text to formulate his characteristic understanding of the necessity of believing in order to gain intellectual understanding — a principle that, not

---

9. So, for example, R. E. Brown, R. Schnackenburg, L. Morris. Exceptional is Ernst Haenchen, who gives considerable space to the interpretation of 7:17 in relation not to Augustine but to Albrecht Ritschl (1822-89), affirming that 7:17 is famous "as a consequence of the theology of Ritschl" and defending Ritschl from Bultmann's (apparent) misreading of him. Ernst Haenchen, *A Commentary on the Gospel of John*, Herm (Philadelphia: Fortress, 1984; ET from German of 1980), 2:13, 14, 19.

10. See M.-F. Berrouard, trans. and ed., *Oeuvres de Saint Augustin 72: Homélies sur l'Evangile de Saint Jean XVII–XXXIII*, BA (Paris: Desclée de Brouwer, 1977), pp. 596-613. Berrouard usefully discusses the date, context, and purposes of the homilies in his introduction.

least in light of St. Anselm's later formulation "credo ut intelligam" ("I believe so that I may understand"), many have taken to be a good definition of the enterprise of theology as a whole.[11] This patristic construal, and the tradition rooted in it, finds great significance in our text and so should be a promising place to begin.

St. Augustine's Exposition of John 7:16-17

Although one may rightly find in *Homily* 29 a general principle of Augustine's thought about belief and understanding[12] — and this is the reason for our interest in his text — Augustine's primary concern in the homily is in fact christological and trinitarian. If we abstract a general principle of epistemology in isolation from Augustine's desire rightly to respond to the triune God revealed in Jesus, then we will not do justice to Augustine's thought. It is the mystery of Christ as Word and Son in relation to the Father within the unity of the Trinity — which Augustine takes to be the meaning of v. 16 — for which the understanding born of faith, the concern of v. 17, is needed.

After some preliminary remarks, Augustine observes that the questioning of the Jews gives Jesus "an opportunity for more deeply inculcating the truth" through a "profound saying deserving more than usual care in its examination and explanation" (29.2). Augustine then focuses on the apparent contradiction between Jesus' depicting his teaching as both "mine" and "not mine." How can both be true? He resolves the problem by appealing to John's prologue, John 1:1. Jesus, as the Word, is himself the teaching of the Father. Yet a word must also be someone's word. Herein lies the solution to the apparent contradiction. Christ calls his teaching both "his," for it is himself, and "not his," for he is the Word of the Father (29.3). After an elaboration of different senses of "word" (29.4), Augustine introduces a trinitarian exposition of the equality between Son and Father, who definitionally exist in relation to each other as Son and Father, by a neat linking together of 7:16 and the latter part

11. The way in which Anselm (and Luther, Schleiermacher, and Barth, among others) follows Augustine's lead, and what the "credo ut intelligam" formula does and does not mean, is nicely spelled out by Nicholas Lash, "Anselm Seeking," in *The Beginning and the End of 'Religion'* (Cambridge: Cambridge University Press, 1996), pp. 150-63.

12. See Berrouard's listing of similar formulations both in the homilies on John and elsewhere in Augustine's works. Berrouard, *Homélies*, p. 57 n. 82, p. 607 n. 31. See also "Sermon 43: On What Is Written in Isaiah: 'Unless You Believe, You Shall Not Understand' (Is. 7:9 LXX)," abr. and trans. in *Augustine and the Bible,* ed. Pamela Bright (Notre Dame: University of Notre Dame Press, 1999), pp. 313-15.

of 7:17: "It seems to me that the Lord Jesus Christ, in saying 'My teaching is not mine' was in effect saying 'I am not from myself'" (29.5).

So deep a reality is this that some may not understand it. Jesus himself anticipated this, which is why he continues with the counsel of 7:17, summed up as "Do you want to understand? Believe" (29.6).[13] Augustine explicates this in two ways. First, there is precedent in the Old Testament prophetic text most used by the Fathers in this regard, Isaiah 7:9 in the Septuagint, "If you do not believe, you will not understand,"[14] on which basis Augustine affirms that "understanding is the reward of faith" and "therefore do not seek to understand so as to believe, but believe so as to understand." Second, Jesus' "if anyone is willing to do God's will" means "to believe," as emerges from John 6:29, "This is the work of God, that you believe in him whom he has sent." And what does believing in Jesus mean? It means loving Christ, going to him, and being incorporated into the members of his body. What God requires is faith itself — faith, as Paul says in Gal 5:6, that works through love. Such faith will yield understanding. And what is that understanding? That Jesus' teaching is not his but his who sent him; that is, that Christ the Son of God, who is the teaching of the Father, is not from himself but is the Son of the Father (29.6).

After noting that this affirmation undoes the Sabellian heresy, Augustine comments on 7:18, whose principle of self-exaltation, the fundamental sin of unwarranted pride, he sees as depicting Antichrist. This is the opposite of the way of Christ, who, although God of God, God with God, came humbly in the created order as a servant and sought the glory of the one who sent him. If that is the way of Christ, then the closing challenge is that Christians should resist the self-seeking way of Antichrist and follow in Christ's way.

Such, in outline, is Augustine's homily. It well illustrates both the strengths and the weaknesses of Augustine's scriptural interpretation. On the

---

13. "Intellegere vis? Crede."

14. The use of Isa 7:9b is a rich and complex issue in its own right. In its literary context, Isaiah is challenging Ahaz to trust YHWH in the face of apparently overwhelming opposition to Jerusalem, yet in v. 9b the address is to "you" *plural,* thereby apparently enunciating an axiom with significance beyond its immediate context. In the Hebrew there is a wordplay between the Hiphil and Niphal of אָמַן *('aman):* "If you do not stand firm in faith, you shall not stand at all" (NRSV). The Greek of the Septuagint, ἐὰν μὴ πιστεύσητε οὐδὲ μὴ συνῆτε *(ean mē pisteusēte oude mē synēte),* gives a different sense to the axiom. Why the Greek took this form is unclear, for συνῆτε *(synēte)* would naturally render Heb. תָּבִינוּ *(tavinu)* rather than תַּאֲמִנוּ *(te'amenu),* and we are not in a position to determine whether textual corruption or interpretative modification is the cause. As the Greek stands, it has a double contextual rationale — the pronouncement that immediately precedes and is hard to understand (7:7-9a) and Israel's lack of understanding in the previous chapter (6:9-10).

one hand, his meditation on John's Gospel is profound. Augustine makes his key interpretative cross-references within the Johannine text (esp. 1:1 and 6:29) and appeals to other scriptural texts that are genuinely apposite (esp. Isa 7:9 LXX; Gal 5:6). He expounds Jesus as God's self-communication in a way that is consonant with the heartbeat of Christian thought down the ages. And he depicts the relationship between believing and understanding in a way that has been formative in Christian theology. On the other hand, Augustine's crucial interpretative move does not ring true. He so quickly links Jesus' "being sent" with his being the "Word of the Father" and with the trinitarian relation of Son and Father that the words of 7:16 take on a meaning alien to the context of John 7; the issue of the text too quickly becomes the trinitarian concern of Augustine's own context.

Van Mildert's Interpretation of John 7:17

Before moving on from considering the use of our text, one other example will indicate something of its historic significance.[15] I choose the 1814 Bampton Lectures at Oxford by William Van Mildert, then Regius Professor of Divinity at Oxford (and subsequently bishop of Durham, where he played a leading role in the founding of the University of Durham, my current workplace). These lectures are not famous and have made no obvious lasting impact. But that makes them no less revealing of the kind of assumptions that a competent and tradition-rooted Anglican theologian could make at the outset of the nineteenth century.[16]

The overall title of the lectures/sermons is *An Inquiry into the General Principles of Scripture-Interpretation*. The second of the eight, which will be our focus here, is titled "Dispositions and Qualifications previously requisite in the Interpreter of Scripture." The text at its outset, which is subsequently expounded, is John 7:17, "If any man will do his will, he shall know of the doctrine, whether it be of God."[17] The basic question Van Mildert addresses is,

15. Also noteworthy is Calvin's comment on 7:17 that "the principle is universal in its application," indeed, that "these words of Christ contain a definition of true religion." John Calvin, *Calvin's Commentaries: John's Gospel*, vol. 1 (Edinburgh: Calvin Translation Society, 1847), pp. 290-91.

16. For the context and purposes of the lectures, see E. A. Varley, *The Last of the Prince Bishops: William Van Mildert and the High Church Movement of the Early Nineteenth Century* (Cambridge: Cambridge University Press, 1992), pp. 57-62.

17. William Van Mildert, *An Inquiry into the General Principles of Scripture-Interpretation, in Eight Sermons Preached Before the University of Oxford in the Year MDCCCXIV*, 3rd ed. (Oxford: Oxford University Press, 1831), pp. 23-46.

"Whence comes religious error?" (p. 23), and he argues that in light of Scripture generally, it becomes clear that "the will of man . . . is deeply concerned in every departure from the truth" (p. 25). This brings him specifically to John 7:17, which is "couched in general terms" and makes the point that "every error respecting the Christian Faith proceeds, more or less, from some perverseness in the mind; or, at least, that an earnest desire to know and to do the will of God, is so far a necessary preparative for a right understanding of its doctrines, that without it no proficiency in that respect is reasonably to be expected" (p. 28).

Specific discussion of his key text in itself (pp. 29-32) reveals that "The *disposition* to do the will of God appears to be the point on which the great stress of our Lord's observation is laid: — ἐάν τις θέλη, if any man *be willing*. . . ." However, "it is not . . . the general disposition of a person habitually practising moral and religious duties, which is here intended (though this is unquestionably of great importance in all inquiries after Sacred truth), but it is the specific character of a person free from prejudices unfavourable to the object of inquiry, and prepared, nay desirous, to profit by its researches." He then discusses the relationship between the understanding and the will, which he sees as complex and variegated, but he nonetheless concludes, "If there be, from whatever cause, an indisposition to do the will of God, there will ever be a proportionate difficulty in coming to the knowledge of the truth: and if the mind be free from adverse prepossessions, obstacles will be so much the more easily removed. This we may conceive to be the full scope and meaning of the text."

Van Mildert then applies the text, so understood, to his wider concern with scriptural interpretation. Other scriptural passages concur with John 7:17 that "the first requisite in the study of Divine truth . . . is a genuine singleness of heart, which has one main object in all its researches, that of knowing and obeying the will of God." He applies the principle both to "avowed unbelievers," where "strong presumptive evidence will almost always appear of a radical indisposition in the will to a careful investigation of the subject" (p. 36), and to "those who, professing a general belief of Christianity, maintain opinions at variance with its essential doctrines," where the "evident prepossessions of the mind against [essential doctrines]" is indicative of "that perversity of will which our Lord teaches us to regard as the proximate cause of all religious error" (p. 37). However, this principle should always be applied to others with "the greatest charity and discretion," while we should "scrutiniz[e] our own opinions . . . with unsparing freedom" (p. 38).

Van Mildert sums up: "The dispositions repugnant to that character [namely, of a sound and faithful interpreter of the Word], are carelessness, indifference to truth, indolence, rashness, a spirit of scepticism and self-conceit, pertinacity in retaining opinions hastily taken up, love of novelty, and a proneness to abandon what is sanctioned by long established authority and well tried experience. It is easy to perceive how these dispositions must operate on the intellectual powers . . ." (pp. 42-43). "In a word, that which we understand by the term, docility, or an aptitude to receive instruction, is the first requisite towards the acquisition of Scriptural knowledge" (p. 43). "Our Lord's admonition in the text demands the most profound consideration, as a fundamental maxim on which all consistency and correct knowledge of religion must depend" (p. 45).

Nearly two centuries later, Van Mildert's text is striking. It illuminatingly presupposes a framework of thought in which the issue within the Gospel context (whether Jesus' teaching is "from God" or "from himself," 7:16) needs no discussion, for 7:17 is understood to stand on its own as a general axiom.[18] Van Mildert does not show any of Augustine's concern with specifically Johannine theology, but his use of Scripture is guided by a disciplined sense of its general tenor. He makes no use of the incipient biblical criticism then current in Germany but remains firmly rooted in a context where Bible and Christian theology belong integrally together. Although his text contains much that sounds strange to contemporary ears and various points at which one might properly seek greater distinction or question his categories, there remains in Van Mildert a genuine challenge. Despite the characteristic tendency of modern biblical criticism to play down issues to do with the will and character of the interpreter (for there are, of course, numerous philological and historical issues in the handling of which questions of character may have little bearing),[19] there is recent renewed recognition of the crucial role that they can play.[20]

18. Van Mildert includes with the lectures an appendix where he cites his many sources (for lecture 2, pp. 261-70). Varley summarizes: "The Appendix acknowledged well over a hundred works: Fathers, Reformers, Caroline Divines, trinitarian controversialists, continental exegetes and sympathetic contemporaries. His principal sources were Horsley, Waterland, Leslie and St. Augustine." Varley, *Last of the Prince Bishops*, p. 57.

19. In public universities there are many other complicating factors. In older universities with religious foundations, the twentieth century saw many moves away from the founding concerns; in departments of theology and religion, there have been many attempts to overcome the restrictions (as to the nature of the subject and who may study it) imposed both by Christian denominations against each other and by Christian faith as a whole in relation to those with other or no religious profession. For trenchant observations from a sophisticated and observant Jewish perspective, see Jon D. Levenson, "Theological Consensus or Historicist Evasion? Jews and Christians in Biblical Studies," in *The Hebrew Bible, the Old Testament, and Historical Criticism* (Louisville: Westminster/John Knox, 1993), pp. 82-105.

20. See L. Gregory Jones, "Embodying Scripture in the Community of Faith," in this volume.

More generally, what both Augustine and Van Mildert show in their different ways is an understanding of the task of scriptural interpretation as integrally related to the doctrine, ethics, and spirituality of Christian faith — an understanding they find spelled out in its essence within Scripture itself, in John 7:16-17. This provides a frame of reference within which we may now turn to our text within its Johannine context.

John 7:14-18 in Its Johannine Context

The placement of our text in its Johannine context raises at least four significant issues. First, the critical concern around which the text revolves — whether or not Jesus' teaching is "from God" or only "from himself," and how one might be able to tell the difference — resonates with a fundamental polarity that runs throughout John's text. The polarity is between that which is "from God," "from above," "from heaven," "from the Spirit," "not from this world," and that which is "from the world/earth," "from the flesh," "from oneself." This polarity is expressed with many variations of terminology, though probably little difference in meaning, in many passages, some of them of prime structural importance (e.g., 1:12-13; 3:1-8, 31-32; 8:23, 28; 18:36-37). Thus the concerns of our passage are not marginal but central within the Gospel.

Second, the meaning of this polarity in its Johannine context is perhaps best spelled out in the prologue. It has to do with an understanding of humanity as made by God and for God, such that the true nature of being human is realized only when people are rightly responsive to God. This is expressed by John in terms of all being made by God through the Logos/Word — "all things were made through him, and without him nothing that has been made was made" (1:3) — which means that in appropriate responsiveness to Jesus, the Logos/Word become flesh, people do not undergo some arbitrary or optional religious experience but rather discover that for which they are made. The problem is that people are not responsive as they should be, not even those (i.e., Israel) who were given most understanding of God — "He [namely, the true light] was in the world, and the world was made through him, yet the world did not know him. He came to what was his own, yet those who were his own did not accept him" (1:10-11). The Gospel's portrayal of Jesus is simultaneously an exploration and an exposition of the dynamics of what causes people both to miss and to discover their true nature in God — in other words, the respective dynamics of being "from the world" and "from God."

Third, the passage is about the teaching (διδαχή, *didachē*, vv. 16, 17) of

Jesus. Despite the importance of the prologue for clarifying the passage's theological categories, John 7:16 is not (*pace* Augustine) about Jesus himself. That is, while within the total context of John's Gospel, questions about the nature and status of Jesus' teaching become ultimately inseparable from christological questions about Jesus himself, it does not do justice to our text to assimilate too quickly its concern with teaching to the Gospel's overall concern with Christology.[21] Things that may need ultimately to be held together may sometimes proximately, and for particular purposes, be validly and usefully distinguished.

In general terms we need to keep in mind the distinction between a prophet, whose message may be considered to come truly from God (cf. 1:6-8), and Jesus, whose whole being is said by John to come from God. Yet even if there is ultimately a major difference between Jesus and the prophets, we should not jump to the affirmation of difference too quickly. For the biblical prophetic concept of being "sent" by God[22] is regularly used of Jesus (as, in our text, in vv. 16, 18) in a way that does not suggest any intrinsic difference of kind between Jesus and the prophets. Moreover, the words of the risen Jesus to his disciples "As the Father has sent me, so I send you" (20:21) emphasize the continuity between the mission of Jesus and that of his disciples. The disciples are not "from God" as Jesus is in terms of being, yet they are "from God" as Jesus is in terms of their mission. The uniqueness of Jesus is not in doubt for John, yet this uniqueness does not preclude fundamental continuities between Jesus and others, and John does not seem to regard it as important to provide definitional clarity as to where the "break" comes.[23]

Fourth, the strong rhetorical polarity ("not this but that"), as in 7:16, "My teaching is not mine but his who sent me," must be taken seriously, but not woodenly. In analytic terms the "not this but that" can regularly mean "not only this but also that." When Jesus ascribes his teaching not to himself

21. So also John Ashton argues that the issue in context is prophecy and is separable from high Christology. John Ashton, *Understanding the Fourth Gospel* (Oxford: Clarendon, 1991), pp. 308-17, esp. 310, 312. However, Ashton's analysis is related to a thesis about the historical development of the Johannine community and its christological formulations, whereas my argument is in terms of the intrinsic logic of the text.

22. Hebrew שָׁלַח (*shalakh*), as in Exod 3:13-15; Isa 6:8; Jer 23:21; 29:31. John's corresponding verbs are ἀποστέλλω (*apostellō*) and πέμπω (*pempō*), which he seems to use synonymously; see C. K. Barrett, *The Gospel according to St. John*, 2nd ed. (Philadelphia: Westminster, 1978), p. 569.

23. Sensitivity to the totality of the Johannine portrayal should discourage any easy privileging of "prophetic" Christology over against a traditional "incarnational" Christology, a move already made by Schleiermacher; see conveniently Francis Watson, "Trinity and Community: A Reading of John 17," *International Journal of Systematic Theology* 1 (1999): 168-84, esp. 168 n. 1.

but to God, he does not mean that he is a mere passive mouthpiece for something originating elsewhere that he passes on without enhancing in any significant way (which would be one possible way of construing his words). On the contrary, Jesus has so absorbed, appropriated, and made his own his Father's teaching that he can speak of a oneness of will and purpose and action between them (e.g., 5:19-24), a oneness that is open to others also who similarly respond to God as Father (17:20-23). The point is that Jesus' teaching that is indeed his own, in the sense that it characterizes and identifies him, is that which is not his own, in the sense that it does not originate with him but is from God.

The Wider Resonances and Implications of John 7:16

Jesus' claim about his teaching, despite its specific Johannine formulation and context, can readily be seen to have wide resonances elsewhere in Scripture. There are similar claims by, or on behalf of, prophets and apostles that these are people whose human words convey the divine word. Thus, for example, the introductory heading to the book of Jeremiah, "The words of Jeremiah . . . to whom the word of YHWH came . . ." (Jer 1:1-2), is presenting Jeremiah's human words as having their source in God. Similarly, Paul can write to the Thessalonians with the same affirmation about his preaching, expressed with the same "not human but divine" rhetorical idiom as characterizes the teaching of Jesus in John 7: "We thank God unceasingly that when you received the word of God you heard from us, you accepted it not as a human word but as what it really is, a divine word, which is also at work in you believers" (1 Thess 2:13).[24]

How are such claims to be understood, and how are they to be evaluated? Particularly at the present time, when many voices emphasize that we construct all our knowledge, it is incumbent upon believers to give an adequate account of what is meant by their affirmation that it is possible for some knowing to be given by God and received by humans so that the constructive work of the human mind is still constructing that which is antecedently given. Alternatively, the resurgence of hermeneutical suspicion — that is, that claims to speak for God may show nothing so much as self-deception and/or manipulation of others — needs to be taken with full seriousness,

---

24. Paul is particularly fond of a rhetorical "not I . . . but God/Christ" to express his self-understanding of what he says and does in relation to God; see, for example, Gal 2:20; 1 Cor 15:10b.

though, significantly, such suspicion in effect renews a sharp critical awareness already present within Scripture and classic Christian spirituality.[25]

Given the need to be able in some way to substantiate claims to speak
from and for God, it is unsurprising that the Johannine text moves on directly
from the claim of Jesus to the question of how one might know when such a
claim is justified.[26]

An Interpretation of John 7:17-18

If "being prepared to do God's will" is the precondition for knowing whether
or not Jesus' teaching is from God, and if, as Augustine already pointed out,
"doing God's will" in a Johannine context is illuminated by John 6:29, where
the work of God is said to be "believing in the one whom he [i.e., God] sent,"
then the sense of v. 17 would seem to be, as Bultmann puts it:

> Only the man who hears the challenge of the Revealer's word and obeys
> it, i.e. the believer, will be able to judge whether it is the Word of God or
> the assertion of an arrogant man. For ποιεῖν τὸ θέλημα αὐτοῦ means no
> more nor less than believing. . . . For John there is no "ethics," no doing of
> the will of God, which is not primarily the obedience of faith; it is the ac-
> tion demanded by God (cf. 6.29).[27]

But if, in John, believing is not a matter of moral practice and integrity of
character (in the kind of way that Van Mildert interpreted the text), then is
there not a danger of the criterion for knowing becoming circular? As
Haenchen puts it:

> But if the "fulfillment of God's will" is the same thing as the acknowledg-
> ment that God has sent Jesus, and if Jesus' teaching consists essentially in
> proclaiming that he is the one sent by God, are we not then stuck in a tau-
> tology: Whoever believes that Jesus is a divine emissary will recognize
> that he has been sent from God?[28]

25. A lucid account is Merold Westphal, *Suspicion and Faith: The Religious Uses of Modern
Atheism* (Grand Rapids: Eerdmans, 1993).

26. Comparably, Paul's statement in 1 Thess 2:13 is preceded by extensive statements
about his integrity and selflessness, which function to provide warrant for the affirmation of a
message from God.

27. Rudolf Bultmann, *The Gospel of John: A Commentary* (Oxford: Blackwell, 1971; ET
from German of 1964), p. 274.

28. Haenchen, *Commentary on the Gospel of John*, 2:13.

The Johannine argument is indeed, in a certain sense, circular; and, in a certain sense, there may be no escape from it, even when criteria of recognition may be available. Bultmann, for example, recognizes that v. 18 "gives us the criteria for recognising the Revealer as such" but says that this makes no real difference to the point of v. 17 because "faith alone can see whether this criterion applies in the particular instance, whether, that is, it applies here to Jesus. In other words v. 18, on the lips of Jesus, is simply a challenge to men to accept him as the true Revealer."[29]

So fundamental, indeed, to Johannine theology is this "circle" that it recurs constantly. For example, the depiction of Jesus as "true" (ἀληθής, *alēthēs*, 7:18) is part of a wider Johannine concern with "truth" (ἀλήθεια, *alētheia*). In the trial before Pilate, Jesus defines his kingship (i.e., his messiahship, that life-giving understanding of Jesus that the Gospel is written to promote, 20:31) first negatively, as "not from this world," "not from here" (18:36), and then positively, in terms of witnessing to the truth, which he combines with saying what is necessary to perceive and respond to this witness: "For this I was born and for this I came into the world — to bear witness to the truth; everyone who is of the truth hears my voice" (18:37). This language recalls the earlier account of the purpose of Jesus' life (3:16-21), which itself recalls the prologue (esp. 1:5, 9-13). The truth is a light — a searchlight that shines into the darkness of the world and, when it shines on people, compels a choice: either to shrink back into the darkness lest what they do be exposed or to come forward in glad response to the light and so realize the true God-derived nature of those good intuitions and practices they already had (3:19-21). We could thus express the "circle" formulated by Haenchen in a different way: Jesus comes to enable the truth to be grasped, but only those who already in some way possess the truth will recognize that this is what Jesus does.

But what kind of "circle" is this? There is a world of difference between a closed, or vicious, circle (with no apparent points of entry or exit, where all is predictable in terms of certain premises) and an open circle (where the necessary and mutual relationship between certain factors can be engaged or evaded according to a person's degree of openness and where the outworking may be endlessly variable) — a circle that is really an ascending spiral.[30] In general terms, the Johannine conception is something people widely recognize and often express in other terms — "heart speaks to heart," "deep calls to

29. Bultmann, *Gospel of John*, pp. 275-76.

30. Hermeneutical theory has repeatedly shown how the necessarily "circular" relationship between preunderstanding and text need not be closed and predictable (though sadly it can become such) but rather should entail dialectical processes that lead to correction and true growth in understanding.

deep." Human awareness is complex and variegated, formed by many factors and responding variously in varied contexts; yet it is possible, at least sometimes, to recognize certain factors that form a person more fundamentally than do others and that may, from sometimes ambiguous beginnings, come over time to be determinative. Love is one such factor, and the close relationship between "love" and "faith" in a Johannine context (as, in varied ways, in other New Testament contexts as well) helps the interpreter see what is at stake in John's characteristic formulations.

The Johannine conception is further illuminated by at least two other factors. First, there is a recurrent use of the verb "come" or other analogous verbs of response ("follow," "eat," etc., all variations on "believe")[31] to depict that which a person needs to do when confronted by the truth that Jesus represents: "The light has come into the world . . . ; the one who does the truth comes to the light" (3:19-21); "I am the bread of life . . . ; the one who comes to me shall not hunger" (6:35). Thus *responsiveness,* envisaged in terms of *movement,* gives content to the hermeneutical spiral of revelation and reception depicted by John. Second, there are the narrative portrayals of Jesus' encounters with particular people in which the dynamics are rarely straightforward and a sense of movement, for good and for bad, characterizes the response to Jesus. The movement may be hesitant and partial, and it cannot be predicted at the outset of the encounter. The steady journey into light of the man born blind is paralleled by the authorities' progress in embracing darkness (John 9, the story that most clearly portrays the dynamics of right and wrong response, dynamics that are worked out even when Jesus is most of the time off-scene); Pilate moves first a little forward but then right back when his incipient intuitions that Jesus is innocent are snuffed out by his concern for self-preservation (18:33–19:16, esp. 19:12).

One of the difficulties in understanding the Johannine spiral of divine revelation and human response is the poverty of our categories for depicting the kind of human reality that is envisaged — and our awkwardness in using such categories as we do possess. To classify the spiral as "moral" would rightly draw attention to the demand made of a person's will and way of life but could mislead if taken to imply adherence to specific moral injunctions, for John's Gospel (as distinct from the Synoptics) is markedly lacking in such. To classify it as "spiritual" would rightly draw attention to the focusing of life upon God but could mislead if taken to imply concern for "feeling good" or showing interest in unusual psychic experiences,[32] both likewise absent in

---

31. Typically, at 6:35 "coming" and "believing" are used in parallel.

32. For a critique of William James's famous approach to religion via unusual and "special" experiences — not dissimilar to the assumptions that have made *The X-Files* a cult attrac-

John's text. To classify the spiral as "contemplative" (perhaps the prime term in much classic Christian parlance) would rightly indicate a searching human openness and loving attention toward God and all that is in God's creation but could mislead if taken to warrant any kind of passivity or introspective self-absorption. In short, there is no easy way of characterizing the content of John's text without the renewal of our conceptual categories in ways that have become foreign to contemporary culture.

Finally, there is the criterion of recognition specified in 7:18. The notion of seeking either "one's own honor" or "God's honor" — an alternative that embodies the basic polarity between a way of living that is "of this world" and one that is "of God" — is another recurrent Johannine emphasis. Indeed, to seek one's own honor is explicitly the opposite of, and that which in effect by definition prevents, having faith: "How are you able to believe, when you receive honor from one another and do not seek the honor that comes from the one who alone is God?" (5:44; cf. 12:43). Thus Jesus' giving teaching that is from God rather than from himself may be redescribed as a kind of self-dispossession that seeks only the honor of God. Only one in whom this kind of self-dispossession is evident can be trusted to be true.

How is this self-dispossession to be seen? The short answer, in John's wider context, is Jesus' way to the cross. In the immediate context, however, we are given a clue by the further specification that such a person not only is "true" but also "does not deceive." The Greek for this is initially a little puzzling, for ἀδικία (adikia, "injustice") must, in context, be the opposite of "true" and so indicate not just "injustice" but "falsehood." However, the choice of terminology may be on account of the Septuagint. As Bultmann puts it, "Ἄδικος and ἀδικία in the LXX are used frequently (for שֶׁקֶר) in the sense of 'liar,' 'lie.'"[33] The characteristic Old Testament use of שֶׁקֶר (sheqer, "falsehood") is well illustrated by Jeremiah's temple sermon (Jer 7). The repeated saying of the people of Judah about the Jerusalem temple, "This is the temple of YHWH" (which on one level is obviously factually correct), is roundly denounced as false (שֶׁקֶר, 7:4, 8), for it is part of a claim to God's presence and protection (7:10) even though the people are living in a way that disregards God's fundamental moral and religious requirements (7:5-6, 9); when the people live thus, the only way in which God's presence will be displayed is in the sweeping away of temple and people alike (7:12-15). That is, what the people say is false because it is a complacent and self-serving use of

---

tion — see Nicholas Lash, *Easter in Ordinary: Reflections on Human Experience and the Knowledge of God* (London: SCM, 1988).

33. Bultmann, *Gospel of John*, p. 276 n. 2.

language. Its opposite is an integrity that is truly responsive to God — as in our Johannine context.

Of course it is always possible, for a variety of reasons, to fail to see integrity when it is present (hence Bultmann's point that John 7:18 does not dispense with the need for faith), but that may ultimately be only to say that people often fail to see what they should see.

In sum, John 7:17-18 says that recognition of the true — that is, God-derived and God-revealing — nature of Jesus' teaching is possible only in the context of a faith that represents a certain kind of self-dispossession, when the human heart opens itself to the heart of God as encountered in Jesus. This is finely expressed by Kenneth Grayston, who in his commentary on this verse draws on the profound resonances of the Synoptic depiction of Jesus' engagement with the will of his Father in Gethsemane: "Only someone who says: 'Not my own will, but the will of God' will know whether *Jesus* truly says 'Not my own will, but the will of God.'"[34]

Conclusion

This essay approached John 7:14-18 via two case studies, St. Augustine and Van Mildert, which illustrate something of the historic use of the text and which, despite certain problems, have much of enduring value. It is striking to the modern reader how readily Augustine (with his trinitarian concerns) and Van Mildert (with his concerns about intellectual character) move beyond the horizons of the Johannine text in itself. We have therefore complemented their use by attending also to our text in its Johannine context. Nonetheless, when John is read as a canonical text whose context is the other writings of the Old and New Testaments, themselves situated within the continuing life, worship, and witness of the church, it becomes natural to extend the study so as to engage with comparable concerns elsewhere within Scripture and to relate them to recurrent issues in the life of faith.

Both Augustine and Van Mildert generalize the specific issue of vv. 16-18 — that faith is necessary to know whether or not Jesus' teaching is truly from God — into the wider issue of faith as the general precondition for religious understanding. In so doing, they are clearly guided by a sense of the general tenor of Scripture, for their epistemological principle is characteristic of the Old Testament as well. The Old Testament's own major axiom about the importance of faith for understanding is not, however, Isaiah 7:9b LXX but rather

---

34. Kenneth Grayston, *The Gospel of John* (London: Epworth, 1990), p. 70.

"the fear of YHWH is the beginning of knowledge/wisdom," which (with variations) occurs in a number of passages, once in keynote position at the beginning of the book of Proverbs (Prov 1:7; see also Prov 9:10; 15:33; Ps 111:10; Job 28:28; it is also a recurrent note in Ben Sira, e.g., Sir 1:14-20). "Fear of God" is the Old Testament's primary term for appropriate human responsiveness to God and so plays a role within the Old Testament somewhat analogous to that of "faith" in the New Testament and Christian parlance. On the significance of "the fear of YHWH is the beginning of knowledge/wisdom," von Rad commented:

> There is no knowledge which does not, before long, throw the one who seeks the knowledge back upon the question of his self-knowledge and his self-understanding. . . . The thesis that all human knowledge comes back to the question about commitment to God is a statement of penetrating perspicacity. It has, of course, been so worn by centuries of Christian teaching that it has to be seen anew in all its provocative pungency. . . . It contains in a nutshell the whole Israelite theory of knowledge.[35]

To conclude: If the claim of John 7:16-18 is characteristic of prophets and apostles elsewhere in Scripture, it is also characteristic of the Christian understanding of Scripture as a whole — that, with whatever provisos and caveats Christians make in one way or another, the Bible is the word of God in human words. And Christian preaching makes a comparable claim as well (again with appropriate caveats) — that in the human words of the preacher, it is possible to hear the word, the voice, the call, of God. But what difference, if any, should such claims make in the way one studies the text? This brings us back to the questions with which we started.

While it may indeed often be a practical necessity to subdivide the tasks of Christian biblical interpretation, our text gives no support to a characteristic post-Gablerian way of conceiving this. What our text prescribes as necessary for engaging with the text's claim to speak from and for God is a mode of being — "being prepared to do God's will" — that is neither precluded by, nor incompatible with, the philological and historical dimensions of the task of understanding what the Bible actually says and what kinds of texts it contains, nor is it in any way guaranteed by engagement with the tasks of dogmatic or systematic theology. Rather, John 7:16-18 would transpose the interpretative task as a whole into a different key by envisaging a particular mode

---

35. Gerhard von Rad, *Wisdom in Israel* (London: SCM, 1972; ET from German of 1970), p. 67.

of being — faith — as the enabling factor in inquiry. Johann Bengel (who died a year before Gabler was born), gave advice that is congruent with the implications of our Johannine text when it is situated within the total context of Scripture: "Te totum applica ad textum, rem totam applica ad te" — "Apply your whole self to the text; apply the whole matter to yourself."

"His Own Received Him Not": Jesus Washes the Feet of His Disciples

Marianne Meye Thompson

The discourses and narratives of the Gospel of John, brimming with metaphors, have lent themselves to a variety of interpretations. Although the account of Jesus' washing the feet of his disciples in John 13 seems at first glance rather more straightforward, it too has generated a multiplicity of interpretations of its significance. In fact, a recent monograph on the footwashing in John 13 identified at least eleven different major interpretations of it in the modern era alone.[1] But in current Johannine studies, one particular approach has risen to prominence. This approach argues that there are two interpretations of the footwashing in John 13. The soteriological interpretation, found in 13:6-11, sees Jesus' act of washing his disciples' feet as a prefiguration of his saving death on the cross; the ethical interpretation, found in 13:12-18, presents Jesus' action as a model of humility and service that his disciples are to emulate (13:12, 14-15).

Commentators speak frequently of the differences and tensions between these two interpretations. For example, Rudolf Schnackenburg states that

> The second interpretation seems to have nothing to do with the first and indeed would appear to be in conflict with it. . . .
> The prospect of Jesus' death and the disciples' share in his glory seems to be forgotten here. In this passage, the author is exclusively concerned with the washing of the feet that has just taken place. Here we have an interpretation that is independent of the first and is concerned with the exemplary aspect of Jesus' action.[2]

1. John Christopher Thomas, *Footwashing in John 13 and the Johannine Community*, JSNTSup 61 (Sheffield: JSOT Press, 1991).

2. Rudolf Schnackenburg, *The Gospel according to St. John*, vol. 3 (New York: Crossroad, 1982), pp. 12, 23.

At least one commentator has gone further, stating that the two interpretations are not merely different but incompatible, offering *irreconcilable* perspectives on the significance of Jesus' action.[3]

To speak of the two interpretations, soteriological and ethical, as existing in conflict with each other or as having nothing to do with each other severs the intrinsic connection between God's action in Christ, which constitutes the community of his followers, and the life of that community. The cross provides a touchpoint for the community only as a sort of common good to which the community subscribes, but it leaves no indelible cruciform impression upon that community. Put differently, in this dichotomizing approach, there is no kerygmatic urgency that underlies Jesus' command to his disciples, no pressure brought to bear on the disciples by virtue of Jesus' saving death on the cross. There is an example — and a noble one at that — but there is no gospel. In light of the fact that preachers are charged with proclamation of the gospel, it is intriguing to inquire how preachers handle John 13. In a number of sermons that I have examined, some discernible patterns emerge in the use and preaching of this text.[4]

First, all of these sermons use historical or exegetical research to explain the significance of footwashing as a common act of service in the ancient world, where roads were dusty and people wore sandals. Interestingly, however, quite a number of sermons dwell at some length on the probable embarrassment that Peter felt in having his feet washed by someone else, since, after all, no one likes to display his dirty, smelly feet in public. To make this point, they have to overlook what their research has turned up — namely, that having one's feet washed by others was in fact routine. More significantly, this is a rereading of the text that shifts the attention from Jesus' service to Peter's dirty feet and presumed self-consciousness. But in the text the issue is clearly Peter's profound scandal that Jesus, his Lord, should perform for him a deed expected of servants. It is what Jesus does, not who Peter discovers himself to be, that so scandalizes Peter.

Second, these sermons reveal a common quest for a timeless principle, usually in the form of a moral exhortation, something that human beings are to do. To be fair, John's text has a command for the disciples. But quite a number of sermons speak of the various "lessons" of the text. One sermon comments, "This footwashing has several lessons for the disciples"; another

---

3. So Jürgen Becker, *Das Evangelium nach Johannes,* vol. 2 (Gütersloh: Gerd Mohn; Würzburg: Echter-Verlag, 1981), p. 419. See also the survey in Thomas, *Footwashing in John 13,* pp. 11-18, 115-25.

4. The sermons to which I refer in the following section of the essay come from some of the many specimens available from various sites on the Internet.

speaks of "three powerful lessons" about humility; still another, of four lessons about Christian love. On the presumption that the passage speaks of humility and love, the sermons use the historical observation as a springboard for an exhortation on the character of Christian service and love. But the sermons contain few, if any, "lessons" about the character or purposes of God or about the church's mission in the world as it seeks to follow a Lord who performs the service of a slave.

Third, none of the sermons deals in any depth or at any length with Jesus' statement "Unless I wash you, you have no share with me." A number point it out, interpreting it as symbolizing Jesus' saving death on the cross and commenting on the importance of Jesus' death and forgiveness of sins as the basis for loving each other. But the ethical dimension of the text seizes the spotlight, and does so in a way that virtually ignores the text's christological, or soteriological, dimension.

Fourth, the overwhelming majority of these sermons are individualistic and moralistic. Attention repeatedly shifts from Jesus' action to human achievement and activity. One sermon exhorts its hearers, "Think of as many ways as possible in which modern Christians can wash each other's feet." While pointing out that Peter originally resisted Jesus' attempt to wash his feet and so manifested a lack of receptivity and responsiveness to Jesus' deed, few sermons suggest that what the text seeks is a radical reorientation of one's way of living and that precisely this demand will scandalize human beings whose natural inclinations lead them into quite different patterns of conduct.

In other ways, the text is repeatedly made to serve the ends of self-discovery rather than to disclose the character of Jesus to its readers. One sermon comments that Jesus knew who he was, where he was from, where he was going, and what power and authority he had (13:3). It then goes on to ask, "Do you fully know this about yourself? Why does knowing these things about yourself make it possible for you to wash others' feet without pride or resentment? Ask God to enable you to know who you are." Still another sermon gently urges that "unless we can become a little vulnerable, a little less self-sufficient and overly modest, we cannot fully share the life that Jesus is holding out to us." On this reading, Peter apparently needs just a washcloth to remove a bit of self-sufficiency here and a bit of modesty there. There is a persistent inclination to read the Bible as the scriptural Aesop's fables: charming stories with a lesson to be learned. Even the most profoundly christological and soteriological claims are thus routinely but subtly turned into "lessons" about self-discovery or even self-improvement.

In spite of the sharp difference in interpretation offered by the historical critic and the contemporary preacher, they do have some things in common.

It is striking how difficult both find it to hold together the text's soteriological and ethical dimensions. Many a historical critic explicitly denies a connection; many a preacher simply ignores it. The biblical narrative of God's seeking out and patiently forming a people who will "do justice, love kindness, and walk humbly with their God" (Mic 6:8) — a narrative in which God's action and human conduct belong intrinsically together — plays little role in these interpretations. While the historical critic resists reading Scripture as a unified dramatic narrative and so seeks difference and diversity, the contemporary preacher seems simply to lack the interest or guidance for reading this particular story as part of the larger, coherent narrative of Scripture.[5] For both, it is as if the stories of Israel were alien accounts of another people, of little significance for understanding either the New Testament or the life of the people of God today. And there is little sense from either that what scandalized Peter in this story poses the same ongoing scandal not only to the world but to the church, requiring a continuous radical reorientation of one's life and values, so radical that one might even speak of it as being "born again."

In the balance of this essay, I do not intend to offer the "definitive" reading of John 13 or to suggest that there is really only one way to understand this text. Rather, I hope to offer a reading of John 13 that attends to the *theological* dimension of the text, where *theological* is taken in its proper sense as discourse about God and God's "action of creating, judging, and saving the world."[6] Specifically, the following exegesis of John 13 offers a reading that takes into account God's action and the human response from the vantage point of the claims in John 1:14 and 1:11-12 — that in Jesus Christ "the Word became flesh and dwelt among us, full of grace and truth" and that "he came to his own home, and his own people received him not. But to all who received him, who believed in his name, he gave power to become children of God" (RSV). John's Gospel recounts a series of incidents that illustrate humans' persistent rejection of the manifestation of God in Jesus of Nazareth and hence their need for divine empowerment, an act of God's enlivening spirit, to engender faith and new birth. Cast in different terms, John's Gospel recounts a series of incidents that graphically depict human resistance to divine love.

The account of Jesus' washing the disciples' feet presents Jesus' willing self-giving in death as the supreme manifestation of God's love for the world,

---

5. To speak of Scripture as a coherent dramatic narrative is not to require that all the rough places be smoothed out. See Thesis 2, "Nine Theses on the Interpretation of Scripture."

6. See Thesis 1.

a love that triumphs over the cosmic forces of evil and will not be thwarted by the tenacity of human resistance to it. The love that triumphs over evil and persists in the face of resistance and rejection takes the form of humble service; it is the appearance of divine grace in the form of humble service that elicits human resistance to it. That resistance finds its starkest embodiment in Judas' betrayal of Jesus. Peter's objection to allowing Jesus to wash his feet manifests another form of human resistance, resistance that comes from "his own" and shows how misguided human judgments are, how prone to reject the grace that alone can heal. The manifestation of God's grace and truth in Jesus receives no ready welcome, either from the world or from "his own." And this is not simply a narrative that recounts "what happened back then." It depicts as well what happens now when God's grace confronts humankind and what always happens apart from the revivifying work of the Spirit that blows where it wills. We turn, then, to an exposition of John 13.

> [1]Now before the festival of the Passover, Jesus knew that his hour had come to depart from this world and go to the Father. Having loved his own who were in the world, he loved them to the end. [2]The devil had already put it into the heart of Judas son of Simon Iscariot to betray him. And during supper [3]Jesus, knowing that the Father had given all things into his hands, and that he had come from God and was going to God, [4]got up from the table, took off his outer robe, and tied a towel around himself.[7]

With this densely packed description of Jesus' deliberate preparation for washing his disciples' feet, John begins the narrative of Jesus' last hours. Throughout the Gospel of John, as here, the incidents of Jesus' life are deliberately linked to the feasts of the Jewish calendar, particularly Passover and Tabernacles. The first "temporal" reference in the entire Gospel, however, does not refer to a specific feast on the Jewish calendar but rather echoes the opening words of Genesis, "In the beginning . . ."[8] The Gospel's narrative demands to be connected with and set in the context of the scriptural account of God's act of creation, an act that implies God's continuing sovereignty over the workings of the world. By noting that God's creation of the world occurred through the agency of the Logos, John asserts that God's sovereign purposes for the world will not be realized apart from his Word, incarnate as

---

7. Scripture quotations, unless otherwise noted, are from the New Revised Standard Version (NRSV).

8. The opening phrase of John's Gospel (Ἐν ἀρχῇ, *En archē*) is identical to the opening of Genesis in the Septuagint.

Jesus of Nazareth. Hence, the note that Jesus' hour "had come" indicates that God's purposes in creating the world are brought to a decisive stage. John identifies the hour of Jesus' glorification, his crucifixion and resurrection, as the hour of the world's judgment (12:31), in which evil is exposed and condemned. Because it is the hour in which Jesus gives his life, it is the hour also of the world's salvation (3:16-18; 6:51). The footwashing, then, must be set against the backdrop of the story of Israel's God, by whose word the world was created and by whose word the world is judged and saved.[9]

The footwashing is set near Passover. At the time of an earlier Passover festival (ch. 6), Jesus reenacted God's giving of manna, the "bread from heaven," in the feeding of the five thousand, an act in which Jesus was among his people "as one who served" (Luke 22:27), even as God had been among his people in the wilderness as one who served. Jesus' subsequent presentation of himself as "the bread of life" and of his flesh and blood as "life for the world" indicates that God's supreme gift of "bread from heaven" is none other than Jesus himself. Jesus not only serves bread and fish to his people; in the end, he gives himself in service to them. To know Christ is to know his benefits; indeed, the benefits are not separable from Christ. Furthermore, Jesus' assumption of the role of a slave at Passover recalls that even as God freed his people from slavery in Egypt and sustained them in their wanderings in the wilderness in spite of their murmurings and recalcitrant ways, so now God grants freedom from the slavery of death and offers the abundant sustenance of eternal life. It is Jesus, the full embodiment of God's wisdom, who in sign and teaching, death and resurrection, provides the sustenance for God's people.[10] Passover is "the festival which gratefully remembers God's past protection, and claims it for the present generation when it too moves from slavery to freedom, from shame to glory, from darkness to light."[11] Now, at the final Passover, Jesus will give his own flesh and blood so that God's life-giving purposes will come to fruition.[12]

9. This observation may be compared to Thesis 1, which asserts that "God is the primary agent revealed in the biblical narrative"; accordingly, God's agency is disclosed through the particular events of Israel's history, climaxing in the death and resurrection of Jesus.

10. This interpretation assumes that John 6 calls on the scriptural and Jewish traditions that fuse bread, manna, wisdom, and Torah, locating the fullness of God's gift in the person of Jesus.

11. Kenneth Grayston, *The Gospel of John*, NC (Philadelphia: Trinity Press International, 1990), p. 105.

12. When Scripture is regarded as a "coherent dramatic narrative" and read "back to front," as Theses 2 and 3 propose, then the figure of Jesus stooping to wash the feet of his disciples illumines the character of Israel's God as one who takes the form of a slave by identifying with the oppressed and lowly of the world.

As John also notes, Jesus knows that the Father has "given all things into his hands," or "put all things under his power" — including the hour of his death; the security of his disciples, the sheep whom he holds in his hands (10:28); and the fate of Judas, his betrayer. Jesus exercises the unique divine power over life and death, for the Father has given it to the Son "to have life in himself" (5:26). His power to raise Lazarus from the dead is also the power to dispose of his own life, "to lay it down and to take it up again" (10:18). Jesus has been entrusted by the Father with the power also to judge (5:27, 30). Here, then, he is shown advancing toward his own death holding in his hands the power not only over his own life but also over the life and destiny of those for whom he will lay down his life. In washing the disciples' feet, Jesus will offer a memorable portrait of the way that his God-given power — the power that brought the world into being, the power to judge, the power over life — expresses itself in humble service and love.

The expression of Jesus' sovereignty and power in the form of humble service and love is further emphasized by the assertion "he loved them to the end." This is the main clause of its sentence; all the other phrases, which identify the time of the act and underscore Jesus' knowledge, are subordinated to "he loved them to the end." The grammar of the sentence is the grammar of the passion narrative, for Jesus is as much the subject, or initiator, of the action that follows as he is its recipient, and the passion is the ultimate manifestation of Jesus' love for his own.[13] Knowing that his hour has come, knowing that he is going to the Father so that his earlier promise that he will be the bread of life for the world might be fulfilled and that he is subjecting himself to the forces of evil arrayed against him — knowing all this, "he loved them to the end." Jesus knows even of Judas' imminent betrayal. It is Jesus' knowledge of Judas' imminent treachery that makes the inclusion of Judas in the washing of the disciples' feet all the more striking as a characterization of Jesus' love. It also defuses the indictment that John knows nothing of love for one's enemies. "He loved his own to the end" encapsulates the passion of Jesus as his self-gift for the world.

A second statement that focuses on Jesus' sovereign initiative is found in vv. 3-4: "Jesus, knowing that the Father had given all things into his hands, and that he had come from God and was going to God, got up from the table, took off his outer robe, and tied a towel around himself." The staccato verbs "got up . . . took off . . . tied . . ." graphically depict Jesus' initiative — indeed, throughout John's passion narrative, Jesus directs the actions and actors. John thus

---

13. In the Greek, εἰς τέλος *(eis telos)* can mean either "to the end" of something or "to the fullest extent"; the English words "ultimate" and "final" can carry both these senses as well.

puts into narrative form Jesus' description of himself as the Good Shepherd: "I lay down my life in order to take it up again. No one takes it from me, but I lay it down of my own accord. I have power to lay it down, and I have power to take it up again. I have received this command from my Father" (10:17-18). Even the wording of Jesus' action at the footwashing alludes to his actions as the Good Shepherd, for as is often pointed out, Jesus is said to "put aside" his garments (τίθησιν τὰ ἱμάτια, *tithēsin ta himatia*), just as he "put aside" his life (τίθημι τὴν ψυχήν, *tithēmi tēn psychēn*). Jesus is the Good Shepherd who lays down his life for the sheep so that they may have abundant life (10:10-18), the one who by laying down his life exemplifies the greatest love one can have for one's friends. The cross is not what people do to Jesus or what God does to Jesus; the cross is the manifestation of God's love through Jesus.

Even though Jesus' act demonstrates that he "loved his own to the end," his chosen way of expressing his love is counterintuitive to the human way, which judges by appearances (7:24), a way that loves "human glory more than the glory that comes from God" (12:43). Peter's response to Jesus' washing his feet, an enacted parable of Jesus' self-giving on the cross, graphically illustrates Peter's peril, for when the Word "came to his own home, . . . his own . . . received him not."

> ⁵Then [Jesus] poured water into a basin and began to wash the disciples' feet and to wipe them with the towel that was tied around him. ⁶He came to Simon Peter, who said to him, "Lord, are you going to wash my feet?" ⁷Jesus answered, "You do not know now what I am doing, but later you will understand." ⁸Peter said to him, "You will never wash my feet." Jesus answered, "Unless I wash you, you have no share with me." ⁹Simon Peter said to him, "Lord, not my feet only but also my hands and my head!" ¹⁰Jesus said to him, "One who has bathed does not need to wash, except for the feet, but is entirely clean. And you are clean, though not all of you." ¹¹For he knew who was to betray him; for this reason he said, "Not all of you are clean."

The interaction between Jesus and Peter in this passage holds the key to the significance of the footwashing in the Gospel of John. Often this dialogue is taken as an exemplar of the so-called Johannine misunderstandings, narratives in John where Jesus does or says something that is misunderstood, leading Jesus to offer the proper interpretation of what he has said. But in this particular incident, Peter does grasp, at least in part, what Jesus is doing, and that is precisely why he objects to it. Jesus has assumed the role of a servant rather than the proper role of Teacher and Lord (13:13-14), and Peter objects in the most vehement terms to Jesus' assumption of that role. When Jesus warns Peter that unless he washes Peter's feet, Peter will forfeit his place with Jesus, Peter shows again that he grasps the magnitude of what is at stake. But what he does not comprehend, what he will comprehend only later, is that Jesus' act of humble service prefigures Jesus' death on the cross and that the cross rewrites the script for the identity and conduct of Jesus' followers, both corporately and individually. Peter scarcely understands that the cross is imminent; therefore, he can hardly be imagined to grasp that it will be this way of death that embodies most fully Jesus' self-giving love — and that it serves as the model of life and love, and of death, that will be asked of Peter as well (21:17-19). In fact, inasmuch as the Gospel of John implies that Peter's fate will someday parallel that of his master, Jesus' words "later you will understand" refer not only to a time distant from the setting of the Last Supper but to "a dimension in the story that [Peter] will only learn to understand over a long period and in a way that is painful."[14]

There is indeed much that Peter does not yet understand. But he does see perfectly well that Jesus is about to perform an act always offered by an inferior to a superior, never by a superior to his subordinates. It is an act expected of a slave, just as crucifixion is often the form of execution for a slave. Peter's objection is not to having his feet washed but to having his feet washed by Jesus, to Jesus' inappropriate donning of the slave's towel — inappropriate, at least, to Peter's way of judging. The address to Jesus as "Lord" and the emphatic placement of the Greek pronouns make this clear: "Lord, do *you* wash *my* feet?" (κύριε, σύ μου νίπτεις τοὺς πόδας; *kyrie, sy mou nipteis tous podas*). It is the fact that *the Lord* washes *his* feet that Peter finds objectionable. As Sandra Schneiders puts it, "the indication of the true meaning of Jesus' action is Peter's instinctive and profound scandal."[15] When Jesus insists upon the necessity of his action, Peter's assertive response, "By no means shall *you* ever wash *my* feet!" — again with the emphatic pronouns "you" and "my," as well as with a strong and forceful negative — intensifies Peter's adamant refusal of Jesus' taking to himself the role of a slave.

Peter's words to Jesus indicate that, while he rightly acknowledges Jesus as Lord, he has yet to grasp that Jesus' path follows the way of humility, service, and death. In this regard, Peter articulates the same objection to the cross that surfaces throughout the New Testament. For example, in the Synoptic Gospels, Peter likewise voices resistance to the way of the cross when he

14. Herman Ridderbos, *The Gospel of John: A Theological Commentary* (Grand Rapids: Eerdmans, 1997), p. 459.

15. Sandra Schneiders, "The Foot Washing (John 13:1-20): An Experiment in Hermeneutics," *Catholic Biblical Quarterly* 43 (1981): 83; reprinted in *Written That You May Believe: Encountering Jesus in the Fourth Gospel* (New York: Crossroad, 1999).

rebukes Jesus' explanation of his destiny as the way of suffering, rejection, and death: "God forbid it, Lord! This must never happen to you." Jesus' response, "Get behind me, Satan! You are a stumbling block to me; for you are setting your mind not on divine things but on human things" (Matt 16:22-23), exposes the contrast between God's way and human ways that would reject a Messiah who is himself rejected, who suffers and dies. But Peter protests that God's Messiah must not experience rejection and death, for to do so would spell the failure of his mission, dying as a slave rather than ruling as a king. Here, the basic protest against the cross as God's way of salvation remains the same. A crucified Messiah, an enslaved Lord, can be understood only as a failure, as a stumbling block (1 Cor 1:23).

The dialogue between Jesus and Peter further underscores Jesus' insistence on the way of self-giving in death as God's way of salvation by emphasizing that it is the washing of Peter's *feet* that is at issue. As we saw, Peter's initial troubled question, "Lord, do *you* wash *my* feet?" and his subsequent objection, "*You* shall never wash *my* feet!" point to the fact that it is Jesus' assumption of the role of a servant that so distresses Peter. Jesus then insists, "Unless I wash you, you have no share with me." It now appears that Peter understands, for he responds, "Lord, not my feet only but also my hands and my head!" If Jesus wishes to wash his feet, why not his hands and head as well! But Jesus' response is telling here, for he repeats the point that he must wash Peter's *feet*: "Jesus said to him, 'One who has bathed does not need to wash, except for the feet, but is entirely clean.'"[16] Peter's objection is not just that it is the Lord who washes but that it is the Lord who washes his *feet*: "Lord, do you wash my *feet?*" Again, his determined resistance is to Jesus' washing his *feet*: "you shall never wash my *feet!*" When Jesus insists, Peter is willing to have his hands and head washed as well, thus shifting the attention away from his feet. But Jesus pushes the conversation and action back toward the original act: he desires only to wash Peter's feet. In other words, Jesus is resolutely oriented toward carrying out this act that portrays his love for his own in the form of service — service that overturns human categories of judging and human standards of glory or honor and so foreshadows the cross. In his last act among them, he will "present himself to his disciples, as he leaves them, for all time to come in the form of a servant."[17]

There is yet more for Peter and the other disciples to absorb, however, in grasping the way of Jesus. For they are called upon to walk the same path that

---

16. Some ancient manuscripts include the phrase "except for the feet," while others do not. For an argument for the longer reading, see Ridderbos, *Gospel of John,* p. 462.

17. Ridderbos, *Gospel of John,* p. 460.

Jesus does. "If any want to become my followers, let them deny themselves and take up their cross and follow me" (Mark 8:34). If they desire to share his glory, they must drink his cup. The cup that Jesus drinks is ultimately a cup of death, and the implication for Jesus' followers is not simply that they must serve as Jesus served but that they must die as Jesus died. Throughout the Gospels, Jesus regularly presents his own destiny as one that his disciples are to share, not necessarily in the form of the fate of physical death or martyrdom, but surely in the form of death to the desire for power, the desire to be first, the inclination to "lord it over" one another, the complicity in oppression, and the desire to be master rather than slave. As "the Son of Man came not to be served but to serve, and to give his life a ransom for many," so among Jesus' disciples "whoever wishes to become great among you must be your servant, and whoever wishes to be first among you must be slave of all" (Mark 10:42-45). Sharing Jesus' lot means not only participating in his glorious kingdom but identifying with "the dominated and the wretched, the powerless and the marginal, . . . with the human condition at its most wretched and degraded, the death of the slave or the criminal."[18]

This is exactly what Jesus means when he tells Peter, "Unless I wash you, you have no share with me." Jesus denies the possibility of inheriting eternal life apart from his own act of cleansing; his statement refers to "the solidarity in destiny of the two men. Only by humbling himself before his own as a servant could Jesus come to glory and make his disciples participants in that glory. If Peter stands by his refusal, their ways will part and he will lose all that he thinks he has found in Jesus."[19] The footwashing prefigures the cross because it demonstrates the means by which Jesus' disciples are united to him and so derive their identity from him. Even as the disciples are united to Jesus not by a triumphant display of power but by an act in which Jesus cedes his power, assuming the role and dying the death of a powerless slave, so the identity that they receive in him is permanently marked by his self-giving in death. Living in union with him, as do the branches with the vine, implies both living in communion with the source of life that assures one's final destiny, one's "share" with Jesus, and receiving an indelible identity from him, even as the branches bear fruit only as they remain on the vine and bear only such fruit as the vine produces.

The union of the disciple with Jesus, of the branches with the vine, commences with death: "Very truly, I tell you, unless a grain of wheat falls into the earth and dies, it remains just a single grain; but if it dies, it bears

18. Richard Bauckham, "Reading Scripture as a Coherent Story," p. 52 in this volume.
19. Ridderbos, *Gospel of John*, p. 460.

much fruit. Those who love their life lose it, and those who hate their life in this world will keep it for eternal life" (John 12:24-25). But the human instinct for self-preservation is strong, and human beings do not naturally seek their own death; they will resist attempts to take life from them. Peter's statement "By no means shall *you* ever wash *my feet!*" encapsulates his dilemma: he resists the role reversal he understands to be implied in Jesus' service of washing his feet; he resists the self-surrender of the cross; he resists Jesus' death, and, in so doing, he resists his own salvation. When encountered by the ultimate manifestation of Jesus' gracious love in the form of a slave's service, Peter resists. To do otherwise would be to accept the inextricable link between the fate of the master, Jesus, and his disciple, Peter, and it would therefore be to accept his own death. Jesus' act demonstrates at one and the same time God's initiative to humankind in the form of self-giving love and human resistance to it, for if God approaches them under the guise of a slave, the implications can only be that the same stance will be asked of those who acknowledge such a Teacher and Lord.[20] The profound irony of this passage is that Peter resists both Jesus' death and his own death and thus resists the means by which God brings life to the world — and to Peter. Still, his hope is that, as the Good Shepherd, Jesus holds him in his hands and will not let him be lost (10:28-29).

> [12]After he had washed their feet, had put on his robe, and had returned to the table, he said to them, "Do you know what I have done to you? [13]You call me Teacher and Lord — and you are right, for that is what I am. [14]So if I, your Lord and Teacher, have washed your feet, you also ought to wash one another's feet. [15]For I have set you an example, that you also should do as I have done to you."

With these words Jesus presents the footwashing as a model of conduct for his disciples in their relationships with each other. Commentators sometimes stress, almost inordinately, the degradation, humiliation, and condescension involved in Jesus' assumption of the role of a servant. The action itself is spoken of as "reserved for the lowliest of menial servants,"[21] "too menial *even for his disciples*,"[22] as demeaning and humiliating.[23] But as C. K. Barrett

---

20. As Thesis 3 proposes, "Faithful interpretation of Scripture requires an engagement with the entire narrative." When the narratives of the exodus and the footwashing are read as mutually illuminating, the portrait of a God who identifies with the human condition is sharpened in both.

21. D. A. Carson, *The Gospel according to John* (Grand Rapids: Eerdmans, 1991), p. 462.

22. Andreas J. Köstenberger, *Encountering John: The Gospel in Historical, Literary, and Theological Perspective*, EBS (Grand Rapids: Baker, 1999), p. 146.

23. George R. Beasley-Murray, *John*, 2nd ed., WBC 36 (Nashville: Thomas Nelson, 1999), p. 233.

aptly comments, "The degrading character of the task should not . . . be exaggerated. Wives washed the feet of their husbands, and children of their parents."[24] In fact, women are shown washing or weeping at Jesus' feet elsewhere in the Gospels, and the narrative of Mary's anointing of Jesus' feet appears at the beginning of John 12 as the Gospel moves into the account of the Last Supper and passion of Jesus.[25] The anointing of Jesus' feet is the other side of the coin of Jesus' washing of his disciples' feet. Just as Jesus' footwashing indicates the service of love that he will render for his disciples on the cross, so Mary's anointing of his feet rather than his head points to the hidden and humble way in which he exercises both his kingship, not as one who wears a crown but as one who himself will wash the feet of his disciples in love, and his authority, not in the display of power and might but in the service of love. Jesus willingly identifies himself with those — including slaves and women — who perform this act of service for others, and he calls on his disciples to do the same. After all, he who is Teacher and Lord has called them friends (15:13-15). It is unthinkable that their life together should be marked by an insistence on rights or prerogatives rather than by the service friends gladly render to each other. Those who choose another way are "setting [their minds] not on divine things but on human things" (Matt 16:23); in the words of John, they love "human glory more than the glory that comes from God" (John 12:43).[26]

Human beings do not naturally set their minds "on divine things" or seek "the glory that comes from God."[27] Peter's response to Jesus makes that clear. In John's Gospel, people do not instinctively search for God, and when God seeks them, often as not they see neither the presence of God nor the gift that God offers. This is clearly true of the world. As we read in the prologue, "He was in the world, and the world was made through him; yet the world did not know him." Even the much quoted John 3:16, "God so loved the world that he gave his only Son," is followed by the recognition that God's revelation receives a mixed welcome: "Those who believe in him are not condemned; but those who do not believe are condemned already, because they have not

---

24. C. K. Barrett, *The Gospel according to St. John*, 2nd ed. (Philadelphia: Westminster, 1978), p. 440. "Washing the feet of the saints" is included in the list of good deeds necessary for a widow to be enrolled (1 Tim 5:9-10).

25. I have not found any commentators who speak of the actions of these women in terms of their humiliating or demeaning nature!

26. See John Painter: "The moral cause of unbelief can be described as perverted or false love." John Painter, *Reading John's Gospel Today* (Atlanta: John Knox, 1975), p. 73.

27. Human resistance to God's ways and disobedience to God's commands is a virtual subplot of Scripture. This plight is illumined for modern Christian readers by the Old Testament no less than the New (see Theses 1, 2, and 3).

believed in the name of the only Son of God. And this is the judgment, that the light has come into the world, and people loved darkness rather than light because their deeds were evil" (3:18-19). And it is not only the world that fails to receive God: "He came to his own home, and his own . . . received him not." This reference to his "own" almost certainly refers to Israel, the people of God, Jesus' own people. Jesus' own people receive him no more readily than does the world.

But then, even more surprisingly, there are disciples in Jesus' own cadre of followers who desert him. A prime example is found in John 6, where the people murmur and grumble at Jesus' claims to be God's gift of the bread of life. The dissension increases until, at the end of the chapter, many of Jesus' own followers no longer walk with him. Finally, there is Judas, one of the Twelve, the inner circle, who turns against Jesus. In some way, all take offense at Jesus; they all love human glory more than the glory that comes from God. This is the natural human condition. Lesslie Newbigin sums it up most pointedly:

> [Peter's horrified reaction] is the reaction of normal human nature. That the disciple should wash his master's feet is normal and proper. But if the master becomes a menial slave to the disciple, then all proper order is overturned. . . . All of us except those at the very bottom have a vested interest in keeping it so, for as long as we duly submit to those above us we are free to bear down on those below us. The action of Jesus subverts this order and threatens to destabilize all society. Peter's protest is the protest of normal human nature.
>
> . . . This is not just an acted lesson in humility; Peter could have understood that. . . . The footwashing is a sign of that ultimate subversion of all human power and authority which took place when Jesus was crucified by the decision of the "powers" that rule this present age. In that act the wisdom of this world was shown to be folly, and the "powers" of this world were disarmed (Col 2:15). But "flesh and blood" — ordinary human nature — is in principle incapable of understanding this. It is "to the Jew a scandal, and to the Greek folly." Only those whom the risen Christ will call and to whom the Holy Spirit will be given will know that this folly is the wisdom of God, and this weakness is the power of God. But this will only be "afterward." At the moment, as the man that he is, Peter cannot understand. The natural man makes gods in his own image. . . . How can the natural man recognize the supreme God in the stooping figure of a slave, clad only in a loincloth?[28]

28. Lesslie Newbigin, *The Light Has Come: An Exposition of the Fourth Gospel* (Grand Rapids: Eerdmans; Edinburgh: Handsel, 1982), p. 168.

In other words, Peter's reaction to Jesus demonstrates that he needs the very act of service that he now so vehemently protests, the act that will give Peter "a share" with Jesus, through which he will participate in Jesus' destiny. But at this point in the narrative, Peter scarcely stands on firmer ground than Judas, than the disciples who deserted Jesus, than the Jews who did not believe, or than the world that "did not know him." Like the uncomprehending Nicodemus, Peter needs the "birth from above." Peter needs God to do for him what he cannot do for himself, so that he may abandon the way of judging by human standards (8:15), by appearances, and instead judge with right judgment (7:24). Then he will demonstrate the truth, not of the assertion that "he came to his own home, and his own . . . received him not," but of that other great statement of John's prologue, "But to all who received him, who believed in his name, he gave power to become children of God, who were born, not of blood or of the will of the flesh or of the will of man, but of God" (1:12-13). Peter's birth from above, like his washing and the washing of his feet, is out of his own hands. This denial of autonomy and self-sufficiency is in fact his "only comfort in life and in death."[29] For his destiny lies in the hands of the Good Shepherd, who, "having loved his own who were in the world, loved them to the end."

*   *   *

This reading of the washing of the disciples' feet in John 13 pays attention to literary, historical, and theological issues. It takes seriously the flow of the narrative and the dialogue between Peter and Jesus, the historical meaning of footwashing, the particular emphases of Johannine theology that come to expression in this pericope, the dimensions of the text that are highlighted when read against the backdrop of the entire canon of Scripture, and the horizon of the contemporary reader. None of these need be sacrificed or made the sole concern of the interpreter; indeed, to discard or isolate any of them is to risk producing a stunted interpretation that does justice neither to the richness of the text nor to the concerns of most of its readers. While this interpretation has aimed specifically to highlight the theological dimensions of the text and to engage those who read the Bible in faith, such interpretation need not — indeed, must not — be oblivious to historical or critical matters; rather, it gladly engages historical, literary, and grammatical concerns precisely because they provide the texture of the text. Without attention to the historical and literary features, interpretation would have no connection to

---

29. From Question 1 of the Heidelberg Catechism.

the text. But merely to enumerate or to explicate such features does not yet tell us what the text is about.

It is my contention in this essay that the narrative of Jesus' washing of his disciples' feet, when set in the larger context of Scripture, reveals the tenacity of human resistance to the self-giving love of God. Human beings do not naturally respond either to God's moral commands or to God's saving initiatives; rather, it is precisely in encounter with God's activity that human recalcitrance and resistance disclose themselves most fully. Apart from God's steadfast faithfulness in seeking and shaping a responsive people, human beings will pursue their own ways, resisting the call to align themselves with God's ways in the world. As this passage so graphically illustrates, human beings instinctively seek to protect their own positions of power and privilege, and they recoil at the thought of power embodied in self-giving and humility. Peter objects to Jesus' act of service because Jesus, who is rightfully called Teacher and Lord, improperly assumes the role of a slave. But Jesus becomes a model for Peter not because he demonstrates the condescension of power to weakness — for Jesus alone has the status of Lord. Rather, Jesus embodies the virtue of a generous humility, freely chosen, that seeks the good of the other. To be sure, Jesus' subversion of the human tendency to seek power and domination is open to misinterpretation: some might read the story as a warrant for forcing those with less power or status into a perpetual role of passive response. But passivity is not humility, and enforced service is not the freely chosen self-giving that Jesus gladly renders here. It is precisely those with power and privilege who are challenged most radically by Jesus' example. Those who interpret the text as exempting them from Jesus' example and command seriously misread it — perhaps precisely because they embody what it warns against.

Reading this story in the context of Scripture illumines the point that human puzzlement and even dismay at God's ways in fact permeate Scripture. Repeatedly, Israel learns that to be the elect of God is not to triumph but to suffer; it is not to know defeat of and power over one's enemies but often to suffer at the hands of one's foes while simultaneously experiencing God's presence in the most dire circumstances. Even as Joseph experienced God's deliverance and providence in a situation that human beings intended for ill, so Peter will experience God's salvation only through an act that human beings intended for ill but God intended for life. That this is so scarcely baptizes all human suffering as cathartic, full of meaning, or salvific, but it does echo the scriptural insistence that God's saving and judging presence calls into question all human aspirations to power, domination, and security. Those who share the lot of the One who gave himself up to death find life.

SELECTED SERMONS

Vulnerability, the Condition of Covenant

Ellen F. Davis

Here we are, only twenty-two chapters into the Bible, and already our skin is crawling. Why is this story in the Bible at all? You've got to wonder. And why is it here so close to the beginning, when we readers are just getting our feet wet in this deep sea of the Bible, when we are just getting to see and know God as Israel did? But if this is what "the God of the Old Testament" is like, then who wants to know more? Another question to increase our discomfort: Why is Gen 22, arguably the consummate story of divine brutality — why on earth is it appointed for this day of violent death, the torturous death of the wholly innocent One? On this day above all, it would be good to be given some explanations, some clear scriptural assurance of God's unwavering goodness. Instead, we get one horrific story on top of another.

God did a strange thing in consenting to be known to Israel through the slippery and always ambiguous medium of stories. Now if I were writing the Bible, I would put at the very beginning what we all need and long for: clear explanatory statements about who God is and what God has in mind in setting up and running the world. Yet those are strikingly absent. Rather, we are given these stories, and somehow we are supposed to find our way to God through them, following an uncertain trail of words that we affirm are somehow "the word of the Lord." It was an enormous risk on God's part, choosing to be known to Israel and to us through stories, some of which bewilder and offend us. Yet God had to take the risk, and for this reason: stories lead us into mysteries we cannot grasp through ordi-

These three meditations on Gen 22 were preached on Good Friday, 2002, to the Sisters of the Community of the Holy Spirit (an Episcopal religious order), St. Hilda's House, New York City.

nary explanatory language, the language of the classroom lecture or the news report.

The mystery I wish to explore with you today is this: vulnerability as the condition, the enabling condition, for covenant relationship with God. Vulnerability is an obvious theme for this day, as we spend the next three hours gazing at the wounded body of our Lord on the cross. Vulnerability, the capacity to be wounded — what does that mean for us who claim to be the body of Christ in the world? For the sign of the cross marks us, the church, as placed in the world specifically with a capacity, a vocation, to be wounded. Calling vulnerability a capacity means that it is something more than a negative — the situation or posture in which we are left when our luck runs out. A capacity is a positive thing, a kind of strength. So what does that capacity to be wounded look like on the ground, in our souls, from generation to generation in the church? These are questions for us to pray into on this day.

Vulnerability is a fitting subject for us this year. As a nation, and especially in this city, we are living for only the second time in my life with a widespread sense of vulnerability, for the first time with a widespread sense of having actually been deeply wounded. So now, much against our will, we all know more about vulnerability than we did last Good Friday. Perhaps now we are ready to pray our way into Gen 22, a story that comes near the beginning of the Bible precisely to give us a glimpse of this terrible mystery. As I read it now, this is a story of the total vulnerability of everyone involved in covenant relationship: Abraham, God, the child Isaac — each of them subject to fearful pain with respect to the others. If I read this story aright, then it is hinting at the truth that vulnerability is, paradoxically, the strength of covenant relationship. The capacity to be wounded to the core of our being, wounded even unto death, wounded precisely for the sake of being in intimate relationship with the other — that is what binds Israel to God and God to Israel, to us.

So my three meditations focus on the vulnerability of each of the three persons in the drama of Mount Moriah: first Abraham, then God, and finally the boy Isaac. Each of them has something different to teach us about what most concerns us this day, the capacity of our Lord to be wounded and die on a cross.

I. Abraham

It was after these things that God tested Abraham, and he said to him, "Abraham," and he said, "Here I am." And he said, "Now take your son, your only one, whom you love, Isaac, and get going to the land of Moriah, and offer him up there as a burnt offering on one of the mountains, where I tell you." And Abraham rose early in the morning and saddled his ass and took his two servants with him, and Isaac his son. . . . And he set off and went to the place of which God had told him.

Why does Abraham go along with it? This is for most of us the first question we are compelled to ask: How can he possibly pull a knife on his own child? — and not even in a sudden access of religious passion, but in a considered, agonizingly protracted act of obedience to God's word. Abraham loads the donkey with wood and knife, travels three days to get to the slaughter site, builds an altar, and then trusses up his son like a sheep. "Nobody could do that!" objected Martin Luther's wife, Katie — and yet Abraham does. So what are we to make of that? Either we must despise Abraham as satanically possessed, or we must consider the more difficult option, that even here Abraham is somehow the father of our faith, as Jews, Muslims, and Christians have always claimed. My bias is toward the more difficult option, because I am convinced that in every place the Bible is pushing us to think in ways that do not come naturally. So what could it be that we stand to learn from Abraham, even — or maybe, especially — in this most awful part of his story?

The answer commonly given is that Abraham is a model of obedience, of unquestioning submission to the inscrutable will of God. For a long time, that seemed to me a sufficient answer. After all, obedience is a fundament of the faithful life, and nobody knows that better than do the women who pray in this chapel day by day whether they feel like it or not. But I've come to think it takes more than obedience to justify the existence of this chilling story within the pages of the Bible. For obedience is a good thing only when it serves a cause that is decent, humane, even noble. Obedience that furthers an inhumane cause is servile, detestable, criminal. That kind of obedience was condemned at Nuremberg — how then can we condone Abraham's willingness to obey the ghastly order "Now take your son . . ."?

The only answer that makes sense in light of the whole biblical tradition is this: Abraham obeys because he trusts God. Abraham has something to teach us about the life of faith because in him — and maybe, except for Jesus, uniquely in him — we see a trust grown so total that there is not the slightest possibility of his choosing against it. I learned this from the Orthodox Jewish theologian Eliezer Berkovits. In his remarkable book about the Holocaust, *With God in Hell*, Berkovits works with this problem: Why did so many Jews keep their faith in the ghettos and in the death camps; why did so many gather, at great danger to their lives, to say their prayers and study Torah and

Talmud? Why did they circumcise their babies, praising God for the gift of a child, even while the SS literally beat down the door? Why did so many walk to the ovens or the gallows or the death pits loudly blessing God's holy name rather than cursing the God who had abandoned the Jews?

As he meditates on this problem, Berkovits returns repeatedly to the figure of Abraham, and especially to this event on Mount Moriah. Here he discovers the depth of trust that characterizes the life wholly bound in covenant, the infinite depth of trust that holds Abraham with God in the hell of Moriah. In the Bible, Abraham is almost speechless, but Berkovits gives him words to address to God:

> "In this situation I do not understand you. Your behavior violates our covenant; still, I trust you because it is you, because it is you and me, because it is us."
>
> . . . "Almighty God! What You are asking of me is terrible. I do not understand You. You contradict Yourself. But I have known You, my God. You have loved me and I love You. My God, You are breaking Your word to me. What is one to think of You! Yet, I trust You; I trust You."[1]

What Berkovits shows, better than any theologian I know, is that Abraham and God are intimates. These are two who know each other, who have chosen to make life together, for better, for worse. Abraham is with God like someone who has long been in a marriage that works, works well enough for competing interests to prove complementary, for two to grow eventually into one. And these two have been together for decades now. We're not sure how long exactly, but Abraham was 75 when they met, and he is now something over 110. In the early years, Abraham did not always trust God enough. As we shall see, the relationship still bears scars of that old mistrust. So God does not know (and probably Abraham himself does not know) how consuming his trust has grown until Abraham finds himself doing the unthinkable thing that God has told him to do: "Now take your son. . . ."

The metaphor of marriage gives us a context for understanding this crucial fact: Abraham is not relinquishing his fatherhood, his protective responsibility for the boy. Abraham and God are in a relationship something like a marriage, and they share a child; Isaac is the child of the covenant bond. So, in the strangest of all paradoxes, Abraham is not giving up his child to death. Rather, he is trusting God totally with the life of the child they share. In the end, Abraham knows only one thing for sure: life and life with God are the

---

1. Eliezer Berkovits, *With God in Hell: Judaism in the Ghettos and Deathcamps* (New York and London: Sanhedrin, 1979), p. 124.

same thing. Like the Jews who prayed and studied Torah in the death camps, Abraham will not — can not — choose survival, even for his child, over life with God. For better, for worse, it is simply too late for him to choose another way to live.

So when God calls him, Abraham responds with only one word: "הִנֵּֽנִי (*Hinneni*, 'Here I am')." That's it; he never expostulates, never argues, never murmurs. Because Abraham speaks only one word to God through the whole story, that word *hinneni* lingers in the silence and grows more significant. It is first of all a declaration of attention: "Here I am, listening." But as Abraham continues in silent fulfillment of God's command to him, the one word *hinneni* acquires deeper resonance: "Here I am, God, with you, in the covenant. Because I cannot live apart from the covenant with you." Already, just a few chapters after God makes the covenant with Abraham, we know for sure that this form of life is not one in which pain can be avoided. Instead, what the Bible tells us is that the covenanted life is the only one in which pain can finally be overcome.

"Here I am" — thus Abraham declares his total, excruciating vulnerability to God. Maybe that is the mantra that keeps his feet on the road and his soul in life for that unimaginable three-day journey from Beersheba to Moriah: *Hinneni; hinneni; hinneni.* One word sums up decades of prayer, decades of intimacy between Abraham and God:

> *Hinneni,* here I am;
> *hinneni,* here I am, with you still;
> *hinneni,* here I am, trusting in you.

O Lord, in thee have I trusted; let me never be confounded.[2]

Now perhaps we may begin to understand why it is that this bone-chilling story is appointed for reading today, as we walk again with special intention the way of the cross. The road from Beersheba to Moriah is the first *via dolorosa* in biblical history. Abraham trailblazed that path, now tragically well worn by millions of his children, who through the millennia have in trust and pain chosen life with God over survival. Strange to say, Abraham pioneered this way of the cross even for Jesus of Nazareth, the one who makes it possible for us to know Abraham's God at all. As children of Abraham, then, and disciples of Christ, let us pray:

---

2. From the Suffrages for the office of Morning Prayer, *The Book of Common Prayer* of the Episcopal Church, USA (1979), p. 55; cf. Ps 25:2.

Almighty God, whose most dear Son went not up to joy but first he suffered pain, and entered not into glory before he was crucified: Mercifully grant that we, walking in the way of the cross, may find it none other than the way of life and peace; through Jesus Christ your Son our Lord. Amen.[3]

II. God

It was after these things that God tested Abraham. . . . And God said, "Now take your son. . . ."

What kind of God would conduct such a test? There are, I think, only two possible answers, and both of them are hard answers: one, a god who is sick beyond imagining, a sadistic god who takes pleasure in human pain for its own sake; or two, a God who has been hurt beyond imagining, hurt so badly that an unimaginable demonstration of human trust is necessary in order to heal God's pain.

The first answer is, biblically speaking, impossible. If indeed God is demonic, deranged, and sadistic, then this one chapter shows the rest of the Bible to be transparently false, and our faith is entirely in vain. So we are left with the second difficult answer, which is, I am convinced, true. Only a God in pain would ask for this. Far from demonstrating God's tyranny, this chapter shows us a divine vulnerability so profound it staggers the religious imagination. Genesis 22 shatters any ordinary understanding of "God the Father Almighty, Creator of heaven and earth." How can we speak of the God of Genesis as vulnerable? — the God who spread out the heavens like a sequined veil, pulled continents out of the ocean and then inundated them again a few chapters later, heartsick that the still-new earth was already rotten with human violence. Yet there it is, probably the one most astonishing thing we learn in those early chapters of Genesis: God is powerful yet also sick at heart (6:6) — wounded, over and over again, by acts of unfaithfulness, from the disobedience in Eden to Cain's bloodshed to Babel's arrogance. Already, in its early generations, the world is a cruel and desperately lonely place for God.

That must be why God calls Abraham, so as not to be alone in a world that knows so well how to hurt God. With Abraham, God finally has someone to count on. Remember when God cuts the covenant with Abraham and says,

---

3. A collect for Fridays and for Monday in Holy Week, *Book of Common Prayer*, pp. 99, 220.

"Walk before me, and be wholehearted" (17:1)? Normally, we hear that as a magisterial command, spoken in a resonant, assured tone of voice: "Walk before me. . . ." But what if we hear it instead as God's plea to Abraham, thus:

> Walk before me — *be with me always;*
> and be wholehearted — *be wholly there for me.*

If that is the right tone to catch here at the moment when the covenant is being created, then it means that the covenant is a sign that God needs to have faith in Abraham as much as Abraham needs to have faith in God. This is surely the key to our terrible story: God needs to have faith in Abraham as much as Abraham needs to have faith in God. Only a wounded God, badly burned by humankind and desperate to trust again, would ask for something like this.

Yet reading between the lines of the story, we can see that God has reasonable doubts even about Abraham, and that is why God now tests him so severely. For Abraham is not above looking out for his own interests. You remember that unsavory business about Abraham passing off Sarah as his sister, not once but twice, when God sent him sojourning in foreign territory — and Sarah wound up in one or another royal harem (12:10-20; 20). Abraham did it because he was scared and he was not sure God would pull them through. Feminist readers rightly take offense for Sarah's sake, but shouldn't we also be offended for God? God has staked everything on the relationship with Abraham. Through Abraham, "all the families of the fertile earth will be blessed" (12:3) — but only through Abraham. God's first, direct approach to humanity did not work. So now God has chosen Abraham to be a kind of prism, catching the light of blessing and diffusing it into every corner of our sin-darkened world. Do you see, then, how dependent upon Abraham's faithfulness God now is? If Abraham goes his own way, if he tries to secure his own life apart from God's plan, then all God's hope of overcoming our evil is lost. If Abraham holds back anything at all from God, even the child Isaac, if Abraham is not wholehearted toward God, then the light of divine blessing cannot pass through him to bathe and reinvigorate our world. If Abraham is not wholehearted toward God, then it would be better if the world had never been made. That is what this terrible test is about.

"Abraham, now take your son. . . ." The talmudic rabbis perceive how vulnerable God is at this moment. With typically grammatical reasoning, they point out that God uses a "particle of supplication" that we would elsewhere translate something like "please": "Abraham, take (קַח־נָא, *qakh-na*) — take please; take, I beg of you — your son . . ." (*BT Sanhedrin 39b*). And when Abraham grants God's request and binds his son and raises the knife,

God stops him, yes — but not indignantly. On the contrary, God's gratitude is unmistakable: ". . . do not do anything at all to him, for now I know that you fear God, and you have not held back your son, your only one, from me!" (22:12). "Now I know" — as a result of this grueling test, God knows what God *has* to know about Abraham and cannot know for sure any other way.[4]

This story never ceases to stun our theological imaginations. Preachers have yet to domesticate it, or biblical scholars to explain it. Here we have, in the first pages of the Bible, a picture of God such as no one had ever before conceived. God, fathomless in power, who alone created heaven and earth, starting from nothing or worse than nothing, now pleads with one human being, whom God already knows to be fallible, to restore God's shattered faith in creation. God, author of the covenant "with all flesh" (9:15), is pleading with Abraham to heal the wounds God has suffered in the course of history. It may be absurd, but this is what covenant finally means: God is bound to the world past the point of escaping the pain that comes from our evil. God is so bound to humankind that God turns to us, or one of us, to assuage the pain in God's heart that human sin has inflicted.

How weird is this? No wonder Israel exclaims at the Red Sea, in something like incredulity, "Who is like you, O LORD, among the gods?" (Exod 15:11). Unlike the old high gods of Canaan or Mesopotamia or Egypt, Israel's God is not really transcendent *over* our world, distant and untouchable as the sun at high noon. Rather, the covenant means that God's transcendence works, you might say, from the bottom up. It begins with God willingly enmeshed in creation, taking hits. "Who is like you, O LORD, among the gods? Who is like you?" So Israel sings at the Red Sea, to celebrate the victory of their God over Pharaoh. But God's victories in the world are hard-won, and they are often overshadowed by defeats for God's side, defeats that look permanent. Mindful of those bitter defeats, a line of Jewish commentators stretching from the destruction of the temple to the Holocaust draws out that question thus: "Who is like you, O LORD, among the gods? — enduring insults and remaining silent."[5] Who is like you among the gods? — humiliated by your own creatures, continually assailed, yet bearing and forbearing. Holocaust theologian Eliezer

---

4. James Luther Mays focuses on the same phrase in his study "'Now I Know': An Exposition of Genesis 22:1-19 and Matthew 26:36-46," *Theology Today* 58 (2002): 519-25. Mays's study, like this meditation, puts primary emphasis on the figure of God and God's need to know "that there was in this human a way for God to work with and for all" (p. 520). For a fuller exposition of my view in essay form, see my *Getting Involved with God: Rediscovering the Old Testament* (Cambridge, Mass.: Cowley, 2001), pp. 50-64.

5. Cf. Eliezer Berkovits, *Faith after the Holocaust* (New York: Ktav, 1973), p. 108, citing Talmud *Gittin 56b*.

Berkovits observes: "The mightiness of God is shown in his tolerance of the mocking of his enemies; it is revealed in his long-suffering. . . . God is mighty in the renunciation of his might in order to bear with [humankind]."[6]

"Who is like you, O LORD, among the gods?" — mocked, abased in the midst of all that you have made, yet enduring in suffering love. We have, of course, come back to the cross by another way. We came first by way of Abraham's uncomprehending and incomprehensible trust in God. Now we come by way of our vulnerable, wounded God, who, with a need we hardly dare to name, seeks still to trust in humanity. Jesus, in a sense, is both of them, Abraham and God — those two old-covenant partners now mystically one, wholly indistinguishable in the God-Man who dies on the cross. Here is Jesus: a vulnerable human being, trusting wholly in God against all the evidence, even against his own will; and at the very same time, here, in Jesus, is our vulnerable God, terribly insulted in the midst of the world.

In exquisite lines, William Sparrow-Simpson expresses that double vulnerability, terrible and wondrous:

> Cross of Jesus, cross of sorrow,
> where the blood of Christ was shed,
> perfect Man on thee did suffer,
> perfect God on thee has bled![7]

Perfect man and perfect God, the One through whom God's blessing continues to pour into our world, raising up things which were cast down, making new things which had grown old, bringing all things to their perfection in him through whom all things were made, Jesus Christ our Lord. Amen.[8]

III. Isaac

"Take your son, your only one, whom you love, Isaac. . . ."

Of the three characters in this drama on Mount Moriah, Isaac is the one who is most evidently vulnerable, lying there on the altar, tied up like a sheep.

---

6. Berkovits, *Faith after the Holocaust*, pp. 108-9.

7. From the hymn "Cross of Jesus, Cross of Sorrow," words by William J. Sparrow-Simpson. *The Hymnal 1982* of the Episcopal Church, USA, #160.

8. Cf. the Collect for Good Friday, *Book of Common Prayer*, p. 280. The same collect is used for ordinations of bishops, priests, and deacons.

Yet it is hard to speak about Isaac; we know so little about him. Through all of Genesis, he has only a few words, a skimpy personal history, almost no personality. We have no idea how old Isaac is when he is laid on the altar. The Bible describes him as a "youth." Maybe a small boy, who has no real choice but to do what his father tells him. Or maybe, as the ancient rabbis supposed, he is a young man in his early prime, who could easily overpower the old man but instead consents to be bound because — well, he trusts Abraham, and therefore he trusts God. So when it seems that his own life is required, Isaac offers it willingly.

But of course all that is speculation. The Bible tells us so little about Isaac that we must fill in large parts of his identity, and maybe that is just the point. Because Isaac lacks a distinctive personal history, because he is faceless, he can acquire a thousand faces, or ten million. He can take on the identities of countless numbers of Abraham's children. Isaac stands for all those innocents within the household of faith who are vulnerable to sacrifice, to suffering and death. I think of war-affected children in Israel and Palestine, the "lost boys" of the Sudan. Their stories scandalize us, and not only because faith in Abraham's God does not protect them against suffering. The greater scandal is that faith in Abraham's God makes these countless Isaacs *more* vulnerable to suffering. It is precisely faith in God — their parents' faith and their own — that puts their earthly lives in jeopardy. The deep scandal of Isaac's story, borne out in the lives of so many children, is that the cost of faith is not evenly distributed among the members of the household. Generation after generation, very much of the cost is borne by those who are, it seems to us, least able to afford it.

So often, as with Isaac, the vulnerability of a child begins with the strong faith of a parent. Some years ago, a young couple sensed a calling to live as medical missionaries in the African bush country. Their three children were under the age of five when they left for what has now been more than ten years of work in African villages. In the last stages of preparation, the mother knelt beside her bed and prayed. She was in anguish, knowing they were taking risks with the children's safety and making sacrifices in their education that most American parents would regard as irresponsible. "How can you ask us to choose this life for our children?" she demanded, and the answer she heard was this: "Don't you know that I love them even more than you do?"

"Don't you know that I love them even more than you do?" Probably that is the only assurance that God can give an anguished parent, a parent whose heart is tearing open at what seems to be the irreconcilable conflict between love of God and love of a child. It is the answer expressed in the wood-

Margaret Adams Parker's woodcut *"And Abraham stretched forth his hand . . ."* (2001. Permission granted.)

cut by printmaker Margaret Adams Parker (see p. 287). "And Abraham stretched out his hand and took the knife. . . ." But notice, the hand with the knife is still locked behind his back. Abraham is stretching out his *other* hand to the boy, as countless times in the past he has reached out to caress his sleeping child. And as Abraham bends over his son, so likewise the angel bends over Abraham, with the same gaze, intensely protective; with arms outstretched, ready to enfold them both. The angel protects Abraham protecting his boy. Looking at this portrait of God's family, it is easy to believe that Isaac is curled up, not in fear, but fast asleep; and this is his own specially appointed angel who, as Matthew tells us, continually "see[s] the face of [our] Father in heaven" (Matt 18:10). Looking at this portrait of God's family, we might hear the angel asking, "Don't you know that I love him even more than you do?" Peggy Parker has given us an unforgettable image of the covenanted life, the life in which vulnerable beings seek and give assurances to one another, assurances of love and trust. A fallible but faithful human being assures God, "You are not alone in this world." God assures an anguished parent, "You and your child are never for a moment outside the reach of my love."

Today, looking at this family portrait through the lens of the passion, we see that each of the three figures is in fact a representation of God. The protecting angel is God; the anguished father is also God; and of course the beloved Son bound on the wood is Jesus the Christ. So we have come to the cross by yet a third way: first by Abraham's painful vulnerability to God, then by God's awe-ful vulnerability to Abraham, and finally through the child, infinitely precious and absolutely vulnerable to them both. "Don't you know that I love him even more than you do?" Yes, today we do know that. Now, as we read this story on Good Friday, it is at last clear why Abraham can afford to trust God with his only and beloved son. In every circumstance and beyond all reason, God can be trusted with the child, for God's heart is wholly the heart of a parent. Today with faith's eye we see our God standing, just as Abraham does, an anguished parent yearning over his "adorable, true, and only Son"[9] bound on the wood. So, in the strange idiom of Christian faith, we know God as the One whose heart has been torn wide open by the conflict between love for his Son and love for the world — and, stranger than strange, God's heart, once ripped open, has the capacity to love all the more.

And what of the child Isaac; what does he experience? Peggy Parker sees him as a wholly passive figure, immobilized on the wood, like Jesus on the

9. Te Deum Laudamus, a canticle for the office of Morning Prayer, *Book of Common Prayer*, p. 53.

cross, awaiting God's deliverance. She is hinting at the obvious yet widely overlooked fact that faithfulness is measured not only by what we do but also by how we endure what is done to us, what just happens to us. A lot of the raw material for holiness of life comes from things that we in no way choose, such as being born into a certain society and family and body, with their own particular weaknesses. In the course of a lifetime, those accidents of birth can cause — will cause — suffering that has nothing to do with our deserving and is well beyond our control. These and other things that happen to us are for each of us the elements of our own "passion" — for the Latin root *patior* means simply "to undergo" something, "to be done to." To be made flesh is to be done to. No one escapes that reality, not even the Word made flesh. The creedal account of God's human life is told almost entirely in the passive voice: Jesus "was born of the Virgin Mary, suffered under Pontius Pilate, was crucified, died,[10] and was buried." All those passive verbs — it is a startling fact that when we speak of the most faithful human life ever lived, we tell mostly what was done to our Lord. To be made flesh is to serve God in the passive voice, sometimes and maybe often.

There is a sense in which all of us know what it is to be bound and rendered passive, like Isaac or Jesus — bound on wood, awaiting God's deliverance. We are bound to things that seem to us hard and unyielding: a recalcitrant church, a Scripture whose harsh words often assault our religious sensibilities. We are bound to family relationships that seem to have been stalled in the same rut for years; or perhaps we are bound by isolation, by unrelieved loneliness. We are bound to aging or ailing bodies that no longer do what we want or expect, to the same nagging emotional weaknesses that have plagued us for years. All of us know these ways of being bound, or some of them, only too well, and we know the danger that attaches to them. If we are pressed to the wood over a long time, we can ourselves become rigid, embittered. So how do we say that being bound and "done to" is an essential part of the covenanted life? Serving God in the passive voice — is that any more than a whitewash for unredeemed suffering?

The answer for us must come from the cross, the place where Jesus is reduced to serving God wholly in the passive voice. Yet today the church glorifies the cross as the source of all our joy:

We glory in your cross, O Lord,
and praise and glorify your holy resurrection;

---

10. In Latin (the original language of the Apostles' Creed), *morior,* "die," is conjugated as a passive verb.

for by virtue of your cross
joy has come to the whole world.[11]

"We glory in your cross," because that is where God comes to us in power. On the cross, the place where all faithful human striving is finally exhausted, finished, stopped dead — on the cross, where even Jesus does nothing but die, there God's power is fully unleashed against our last and worst enemy. By the alchemy of the cross, Jesus' passion becomes divine action. His being done to becomes God's unprecedented doing. Jesus' long-practiced passion, his unconditional receptivity to God, is the channel whereby joy comes to our whole world.

That kind of passion, that practiced and gradually total receptivity to God, is what we see in the lives of the saints; it's what we hear in the prayers of the psalmists. It is what we are practicing here today: when we do as little as possible, when we don't worry about eating to keep up our strength, when we are relieved of the necessity to think of something helpful, clever, or convincing to say. But our practice of passion, of being done to — that can be holy only if it is aimed at the right goal. The goal is not that we should become docile — in the church, in this Community, at home or at work — wherever the hard wood may be in our lives. The goal is that we should be delivered. If gradually our own wills should grow less assertive, if our own doing should seem less urgent than once it did, if even what is done to us should seem less oppressive — that change in us will be holy only if we are at the same time becoming more receptive, yes, more vulnerable to God's action . . . like Isaac, lying still on the wood, as angel arms reach down to enfold him. Amen.

A Note on Divine Changelessness

When these meditations were discussed among the members of the Scripture Project (some months after they had been preached), strong objection was raised to the representation of God in the second meditation. The objection focused on the portrayal of God as having suffered "wounds . . . in the course of history" (p. 284) and therefore being "desperate to trust again" (p. 283) — a representation taken to be at odds with central and ancient strands of Christian theology. The question that emerged is whether my treatment of Gen 22 has an adequate exegetical base and, further, whether it can be reconciled with the patristic and medieval doctrine of divine impassibility, or *apatheia,*

---

11. An anthem for Good Friday, *Book of Common Prayer,* p. 281.

which maintains that God "is impervious to any force — any pathos or affect — external to his nature and is incapable of experiencing shifting emotions within himself. . . ."[12] The practice of reading "by the rule of faith" is basic to the Project that produced this volume, and I take the objection seriously. Although I cannot change what I have preached — and in fact, what I still consider to be *part* of a satisfactory interpretation of the text[13] — I shall try to formulate at least an initial response to that objection here.

The exegetical base for my treatment lies within the first chapters of Genesis — to which, I argue elsewhere,[14] this story alludes with its opening words: "*After these things,* God tested Abraham." The early history of the world, preceding the call of Abraham, brings God bitter disappointment and, indeed, pain: "And YHWH was sorry that he had made the human being on earth, and he was hurt (וַיִּתְעַצֵּב, *vayyit'atsev*) to his heart" (Gen 6:6). The Hebrew root עצב (*'-ts-v*) denotes acute pain, either mental or physical; its only occurrences in the Bible before this one refer to the experiences of childbirth and hard physical labor (Gen 3:16-17; 5:29). The Hitpael form of the verb (used here) occurs elsewhere only in Gen 34:7, where it expresses the reaction of Dinah's brothers when they hear of her rape. From these several instances, I conclude that the reader of Genesis is to understand that God's early experience of humanity occasioned the sharpest pain in the divine heart.

Can that exegetical conclusion be squared with a doctrine of divine impassibility? I recognize that the patristic theologians who formulated the doctrine were fundamentally biblical theologians who saw the textual evidence as clearly as I do. The patristic theologians understood *apatheia* as both an attribute of God and a fundamental disposition of the healthy Christian soul. Gregory of Nyssa in his *Commentary on the Song of Songs* frequently speaks of the necessity of cultivating *apatheia,* sometimes translated as "detachment."[15] But surely Gregory, whose theological imagination is riveted on divine love, does not imagine that detachment from humankind and the world is characteristic of God. On the contrary, *apatheia,* as described by Da-

---

12. David Bentley Hart, "No Shadow of Turning: On Divine Impassibility," *Pro Ecclesia* 11 (2002): 185.

13. There is of course more that can and probably should be said. For a treatment of Gen 22 as a story of Abraham's "effective self-sacrifice," which becomes a model for all Israel, see R. W. L. Moberly, "Living Dangerously," in this volume. While Moberly and I agree that Abraham's trust in God is central to the story, Moberly does not accept the representation of God that I offer in the second meditation.

14. Davis, *Getting Involved with God*, pp. 59-61.

15. So Casimir McCambley, OCSO, in his translation of Gregory's *Commentary on the Song of Songs* (Brookline, Mass.: Hellenic College Press, 199_), p. 48 et passim.

vid Hart, is "a condition of radical attachment"; Hart cites Evagrius of Pontus to the effect that "*apatheia* has a child called *agapē* who keeps the door to deep knowledge of the created universe."[16]

The connection between *apatheia* and self-giving love *(agapē)* is crucial. In teaching *apatheia* as a spiritual discipline, the constant emphasis of the patristic theologians is on growing to be free of irrational feelings and fantasies that stem from self-love, from vanity and wounded pride. That is, *apatheia,* as either an attribute of God or a Christian virtue in this world and "beatitude" for the world to come,[17] is the opposite of what we normally call an emotional reaction. It is, rather, an aspect of the "eternal changelessness"[18] of divine love, "God's everlasting outpouring,"[19] flowing in and from the Godhead and at work also in the human creature.

Viewed in relation to divine love, it seems clear that the doctrine of *apatheia* functions to make two crucial assertions about God's involvement with the world. Negatively, it refutes the possibility that the God known to Israel can ever become estranged from humanity or any part of it — unlike the highly emotional and therefore fickle gods worshiped by the Mesopotamians, the Greeks, or the Romans. Positively, the doctrine of *apatheia* affirms that God can be genuinely involved in events that happen in time, in human events, without being either formed or diminished by them.

It is especially apt to consider the patristic teaching of *apatheia* in connection with these meditations (although I did not consider it when I wrote them), because I believe that the biblical concept of covenant is a way of making, through the medium of narrative, these same crucial assertions. Covenant is the stabilizing mechanism that allows God to remain profoundly involved in the contingent events of history, responding in various ways to the often distressingly unstable human situation and heart, yet without *essential* change in either the divine being or the divine disposition toward those whom God has made. The first indication of this function of covenant occurs within the early chapters of Genesis, when the original covenant is established, through Noah, with "all flesh" (Gen 9:17). It is telling that the recognition that hurts God to the heart and leads to the flood — namely, that "every

16. Hart, "No Shadow of Turning," pp. 193-94.

17. Hart points out that Augustine did not think perfect impassibility either possible or advisable in this world. "No Shadow of Turning," pp. 194-95.

18. The phrase comes from a collect traditionally prayed at the close of the day: "Be present, O merciful God, and protect us through the hours of this night, so that we who are wearied by the changes and chances of this life may rest in your eternal changelessness; through Jesus Christ our Lord." *Book of Common Prayer,* p. 133.

19. See Hart, "No Shadow of Turning," p. 205.

inclination of the thought of [the human] heart is purely evil all the time" (Gen 6:5) — is the very recognition that, immediately after the flood, moves God to forswear further destruction and enter into covenant with this creature whose heart inclines to evil "from his youth" (8:21). And from this recognition the whole of biblical history unfolds. Now, it is foreseeable that there will be other occasions for God to be "hurt to the heart," yet covenant represents God's own renunciation of an emotional reaction. It is God's choice, one might say, of the spiritual discipline of *apatheia*.

I believe it is such a reading of biblical history that moves some more recent Christian theologians to speak categorically of the sufferings of God. I think of George Herbert and Dietrich Bonhoeffer, whose imaginations are fed primarily by the Bible in both Testaments. Thus Bonhoeffer writes in one of his poems composed in prison ("Christians and Unbelievers"): "Christians stand by God in his hour of grieving"; and in a letter (of July 18, 1944): "[Humanity] is challenged to participate in the sufferings of God at the hands of a godless world."[20] The larger context of both statements shows that Bonhoeffer has in mind the passion, but it is noteworthy that he does not confine divine suffering to the experience of the Son. Herbert, in a poem that clearly distinguishes between Father and Son ("Ephes. 4.30: Grieve not the Holy Spirit, &c."), says of the former:

> Almighty God doth grieve, he puts on sense:
> I sinne not to my grief alone,
> But to my Gods too; he doth grone.

The language of acute divine anguish is important, no less so than the language of divine changelessness, in giving substance to Christian hope.

---

20. Dietrich Bonhoeffer, *Letters and Papers from Prison* (London: Collins/Fontana, 1953), pp. 122, 174.

Self-Inflicted Violence

Ellen F. Davis

"Let the high praises of God be in their throat and a two-edged sword in their hand." It's bothersome, that cry of violence and praise that erupts in the next-to-last psalm, disturbing the long crescendo of alleluias with which the Psalter ends. Most modern commentators are agreed that the sentiment is, if not blatantly primitive, then at least pre-Christian, another instance of Israel's colorfully warlike mentality. (Gunkel imagines sword dancers in the Temple, and you can't help but feel that he finds the idea intriguing, if distinctly non-Protestant.) "Let the high praises of God be in their throat and a two-edged sword in their hand." The well-armed psalm singers disturb our genteel notion of praise, yet the church in her habitual perversity has chosen this psalm out of all the others to honor the saints. And because of that peculiar choice, we are constrained to wonder what it is in these words that might befit the honor of a Christian saint:

> Let the high praises of God be in their throat
>   and a two-edged sword in their hand;
> To wreak vengeance on the nations,
>   reproof upon the peoples;
> To bind their kings in chains
>   and their nobles with links of iron;
> To inflict on them the judgment decreed;
>   it is glory for all his saints.

(Ps 149:6-9)

The sermon was preached at a eucharistic liturgy in celebration of All Saints' Day at Berkeley Divinity School (Episcopal) at Yale. The readings appointed for the day are Ps 149, Rev 7:2-4, 9-17, and Matt 5:1-12.

The uncomfortable choice of this psalm for this occasion points to a disturbing phenomenon to which Scripture regularly attests: the connection between violence and praise that lies at the heart of sainthood; the strange, discriminating combination of violence and praise that brings on the kingdom of God and carries us into it. Indeed, the connection between violence and praise underlies both pictures of Christian sainthood that we have just read: Jesus extolling the privilege of those lucky folk who have been reviled, persecuted, and lied about to the greater glory of God, and also St. John's vision of the choir of the blood-washed sanctified. Strange — or is it? — that the book of Revelation, which is the most saint- and song-filled book of the New Testament, is also the most violent. If the Revelation to John of Patmos can be said to make anything clear, it is this: you don't get to be in the heavenly chorus by passing through life untouched and impervious to harm, like a friendly ghost. The saints are those who have gone all the way through the great ordeal, suffered, bled, and wept. But God's blood washes saints' wounds, and now they stand on the other side, their tears dried, singing in full voice, choir robes bright white from the blood of the Lamb.

We must be clear about the ordeal of the saints. It is not a calamity inflicted upon the church from the outside, by the enemies of God. Rather, the ordeal is the necessary confrontation with evil that God requires of us, and the first form the ordeal takes is bitter confrontation with the evil in ourselves. The saints are fanatical types, people of violence, taking the kingdom of heaven by main force, and this is their strategy: laying siege to the powers within themselves that are opposed to God, waging war and giving them no quarter, "binding their rulers in chains, and their nobles with links of iron." There is a regular pattern of sainthood: first withdraw and do battle in your own heart, then do battle in the world. It is the pattern of Jesus driven by the Holy Spirit into the wilderness to be tested by the devil, put into fighting trim to do battle on the streets of Capernaum and Nazareth against those old enemies of ours: sickness, despair, and unbelief; Jesus made proof against intimidation, to take his stand in the Temple and on Golgotha, finally waging war on death itself.

Withdraw and do battle against the powers that have made your own heart occupied territory. It is the pattern of Anthony of Egypt in the fourth century, tormented by demons, living alone for twenty years in a cave by the Nile. At last, battle-hardened and cleansed by solitude, he left the cave to become one of the founders of monasticism. Withdraw for a time, for only then can you see how much of the world and its ways you have taken into yourself: imbibed, absorbed, assimilated, even from infancy. It is the wisdom of Catherine of Siena, twenty-fifth and youngest child of a rich dyer, whose life was transformed by a vision of Christ at the age of six. From then on she gave herself to prayer, cutting off her beautiful hair to end her mother's attempts to make her "be like the other girls," until at last stubbornness won her permission to live a monastic life in her family home. Catherine grew to womanhood tough enough to nurse victims of leprosy, plague, and cancer that no one else would touch, clear-eyed enough to fight schism in the papacy until she died, exhausted, at the age of thirty-three.

There is a clear marker that distinguishes the violence that takes hold of God's kingdom from that which wreaks destruction in our world — a difference between the saints' violence, always conjoined with God's high praise, and the unholy violence that rings as shrill mockery in God's ears. The difference is this: every kind of godless violence is directed at getting something or holding on to it — power, oil, satisfaction, vengeance, personal or national security. But the battle of the saint is always fundamentally directed toward giving, giving praise to God, and that cannot be fully, freely given without first giving up what we normally value above all else, namely, a good opinion of ourselves. The saints are those who have given themselves completely to that lifelong work of self-inflicted, surgical violence which the tradition calls repentance. The saints' sacrifice — literally, what "makes holy" — the sacrifice of the saints is their willing disillusionment with themselves, and that is what frees them for praise. You have to be empty of yourself to be full of God's praise.

My friend Suzanne is one of the relatively few clergy whom I very much suspect of the ambition to be a saint. (And the saints are highly ambitious, all of them, for they are satisfied with nothing less than God.) Suzanne recently told me a story about where the battle for holiness began in her own life. When she was four years old, she was playing with a kitten in a neighbor's yard, and it scratched her. In a rage, Suzanne picked up the tiny kitten and threw it, she thought, in the well. Suzanne was too short to see that the well was covered, and so the kitten survived, but Suzanne got the point about herself: she would kill a kitten for scratching her. It is, of course, not remarkable that a four-year-old should be capable of cruelty and vengefulness grossly disproportionate to the offense. What four-year-old, or twenty-four-year-old, or forty-year-old is not? What is remarkable, and graced, is that Suzanne saw that evil in herself, did not dismiss it as an aberration, and has remembered it ever since. Early and thorough disillusionment with oneself — that is one way a saint is made. Yet early or late, each of us must experience that bitter recognition of our own evil if we are to be saints, whether of the technical variety or the more ordinary kind of saint who frequently shows up "in shops, or at tea."[1]

---

1. A phrase from the hymn "I Sing a Song of the Saints of God," words by Lesbia Scott. *The Hymnal 1982* of the Episcopal Church, USA, #293. The hymn is often used on All Saints' Day.

And we must become saints. For if we do not, there is only one alternative: we will be dangerous, and all the more dangerous for the advantage of a theological education. Anyone who is innocent about herself is dangerous, but particularly the self-deluded person engaged in Christian ministry, wielding pastoral skills, theological sophistication, ecclesial and spiritual clout like unlicensed firearms. The key to responsibility in ministry is precisely the saints' practice of self-inflicted violence, rigor in naming and opposing the evil we find in ourselves. It is the toughness gained from fighting the battle within that enables us to be gentle toward others — not naive about the seriousness and insidiousness of sin but compassionate toward the sinner, able to encourage and guide him in the way of healing.

Habitual rigor with ourselves makes us gentle toward others. The habit of repentance is also a kindness to ourselves, the most necessary kindness. When we refuse to make an easy peace with ourselves, to console ourselves too quickly — "After all, comparatively speaking, we're not that bad" — when we refuse those easy consolations, then we open ourselves to the deep, penetrating compassion of our God, the consolation that heals rather than simply soothing.

And if you do consent to become a saint, to fight the battle within, then what may you expect for your ministry? More battle, "strife closed in the sod."[2] "Let the high praises of God be in their throat and a two-edged sword in their hand." The sword-wielding singers of praise — this is an image that clarifies the conditions of Christian ministry and strengthens us against intimidation. It is an icon of the saints standing firm through the great ordeal, the ordeal that every one of you, and everyone you serve, will pass through in this life; an icon of the imperiled saints, literally singing for their lives, singing God's praise as they hold fast to the one piece of equipment that will bring them safely through: "the sword of the Spirit, which is the word of God" (Eph 6:17), the sword of God's cutting and healing word, the sharp instrument of discernment that we learn to wield accurately only through the discipline of prayer.

Hold that icon before you, for as a Christian you are charged not to hope for the best but to face the worst squarely, to head into evil full tilt and transmute it with your prayer. As a saint in the making, you are called to spend yourself in ways you cannot now imagine, fighting and suffering, not for what you hope to achieve in this world, not even for the sake of winning a place in heaven (although that is a far more practical goal). The reward for sainthood is just that: sainthood, the blessed life of simple, consuming desire

2. "The peace of God, it is no peace, but strife closed in the sod" — this is a line from the hymn "They Cast Their Nets in Galilee," words by William Alexander Percy. *Hymnal 1982*, #661.

for God. You will not win the battle over evil, in yourself or in your ministry. But through your baptism, you have been honored with the charge to fight it, fight to the death in a battle whose outcome is certain. With the logic peculiar to our God, you are called to give yourself wholly for a victory that is already assured but remains incomplete, to give praise — not only with your lips but in and with your life — for a sure victory that is still infinitely costly, and costly above all to God. For over all the fighting and suffering and singing of the saints stands the cross of Christ, the towering sign of that world-shattering conjunction between violence and praise that is the focus of all our hope and the source of all our peace. Amen.

Interpreting the Text

As an Episcopalian, I am a lectionary preacher, and so I often begin to think about a sermon by focusing on something that puzzles or bothers me in one of the texts appointed for the day. (Generally, my sermon will deal primarily with a single text, although I may develop its thought, as I do here, with reference to the other texts appointed.) Here, the puzzling thing is the seemingly strange fit between the occasion — All Saints' Day — and the Psalm text. Of course, we are never told exactly why liturgical theologians of an earlier age (lectionary choices for the major feasts of the year often date back a number of centuries) might have chosen a particular text to be read on a given day in the church year. On All Saints' Day, presumably, it was the fact that the psalm, at least in its Latin translation, speaks of what constitutes the glory of God's "saints" *(sanctis)*.

The sermon, then, becomes a reflection on the nature of sainthood, and the text itself provides the essential clue that some kind of violence is essential to the saints' "glory" of offering praise to God. This is, of course, exactly the element of the psalm that might lead contemporary preachers to judge the psalm "unpreachable."[3] And if the psalm is read at the literal level, it may well be unpreachable for First World Christians, since it seems to call for exactly the kind of aggressive national policy ("to wreak vengeance on the nations") that many of us consider incompatible with our faith.[4]

3. See Christine McSpadden's advice to preachers to begin by "crossing out" the things on which they could easily preach. Christine McSpadden, "Preaching Scripture Faithfully in a Post-Christendom Church," p. 138 in this volume.

4. I confine this judgment to First World Christians because to Christians in a situation of oppression, it could read quite differently. It might be offered as a protest against oppression and a prayer for divine intervention by those who have no realistic possibility of throwing off oppression by force of arms.

Therefore I read the psalm, not literally, but for what medieval theologians and exegetes (who were, of course, the same individuals) would have called its "moral sense" *(sensus moralis)* — that is, I read it as a source of practical guidance for the life of Christians in this world. The essence of my reading is that the violent language of this psalm (reinforced by the echo of its language in Ephesians and the equally striking violence of Revelation) points to the well-tested truth that sainthood involves a willingness to "do violence" to our pride in order that we may be capable of offering genuine praise to God. Although the reading I offer is my own, I believe it to be congruent with the theological style and assumptions of earlier centuries. The most fundamental of these assumptions (not widely shared in contemporary preaching or, indeed, in biblical scholarship) is that the Bible in all its parts and, further, in the details of its language is a trustworthy guide for our life with God. The sermon illustrates the kind of exegetical work that proceeds from the conviction that we may *safely* look to a text that initially seems "un-Christian" for both instruction and essential correction.

Prisoner of Hope

Ellen F. Davis

Lent is the most intimate season of the church year. Its intimate character is evident when you compare it with the evangelical seasons that bracket it on either side. The whole point of Epiphany and Easter is that nations should stream to the light of Christ, that the unprecedented good news of the resurrection should be spread far and wide. But in Lent we traditionally receive the instruction to go into a closet, shut the door, and there pray to our Father who is "in secret" (Matt 6:6).[1] In those closet conversations, we might find ourselves praying somewhat differently than we normally do, erupting in prayers that sound strange to our own ears and might even cause God's ears to tingle. Prayers like this one, offered by some ancient Israelite in pain:

> Hear my prayer, O LORD,
> and give ear to my cry;
>   hold not your peace at my tears.
> For I am but a sojourner with you,
>   a wayfarer, as all my forebears were.
> Turn your gaze from me, that I may be glad again,
>   before I go my way and am no more.
>
> (Ps 39:13-15 BCP)

---

1. The Episcopal Church Lectionary appoints this text for reading on Ash Wednesday.

This sermon was preached at a combined eucharistic and healing service at the Virginia Theological Seminary (Episcopal). The readings for the service were Mark 14:26b-42 and Psalm 39. This psalm is not in the Eucharistic Lectionary; it was specially chosen for this service. Contrary to the normal custom of the Psalm being read by the congregation in unison, at this service it was presented by two readers in dialogue.

"Turn your gaze from me, that I may be glad again, before I go my way and am no more." This is not the prayer of the spiritually triumphant. Indeed, Psalm 39 stands almost alone as a psalm that contains not one note of spiritual triumph. As you know, the psalms of lament almost always express confidence in God's saving power, and often they end by looking forward to some feast of thanksgiving. That is what makes the Psalms so inspiring and inspired: even in times of acute pain, the psalmist almost invariably praises God as the merciful and strong deliverer. Almost invariably — but not this time. Psalm 39 ends with what I take to be one of the most forlorn statements, or pleas, that ever came to God's ears:

> As for me, I am a sojourner with you,
>   a resident alien, like all my ancestors.
> Look away from me, so that I may feel better,
>   before I go away and am no more.
>
> (vv. 14-15)

"I am a resident alien with you" — what child of God would pray like that, end a prayer like that? Someone who cannot be at ease in God's presence, who experiences the nearness of God as a gaze of judgment: "Look away from me!" Isn't this the cry of a frantic child, whose small world has just collapsed, railing against her parent: "Don't look at me like that! I can't stand for you to look at me!" There are moments when even the one who loves you most in the world cannot shield you from the mess of your life. His presence, for a time at least, seems to make matters worse. Her suffering compounds yours; her gaze burns you like fire. "Look away from me, so I can feel better. . . ." In fact, God's gaze is intolerable because the psalmist knows just how much God is involved in the mess. This prayer comes from a fierce and desperate believer, like Job and Naomi, who knows that his sufferings come, in some sense, from God.[2] And like Job or Naomi, he would be glad for God to take an interest in someone else:

> Relieve me of your touch;
>   I'm finished off by the hostility of your hand.
>
> (v. 11)

Our psalmist tells God to lay off, but it's an empty demand. For even if God's hand were removed, she would be no less painfully bound to God, bound by a desperate and indestructible hope:

---

2. See Ruth 1:20-21 and Job 1:21; 6:4; 9:13-24; 10:1-22; etc.

And now, what am I hoping for, Lord?
  My hope? — it's in you.

(v. 8)

This "confession of faith," if you can call it that, erupts from her as a protest. She cannot help but hope in God, and it brings no comfort at all. The opposite, in fact: this psalmist is, in the remarkable phrase of the prophet Zechariah, a "prisoner of hope" (Zech 9:12), unwillingly and inescapably bound to God.

In this psalm, hope placed in God remains desperate to the end. We don't know exactly why. Maybe the hope is ill conceived, at odds with God's will. Maybe the times are so badly out of joint that the more righteous the hope, the more desperate it is bound to be. Or maybe the psalmist is what we would call clinically depressed, and any number of factors — emotional, spiritual, physiological, circumstantial — conspire to prevent him from making the move that most psalmists do make, that edifying move beyond lamentation to strong confidence in God, to confidence that emanates in praise.

Yet here we have a prayer that doesn't make it to praise, that utterly fails to be uplifting. So why should we pray it at all? The lectionary architects seem not to have found a good answer to that question, so they sidelined this psalm; I believe it occurs only once, on a weekday in Advent. But I asked to have it read with special care this evening, because I have a hunch that this psalm could be especially valuable to us in our Lenten prayers. If we pray it now, I think it will help keep us honest when in a few weeks the church moves forward to claim the victory of Easter. The fact is that some among us will not experience much Easter triumph this year, and maybe not next year or the year after. This psalm makes their voice audible, the voice of the resident aliens within the household of God: people who feel God's presence but feel it painfully, feel it as judgment. People who put their hope in God and are perpetually disappointed — or feel that God is disappointed in them. There are more than a few such resident aliens in the church, and they are the saddest members of any congregation — and also, I suppose, the most difficult for clergy or anyone else to deal with.

It seems to me that the presence of this psalm in our Bibles and prayer books challenges a way of thinking that is almost instinctual, at least in me. I generally fail to consider what I might learn about my faith from the despondent members of God's household. I might sometimes try to offer them consolation, but when I'm on the receiving end, when I am looking for strengthening in my faith, I normally look to my more buoyant sisters and brothers. Yet this psalm devoid of praise makes a witness that surprises me in its strength: "As for me, I am a resident alien with you [God], like all my ancestors." The psalmist speaks with a pedigree. Taking her place in a long line of resident aliens in the household of God, the psalmist speaks with a kind of authority: "I am a resident alien *with you*." She knows herself to be with God, though she doesn't even try to keep up with the triumphal procession marching in the light of God.

Moreover, the Gospel takes us deeper into this psalm, for it reveals how true is the resident alien's claim to be "with God." The Psalter in many places attests that God is present with the desperate, and that is much — very much. Yet it is not enough. Our situation is too far gone for that. God must become one of the desperate. So in the fullness of time, God becomes a resident alien in the person of Jesus Christ — alien to humanity, rejected by us, and alien to God, forsaken. Unimaginable alienation: God in Christ is forsaken by God the Father. Psalm 39 should be a privileged text for this season, for almost unique in the Psalter, it sustains a prayer of total alienation. We might well imagine that this is the psalm Jesus prayed in Gethsemane:

> Hear my prayer, O LORD,
> and give ear to my cry;
>> hold not your peace at my tears.
> As for me, I am a sojourner with you,
>> a resident alien, like all my ancestors.
> Look away from me, so that I may feel better,
>> before I go away and am no more.

Jesus' prayer in Gethsemane is the most intimate prayer in the history of the world, and the most remote. There is an infinity of distance between Gethsemane and the throne of God. It is the most profound prayer ever spoken — "deep calling to deep," as another psalmist says (Ps 42:8 Heb)[3] — the most profound, and yet the most impotent. In Gethsemane, prayer drops into the abyss. Jesus does indeed go away to die as an alien — betrayed by friends; imprisoned, but not by Roman soldiers. They hold his body for a few hours, but what really imprisons Jesus and sends him to Golgotha is hope, hope in God, just as Zechariah foretold.

We would none of us be here if that were the end of the story, if this Gethsemane psalm were the last word on prayer. Yet each one of the 150 psalms is given us to hold us close to God through a lifetime of prayer, to keep us in true prayer through all the varied moments of our life and God's life

---

3. Psalm 42–43 (two parts of a single poem) finds an explicit echo in the part of the passion narrative that was read in this service: Mark 14:34 echoes the psalmist's refrain, "Why are you cast down, my soul . . . ?" (Ps 42:6, 12; 43:5 Heb).

with us. In this most intimate season of the year, we are asked to stay awake with Jesus in his distress and pray with him, if only for an hour (Mark 14:37-38). If we can do that, it will enable us to know ourselves differently. "Let me know my end," the psalmist prays, ". . . how short my life is. You have given me a mere handful of days" (vv. 5-6 BCP). Praying in Gethsemane with Jesus means facing the terrible human frailty that seems to mock our faith in the eternal God. And what happens in Gethsemane is that our frailty ceases to be terrible, not because it is overcome — that never happens in any human life, including Jesus' — but because frailty is transformed into obedience: "Not my will but yours be done." It is precisely our frailty, transformed into perfect submission to God's will, that drives us into God's hands, there to shelter and find whatever peace and joy there is for us in this life, from now until the hour of our death.

> And now, what am I hoping for, Lord?
> My hope? — it's in you.

Amen.

Interpreting the Text

This sermon represents a rare exception to my normal practice of preaching from the texts that the lectionary has appointed for the day. I chose Psalm 39 because I wanted to explore homiletically — that is, to discover the gospel in — this disconsolate psalm. The Psalter offers prayers for all the widely varying moods and moments in the life of faith, and my hunch was that this psalm would prove to have a good fit with the mood of Lent.

Like the preceding sermon, this one follows a model of interpreting Scripture (and especially the Old Testament) that was developed by the ancient and medieval church. The earliest form of the model was to read a text in three "senses": the literal sense, the allegorical sense (reading the text as pointing to the life of Christ), and the moral sense (focusing on the guidance it offers for Christian life). As noted above, the previous sermon offers a reading of the Psalms according to the moral sense. But according to Origen, the first systematic expositor of Scripture according to the threefold model, the priority belongs to the allegorical sense. Hearing the text in conjunction with the story of the life, death, and resurrection of Christ gives clarity to the way we apply the text to our own lives; the allegorical sense illumines the moral sense.

So I found (I admit, somewhat to my own surprise) that my way into preaching the psalm came through hearing this as Jesus' prayer in Gethsemane. While that suggestion is of course imaginative, it is both historically possible and related to the existing witness of Scripture. The book of Psalms is among the Old Testament books most frequently cited in the New Testament, and we do hear fragments of other lament psalms on Jesus' lips. However, the crucial connection with the gospel is not historical or literary but theological. The conjunction of despondency in the presence of God and hope in God, which the psalm articulates so fully, is expressed several times in Scripture, but nowhere is that conjunction so powerful for Christian faith as in the passion. When the Psalm and the Gospel were read together (not incidentally, by skillful readers) in the context of the liturgy, I believe it was already evident to the congregation that they are mutually illumining. My sermon built upon that liturgical reading.

Who Is the God That Will Deliver You?

Richard B. Hays

Shadrach, Meshach, and Abednego — the three Jewish heroes with the rhythmically irresistible names — were miraculously saved from the fiery furnace, where they had been thrown by order of the Babylonian King Nebuchadnezzar. Many of us learned that from Bible story picture books as children. But few of us had any real idea of what the story was about. It seemed like one more instance of the good guys miraculously triumphing over evil — like Superman escaping from the traps set by the villains or Luke Skywalker escaping from the evil clutches of Darth Vader — an ancient precursor of our modern action thrillers. But if we only revel in the special effects, cheering our heroes as they burst from the superheated blaze, we are missing something much more important in the tale.

This story was told and retold by the Jewish people during long years of exile in Babylon. Even after they returned to the land of Israel, they found themselves under the thumb of foreign rulers. Some of those rulers, like the notorious Syrian King Antiochus IV Epiphanes, defiled their holy temple and persecuted them for their fidelity to the one God of Israel. It was precisely for such a time that the book of Daniel was written. The tale of the three heroes in the fiery furnace came to be understood as a parable of political resistance: no matter what unjust laws might be passed, no matter what pressures were brought upon the people to worship false gods, the story of Shadrach, Meshach, and Abednego called the people of Israel to resist. The book of Daniel is indeed a great charter for all subsequent civil dis-

---

This sermon was preached at Westminster Abbey, London, on May 21, 2000, the Fifth Sunday of Easter. The texts appointed for Matins were Dan 3:16-29 and Heb 11:32–12:2.

obedience, an encouragement to all who confess that they must obey God rather than men.

King Nebuchadnezzar set up an enormous golden statue, nearly as high as the ceiling of this great Abbey. When the band played the fanfare, everyone was to fall down and worship it on cue. But our three heroes refused. Nebuchadnezzar was furious. He gave them one more chance, warning that if they refused again he would throw them into the furnace. He taunted them: "Who is the god that will deliver you out of my hands?" (Dan 3:15).[1] In other words, "It's all very well for you to talk about this god of yours and to tell those old stories about how he delivered you from bondage to Pharaoh in Egypt, but this is the real world now. I'm the one who holds the power here, and you'd better get with the program. Your so-called god is nothing."

But still they refused, and, as we have heard, God vindicated their trust in him by saving them. At the end of the story, the astonished King Nebuchadnezzar orders his entire kingdom to honor Israel's God, for, as he confesses, "There is no other god who is able to deliver in this way" (3:29). Only Israel's God holds the power that trumps the lesser authority of the king and shows how foolish and powerless his gaudy statue actually is.

That is what Nebuchadnezzar has learned. But what have we learned? In free societies like Britain and the United States, we like to think that we are not being pressured by any ruler to worship idols. The church is not being persecuted here as it is in the Sudan or in China, thank God. So if Daniel is a parable of resistance, does it speak to us? Indeed it does: the pagan powers of our time are more subtle in their demands, but no less relentless. We are surrounded and coaxed by images seeking our worship — on our television screens and in our shopping malls. We are surrounded by images of gold: tantalizing displays of wealth, power, and security. When we hear the fanfare, we fall down and worship. We don't know how to say no.

But Shadrach, Meshach, and Abednego show us how to say no to the glitter, how to resist. Everyone else was worshiping the golden statue, but they said no, because they trusted God. They trusted God without knowing how the story was going to turn out. Did you notice what they said to the king? "If our God whom we serve is able to deliver us from the furnace of blazing fire and out of your hand, O king, let him deliver us. But if not, be it known to you, O king, that we will not serve your gods and we will not worship the golden statue that you have set up" (3:17-18). They preferred to die rather than be unfaithful to the one true God who made them and loved them. It's important to hear that, because otherwise the story rings false. Not all stories

---

1. Scripture quotations are from the New Revised Standard Version (NRSV).

end as happily as theirs. After a century when millions of Jews actually died in furnaces, we would be fools to think that trusting God leads always to a triumphant ending. The story rings true only if we know that our resistance to idolatry may get us thrown into the furnace too — and that the outcome of that trial remains open to a future that lies only in the hands of God.

But there is one more element in the story that we must not overlook. Who is that mysterious fourth figure in the fire? Nebuchadnezzar says, "Didn't we just throw three men into the fire?" . . . "But I see four . . . , and the fourth has the appearance of a god" (3:25; the original Aramaic text says "the appearance of a son of the gods"). Ah, the plot thickens! Daniel gives no explanation, but those who know the story of Israel need no explanation: this is the presence of God — with us in our suffering, sustaining us and saving us.

Did you notice, though, a strange thing? When Nebuchadnezzar opens the door of the furnace, only Shadrach, Meshach, and Abednego come out. The one whose appearance is like a son of God does not come out of the furnace of suffering. He is not miraculously preserved from the fire: he remains within it.

And that is precisely why the author of the Letter to the Hebrews points to Jesus. The Old Testament offers a long roll call of heroes of the faith who conquered kingdoms, shut the mouths of lions, escaped the edge of the sword, quenched raging fire. But it also tells the story of those who were imprisoned, tortured, killed for bearing witness to the one God who has the power to deliver — even if they did not see the fulfillment of the truth to which they testified. At the end of this story stands Jesus, the pioneer and perfecter of faith. Jesus did not escape the clutches of his enemies; he did not emerge unscathed out of the furnace. No, he remained within it. He "endured the cross, disregarding its shame," precisely in order to deliver us to freedom and hope.

Therefore, because we are surrounded by a great cloud of witnesses — by the examples and memories of Dietrich Bonhoeffer and Martin Luther King Jr. and Oscar Romero and all the other martyrs above the Great West Door of the Abbey, martyrs who said no to the powers — because we are surrounded by a great cloud of witnesses, let us struggle to resist idolatry. And let us look to Jesus, the fourth figure in the fire.

He is our sustainer and protector in time of trial. He suffers both with us and for us, a perfect exemplar of faith lived to the end. Who is the god who will deliver us? It is the God who enters the furnace with us. His promise stands:

> When you pass through the waters, I will be with you;
> and through the rivers, they shall not overwhelm you;

> when you walk through fire you shall not be burned,
>> and the flame shall not consume you.
> For I am the LORD your God,
>> the Holy One of Israel, your Savior.

(Isa 43:2-3a)

Amen.

Interpreting the Text

My hosts at Westminster Abbey gave me three guidelines to observe in preparing this sermon: "First, you must bear in mind that you will be preaching to a congregation of tourists; you cannot assume they know anything about the Bible or Christian theology. Second, your sermon should be no longer than ten minutes. Third, because of the acoustics in the Abbey, you must speak slowly and distinctly." This challenging set of constraints — combined with the fact that the Church of England's lectionary for this Matins service prescribed no Gospel text — shaped the sermon in some unexpected ways. In this case, I preached the gospel directly out of Daniel, in a way intended to recall early Christian exegesis of the Old Testament's stories of deliverance.

Most of the sermon simply retells the story of Daniel 3. (The lectionary reading, beginning in v. 16, would surely be puzzling to any hearer who did not already have the story clearly in mind.) The retelling seeks to highlight two important themes: the people of God may be called to resist the violent political systems under which we live, and the danger of idolatry is omnipresent. These motifs are powerfully reinforced by a series of statues recently installed above the exterior west door of the Abbey, paying tribute to twentieth-century Christian martyrs from various nations around the world. Visitors to the Abbey who heard the sermon might later walk around the outside of the building and find the sermon's themes of resistance and suffering evoked once again by this moving sculptural program (see Thesis 7 on the example of the saints as a key to interpretation). The exhortation to resistance, however, is not yet the heart of the text's message.

On rereading Dan 3 closely, I found my attention captured by the mysterious fourth figure who appears in the furnace, the one whom the Aramaic text describes as having the appearance of "a son of the gods" (rendered by the Septuagint as "a son of God"). I had not noticed before that the text of Daniel neglects to tell us what happens to this fourth figure when Shadrach, Meshach, and Abednego emerge from the furnace unscathed. The unexplained figure in the fire, then, became the focus of the sermon. Emboldened by our discussions in the Scripture Project, I read this fourth figure as a christological sign, a prefiguration of God's presence with and for us in our suffering.

This reading provides a surprising but resonant answer to the key question on which the story hinges, Nebuchadnezzar's rhetorical taunt: "Who is the god that will deliver you out of my hands?" (3:15). The God who will deliver us, the sermon affirms, is the Holy One of Israel who promises in Isa 43 to be with his people when they pass through flood and fire — the same God who was in Christ, enduring the cross in order to reconcile the world to himself.

Thus the sermon exemplifies a number of the Scripture Project's theses. It turns out to be a sermon principally about God's saving activity (Thesis 1 — note the sermon's title), and it presumes the unity of the Old and New Testaments in bearing witness to the continuing story of God's saving intervention (Theses 2 and 3). Most importantly, the sermon turns on a claim about Scripture's multiple senses (Thesis 4): the sermon performs a figural reading of Dan 3. I do not mean to assert that the author of Daniel *intended* to write christological prophecy;[2] rather, I mean to suggest that he wrote *figuratively* about the embodied saving presence of God in a way that articulates and prefigures what the New Testament later claimed about Jesus. In this case, the figural reading shifts the sermon's emphasis from moral exhortation to assurance and consolation. Or, to speak more precisely, it *grounds* the moral exhortation in a christological word of assurance.

Prior to my participation in the Scripture Project, I would not have preached Daniel in this way. Now it seems to me that I could hardly preach it otherwise.

---

2. Indeed, the sermon presupposes the historical hypothesis that the book of Daniel is principally intended as an apocalyptic manifesto of resistance, composed during the second century B.C.E. in the era of Maccabean opposition to Antiochus IV Epiphanes. (This information is explained briefly in the second paragraph of the sermon.) Thus the sermon illustrates the point that figural reading does not abolish the original historical reference of the text.

Netted

Richard B. Hays

Today we celebrate one of the most solemn and joyous festivals in our liturgical calendar: the Duke-North Carolina basketball game. And so it is fitting that in today's Gospel reading we find a story about filling up the net!

But, as always, the gospel story is full of surprises. There's a catch in the story, so to speak. . . . And I want to propose to you that the catch in *this* net turns out to be something slightly different from what we were expecting.

Luke's story of the miraculous catch of fish is a call story; it explains how Simon Peter and James and John left their fishing business on Lake Gennesaret and began to follow Jesus. We love this call story, because many of us have an experience of being called to leave behind a secure livelihood to follow Jesus and preach the good news. We've given up a lot. So this story comforts us as we encounter our culture's increasing obliviousness to the gospel. Even if we've labored all night and caught nothing, we see in this story a promise of success: just as the fishermen hauled in nets teeming with fish, so our work in ministry will bring an abundant catch, if only we are persistent and obedient to Jesus' command.

But when we read Luke's story against the background of Isaiah's call story — as it's meant to be read — we hear a more complex message, a darker word. When we Christians read the New Testament apart from the Old — as we are accustomed to do — we tend to spin the tale into a cotton-candy Marcionite fantasy. Dietrich Bonhoeffer, late in his tragically short life, la-

---

This sermon was preached in the Thursday eucharistic service at York Chapel, Duke Divinity School, on February 1, 2001. The texts were those appointed by the Revised Common Lectionary for the Fifth Sunday after the Epiphany: Isa 6:1-8 and Luke 5:1-11.

mented that we "read the New Testament all too little from the point of view of the Old." Indeed, for that reason he warned, "I don't think it is Christian to want to get to the New Testament too soon and too directly."[1]

So, before we reflect again on the miraculous catch, let's first listen carefully to the account of Isaiah's temple vision. Isaiah sees the Lord — the *kyrios* — exalted on a throne, with his robe filling the temple. The seraphs — heavenly creatures around the throne — cover their faces and cry out, "Holy, holy, holy is the LORD of hosts; the whole earth is full of his glory" (Isa 6:3).[2] The temple quakes and fills with smoke. And the response of Isaiah is the only possible one: terror.

A century of sentimental depictions of a domesticated deity has rendered us nearly incapable of imagining this fearful holy presence. When we hear the word "awesome," we think of Dick Vitale describing a slam-dunk — rather than envisioning the terrifying presence of the living God. So we need Isaiah to model for us an authentic response to God's presence: "Woe is me! I am lost, for I am a man of unclean lips, and I live among a people of unclean lips; yet my eyes have seen the King, the LORD of hosts!" (6:5).

Do we live among a people of unclean lips? I'm not talking about just the profanity that pollutes our airwaves and movie screens, what we usually call "dirty" words and sexual innuendo. No, I mean the pernicious babble that passes for public discourse; I mean the smooth, relentless stream of advertising that shapes us into docile consumer units.

Am I a man of unclean lips? Certainly, I am. How often have I wished to draw back the stupid, unthinking remark, the self-serving half-truth, the deft put-down that proves I'm smarter than you! Our speech is polluted because *we* are polluted. As Jesus warned, it is the things that come out of our hearts that defile.

So Isaiah models for us our true identity before the Holy One of Israel. We are lost, unclean. But that's not the end of the vision. One of the seraphs touches Isaiah's mouth with a burning coal from the altar and declares his sin blotted out. And at just that point, he hears the Lord speaking to the heavenly court, asking, "Whom shall I send?" And Isaiah volunteers: "Here am I; send me!" (6:8). So recognizing our true identity includes knowing that we, a people of unclean lips, are purified by an initiative not our own and that we, like Isaiah, are sent to speak in the name of God. Here ends the lectionary reading.

---

1. Dietrich Bonhoeffer, *Letters and Papers from Prison* (London and Glasgow: SCM, 1953), pp. 93, 50. I am indebted to Ellen Davis for drawing my attention to these comments.

2. Scripture quotations are from the New Revised Standard Version (NRSV).

But if you've read Isa 6, you'll recognize immediately that the lectionary stops the story right in the middle. Why? Here's how it continues: God says, "Okay, Isaiah, I'll send you. When you get to your first parish appointment, here's what I want you say to my people: 'Keep listening, but do not comprehend; keep looking, but do not understand' . . . until all the cities are laid waste and the land is desolate and all of you are sent away into exile." That's Isaiah's prophetic commission. Do you see why our sweet, sentimental lectionary brackets out vv. 9-13? We don't want to hear this, and we don't want this kind of ministry. But that's the way it is in the Bible. When the word of God meets the people of unclean lips, the result is both judgment and transforming power. You can't have one without the other. The lectionary — and the tepid Protestant church that it represents — tries to have the healing power without the judgment; consequently, it ends up losing both. If we are faithful prophets, we will join Isaiah in speaking God's judgment and, at the same time, crying in supplication, "How long, O Lord?" (6:11).

Now, what does this have to do with the miraculous catch of fish and Jesus' call to discipleship? Just this: the Lord who filled the temple with smoke and set Isaiah trembling in terror is the same Lord who stuffed the nets and swamped the boats with fish. This astounding superabundance is a sign that God has invaded our space. *God has invaded our space.* We might expect Peter to see the massive catch as a terrific business opportunity. If Jesus will join up in partnership with James and John, they can corner the fishing business in Galilee. They'll have to buy bigger boats, set up a new distribution network to maximize profits. . . . But no, there's no such trivial response, because Peter recognizes immediately who it is that has broken into his world. He falls on his knees before Jesus, and his response echoes Isaiah's: "Go away from me, Lord, for I am a sinful man!" (Luke 5:8).

But Jesus does not comply with this request. There's no escape for Peter. The *kyrios* who sent the seraph with a burning coal to purify Isaiah is the same *kyrios* who says to Peter, "Do not be afraid" (5:10). And then, it follows, the *kyrios* who sent Isaiah to proclaim judgment on the people is the same *kyrios* who tells Peter he's been drafted from now on to cast the nets for people. Instead of departing from Peter, he nets him — and Peter follows.

Here we'll go astray if we too quickly suppose that the Old Testament's judgment is replaced by sheer mercy in the New. This image of being netted is an image of being *captured by* God, and we would be truly foolish if we were to suppose that such capture entails no judgment upon our idolatry and violence. When Jesus recruits Peter to catch people, he is drawing on familiar Old Testament imagery. Listen: Jeremiah, speaking the word of the Lord declares, "I am now sending for many fishermen, says the LORD, and they shall catch them. . . . For my eyes are on all their ways; they are not hidden from my presence, nor is their iniquity concealed from my sight. And I will doubly repay their iniquity and their sin, because they have polluted my land . . ." (Jer 16:16-18). Or Jesus may be remembering the dire warning of the prophet Amos: "Hear this, you cows of Bashan who are on Mount Samaria, who oppress the poor, who crush the needy. . . . The Lord GOD has sworn by his holiness: the time is surely coming upon you, when they shall take you away with hooks, even the last of you with fishhooks" (Amos 4:1-2).

So when Jesus summons the fisherman Peter, he is calling him to throw the net to gather in humankind for judgment and mercy — just as in the parable that Jesus tells about the fishing net: ". . . the kingdom of heaven is like a net that was thrown into the sea and caught fish of every kind; when it was full, they drew it ashore, sat down, and put the good into baskets but threw out the bad. So it will be at the end of the age. The angels will come out and separate the evil from the righteous and throw them into the furnace of fire, where there will be weeping and gnashing of teeth" (Matt 13:47-50).

We'll leave it to the angels to do the separating. But our commission, like Peter's, is to cast the net by telling the story. The story goes something like this: We've been laboring all night, catching nothing. Now the *kyrios* has swamped our boats with more fish than we could have dreamed. But here's the strange thing: we've been changed in this encounter with him, and we see that, in fact, we are the ones caught in the net.

May the One who was sent to proclaim release to the captives show mercy upon those who fear him. Amen.

Interpreting the Text

Several features of this sermon were influenced by its original setting in the weekly eucharistic service of the Duke Divinity School community. First, the service happened to fall on the day of the Duke–North Carolina basketball game — an occasion that threatened to distract congregation and preacher alike from the more serious business at hand. The opening remark about the basketball schedule as "liturgical calendar" is not entirely a joke, as anyone who has ever visited North Carolina during basketball season can attest. The remarks about basketball, then, served as a segue from congregational setting to the text. Second, the brevity of the sermon was dictated by the fact that the Thursday Eucharist must be squeezed into the time allotted between classes in the daily academic schedule; this meant that the theme of the sermon had to be sketched in a few bold strokes, with little time for exposition or explanation.

Most important, the congregation for the occasion was composed almost entirely of theological students and faculty. For such a congregation, made up of individuals who have already responded to a call to enter the ministry, there is a danger that the story of Jesus' call of the disciples might become occasion for self-congratulation, along the lines of Peter's later self-approving comment to Jesus, "Look, we have left our homes and followed you" (Luke 18:28). The miraculous catch of fish might then function as a symbolic validation of a decision already made. There is a time and a place for sermons that offer reassurance, of course, but that is hardly the principal message of Luke 5:1-11. It seemed to me, therefore, that for this congregation the sermon should highlight the daunting — indeed, terrifying — character of an encounter with the living God in the person of Jesus. For a different congregation, a sermon on Luke 5:1-11 might highlight the compelling summons to follow Jesus — though it is striking that the Lukan version of the story (in contrast to Mark 1:16-20) does not actually narrate Jesus' calling the disciples to follow.

The linkage of the Gospel text with Isaiah's call story naturally emphasizes the elements of fear and judgment that are signified in Peter's response to Jesus (Luke 5:8), and Peter's address of Jesus as κύριε (*kyrie*, "Lord") echoes suggestively in counterpoint with Isaiah's vision of the awesome *kyrios* on the heavenly throne (Isa 6:1, 3, 5, 8).[3] The lectionary, however, runs the risk of undermining this emphasis by designating Isa 6:1-8 as the unit of text to be read, omitting vv. 9-13. This has the effect of ending the reading on the upbeat note of Isaiah's volunteering his services to God: "Here am I; send me!"[4] Something crucial is lost here if the congregation does not encounter the larger shape of the canonical call story; the prophet's commission is to pronounce judgment on an unfaithful people while also planting a seed of hope for the future. The sermon, then, seeks to narrate this larger story and to restore the delicate balance between the word of judgment and the word of grace.

As I reflected on this dialectic of judgment and grace, I researched the Old Testament background of the image of catching fish and discovered that Jeremiah and Amos use it as a metaphor for God's impending judgment. This became a key to the development of the sermon. Christians tend to assume blithely that the commission to be "fishers of men" is a mandate for evangelism and inclusion, but the canonical picture is a much more sobering one: to

3. Luke, distinctively among the evangelists, applies the title *kyrios* repeatedly to Jesus during his earthly activities. The following passages are especially instructive: Luke 1:43; 2:11; 7:13, 19; 10:1, 41; 11:39; 13:15; 17:5-6; 18:6; 19:8; 22:61; 24:34.

4. The Revised Common Lectionary actually designates the reading as Isa 6:1-8 (9-13), treating the words of judgment as an optional part of the passage.

be caught by God is to be ensnared for judgment. Therefore, the commission of the disciples is to participate in Jesus' prophetic mission of gathering people in for eschatological judgment. This reading of the commission is strongly reinforced by Jesus' parable of the net (Matt 13:47-50). Normally I try to avoid explicating the message of one Gospel by citations from another, but in this case it seemed to me that the Matthean parable neatly confirmed the message of judgment that was already evoked by Luke's intertextual echoes of Isaiah and Jeremiah.

Thus the sermon illustrates Thesis 3, that the Bible must be read both back to front and front to back. The Old Testament prophetic message of judgment illuminates the admonitory challenge of Luke's story of the miraculous catch, while Luke's message of God's saving mercy ("Do not be afraid") highlights the theme of God's covenant faithfulness that is already integral to Isaiah's message.

Whether We Live or Die, We Are the Lord's

Richard B. Hays

Each one of us will give an account to God. . . .

I

I expect that at least some of you have shared my family's experience of trying to figure out how to have a peaceful Thanksgiving dinner when one of the family members is a militant vegetarian. Now, on this issue, I myself belong to the group that Paul calls "the strong": I think it's a wonderful thing to give thanks for a juicy steak and, as Paul says, to "eat to the Lord." But my wife and I have somehow raised a young adult daughter who is a devout vegetarian. So when the holiday comes, she shows up at our house with her earnest vegetarian boyfriend, the two of them — determined to let no animal products pass their lips — carrying in their lentils and tofu and cartons of soy milk. At the same time, our son and his wife, avid devotees of fine cuisine, appear on the doorstep with the new recipe they've found in *Bon Appétit,* a recipe for turkey stuffing, chock full of chicken broth and bacon. So while the turkey roasts in the oven, the rival parties negotiate and dance around each other in the kitchen, preparing two mostly separate meals.

This sermon was preached in York Chapel, Duke Divinity School, on September 19, 2002. The Old Testament and Epistle texts were those appointed by the Revised Common Lectionary for the Seventeenth Sunday after Pentecost: Exod 14:19-31 and Rom 14:1-12. The Gospel text, Matt 18:21-35, had been preached in chapel the previous day; consequently, it was not employed again in this service, though its message may still have been echoing in the ears of the congregation.

When we finally sit down around the table, after the thanksgiving prayer is said, the daughter surveys the rest of us through narrowed eyelids, deploring our carnivorous passions, while the son rolls his eyes condescendingly and shoots us a knowing glance, as if to say, "When is she going to outgrow this?" And so it goes through the evening.

II

This family vignette may help us picture in microcosm the far more serious conflicts that were going on in the church at Rome. We don't know exactly what all the issues were — indeed, Paul himself may not have known the details, since he hadn't yet been to Rome at the time he wrote this letter. But the general drift of the problem is clear: some are concerned about observing the kosher dietary prescriptions of the Torah, while others — who see themselves as "the strong" — are confident that their Christian faith makes such rules needless. And so, apparently, they are squabbling with each other, not only about food but also about other matters such as Sabbath observance. The strong *despise* the scrupulous as "weak" in faith, hung up on outmoded laws. The Torah observers *judge* the meat eaters as libertines flouting God's commandments and skating carelessly along the edge of idolatry. (Paul consistently uses these two verbs, "despise" and "judge," to describe the attitudes of the opposing factions.) The Torah observers can point to what the Bible clearly says about Sabbath and food laws, and to a long chain of authoritative tradition on their side of the argument. The "strong" can point to their own experience of the Holy Spirit's liberating power in a community of Gentile believers no longer constrained by ancient prescriptions.

As you know, Paul refuses to adjudicate these disputes. Even though he himself is clearly on one side of the debate — the side of the "strong" — he refuses to press their case. Indeed, if anything, he gives his sharpest word of rebuke, later in this same chapter of the letter, to those who are partisans of his own law-free position: "If your brother or sister is being injured by what you eat, you are no longer walking in love. . . . Do not, for the sake of food, destroy the work of God" (Rom 14:15a, 20a NRSV). His advice is that the feuding factions should just *welcome* one another and stop "quarreling about opinions."

III

Because Paul counsels mutual acceptance of differing views in the church, this passage has become a favorite proof text for advocates of tolerance and inclusivity. It certainly does look as though Paul is saying that everybody has a right to his or her own opinion. (Of course, as we all know, wearily and regretfully, the opinions that polarize the church now in our day have to do not with food but with sex — a topic on which, by the way, Paul emphatically did *not* think everybody should do his or her own thing. But I digress.) So Romans 14 looks at first glance like a charter for us all to do what is right in our own eyes. But if we read this passage and find only a message about "tolerance" and the sanctity of individual conscience, we have gravely misunderstood the foundation on which Paul's argument is built.

In the laissez-faire free-market individualism that has enveloped the mainline Protestant church I grew up in, we believe that we should tolerate diversity because individual "choice" is sacred in itself and because we really don't believe that God judges anybody. God *affirms* everybody and everything. Because God doesn't judge, we shouldn't either. So the word "God" describes a great foggy cloud of benevolent indifference. (Surely, *our* God couldn't really have drowned all those sincere Egyptians in their high-tech military vehicles.) One of my faculty colleagues used to have a cartoon posted on the door showing the devil, with horns and pitchfork prominently displayed, sitting in a pew and saying to the person next to him, "I just love this church, because it's so *inclusive.*"

But Paul's account of the matter is very different: the reason we are not to judge each other is not because God doesn't judge us; rather, it is because God *will* judge us. We are not moral free agents; rather, each of us is God's servant, and we will be called upon to present a detailed account to the One who is our Lord and master. We should be concerning ourselves with that, not with judging a servant who does not belong to us.

Paul addresses the squabbling Romans: "You — why do you *judge* your brother? Or you, too — why do you *despise* your sister?" He summons the squabblers to look up and into the future that has broken in upon us: "For we *all* will stand before the βῆμα *(bēma)* — the judgment seat — of God." The βῆμα was the place of public tribunals, where Caesar or his representatives handed down what they called justice. (Remember, this letter is addressed to Christians living in the immediate shadow of the imperial power — it's as if Paul were writing a letter to the churches in Washington and saying we all will stand before the Supreme Court of God.) Paul sees Caesar's justice as a pale parody of the real thing, the justice of God that will appear on the day when we present ourselves before the βῆμα of God, the tribunal that really *is* the Supreme Court. That day, Paul has just reminded the Romans, is "nearer now than when we became believers" (13:11). On that day, our squabbling will appear shameful and ridiculous.

God will judge us, but not along the lines of our pet causes, our careful litmus tests for right thinking. We will be judged by the One who is throned in unapproachable light and righteousness. That is the prospect contemplated in the extraordinary prayer of confession that we prayed this morning:

> When thou, O Lord, shalt stand disclosed
> In majesty severe,
> And sit in judgement on my soul,
> O how shall I appear?[1]

When we see our present conflicts from the perspective of that day, recognizing our own failure and culpability, we will treat our brothers and sisters in a very different way. Isabella in Shakespeare's *Measure for Measure* elegantly captures the transformation that occurs when we consider our own judgments before God's βῆμα:

> . . . How would you be,
> If He, which the top of judgment, should
> But judge you as you are? O think on that!
> And mercy then will breathe within your lips,
> Like man new made.[2]

So, knowing that we are to be judged, we should cut one another some slack. This, I suppose, is the Pauline equivalent of the line in the Lord's Prayer that says "forgive us our debts as we forgive our debtors."

So far, so good. . . . But that does not yet reach to the heart of the matter as Paul narrates it. What I've said so far can be heard simply as a threat: you'd better not be unkind to your brothers and sisters, because God is coming after you. You'd better watch out, you'd better not cry, you'd better not pout. . . . In short, this is still a matter of self-interest.

---

1. From the hymn "When Rising from the Bed of Death," words by Joseph Addison, 1712.
2. *Measure for Measure* 2.2.

IV

But the heart of Paul's message is still something else — and it is that something else that makes it *gospel*. The heart of the message is this: The Lord to whom we belong, the One before whose judgment we stand, is Jesus Christ, and he is the one who has the power to make us stand (v. 4). In the phrase "make [us] stand," we hear a hint of the message of resurrection. To "stand" at the last day is to be raised up into a new creation, a restored world of God's making. When we are raised into that new life, we do not stand isolated.

> For none of us lives to himself, and none of us dies to himself.
> For if we live, we live to the Lord, and if we die, we die to the Lord.
> Therefore, whether we live or die, we are the Lord's.
> For this reason Christ died and lived:
> So that he might be Lord of both the dead and the living.
>
> (vv. 7-9)

Jesus Christ has defeated death, and we shall be raised with him. He has claimed us. Therefore:

- In days of terror, when our sleep is disturbed by endlessly repeated nightmare images of jets slamming into buildings, of desperate people leaping to their deaths, we know that whether we live or die, we are the Lord's.
- In days of foreboding, when our sleep is disturbed by the prospect that our blundering Caesar will plunge the world again into violence by deluded visions of imposing a Pax Americana, we know that whether we live or die, we are the Lord's.
- In days of old age or sickness, when our sleep is disturbed by persistent pain or the fear of loneliness, we know that whether we live or die, we are the Lord's.

Professor Gerhard Sauter of Bonn University reminded us in his guest lecture on Monday of the powerful words of the Heidelberg Catechism: "What is your only comfort, in life and in death? That I belong — body and soul, in life and in death — not to myself, but to my faithful savior Jesus Christ. . . ."[3]

I repeat, then: to belong to Jesus Christ and to be raised up by and with

---

3. Question 1 of the Heidelberg Catechism (400th anniversary edition; United Church Press, 1962).

him is not to experience a solitary vindication, but it is to enter with all the saints into a new world of justice, a world where divisions are healed and wrongs put right. The theologian Miroslav Volf tells a story about Karl Barth. When Barth was asked whether it is true that one day in the resurrection we will see our loved ones, he responded, "Not only the loved ones." Volf then comments, "The not-loved-ones will have to be transformed into the loved ones and those who do not love will have to begin to do so; enemies will have to become friends."[4]

Furthermore, according to Paul's gospel, the reconciling power of the resurrection is already at work among God's people. The church is the community of human beings in whom Jesus Christ's authority is not only confessed but also embodied. That is what he means when he writes, a few verses later in Romans 14, "The kingdom of God is not food and drink but justice and peace and joy in the Holy Spirit. . . . Let us then pursue what makes for peace and for mutual upbuilding" (vv. 17, 19).

"Let us pursue what makes for peace." The squabbling in the church at Rome threatens to undermine this embodiment of Christ's lordship. The judging and despising threatens to destroy "the work of God" — by which Paul means this strange new human community in which Jew and Gentile, slave and free, male and female stand together in harmonious praise of the one God of Israel. Therefore, Paul urgently exhorts the Romans to "welcome one another as Christ has welcomed you" (15:7). Only if they do so can they raise their voices together and faithfully represent the truth about God's kingdom.

"Welcome one another." This same urgent exhortation comes to us in our time. We are called to welcome one another, despite our pain-inflicting differences, not because we believe in "tolerance" or "inclusiveness" or individual rights. No, we are called to welcome one another because we have been claimed by Jesus Christ, who has welcomed us into his family. It may be a turbulent family — but it shapes our identity in ways we cannot escape. And our celebration together is a sign and foretaste of the celebration that all creation will offer at the end:

> As I live, says the Lord, every knee shall bow to me
> and every tongue shall confess to God.
>
> (14:11, echoing Isa 45:23)

---

4. Miroslav Volf, "The Final Reconciliation: Reflections on a Social Dimension of the Eschatological Transition," *Modern Theology* 16 (2000): 91-113, quote 91.

This is the God who "loosed from Pharaoh's bitter yoke Jacob's sons
  and daughters."

This is the God who "led them with unmoistened foot through the Red
  Sea waters."[5]

This is the God who raised Jesus from the dead and gave him the name
  above all other names.

Because Jesus is Lord of the dead and the living, we too have passed
  through the waters, and we belong to him.

Because we belong to him, we are one family.

And as one family we look for the resurrection
    and the day that Isaiah proclaimed,
      when all the ends of the earth will turn to him and be saved.

That is where our hope lies. So whatever our differences here — and I do not
minimize their painful reality — whatever our differences, let us sing together
in anticipation of the new creation.

Interpreting the Text

This sermon was preached eight days after the first anniversary of the September 11 terrorist attacks. The terrible images of the collapsing Twin Towers
had been burned anew into our brains by television news reports, and the
grim possibility loomed on the horizon that the president of the United States
would soon launch a preemptive war against Iraq. The sermon, therefore,
sought to speak a word of consolation in a troubled time.

Four exegetical observations about Rom 14 were generative for my
treatment of the text.

First, Paul highlights and repeats the verbs ἐξουθενέω (*exoutheneō*, "despise," vv. 3, 10) and κρίνω (*krinō*, "judge," vv. 3-5, 10, 13). These two contrasting
verbs describe the clashing attitudes of different groups among the Roman
Christians: those who "judge" are horrified by others' violation of a fixed norm,
while those who "despise" assume a stance of condescending superiority over
those who are so rigid as to worry about such things. The sermon's opening
story of my family's Thanksgiving dinner dramatizes the contrast between
Paul's two thematic verbs. This story, therefore, is not merely an amusing open-

---

5. These lines echo the hymn "Come, Ye Faithful, Raise the Strain," which was sung as the
opening hymn of the service. Words by John of Damascus, trans. John Mason Neale. *United
Methodist Hymnal*, #315.

ing anecdote; it engages the congregation in a good-humored recognition of the way in which this dialectic of judging and despising plays itself out again and again in our lives. (Of course, just beneath the surface of the humor lies the tension of the contemporary church's debates about sexual ethics.)

Second, Paul was writing this letter to *Rome,* the imperial capital. If we keep the social and political world of the original readers in mind, the text's references to lordship and judging appear in a new light. When Paul writes, "We shall all stand before the βῆμα of God" (v. 10), he is declaring a new order of justice that supersedes Caesar's authority and all the conventions of Roman political power. By highlighting this declaration, my sermon invites the hearers to rethink our relation to the ruling powers of our own time — and thereby to reckon with our ultimate accountability to the one true judge.

Third, the passage pivots theologically on v. 4c: "he will be made to stand (σταθήσεται, *stathēsetai*), for the Lord has the power to make him stand (στῆσαι, *stēsai*)." This sentence shifts the emphasis from exhortation (what *we* should do) to proclamation (what *God* has done and will do). N. T. Wright has suggested — correctly, I believe — that the future passive verb σταθήσεται alludes to God's action of causing us to "stand" again at the resurrection;[6] in other words, "made to stand" has a double sense. It speaks not only figuratively, of our being vindicated, but also literally — physically — of our bodies being raised up by God. This image of God's restorative eschatological power is the keynote of the last part of the sermon.

Fourth, Paul brings his account of God's eschatological judgment to a climax in v. 11 by paraphrasing Isa 45:23 — a text also echoed at the climax of the great Christ hymn of Phil 2:6-11. My sermon's conclusion draws phrases from the wider context of these passages, as well as from the Exodus reading, to focus the congregation's hope on Isaiah's vision of the time when all nations will abandon their idols and turn, all together, to God. Both the exodus and Isaiah's vision of return from exile are read as typological prefigurations of God's final powerful act of putting all things right and bringing peace.

In sum, then, the sermon follows Paul's strategy of reframing mundane church-dividing squabbles within the great biblical narrative of cosmic reconciliation. To understand who we are and how we should treat each other, we must remember that we are the heirs of the story of Israel, delivered by God from Pharaoh's army.[7] We must remember that we belong to Jesus

---

6. N. T. Wright, *Romans, NIB* 10 (Nashville: Abingdon, 2002), p. 736.

7. The sermon presupposes, but does not explain, the patristic interpretation of God's rescue of Israel at the Sea as a prefiguration of the resurrection (cf. Thesis 4, "Nine Theses on the Interpretation of Scripture").

Christ, who died for us and was raised up by God's power: that is why "we do not live to ourselves and we do not die to ourselves" (v. 7). And we must remember that our hope lies in God's judgment. The ultimate judgment of God is not to be downplayed theologically but highlighted as the frame of reference within which all our actions are to be evaluated.

The tendency of modernist Protestantism has been to skim off a message of "tolerance" from Rom 14 while neglecting its narrative underpinnings. The strategy of this sermon, on the contrary, is to retell the story as the necessary foundation for reconciliation and hope in a time of struggle.[8]

---

8. Thus the sermon particularly illustrates the homiletical outworking of Theses 1-3.

Selected Bibliography

History of Biblical Interpretation

Anderson, Gary A. *The Genesis of Perfection: Adam and Eve in Jewish and Christian Imagination.* Louisville: Westminster/John Knox, 2001. A highly readable survey, extending from antiquity to the present, of the attraction that this story has exercised on the religious imagination and how this is expressed in both literature and the visual arts.

Bright, Pamela, ed. *Augustine and the Bible.* Notre Dame: University of Notre Dame Press, 1999. This collection of essays is the best work on Augustine's exegesis available in English. A companion volume provides an interesting, well-balanced survey of early Greek exegesis: Paul Blowers, ed., *The Bible in Greek Christian Antiquity* (Notre Dame: University of Notre Dame Press, 1997).

Greene-McCreight, Kathryn. *Ad Litteram: How Augustine, Calvin, and Barth Read the "Plain Sense" of Genesis 1–3.* New York: Peter Lang, 1999. The trajectory traced here shows how the "literal" sense of the biblical text may vary over time, and yet certain basic consistencies are evident among three interpreters who heed the Christian rule of faith.

Lubac, Henri de. *Medieval Exegesis.* Vols. 1-2. Grand Rapids: Eerdmans, 1998. A magisterial study of the four senses of Scripture in the medieval period.

Young, Frances. *Biblical Exegesis and the Formation of Christian Culture.* Cambridge: Cambridge University Press, 1997. A brief and profoundly thoughtful survey of how early Christian theologians understood and used the Bible, from the second through the fourth centuries.

Exegetical Works

Brueggemann, Walter. *Cadences of Home: Preaching among Exiles.* Louisville: Westminster/John Knox, 1997. With his profound concern for preaching,

Brueggemann creates a provocative and original conversation between a variety of biblical texts and our own experience of cultural exile.

Childs, Brevard S. *The Book of Exodus*. Philadelphia: Westminster, 1974. This work "broke the mold" of the historical-critical commentary and remains a modern classic. Each passage is considered from the several perspectives of historical criticism, the histories of Jewish and Christian exegesis, and the theology of the whole Christian Bible.

Davis, Ellen F. *Getting Involved with God: Rediscovering the Old Testament*. Boston: Cowley, 2001. A collection of short exegetical essays and sermons, many of them on passages or whole books that pose theological problems for Christian readers.

Grieb, A. Katherine. *The Story of Romans: A Narrative Defense of God's Righteousness*. Louisville: Westminster/John Knox, 2002. This close reading of the Letter to the Romans shows how Paul's argument is grounded in the great story of God's faithfulness to Israel. The book, addressed not just to scholars but also to all serious readers in the church, offers insights about how Paul's apocalyptic message can speak to the theological and political issues of our time.

Mays, James L. *The Lord Reigns: A Theological Handbook to the Psalms*. Louisville: Westminster/John Knox, 1994. This deft study draws on insights gained from historical criticism, traditional Christian interpretation, and careful literary analysis to present the Psalms as liturgical songs directed toward the kingdom of God.

Minear, Paul S. *The Good News according to Matthew: A Training Manual for Prophets*. St. Louis: Chalice, 2000. A wise, seasoned interpreter of the New Testament imaginatively penetrates Matthew's thought world and summons readers to learn, alongside Jesus' original disciples, how to carry on Jesus' work.

Moberly, R. W. L. *The Bible, Theology, and Faith: A Study of Abraham and Jesus*. Cambridge: Cambridge University Press, 2000. A theological study of faithful obedience, sustained through both Testaments.

Seitz, Christopher. *Word without End: The Old Testament as Abiding Theological Witness*. Grand Rapids/Cambridge: Eerdmans, 1998. An excellent anthology of essays by an important Old Testament scholar that treats major issues in biblical hermeneutics and theology, as well as practical matters concerning use of the Bible for teaching and preaching.

Theological and Hermeneutical Studies

Fishbane, Michael. *The Garments of Torah: Essays in Biblical Hermeneutics*. Bloomington: Indiana University Press, 1989. Perceptive essays on ancient, medieval, and modern styles of biblical exegesis, and on interactions between biblical interpretation and culture in Jewish communities up to the present day.

Fowl, Stephen E. *Engaging Scripture: A Model for Theological Interpretation.* Malden, Mass./Oxford: Blackwell, 1998. This thoughtful study argues for a type of biblical interpretation that is closely tied to how Christians worship and live together in the presence of a triune God.

———, ed. *The Theological Interpretation of Scripture: Classical and Contemporary Readings.* Malden, Mass./Oxford: Blackwell, 1997. This fine collection includes essays on several discrete contexts of biblical interpretation (patristic, feminist, and African American), as well as classical and contemporary studies of selected biblical passages.

Green, Joel B., and Max Turner, eds. *Between Two Horizons: Spanning New Testament Studies and Systematic Theology.* Grand Rapids: Eerdmans, 2000. An important collection of essays from an international, interdisciplinary, and denominationally diverse team of evangelical scholars.

Lash, Nicholas. *Theology on the Way to Emmaus.* London: SCM, 1986. This fine collection of theological essays, written in lucid style, treats (among other topics) the nature of theological language and the relationships among Scripture, theology, and Christian living.

Levenson, Jon D. *The Hebrew Bible, the Old Testament, and Historical Criticism.* Louisville: Westminster/John Knox, 1993. An important set of essays that takes up a subject rarely treated: the relationship between historical criticism and religious interpretation of the Bible by Jewish and Christian communities.

Louth, Andrew. *Discerning the Mystery: An Essay on the Nature of Theology.* New York/Oxford: Oxford University Press, 1983. A thoughtful study of the limits of modern historicism, the function of tradition in the work of theology, and the need to reintegrate biblical study with a liturgical apprehension of the mystery of God.

Schneiders, Sandra. *The Revelatory Text: Interpreting the New Testament as Sacred Scripture.* 2nd ed. Collegeville, Minn.: Liturgical Press, 1999. This important work by a Roman Catholic scholar treats hermeneutics as transformation of the Christian imagination within the believing community, testing the theory with a feminist interpretation of John 4.

Watson, Francis. *Text and Truth: Redefining Biblical Theology.* Edinburgh: T. & T. Clark, 1997. A call for a thoroughly interdisciplinary "biblical theology," with reciprocal engagement among Old Testament and New Testament studies and systematic theology.

Scripture Index